MARKETING ETHICS & SOCIETY

SAGE was founded in 1965 by Sara Miller McCune to support
the dissemination of usable knowledge by publishing innovative
and high-quality research and teaching content. Today, we
publish more than 850 journals, including those of more than
300 learned societies, more than 800 new books per year, and
a growing range of library products including archives, data,
case studies, reports, and video. SAGE remains majority-owned
by our founder, and after Sara's lifetime will become owned by
a charitable trust that secures our continued independence.

Los Angeles | London | New Delhi | Singapore | Washington DC

MARKETING ETHICS & SOCIETY

Lynne Eagle &
Stephan Dahl

Los Angeles | London | New Delhi
Singapore | Washington DC

Los Angeles | London | New Delhi
Singapore | Washington DC

SAGE Publications Ltd
1 Oliver's Yard
55 City Road
London EC1Y 1SP

SAGE Publications Inc.
2455 Teller Road
Thousand Oaks, California 91320

SAGE Publications India Pvt Ltd
B 1/I 1 Mohan Cooperative Industrial Area
Mathura Road
New Delhi 110 044

SAGE Publications Asia-Pacific Pte Ltd
3 Church Street
#10-04 Samsung Hub
Singapore 049483

Editor: Matthew Waters
Editorial assistant: Molly Farrell
Production editor: Sarah Cooke
Marketing manager: Alison Borg
Cover design: Francis Kenney
Typeset by: C&M Digitals (P) Ltd, Chennai, India
Printed and bound in Great Britian by Ashford
Colour Press Ltd

Library of Congress Control Number: 2014959145

British Library Cataloguing in Publication data

A catalogue record for this book is available from
the British Library

ISBN 978-1-44629-661-5
ISBN 978-1-44629-662-2 (pbk)

Contents

CONTENTS

About the Contributors

Stephan Dahl is Senior Lecturer in Marketing at Hull University Business School in England and Adjunct Associate Professor of Marketing at James Cook University. His research interests include health and social marketing, cross-cultural marketing and online/social media marketing, and he has published widely in national and international journals as well as authoring a text on Social Media Marketing (Sage, 2015). Dr Dahl's current focus is on the role of social marketing to increase physical activity, online Word of Mouth and marketing, using social networks and marketing green issues.

Debra M. Desrochers is Senior Lecturer in Marketing & Business Strategy at Westminster Business School. Her research focuses on the impact of marketing activities and practices on the consumer, with significant attention on the policy issues surrounding food marketing. She is associate editor of the *Journal of Consumer Affairs* and on the Editorial Review Board of the *Journal of Public Policy & Marketing*. Her research has been published in the *Journal of Retailing* and the *Journal of Public Policy & Marketing*, and presented at numerous national and international conferences. She has served as a visiting scholar at the Federal Trade Commission and contributed to a research project on children's exposure to television advertising, with a particular emphasis on food advertising.

Lynne Eagle is Professor of Marketing at James Cook University. Her research interests include marketing communication effects and effectiveness, including trans-disciplinary approaches to sustained behaviour change in social marketing/health promotion/environmental protection campaigns; the impact of persuasive communication on children; and the impact of new, emerging and hybrid media forms and preferences and the use of formal and informal communications channels. She has published in a wide range of academic journals, including the *Journal of Advertising* and *European Journal of Marketing*, led the development of both Marketing Communications and Social Marketing texts and contributed several book chapters for other texts, as well as writing commissioned social marketing expert papers and presenting numerous research papers at international conferences. She is on the editorial board of several journals.

Mustafa Ebrahimjee is a general practitioner and partner at the Pall Mall Surgery in Leigh-on-Sea, Essex. Dr Ebrahimjee's research interests include the prevention of health problems and pro-active patient engagement, and he has participated in and published on research projects related to physical activity of the elderly and social marketing interventions in these areas. He is also a qualified trainer, teaching future doctors who wish to train as GPs. He brings extensive experience of medical practice both in the UK and abroad, and speaks English, Kiswahili, Gujarati, Hindi and Urdu.

David R. Low is Dean of the College of Business, Law and Governance and Professor of Business at James Cook University. He has a wide variety of both industry and academic senior management and boardroom experience. His research interests include cross cultural issues; country of origin studies; ethnicity, social media, social marketing, market orientation, firm performance and e-marketing; and innovation, SMEs and the use of technology in business value chains. David has recently co-edited a book on E-Novation and Web 2.0.

Tracey Mahony is Lecturer and PhD candidate in the discipline of Marketing at James Cook University. Her research interests focus on the efficacy of regulation of new and emerging electronic media, brand community development and the use of social media in developing economies. She has a wide variety of industry management experience in business and law, has lectured in Accounting, Management and Business Negotiation subjects, and has extensive experience in developing course material for undergraduate and postgraduate students.

Kathleen Mortimer is Associate Professor of Marketing Communications at Northampton Business School, University of Northampton. She is also chair of the Marketing Communications SIG of the Academy of Marketing and Deputy Editor of the *Journal of Marketing Communications*. Her research focuses on advertising and marketing communications, and she has published widely in numerous scholarly journals, including the *European Journal of Marketing*, *Journal of Services Marketing*, *Journal of Marketing Communications* and *Journal of Customer Behaviour*.

Nadine Waehning-Orga is Lecturer in Marketing at York St John University. She previously worked and completed her PhD at Hull University. Her research interests include consumer behaviour; cross cultural issues; regional product purchase motives; international marketing; and marketing for SMEs. Her expertise is not just focused on the academic side of businesses; she is also a Managing Director of the international marketing consultancy Initio Marketing (www.initiomarketing.co.uk). Additionally she is a Chartered Marketer and an active member in the local branch.

Fannie Yeung is Lecturer in Marketing at Hull University Business School in England. Her research interests centre on the impact of ethics on consumer behaviour with a particular focus on financial products and services. Her interest in financial products and services stems from her many years of professional experience working with a number of leading multinational organisations in the financial services industry prior to joining academia. Fannie has also worked on a number of consultancy projects for clients both in the UK and overseas.

LOOK!

GET ONLINE FOR MORE

LECTURER RESOURCES

* POWERPOINT SLIDES PER CHAPTER

* TUTOR'S MANUAL

STUDENT RESOURCES

* MULTIPLE CHOICE QUESTIONS PER CHAPTER

* SAGE JOURNAL ARTICLES PER CHAPTER

* SAGE PINTEREST MARKETING PINS

* LINK TO AUTHOR BLOG

with

companion website

study.sagepub.com/eagle

100% FREE

1 Introduction to Marketing Ethics

Lynne Eagle

CHAPTER OVERVIEW

In this chapter we will discuss:

- The changing nature of ethical criticisms of marketing over time
- The scope of ethics overall, business ethics and marketing ethics
- The relationship between ethics, religious beliefs and values
- The relationship between ethical and legal or regulatory actions
- The range of ethical challenges facing marketers
- Key theories and frameworks that can be used to make ethical decisions

CHANGING NATURE OF ETHICAL CRITICISMS OF MARKETING

The main criticisms of marketing, often focused on marketing communication as the most visible component of marketing activity, have in the past centred on allegations that marketing was inherently deceptive, manipulative and caused people to buy things that they did not really need, including leading people into excessive debt (Rotfeld and Taylor, 2009; Shimp, 2003). In the last few decades, while these criticisms and others also addressed in the next chapter are still made, the focus has changed to include criticisms of marketing for contributing to unsustainable economic growth and accompanying problems of resource depletion, environmental damage and accelerated climate change effects due to increased levels of **greenhouse gases** in the atmosphere (Dietz and Stern, 2008). To provide a foundation for assessing the validity of the criticisms, we need firstly to be clear as to what the role of marketing is, then what is meant by ethics, business ethics and, specifically, marketing ethics.

Standard definitions of marketing

Consider the definitions of marketing found in many textbooks. It is suggested that 'the definition of our discipline shapes marketing's boundaries for practitioners (public and private), scholars and educators' (Sheth and Uslay, 2007: 305). A review of the definitions used by some of the principal organisations therefore follows. Interestingly, none of the definitions listed contain any specific reference to ethics. While they vary somewhat, the central theme has been that marketing's purpose is to 'create exchanges that satisfy individual and organizational goals' (Sheth and Uslay, 2007: 302). The definitions provided by the American Marketing Association (2008) have been adopted by associations in other countries, but changes in the AMA's definitions to reflect the changing business environment are not always picked up by other associations. For example, the AMA's 1985 definition was that marketing is:

> The process of planning and executing the conception, pricing, promotion and distribution of ideas, goods and services to create exchanges that satisfy individual and organisational objectives.

The definition changed in 2004 to:

> Marketing is an organizational function and a set of processes for creating, communicating, and delivering value to customers and for managing customer relationships in ways that benefit the organization and its stakeholders.

In 2007, the AMA again changed their definition to:

> Marketing is the activity, set of institutions, and processes for creating, communicating, delivering, and exchanging offerings that have value for customers, clients, partners, and society at large.

The Chartered Association of Marketers in the UK also changed their definition in 2007 to:

> The strategic business function that creates value by stimulating, facilitating and fulfilling customer demand. It does this by building brands, nurturing innovation, developing relationships, creating good customer service and communicating benefits. By operating customer-centrically, marketing brings positive return on investment, satisfies shareholders and stake-holders from business and the community, and contributes to positive behavioural change and a sustainable business future. (Charles, 2007)

The Marketing Association of Australia and New Zealand continue with an (undated) definition more akin to the AMA's 2004 definition:

> Marketing consists of activities that facilitate and expedite satisfying exchange relationships in a dynamic environment through the creation, distribution, promotion and pricing of products (goods, services and ideas). (The Marketing Association of Australia and New Zealand, n.d.)

The European Marketing Academy (EMAC) does not have a formal definition; however, a definition was proposed by a prominent European academic in 2006, in response to the AMA's 2004 definition:

> Marketing is a customer focus that permeates organizational functions and processes and is geared towards making promises through value proposition, enabling the fulfilment of individual expectations created by such promises and fulfilling such expectations through support to customers' value-generating processes, thereby supporting value creation in the firm's as well as its customers' and other stakeholders' processes. (Grönroos, 2006: 406)

The pre-2007 definitions support the perception that marketing is successful if customers are satisfied, but what if that satisfaction ignores the potential for societal harm – such as the problems caused by excess alcohol consumption – or environmental harm?

Think points

Should marketing always give the customer what they want? What are the long-term consequences of 'consuming beyond the material and environmental limits of the planet's resources?' (Nahser, 2014: 127). What impact are the 2007 definition changes likely to have on marketing practice?

In noting the criticisms of marketing for its role in driving **consumption**, commentators have cautioned that if the growth of consumption patterns in developing countries mirrors that of developed countries, there may be further negative consequences as improved standards of living are linked to resource consumption (Peattie and Peattie, 2009).

Ethics are implicit in **Service-Dominant Logic (S-DL)** which holds that service is the fundamental basis for exchange, that service provision is a part of goods distribution, all economies are service economies and that customers co-create value (Williams and Aitken, 2011). However, the notion of engaging in exchange in order to gain value comes back to what wants and needs are satisfied by exchanges and whether S-DL should contain caveats regarding the social and environmental impacts of consumption decisions.

The wider economic focus on growth

The comments above illustrate a paradox for marketers which has its foundations in the way that economic growth and prosperity are measured, i.e. via **Gross Domestic Product (GDP)** which is usually defined as 'the total market value of all final goods and services produced in a country in a given year, equal to total consumer, investment and government spending, plus the value of exports, minus the value of imports' (Salvaris, 2013).

Think points

Think about the things that are included in this definition, such as production of weapons and cigarettes, and the things that are not included, such as air or water pollution and environmental damage resulting from production, and all the products and services that are produced but not sold through commercial markets.

The standard definition of a **recession** is 'a period of temporary economic decline during which trade and industrial activity are reduced, generally identified by a fall in GDP in two successive quarters' (Nunes et al., 2011). Thus if production decreases, there is a reduction in business profits and incomes, and thus individual and household spending reduces and unemployment rises.

Marketing is seen as playing a major role during periods of recession in stimulating demand for goods and services – but this can result in the original set of criticisms being levelled against marketing activity, i.e. that marketing manipulates people into buying things they do not need and potentially encourages individual debt, repayments for which may not be affordable through credit facilities.

The misuse of GDP data

The fact that GDP is not a good measure of economic growth, well-being or prosperity has been known for many decades:

> It is a great historical irony that no one was more aware of the limitations and the potential for misuse of the GDP than its chief inventor. For Simon Kuznets, American economist and Nobel Prize Laureate, GDP was never intended as a measure of overall social well-being.

> Kuznets famously remarked that 'the welfare of a nation can scarcely be inferred from a measurement of national income as defined by the GDP'. Nor was growth itself necessarily a good thing, he said: 'Goals for "more" growth should specify growth of what and for what' (Kuznets 1934, p. 7). Yet despite this clear warning, and by default over many years, GDP has come to be used as the key measure of national progress and political success, especially by politicians and economists. (Salvaris, 2013: 81)

Despite criticisms, GDP is still used to measure economic success or failure and thus national well-being. GDP trend data have political and social power, being reported in all major media and subject to detailed analysis in terms of national success or failure.

While a global movement to develop new means to measure sustainable well-being or composite indices that include economic, social and environmental measures does exist (Colman, 2010), GDP remains the predominant measure of prosperity. As part of this, marketers must consider the validity of the criticisms directed at marketing activity and consider how to reconcile the satisfaction of consumer wants and needs with long-term measures that include environmental and resource factors and the needs of future generations, i.e. **sustainability**. This is often framed as a '**triple bottom line**' approach as it incorporates economic, social and environmental impacts (Stuart, 2011). This is linked closely to **Corporate Social Responsibility (CSR)**, which will be analysed in more detail in the next chapter. This is a management approach designed to show an organisation's commitment to the social environment in which it operates, with the following assumptions:

1. Corporations *should* think beyond making money and pay attention to social and environmental issues;
2. Corporations *should* behave in an ethical manner and demonstrate the highest level of integrity and transparency in all their operations;
3. Corporations *should* be involved with the community they operate in terms of enhancing social welfare and providing community support through philanthropy or other means. (Banerjee, 2008: 62, emphases in original)

While the aims are laudable, critics dismiss CSR as nothing more than 'smoke and mirrors' (Prasad and Holzinger, 2013), given that its aim is to increase loyalty and brand reputation and thus ultimately achieve financial returns for the organisation. There is evidence that an increasing number of consumers will support firms that can demonstrate environmental and societal responsibility (Hoffmann and Hutter, 2012), and conversely, punish those that are seen to behave irresponsibly.

What the focus on sustainability means for marketers and marketing ethics

There are several dimensions to sustainability. Economic sustainability is important for the long-term survival of organisations. They must generate sufficient revenue to cover their current and likely future costs and provide a financial return for their owners or shareholders.

There is a much wider definition of sustainability, focused on environmental sustainability, which impacts on the way all enterprises, commercial or non-profit, operate and that has the potential to change the way in which enterprises operate. It is based on the recognition firstly that continued pursuit of economic growth based on the exploitation of finite resources is unsustainable (Burroughs, 2010; Kilbourne and Pickett, 2008). Secondly, there is increasing recognition that human activity has disrupted many of the ecological systems on which people depend. For example, it is estimated that '60 per cent of ecosystem services, involving climate regulation, fresh water provision, fisheries and many other services were either being degraded or used unsustainably' (Assadourian, 2010: 187).

There is not, however, recognition – let alone clear communication – of what action should be taken to address these issues and by whom. Closely linked to discussions of environmental sustainability is the concept of externalities. These may be positive or negative, and refer to the losses or gains to individuals, society or the environment as the result of economic activity, such as **production** of goods, by another party. Examples may be air or water pollution as a result of agricultural or industrial production. The producers do not 'pay' for the pollution created, but others, such as those with breathing difficulties suffer from the effects of poor air quality and swimmers (and marine life) suffer from the effects of water pollution. As noted in the previous section, these problems are not captured in GDP measures.

Consider the four definitions of sustainability below. The first two are focused on externalities; the third considers both inputs into production and externalities resulting from that production. The fourth definition encompasses economic sustainability as well as production inputs and externalities, including the effects on society as well as the environment.

> A way of doing business that creates profit while avoiding harm to people and the planet. (Centre for Sustainable Enterprise cited in Connelly et al., 2011: 86)

> Development that meets the needs of the present without compromising the ability of future generations to meet their own needs. (World Commission on Environment and Development, 1987; cited in Chabowski et al., 2011: 55)

> Consumption that can continue indefinitely without the degradation of natural, physical, human and intellectual capital. (Costanza, cited in Crittenden et al., 2011: 72)

> Sustainability ... translates into a 'triple bottom line' responsibility, with the implication that assessment of business results should be based not only on economic performance but should take into account the environment and social impact as well. (Sheth et al., 2011: 21).

These definitions bring with them a number of complications that deserve careful consideration. Reducing the demand for products and services ('**demarketing**'), rather than encouraging this, presents a significant challenge for marketers, given its focus on meeting consumer needs. Widespread reduction of demand for products or services could trigger the factors that are usually seen during recessions, as discussed in the section 'Standard definitions of marketing' above.

Even if demand levels remain static or even increase, organisations must consider environmental sustainability in conjunction with economic sustainability, with implications for the sourcing of raw ingredients, production processes and overall market orientation. From the organisational perspective, there are several reasons for a company to support environmental sustainability. While some organisations still see the issue of sustainability as being at odds with profitability, there is ample evidence that a sustainability focus leads to both organisational and technological innovations that yield positive returns. For example, a commitment to environmental sustainability has resulted in companies such as General Electric with significant cost savings through greater efficiency, reduced waste and increased appeal to some market sectors (Connelly et al., 2011). There is also the added issue of changing consumer perceptions about sustainability as the following mini case study illustrates.

Mini case study 1.1 Consumer pressures on corporations

Consumer pressure has also forced companies to improve their environmental sustainability practices. For example, an integrated social media campaign evolved in 2010 in response to a Greenpeace article criticising Nestlé for sourcing palm oil (used in confectionery products such as Kit Kat) from non-sustainable sources and accused them of depleting areas of rainforest that were a habitat for orangutans (Coombs and Holladay, 2012).

An orchestrated protest campaign led by Greenpeace followed, including a spoof Kit Kat commercial highlighting the plight of orangutans. Several versions of the advertisement in different languages and coverage of protests outside Nestlé offices can be found on YouTube.

While Nestlé officially responded to the criticism by reiterating its support of sustainable sourcing and suspending the supplier whose actions were questioned, a badly managed response by Nestlé to criticism on their Facebook page significantly increased the campaign's publicity (Day, 2011), resulting in over 1.5 million viewings of the Greenpeace commercial and over 200,000 emails to the company demanding that they change to sustainably sourced palm oil. The attempts by Nestlé's Facebook page manager in deleting any negative messages not only increased anger, they also gained news media coverage which continues today.

While Nestlé changed its palm oil sources in response to the pressure, claiming that it had merely accelerated plans to move to sustainable supplies, its actions in initially trying to stifle criticisms led to scepticism and may have created reputational damage, the magnitude of which has yet to be made public.

(Continued)

(Continued)

Pressure is being maintained by organisations such as Greenpeace and Sustainable Brands to get other major manufacturers to move to sustainable sourcing. In late 2013, Unilever pledged to change to traceable, sustainable sources of palm oil (1.5 million tons annually) for its products by the end of 2014 (Hower, 2013).

Questions to consider

How is the growth of consumer pressure groups likely to impact on the **supply chain** – i.e. all the organisations and individuals involved in the production and distribution of raw ingredients, parts and finished products – of other organisations?

What actions should organisations take to:

a) ensure the sustainability of their supplies?
b) ensure the organisation is able to respond credibly to any criticisms?

Consumers' roles in sustainability

There are two parties to a marketing exchange – the marketer and the customer or consumer. Consumers' perspectives are complex: if all things are equal, it is claimed that most consumers will select environmental sustainability, but the decision process becomes more complex when price, quality and status dimensions are considered (Sheth et al., 2011). If the comparison and purchase process is too complex, environmental sustainability criteria are likely to be disregarded (Jones et al., 2008). The issues surrounding consumer perspectives of ethical issues in relation to their own purchase and consumption habits are addressed in Chapter 6. Further research is needed into how these factors vary across population segments and in the types of potential programmes that will engage the public in the issues in order to change individual and community behaviours sufficiently to adapt to changing environmental conditions and more sustainable societies.

MARKETING ETHICS IN THE TWENTY-FIRST CENTURY

The preceding sections have illustrated the much wider extent of ethical issues facing marketers. At this point, we need to be clear regarding what we mean by marketing ethics. To answer this, we need to work through from a general definition of ethics, through to business ethics, and then finally to marketing ethics specifically. Unfortunately, there is no single definition of ethics – different disciplines have provided a range of definitions over time and the advent of the Internet has seen definitions multiply. Many of these definitions are either abstract or refer to 'right' versus 'wrong' decisions, but these latter definitions do not recognise that there may be different perspectives (Lewis, 1985).

Ethics definitions

In terms of ethical choices that may be encountered in everyday life, the following examples may help to illustrate the type of issues covered by ethical decision making:

> Ethics is about norms and values of a certain seriousness, about standards and ideas, i.e. ones that people cannot easily neglect without harming others. (Harvey, 1994: 15)

> [Ethics are] principles, norms and standards of conduct governing an individual or group. (Treveno and Nelson, 2004: 12)

A more expansive definition that captures some of the challenges within ethical dilemmas is:

> Typically defined as the study of standards of conduct and moral judgment. It is particularly useful to us when it helps us to resolve conflicting standards or moral judgments. It is not as simple as deciding what is right and what is wrong. The toughest ethical dilemmas arise when two seemingly right principles are in conflict. (Andreasen, 2001: x)

These definitions imply some sort of explicit governance mechanism, but this does not operate in the formal manner that the legislative system uses. Transgression of ethical norms may result in nothing more than mild criticism from colleagues – or it may result in major adverse media coverage, with potentially damaging effects on company and brand reputations.

Link between ethics and religion/values

While it is assumed that ethics and religion are related, past research has provided mixed conclusions about the exact nature of that relationship. Formal and informal norms, values and beliefs are contained in the teachings of most major religions (Conroy and Emerson, 2004; Parboteeah et al., 2008). Yet while these guides exist, some studies have found no difference between religious and non-religious people with regard to dishonesty or consumer purchasing behaviours (Vitell, 2009).

Business ethics

Business ethics are the values, standards and principles that apply within both commercial and non-commercial business activity. Non-commercial businesses include the not-for-profit/charity sector, governmental sectors, cause-related marketing and social marketing. The challenges confronting these sectors will be discussed in later chapters.

Commercial business ethics has a long history, with the Code of Hammurabi more than 1700 years ago often cited as an example of an early ethics code. The rulers of Mesopotamia (roughly modern day Syria and parts of its surrounding countries) attempted to set fair prices for the sale of goods. The Greek philosopher Aristotle wrote several texts on various aspects of ethics and many major religions provide guidance on business conduct (see, for example, the Christian Bible, the Islamic Koran and the Jewish Talmud) (Marcoux, 2006).

There is now increasing recognition of the difference in ethical perspectives across cultures regarding acceptable versus unacceptable conduct and also methods for dealing with transgressors (Svensson and Wood, 2003). Cross-cultural perspectives will be discussed in more detail in Chapter 3; suffice it to say here that these issues are important and need to be understood within the context of marketing strategy decisions.

Ethical failures in business are frequently blamed on a lack of knowledge about ethical issues – and often educational institutions are blamed for not ensuring that students have an understanding of ethics. The expectation that ethics education provision can somehow result in a major reduction in corporate wrongdoing is, of course, unrealistic. A university is only one of the many institutions that students will encounter and 'no instruction can suffice to turn a scoundrel into a virtuous human being' (Bok, 1974: 7). The organisational environment in which graduates gain employment will have a substantial impact on their subsequent behaviour (Marburg, 2003), with the potential for conflict between personal ethical standards and those that might be perceived as acceptable or expedient within a specific organisation. Indeed, it has been noted that many of those responsible for recent corporate scandals hold MBAs 'from prestigious business schools' (McAlister, 2004: 55). This concept can be extended to suggest that an ethical individual will struggle in an amoral company, as will an ethical company in an amoral business environment (Spence and Van Heekeren, 2005).

Marketing ethics

Ethics are seen as an important part of marketing decision making. The perception of what was ethical to market has changed considerably over time. For example, some historical articles describe in detail the marketing of slaves and the way these 'human assets' were recorded in financial statements ('human capital accounting') (Steen et al., 2011). In the twenty-first century, we find the concept repugnant, but up until the mid-nineteenth century, it was an acceptable business practice in many countries.

More recently, tobacco advertising began to be restricted only in the mid-1960s, being totally banned in many countries only in the 1980s and 1990s – and many developing countries do not yet have such bans in place (see also the discussion in Chapter 3). Consider the examples of historical advertisements shown in Figure 1.1, in terms of the messages that can be conveyed by marketers versus what we now know about the negative health impacts of smoking resulting in marketing messages being restricted in some countries.

Figure 1.1 Historical tobacco advertisements

Source: From the collection of Stanford University (http://tobacco.stanford.edu)

Mini case study 1.2 Did predatory marketing tactics contribute to the global financial crisis?

There are those who suggest that aggressive or **predatory marketing** tactics by the financial sector contributed to (some would say directly caused) the Global Financial Crisis that began to impact on many economies in 2007. The problems began with an increase in subprime lending, i.e. lending via credit, especially via adjustable-rate mortgages, to people whose profiles indicated they were likely to have difficulty in making scheduled repayments of their loans. A high level of defaults on mortgages has been shown to have been a significant contributor to the Global Financial Crisis (Hawtrey and Johnson, 2010). After several years of steady increases, house prices began to fall. At the same time, interest levels increased, making it difficult for people to either refinance loans at what had been expected to be lower interest rates or to keep up with their monthly repayments.

While the problem started in the USA, global investors who had purchased securities backed by mortgages were impacted, leading to a reduction in the purchase of these securities and a tightening of credit around the world. Economic growth stalled and several countries went into recession, with substantial job losses, pushing families into poverty. Some pension funds were badly affected, impacting on current and future retirement incomes. Industry lost output both from the reduced workforce, and from reduced demand for products and services as people lost the ability to spend – or focused on reducing debt rather than spending income (Hawtrey and Johnson, 2010; McKibbin and Stoeckel, 2010).

Questions to consider

While many economies have recovered or are recovering, the question remains: Is it ethical for the financial sector to target consumers who may struggle to pay debts from credit card use or from mortgages?

What is the responsibility of the consumer in making the decision to take on debt?

THE RELATIONSHIPS BETWEEN ETHICS, LEGISLATION, REGULATION AND SELF-REGULATION

Legislation

We need to be clear about the relationship between **legislation**, **regulation** and ethics. Legislation refers to laws – these are universally binding and those who break laws will be prosecuted: penalties may involve fines, jail terms, or orders to cease specific activity which may prevent an organisation from continuing to trade.

Few organisations deliberately violate laws as the penalties, both legal and reputational, are clear. There are exceptions such as major corporate financial failures, for example WorldCom and Enron (Conroy and Emerson, 2004). These scandals illustrate the international financial and reputational costs to the organisations, their employees and their investors. The situation is not so clear with respect to regulation where industry itself is responsible for drafting, maintaining and enforcing regulations as the next section will show.

Regulation takes several forms, but is always subservient to legislation, being used to implement legislation and is usually 'local' in focus, such as applying only to a specific industry sector. Regulation can never be used as an alternative to law, or to supersede legal rulings. It may be enforceable by a governmental authority, or by industry bodies, i.e. self-regulation.

Self-regulation effectiveness

Many industries, including marketing, are self-regulating through the various industry associations that set desired standards for the behaviour of their members. In addition, the marketing communication/advertising sectors are self-regulating, setting their own rules. However, unlike more established professions, there is no means of taking action against those who transgress. For example, an accountant or doctor found to have committed a major breach of ethical provisions could be barred from practising.

The merits of **self-regulation** have been vigorously debated for decades. It has been noted that 'it is too readily assumed that if the market fails, only government regulation can correct its shortcomings' and that 'there are readily observable limits to what regulation, as a form of societal control, can achieve' (Boddewyn, 1989: 20). This raises questions, however, regarding what self-regulation can potentially achieve, whether it is, in reality achieving what can be reasonably expected of it, and if not, what changes to prevailing self-regulatory models should be investigated. Table 1.1 summarises the main arguments put forward for and against self-regulation principles within the context of marketing communication.

The example of advertising and obesity

There is agreement that most countries face a growing 'obesity' epidemic with substantial associated health problems (Stein and Colditz, 2004). Despite considerable debate, there is little agreement regarding the exact causes of the problem, let alone possible solutions; however, restrictions or outright bans on advertising to children are regularly proposed (Jones et al., 2003). There is a growing body of evidence that the influence of marketing activity on dietary and lifestyle choices is small in relation to a number of other factors such as family influence and socio-economic factors (Livingstone, 2005) and that banning advertising of foods perceived to be of low nutrient value and/or foods targeted at children would be ineffective in reducing childhood obesity.

In spite of this, there remain lobbyists who maintain that such bans are central to any serious strategy to reduce the incidence of advertising-related chronic diseases such as obesity, diabetes and cardiovascular diseases. Given the current environment in which policy makers are pressured to be seen to act to remedy increasing obesity levels, it could be expected that marketers would ensure marketing communication programmes

Table 1.1 Overview of arguments for and against self-regulation (adapted from Schumacher et al., 2005)

For	Against
Industry-specific expertise.More effective than legislation which lacks 'nuances derived from an intimate knowledge of business problems and concerns'.	Many decisions come too late, for example, if an advertisement is ordered withdrawn after a campaign is completed, there is effectively no sanction effect at all.
The letter, but not the spirit of legislation, can be observed – self-regulation allows for both. Marketers cannot use technicalities to evade action.	Penalties are often minor, if they are imposed at all; the regulatory provisions are a 'toothless tiger' (Howarth, 2004).
Lower implementation costs and higher effectiveness (public goods).Costs are met by industry with no costs to the complainant or taxpayers.	Cost to industry members will be too high. Free riders as not all marketers/advertisers fund the system; also no penalties on media or advertising agency in the event of a complaint being upheld.
Less adversarial.	Certain factions within the industry will hijack the process for their own ends including using the process against competitors.
Allows members of the public and small companies (for whom litigation may not be economically viable) to challenge the actions of larger companies.	Expertise of experts is used for the benefit of industry rather than the public.
Forestalls more onerous government-imposed regulation.	Operates only when there is a real threat of imminent legislation.
Flexible – can be adapted to deal with new media and easily revised/updated to accommodate new issues.	Danger of collusion.
Protects the right of free speech.	

that demonstrated exemplary responsibility and adherence to self-regulatory principles in order to ensure that their right to self-government was preserved. Given that breaches of the regulatory provisions would indicate that behaviour, albeit from a small number of advertisers, it might be suggested that the existing regulatory provisions be reviewed and strengthened to ensure compliance is obtained – and punitive action against attempted offenders made possible. The alternative for industry is that self-regulation will no longer be a privilege afforded to them and legislative action to restrict their activities may therefore be imposed (Howarth, 2004).

Self-regulatory structures: the example of marketing communication

The advertising industry in many countries is governed by numerous consumer protection laws that apply to all sectors of society. Below the 'layer' of broad legislation, the industry is, in such countries, self-regulating. In these countries, the various communication industry sectors, including advertisers, advertising agencies and the media, have co-operated in drafting Codes of Practice. A major regulatory body, usually titled as an 'Advertising Standards Authority', is established to oversee the processes by which advertising conforms to both the letter and the spirit of the relevant codes.

Supporting this structure, joint industry bodies may exist to maintain advertising standards across specific media such as television. These organisations provide an advisory service, interpreting both relevant statutes and industry codes and applying them to the scripts for proposed commercials as well as 'vetting' final completed commercials prior to their being screened for the first time. Additional restrictions may also apply. For example, commercials that are accepted for screening are given classifications that determine their time placements within programme schedules (e.g., a specific commercial may not be screened before 8.30pm). However, we will show in later chapters that this system lacks accountability.

An additional indirect restriction on advertising is the quota of advertising on electronic media. In many countries, no advertising is permitted in programmes aimed at pre-school aged children; advertising in other children's programmes is restricted to 10 minutes per hour – a move some critics see as an arbitrary restriction on the right of commercial free speech and inconsistent with the total absence of quotas in print media.

Based on an extensive review of the literature, some have contended that self-regulation is the most efficient tool for curbing excesses (Abernethy and Wicks, 2001). However, it should be stressed that programme content is not subject to the same level and type of regulation, and given the concerns noted regarding food portrayal in programmes versus commercials, this is an aspect the media could very well address. This is problematic for countries buying the bulk of their television programmes from overseas.

There is an apparent contradiction between advertising practitioners' acknowledgements that they engage in various forms of **stealth marketing** coupled with, at times, actively seeking to breach regulatory provisions in order to garner publicity and practitioners' apparent disbelief that tighter regulation might be warranted (Cronin, 2004). At best, self-regulatory provisions may be extended to cover evolving media forms. A reality that must be faced is that self-regulation will be replaced by more stringent legislative action likely to restrict marketing activities for specific product categories and/or consumer groups (McAlister, 2004). The potential inadequacy of current self-regulatory systems to adequately oversee and regulate hybrid media activity (Thompson, 2005) is acknowledged in the practitioner literature. Research in related areas such as **advergames** (Dahl et al., 2008) has shown that marketing communications activity in media not subject to formal advertising codes lacks the responsible approach that could reasonably be expected, and that much of this activity would be substantially in breach of the codes that apply to mass media should those codes be extended to other media forms.

It has been observed that marketers engaged with youth-oriented products readily criticise the overall industry but fail to recognise or challenge potential ethical issues stemming from the actions of their own organisations. It is also suggested that this, while not an indicator of deliberate attempts to deceive, has led to a failure to even consider the ethical dimensions of marketing activity (Geraci, 2004). This lack of perception has resulted in inaction on key ethical issues such as the link between food and beverage marketing and childhood obesity.

COMPETING THEORETICAL FOUNDATIONS AND FRAMEWORKS

Think points

How might we use Aristotle's practical wisdom (**phronēsis**) to help understand how, when, where and in what way (Messikomer and Cirka, 2010: 58) to apply theories, frameworks and other factors in our ethical decision making?

Common frameworks

There are several competing ethical frameworks available, including **deontology** (focused on intentions) and **teleology** (focused on outcomes), each with different values (Carter et al., 2011). The frameworks most commonly cited focus either on intentions (often termed deontology, from the Greek word for 'duty') or consequences (often termed teleology, from the Greek word for 'ends', but also referred to in the literature as **consequentialism**). Teleology is also frequently broken down into **utilitarianism** and **egoism** options (Hoffman et al., 2001), with the latter not used in the business context (see the definitions that follow this section). The selection of an ethical framework will impact on the development of marketing strategy. For example, activity that was driven by good intentions without potential negative consequences being considered would be acceptable under deontological reasoning but not under teleological reasoning. While space prevents a detailed analysis of all possible frameworks, the next section gives a brief overview of the main provisions of commonly used frameworks, together with a short commentary on the implications for marketing interventions of the adoption of the different frameworks.

Overview of common ethical frameworks (based on Eagle et al., 2013; originally adapted from Ferrell and Fraedrich, 1994: 54)

Deontology (based on the work of eighteenth-century philosopher Immanuel Kant)

This framework focuses on intentions and holds that there are ethical 'absolutes' that are universally applicable, with the focus on means or intentions. Under deontology, it is accepted that actions intended to do good may have unintended negative consequences, such as creating fear or distress. This is contrary to teleological beliefs that interventions should do no harm, particularly to vulnerable groups who may not be the target of the activity.

Teleology/consequentialism

Teleology/consequentialism focuses on the outcomes or effects of actions and is usually divided into two sections:

a) *Utilitarianism* in which behaviour is ethical if it results in the greatest good for the greatest number, with a recent suggestion that utilitarianism could also be interpreted as the least harm for the greatest number of those affected (Payne and Pressley, 2013).

b) *Egoism*, in which the benefits to the individual undertaking action are stressed and the impact on other people is deemphasised.

Utilitarianism presents challenges when comparing alternative courses of action with different levels of potential impact, for example, a programme that provides minor benefits to all, versus one that provides major benefits to many but no impact or negative impact on others. It also raises questions in relation to who has a mandate to decide whether any harm, or what level of harm might be acceptable. While stigmatising some groups would be unacceptable for many, it is suggested that it can legitimately be used for activities such as reducing smoking rates (Bayer, 2008).

Relativism

Under this framework, there is no universal set of ethical principles as individual cultures, societies or social groups may have their own ethical frameworks; no set of principles is superior to others and no group should judge the ethical standards of other groups. Reasoning under this framework ignores the possibility that:

a) a group's principles are based on incorrect information; and

b) the implications of a group's principles being repugnant to other groups (e.g. sexism or racism).

Two closely related, but less widely used frameworks are:

Social Contract Theory (Kimmel et al., 2011) – this framework posits that an implicit contract exists between the state and/or organisations and individuals or groups regarding rights and responsibilities as a member of society.

Distributive Justice – proponents of this framework hold that there should be assignments of benefits and burdens from all activity according to some standard of fairness.

Given that contracts are implied rather than stated explicitly, there is no shared understanding of which rights and responsibilities and fairness measures apply to the various parties. An additional framework covered in the academic literature is:

Stakeholder theory – holds that there are groups beyond shareholders to whom an organisation has obligations; however which groups should be included as stakeholders is open to debate. Few would argue that workplace conditions for those employed by an organisation should be included, and many high profile brands, including Nike and some major retailers have been heavily criticised for contracting the manufacture of their products to countries where the working conditions and wage rates would be totally unacceptable in developed economies, or where child labour is used in their manufacture (Bair and Palpacuer, 2012; Gilbert and Rasche, 2008). Whether a 'socially responsible' label on clothing would be supported by consumers, or whether consumers would be prepared to pay a premium for items that could be certified as having been made in factories that provided non-sweatshop working conditions has yet to be determined. Additionally, exactly how an organisation can and should take into account the interests of other potential stakeholders remains open to debate. (Gilbert and Rasche, 2008)

Some authors suggest there is no universal set of ethics that can apply across all sectors of society due to the increasing diversity of society and different perspectives may be held within cultures or groups and therefore each group's ethical perspective should be held to be equally valid. The implications of cross-cultural ethics will be discussed further in Chapter 3. A further problem is the lack of a clear and unambiguous interpretation of the frameworks. For example, fear-based interventions, commonly used within social marketing activity such as road safety campaigns, would be acceptable under deontological reasoning given their positive intentions. If they caused distress, teleological principles would render the approach unacceptable. Indeed, as several social advertisers have found to their cost, marketing communication regulators in many countries appear to operate under teleological principles, resulting in the advertising component of an intervention being withdrawn from the media entirely, or requiring modification before being able to be rescheduled (see, for example Advertising Standards Authority, 2012).

CODES OF ETHICS

We note the recent call for a 'transcendental code of ethics' for all marketing professionals (Payne and Pressley, 2013) but suggest these authors grossly oversimplify the magnitude of the task as they merely list broad principles and present an authoritarian approach, including 'the inability of the marketing decision maker to understand that there may be ethical components to a decision being made must be overcome' (2013: 69) without considering what ethical resources might be needed, how support for development and implementation of appropriate resources, and what outcomes might be achieved as a result. Codes of Ethics (CoE), together with support from professional associations, possibly including specific ethics training, may thus help educate inexperienced practitioners and sensitise them to issues they may face in the future (Eagle et al., 2013), but they are not panaceas – there is substantial evidence that the existence of a CoE will not of itself prevent unethical behaviour.

One of the challenges for marketing is that, unlike for members of an established, recognised, profession, there is no mechanism whereby members potentially could lose the right to practise in their profession if found guilty by their peers of a significant transgression of professional ethics. Marketers are not subject to the same level of peer control; there is no requirement that they be licensed and membership of sector organisations is voluntary. The lack of overarching codified legislation and thus the inability to enforce standards or codes in the way that established professional groups are able to do are missing (Hunt and Vitell, 2006).

We have included the links to a number of marketing industry codes of ethics as additional resources at the end of this chapter; they are useful in terms of comparison of how useful they might be for a marketer facing an ethical dilemma. Further research is needed into which types of ethical resources would be most useful to practitioners at all levels in marketing strategy and tactics decisions.

SUMMARY

The discussion in this chapter has highlighted the complexity of ethics within marketing, and their link to wider social, economic and environmental factors. The focus on 'giving the customer what they want' may be at odds with the increasing impetus towards a greater sustainability focus in all spheres of activity impacting on consumers and organisations. The greater awareness of sustainability issues among consumers and their willingness to both reward companies who act responsibly and to punish those that do not will impact on future marketing activity.

There are thus increasing reasons for organisations to act ethically in all aspects of their operations, not just marketing. Unfortunately, breaches of ethics and of consumer trust reoccur, with the ability of the industry to effectively self-regulate itself in an increasingly complex communications environment being increasingly questioned.

While there are a number of ethical frameworks that are frequently cited in both academic and practitioner literature, guidance on which framework should be applied under specific circumstances is lacking and many frameworks remain statements of hope and good intent rather than offering clear guidance for the resolution of specific ethical problems. The lack of enforceable codes of ethics for the industry also remains problematic and this represents an area in which further research is needed.

Case study   Product recalls in the auto and other industries

A test of an organisation's ethical stance occurs during times of crisis. The 'gold standard' of exemplary ethical behaviour is the action of Johnson & Johnson (J&J) in the USA in its handling of the recall of its Tylenol (headache remedy) product in response to a cyanide-poisoning crisis in 1982. The then CEO of J&J had focused on crisis management provisions to ensure that active commitment to the company philosophy statement and the ethical principles it implied would be maintained even in the event of a major crisis situation. This made the subsequent swift and effective product withdrawal, coupled with full, honest discussion of the company's actions in the media, an uncontested course of action (Anonymous, 2003), which, while it cost the company some $US100 million in lost earnings in the short term, allowed it to rebuild and increase its market share in the long term and 'reinforce the company's reputation for integrity and trustworthiness' (Pearson and Clair, 1998: 61).

This case stands in marked contrast to the actions of the automobile industry, starting with the now infamous Ford Pinto case where Ford rushed the Pinto into production in 1971 to try to combat strong competitive pressures from other brands, even though they were aware that rear-end collisions would rupture the car's fuel system, potentially causing the gas tank to explode. Several deaths from rear-end collisions and resultant fires lead to the first ever criminal homicide charge against an American company. Documents produced in court showed that Ford had actually conducted a cost-benefit analysis, weighing likely damages claims due to injury or death against the cost of modifying all cars (at $11 per car). While the criminal homicide charge was dismissed, Ford subsequently paid out millions in out-of-court settlements and mandatory safety standards were eventually introduced despite intensive lobbying to prevent or delay their introduction (Hoffman, 1984).

More recently the case of Ford/Bridgestone (Govindaraj and Jaggi, 2004; O'Rourke, 2001) erupted in 2000, although first reports of problems with Bridgestone tyres had surfaced in 1996. In 2000 Ford unilaterally recalled 13 million tyres, at a cost of US$2.1 billion, after pressure mounted on the company to investigate increasing reports of faulty tyres. The affair lasted for more than five years after the product recall, and resulted in both sides blaming each other publically for the faulty tyres, which resulted in more than 270 deaths and over 800 injuries (BBC News, 2005). The affair finally came to an end in 2005, but not after a massive loss in confidence in both companies.

In early 2010, Toyota announced a number of recalls, totalling over 8.5 million cars across a wide range of models, due to several mechanical problems that were linked to road accidents, some of which were fatal (BBC News, 2010). It remains to be seen as to what the long-term impact on the company will be.

Volkswagen incurred a considerable amount of negative media coverage during 2009–2013 and adverse customer sentiment for differing responses across countries in response to gearbox problems and diesel injectors. For example, Volkswagen Australia refused to issue recalls when Volkswagen of America had done so (Fyfe, 2013). A worldwide 2.6 million vehicle recall in late 2013 for possible fuel leaks, electrical faults and gearbox problems has been attributed in the news media to Volkswagen 'taking shortcuts in its bid to overtake Toyota to become the world's biggest car maker by 2018' (Dowling, 2013: 1). Toyota subsequently made a US$1.32 billion payment to the US Justice Department in early 2014 after admitting it misled consumers, concealed safety issues and made deceptive statements about them (Cowan, 2014).

(Continued)

(Continued)

Questions are being asked about why the auto industry is subject to these types of ongoing problems, and why European and American producers have recall rates that are nearly three times greater than those of their East Asian counterparts (Bates et al., 2007).

Product recalls are not exclusive to the automotive industry. Recent recalls have included toys (Freedman et al., 2012). A 2013 'horsemeat scandal' involving deliberate mis-description of beef burgers and ready meals in the UK led to major product recalls by supermarket chains including Tesco, Iceland, Aldi and Lidl, as well as catering companies, hotel and fast food chains, with similar problems being subsequently found in several European countries. The problem has led to calls for greater food traceability provisions and tighter regulation of food supply chains (Van Vark et al., 2013).

Apart from the direct costs in a product recall, there are also substantial direct and indirect costs associated with such a crisis (Jarrell and Peltzman, 1985); indirect costs will be substantially higher than the direct costs of a product recall, particularly as a result of the negative impact on a firm's goodwill, to the extent that negative externalities for competitors may be larger than those of the company producing the recalled product. These financial strains can be so severe that many companies will need to seek bankruptcy protection when faced with both the direct recall costs and the resulting fines and product-liability claims and/or lawsuits as a result of faulty products (Kwon, 2000).

Often consumers will react to a product recall with total product avoidance, often beyond the affected products. This product avoidance may well last substantially longer than the crisis itself, and therefore remain a major obstacle long after the recall is finished. As a result, after a recall, a company may well struggle to recover its lost market share (Dawar and Pillutla, 2000; Siomkos and Kurzbard, 1994). However, despite these potentially devastating effects of reactive crisis communication, most firms remain ill-prepared to handle a potential crisis effectively – and some argue if most companies face a crisis at best they react ambivalently (Dawar and Pillutla, 2000).

Consumers' interpretations of a firm's response to a product recall crisis are heavily dependent on their prior expectations about the firm (Siomkos and Kurzbard, 1994); a company that is regarded as generally a 'good' company may well find it easier to communicate their point in a crisis situation than a company that is perceived as deceptive or has a poor rapport with the public. Firms with weaker consumer expectations may also have to undertake more brand support either during the crisis or after the immediate crisis is over, for example with extensive advertising and sales promotions, in order to maintain or restore consumer brand equity and **trust** (Kwon, 2000). Recovery rates are an indicator of the success of strategies and tactics put into place to deal with a crisis (Kabak and Siomkos, 1992), as seen via Tylenol. Unfortunately, data from the automotive industry regarding the impact of their recalls are not available.

Brand equity is a term that is frequently used, but often in different ways. There are two distinct ways in which brand equity is measured. The first is financial – the value of a brand as a specific asset when it is sold or included on a balance sheet. The second way in which the term is used relates to customer perceptions and is more relevant here. Consumer-based brand equity is a measure of the strength of consumers' attachment to a brand. Coupled with this are descriptions of the associations and beliefs people have about a brand, brand loyalty and willingness to pay the same price or more than for other brands. Brand equity is therefore closely linked to measures of past satisfaction and intentions to repurchase and can be adversely affected by crises or prolonged negative publicity.

Questions to consider

How should companies develop ethical procedures to be implemented in the event of a product recall or other crisis?

How should they monitor, and respond to, media and consumer comments on any such activity?

Further Reading

Philosophy

You may want to go right back to original philosophies, although some of these are very 'heavy' reading! They are also listed in the supplementary resources at the end of the text.

Aristotle (approx. 350 BCE) *The Ethics of Aristotle* (available as a free ebook from sources such as Project Gutenberg)

Kant, I. (1785) *Groundwork for the Metaphysic of Morals*. Available at: www.justiceharvard.org/resources/immanuel-kant-groundwork-for-the-metaphysics-of-morals-1785/ (accessed 29 June 2015).

Mill, J.S. (1863) *Utilitarianism* (available as a free ebook from sources such as Project Gutenberg)

Rawls, J. (1972) *A Theory of Justice*. Oxford: Clarendon Press.

Business ethics-focused readings

Craft, J. L. (2013) 'A review of the empirical ethical decision-making literature: 2004–2011', *Journal of Business Ethics*, 117: 221–59.

Elm, D.R. and Radin, T.J. (2012) 'Ethical decision making: Special or no different?', *Journal of Business Ethics*, 107(3): 313–29.

(Continued)

(Continued)

Marketing ethics-focused readings

Harrison, P. and Gray, C. (2010) 'The ethical and policy implications of profiling "vulnerable" customers', *International Journal of Consumer Studies*, 34(4): 437–42.

Rodford, P. (2009) 'APACS response to "irresponsible lending? A case study of a credit industry reform initiative', *Journal of Business Ethics*, 86(4): 535–9.

Schlegelmilch, B.B. and Öberseder, M. (2010) 'Half a century of marketing ethics: Shifting perspectives and emerging trends', *Journal of Business Ethics*, 93(1): 1–19.

Van den Bergh, J.C. (2011) 'Environment versus growth—A criticism of "degrowth" and a plea for "a-growth"', *Ecological Economics*, 70(5): 881–90.

Websites

Sustainable Brands: *http://www.sustainablebrands.com/about*

Codes of Ethics (this is not a comprehensive list – we have selected a range of marketing organisations to illustrate the differences in the format, content and detail within their various codes).

American Marketing Association: *http://www.marketingpower.com/AboutAMA/Pages/Statement%20of%20Ethics.aspx*

Business Marketing Association: *http://www.marketing.org/i4a/pages/index.cfm?pageid=3286*

Chartered Institute of Marketing: *http://www.cim.co.uk/about/mktgstandards.aspx*

European Marketing Confederation: *http://www.emcq.eu/index.php?page=code-of-ethics*

European Society for Opinion and Marketing Research (ESOMAR): *http://www.esomar.org/publications-store/codes-guidelines.php*

Market Research Society: *https://www.mrs.org.uk/standards/code_of_conduct/*

Mobile Marketing Association: *http://www.mmaglobal.com/node/1563*

Sales and Marketing Executives International: *http://www.smei.org/displaycommon.cfm?an=1&subarticlenbr=16*

The Incentive Marketing Association: *http://www.imaeurope.com/code-of-ethics/*

The Marketing Association of Australia and New Zealand: *http://www.marketing.org.au/esomar.aspx*

You may also want to search for corporate codes of ethics from a range of organisations.

References

Abernethy, A. and Wicks, J.L. (2001) 'Self-regulation and television advertising: A replication and extension', *Journal of Advertising Research,* 41(3): 31–7.

Advertising Standards Authority (2012) *Public Perception of Harm and Offense in UK Advertising.* Available at: http://www.asa.org.uk/News-resources/~/media/Files/ASA/Misc/ASAHarmOffenceReport.ashx.

American Marketing Association (2008) *The American Marketing Association Releases New Definition for Marketing.* Available at: http://www.marketingpower.com/aboutama/documents/american%20marketing%20association%20releases%20new%20definition%20for%20marketing.pdf.

Andreasen, A.R. (ed.) (2001) *Ethics in Social Marketing.* Washington, DC: Georgetown University Press.

Anonymous (2003) 'James Burke acted before crisis hit', *Fortune,* 138(3): 69.

Assadourian, E. (2010) 'Transforming cultures: From consumerism to sustainability', *Journal of Macromarketing,* 30(2): 186–91.

Bair, J. and Palpacuer, F. (2012) 'From varieties of capitalism to varieties of activism: The Antisweatshop Movement in comparative perspective', *Social Problems,* 59(4): 522–43.

Banerjee, S.B. (2008) 'Corporate social responsibility: The good, the bad and the ugly', *Critical Sociology,* 34(1): 51–79.

Bates, H., Holweg, M., Lewis, M. and Oliver, N. (2007) 'Motor vehicle recalls: Trends, patterns and emerging issues', *Omega,* 35(2): 202–10.

Bayer, R. (2008) 'Stigma and the ethics of public health: Not can we but should we', *Social Science & Medicine,* 67(3): 463–72.

BBC News (2010) *Toyota Recalls Thousands of Prius Cars Worldwide.* Available at: http://news.bbc.co.uk/2/hi/business/8505402.stm.

BBC News (2005) *Bridgestone ends Ford recall row.* Available at: http://news.bbc.co.uk/1/hi/business/4335324.stm.

Boddewyn, J.J. (1989) 'Advertising self-regulation: True purpose and limits', *Journal of Advertising,* 18(2): 19–27.

Bok, D. (1974) 'Can higher education foster higher morals?', *Business and Society Review,* 66(Summer): 4–12.

Burroughs, J.E. (2010) 'Can consumer culture be contained? Comment on "Marketing Means and Ends for a Sustainable Society"', *Journal of Macromarketing,* 30(2): 127–132.

Carter, S.M., Rychetnik, L., Lloyd, B., Kerridge, I.H., Baur, L., Bauman, A., Hooker, C. and Zask, A. (2011) 'Evidence, ethics, and values: A framework for health promotion', *American Journal of Public Health,* 101(3): 465–72.

Chabowski, B., Mena, J. and Gonzalez-Padron, T. (2011) 'The structure of sustainability research in marketing, 1958–2008: A basis for future research opportunities', *Journal of the Academy of Marketing Science,* 39(1): 55–70.

Charles, G. (2007) *A New Definition of Marketing.* Available at: http://www.brandrepublic.com/news/739886/.

Colman, R. (2010) 'Measuring real progress', *Oxford Leadership Journal,* 1(3): 1–8.

Connelly, B., Ketchen, D. and Slater, S. (2011) 'Toward a "theoretical toolbox" for sustainability research in marketing', *Journal of the Academy of Marketing Science,* 39(1): 86–100.

Conroy, S.J. and Emerson, T.L. (2004) 'Business ethics and religion: Religiosity as a predictor of ethical awareness among students', *Journal of Business Ethics,* 50(4): 383–96.

Coombs, W.T. and Holladay, J.S. (2012) 'The paracrisis: The challenges created by publicly managing crisis prevention', *Public Relations Review,* 38(3): 408–15.

Crittenden, W., Ferrell, L., Ferrell, O. and Pinney, C. (2011) 'Market-oriented sustainability: A conceptual framework and propositions', *Journal of the Academy of Marketing Science,* 39(1): 71–85.

Cowan, J. (2014) *Toyota to Pay $1.3 Billion for Deadly Defect Cover-Up.* Available at: http://www.abc.net.au/news/2014-03-20/toyota-pays-1-3-billion-for-defect-cover-up-statements/5332894.

Cronin, A.M. (2004) *Advertising Myths: The Strange Half-lives of Images and Commodities.* London: Routledge.

Dahl, S., Eagle, L. and Baez, C. (2008) 'Analyzing advergames: Active diversions or actual deception. An exploratory study of online advergame content', *Consumers,* 10(1): 17–34.

Dawar, N. and Pillutla, M.M. (2000) 'Impact of product-harm crises on brand equity: The moderating role of consumer expectations', *Journal of Marketing Research,* 37(2): 215–26.

Day, G. (2011) 'Closing the marketing capabilities gap', *Journal of Marketing,* 75(July): 183–95.

Dietz, S. and Stern, N. (2008) 'Why economic analysis supports strong action on climate change: A response to the Stern Review's critics', *Review of Environmental Economics and Policy,* 2(1): 94–113.

Dowling, J. (Producer) (2013) *Volkswagen Issues Second Major Recall in Five Months.* Available at: http://www.news.com.au/business/companies/volkswagen-issues-second-major-recall-in-five-months/story-fnda1bsz-1226761008994.

Eagle, L., Dahl, S., Hill, S., Bird, S., Spotswood, F. and Tapp, A. (2013) *Social Marketing.* Harlow, England: Pearson.

Ferrell, O.C. and Fraedrich, J.B. (1994) *Business Ethics: Ethical Decision Making and Cases* (2nd edn). Boston, MA: Houghton Miflin.

Freedman, S., Kearney, M. and Lederman, M. (2012) 'Product recalls, imperfect information, and spillover effects: Lessons from the consumer response to the 2007 toy recalls', *Review of Economics and Statistics,* 94(2): 499–516.

Fyfe, M. D. and Dobell, G. (2013) *Faults that Trashed a Reputation.* Available at: http://smh.drive.com.au/motor-news/faults-that-trashed-a-reputation-20130607-2nvlc.html.

Geraci, J.C. (2004) 'What do youth marketers think about selling to kids?', *International Journal of Advertising & Marketing to Children,* 5(3): 11–17.

Gilbert, D.U. and Rasche, A. (2008) 'Opportunities and problems of standardized ethics initiatives – a stakeholder theory perspective', *Journal of Business Ethics,* 82(3): 755–73.

Govindaraj, S. and Jaggi, B. (2004) 'Market overreaction to product recall revisited – the case of Firestone Tires and the Ford Explorer', *Review of Quantitative Finance & Accounting,* 23(1): 31–54.

Grönroos, C. (2006) 'On defining marketing: Finding a new roadmap for marketing', *Marketing Theory,* 6(4): 395–417.

Harvey, B. (ed.) (1994) *Business Ethics: A European Approach.* Hertfordshire: Prentice Hall International (UK).

Hawtrey, K. and Johnson, R. (2010) 'On the atrophy of moral reasoning in the global financial crisis', *Journal of Religion and Business Ethics,* 1(2); Online edition, article 4: 1–26.

Hoffmann, S. and Hutter, K. (2012) 'Carrotmob as a new form of Ethical Consumption. The nature of the concept and avenues for future research', *Journal of Consumer Policy,* 35(2): 215–36.

Hoffman, W.M. (1984) 'The Ford Pinto', *Business Ethics*, 419.

Hoffman, W.M., Frederick, R.E. and Schwartz, M.S. (2001) *Business Ethics: Readings and Cases in Corporate Morality* (4th edn). New York: McGraw-Hill.

Howarth, B. (2004) 'Advertisers test the limits', *Business Review Weekly (BRW),* 26(4): 62–3.

Hower, M. (2013) *Unilever Pledges 100% Traceable Palm Oil by End of 2014.* Available at: http://www.sustainablebrands.com/news_and_views/food_systems/mike-hower/unilever-promises-100-palm-oil-will-be-traceable-known-source.

Hunt, S.D. and Vitell, S.J. (2006) 'The general theory of marketing ethics: A revision and three questions', *Journal of Macromarketing,* 26(2): 143–53.

Jarrell, G. and Peltzman, S. (1985) 'The impact of product recalls on the wealth of sellers', *The Journal of Political Economy,* 93(3): 512–36.

Jones, A., Williams, F. and Buckley, N. (2003) 'WHO warns against media obsession with obesity', *Financial Times online edition*, June 24.

Jones, P., Clarke-Hill, C. and Comfort, D. (2008) 'Marketing and sustainability', *Marketing Intelligence & Planning,* 26(2): 123–30.

Kabak, I.W. and Siomkos, G.J. (1992) 'Monitoring recovery after a product harm crisis', *Industrial Management,* 34(3): 11–12.

Kilbourne, W. and Pickett, G. (2008) 'How materialism affects environmental beliefs, concern, and environmentally responsible behavior', *Journal of Business Research,* 61(9): 885–93.

Kimmel, A.J., Smith, N.C. and Klein, J.G. (2011) 'Ethical decision making and research deception in the behavioral sciences: An application of social contract theory', *Ethics & Behavior,* 21(3): 222–51.

Kwon, B. (2000) 'When bad things happen to good companies', *FSB: Fortune Small Bus,* 10(8): 104–7.

Lewis, P.V. (1985) 'Defining "business ethics": Like nailing jello to a wall', *Journal of Business Ethics,* 4(5): 377–83.

Livingstone, S. (2005) 'Assessing the research base for the policy debate over the effects of food advertising to children', *International Journal of Advertising,* 24(3): 273–96.

Marburg, E. (2003) 'Educational impacts on academic business practitioner's moral reasoning and behaviour: Effects of short courses in ethics or philosophy', *Business Ethics: A European Review,* 12(4): 403–13.

Marcoux, A. (2006) 'The concept of business in business ethics', *Journal of Private Enterprise,* 21(2): 50-67.

McAlister, D. (2004) 'Building ethical capacity in business schools', *Marketing Education Review,* 14(3): 55–62.

McKibbin, W.J. and Stoeckel, A. (2010) 'The global financial crisis: Causes and consequences', *Asian Economic Papers,* 9(1): 54–86.

Messikomer, C.M. and Cirka, C.C. (2010) 'Constructing a code of ethics: An experiential case of a national professional organization', *Journal of Business Ethics,* 95(1): 55–71.

Nahser, F.B. (2014) 'Consumption in the un-commons: The economic case for reclaiming the *commons* as unique *markets*', in P.E. Murphy (ed.), *Marketing and the Common Good.* Abingdon Oxon: Routledge. pp. 127–52.

Nunes, J.C., Drèze, X. and Han, Y.J. (2011) 'Conspicuous consumption in a recession: Toning it down or turning it up?', *Journal of Consumer Psychology,* 21(2): 199–205.

O'Rourke, J. (2001) 'Bridgestone/Firestone, Inc. and Ford Motor Company: How a product safety crisis ended a hundred-year relationship, *Corporate Reputation Review,* 4(3): 255.

Parboteeah, K.P., Hoegl, M. and Cullen, J.B. (2008) 'Ethics and religion: An empirical test of a multidimensional model', *Journal of Business Ethics,* 80(2): 387–98.

Payne, D. and Pressley, M. (2013) 'A transcendent code of ethics for marketing professionals', *International Journal of Law and Management,* 55(1): 55–73.

Pearson, C.M. and Clair, J.A. (1998) 'Reframing crisis management', *Academy of Management Review,* 23(1): 59–76.

Peattie, K. and Peattie, S. (2009) 'Social marketing: A pathway to consumption reduction?', *Journal of Business Research,* 62(2): 260–8.

Prasad, A. and Holzinger, I. (2013) 'Seeing through smoke and mirrors: A critical analysis of marketing CSR', *Journal of Business Research,* 66(10): 1915–21.

Rotfeld, H.J. and Taylor, C.R. (2009) 'The advertising regulation and self-regulation issues ripped from the headlines with (sometimes missed) opportunities for disciplined multi-disciplinary research', *Journal of Advertising,* 38(4): 5–14.

Salvaris, M. (2013) 'Measuring the kind of Australia we want: The Australian National Development Index, the Gross Domestic Product and the global movement to redefine progress', *Australian Economic Review,* 46(1): 78–91.

Schumacher, C., Bulmer, S.L. and Eagle, L. (2005) 'The games marketers play: Perspectives on marketing communication, self-regulation and Game Theory', *Massey University Department of Commerce Working Paper Series, 05.30.*

Sheth, J.N. and Uslay, C. (2007) 'Implications of the revised definition of marketing: From exchange to value creation', *Journal of Public Policy & Marketing,* 26(2): 302–7.

Sheth, J.N., Sethia, N.K. and Srinivas, S. (2011) 'Mindful consumption: A customer-centric approach to sustainability', *Journal of the Academy of Marketing Science,* 39(1): 21–39.

Shimp, T.E. (2003) *Advertising, Promotion and Supplemental Aspects of IMC* (6th edn). Mason, OH: Thompson Southwestern.

Siomkos, G.J. and Kurzbard, G. (1994) 'The hidden crisis in product-harm crisis management', *European Journal of Marketing,* 28(2): 30–41.

Spence, E. and Van Heekeren, B. (2005) *Advertising Ethics.* New Jersey: Pearson Education.

Steen, A., Welch, D. and McCormack, D. (2011) 'Conflicting conceptualizations of human resource accounting', *Journal of Human Resource Costing & Accounting,* 15(4): 299–312.

Stein, C.J. and Colditz, G.A. (2004) 'The epidemic of obesity', *Journal of Clinical Endocrinology and Metabolism,* 89(6): 2522–5.

Stuart, M.B. (2011) 'The good, the bad and the indifferent: Marketing and the Triple Bottom Line', *Social Business,* 1(2): 173–87.

Svensson, G. and Wood, G. (2003) 'The dynamics of business ethics: A function of time and culture–cases and models', *Management Decision,* 41(4): 350–61.

The Marketing Association of Australia and New Zealand (n.d.) *Marketing Defined.* Available at: http://www.marketing.org.au/?i=Xn3dEjHBZ5M=&t=jZS6ngCVPug=.

Thompson, S. (2005) 'Food Fight's new fronts: Viral marketing, games', *Advertising Age,* 76(29): 3–4.

Treveno, L. and Nelson, K.A. (2004) *Managing Business Ethics* (3rd edn). NJ: John Wiley & Sons.

Van Vark, C., Humphrey, J., Sampathkumar, R., Nicolaides, L., Robinson, P., Ducharme, H. and Longfield, J. (2013) 'What do food traceability crises in the North mean for people working in food chains in the global South?', *Food Chain,* 3(1): 5-17.

Vitell, S.J. (2009) 'The role of religiosity in business and consumer ethics: A review of the literature', *Journal of Business Ethics,* 90(2): 155–67.

Williams, J. and Aitken, R. (2011) 'The service-dominant logic of marketing and marketing ethics', *Journal of Business Ethics,* 102(3): 439–54.

Criticisms of Marketing

Lynne Eagle, Stephan Dahl and David R. Low

CHAPTER OVERVIEW

In this chapter we will discuss the major generic criticisms of marketing, including:

- fostering of materialism and unsustainable consumption
- deception, including 'greenwashing' and manipulation
- the (mis)use of corporate social responsibility as a mechanism to enhance corporate reputations

We will also examine the specific ethical issues that may arise in developing marketing strategies and tactics, including:

- product design, safety, packaging, labelling
- market research
- promotional activity, including both traditional forms of marketing communications and newer hybrid forms such as product placements, as well as ethical issues in public relations and selling activity

We will conclude the chapter with a discussion of how marketers should address these criticisms and then discuss what concepts such as ethical marketing involve.

MAJOR 'GENERIC' CRITICISMS OF MARKETING (I.E. MADE OVER THE LAST 50 YEARS)

A scan of both academic literature and consumer media shows that marketing has been blamed for a number of issues over the last 50 years. Marketing is the organisational function that brings customers and consumers into contact with an organisation. It does not operate in a vacuum; a firm's overall identity and choice of expectations and standards impacts on all aspects of the organisation including marketing (Martin et al., 2011).

The main generic criticism of marketing over time have been that it is inherently deceptive, manipulative, offensive and wasteful (i.e. adding to costs). In relation to marketing communication specifically, it is also claimed that it persuades people to buy products and services they don't need and plays on fears and insecurities (Shimp, 2003), for example through the marketing of toothpaste for fresh breath and deodorant to combat body odours. More recent criticisms have included the fostering of materialism and **unsustainable consumption**. We now examine the main criticisms in more detail.

Fostering materialism and unsustainable consumption

We discussed some of the implications of marketing's role in driving economic growth in Chapter 1. Does it drive materialism? **Materialism** has existed long before mass marketing and marketing communication activity (Sirgy et al., 2012a). However, there is little doubt some marketing activity reinforces the desire to possess things for more than their purely functional attributes, such as for status. Having material things does not guarantee satisfaction with standards of living. Highly material people may frequently evaluate their perceived relative standard of living, leading potentially to a heightened sense of dissatisfaction with their standard of living and to dissatisfaction with quality of life overall (Sirgy et al., 2012b). This may lead to the desire to possess even more things – how such people might respond to the growing calls for sustainability is as yet unknown.

There is a growing body of evidence that a competitive advantage can be obtained by aligning sustainability with marketing strategies (Mitchell et al., 2010). Achieving this may require a dialogue with stakeholders, including a clear presentation of the financial and non-financial benefits (Crittenden et al., 2011). However, it appears the claim that marketing promotes unsustainable consumption is incorrect. Fifty years ago, there was little recognition of any responsibilities to the wide range of stakeholders recognised today. This modern recognition of responsibility drives the need for an organisation to provide value in the products and services it offers in a sustainable and socially responsible manner (Svensson et al., 2010).

Deception and manipulation

Deception usually focuses on marketing communication and longitudinal studies have shown, over a long period of time, a large majority of people have believed advertising was untruthful (Calfee and Ringold, 1994). There is a difference between the use of **puffery**, being the obvious and recognised exaggeration of a product's benefits, and deliberate deception. The latter is prevented, in the mass media at least, via the complex regulations that apply in many countries. We will show in Chapter 5 that newer media forms present challenges regarding effective regulation.

The charge of **manipulation** implies advertising is a strong force capable of making people act in ways they would not normally (Shimp, 2003). This view has been more popular in the US than in Europe but a growing body of evidence indicates advertising, via traditional media at least, is a relatively weak force, particularly in mature markets (Eagle et al., 2005). Thus, advertising is unlikely to create fear and insecurity to an extent that people will suddenly start to buy products for which they previously had no use. Ideally, it presents people with potential solutions to problems they recognise.

Manipulation is also claimed in relation to **subliminal advertising**, i.e., where messages are presented in a way that people are not consciously aware of them (Rotfeld and Taylor, 2009). Concerns regarding the possible effects of subliminal advertising have existed since the 1950s when a US study claimed to show significant increases in popcorn and cola sales as a result of subliminal messages in movies. While this study has been shown to have been falsified, popular media have continued to claim behavioural effects (Broyles, 2006; Keys, 1973). Short-term effects have been created in artificial laboratory situations and there is no evidence of real-world effects (Cooper and Cooper, 2002). Even in recent academic literature, there is evidence of confusion as to what subliminal advertising is, such as classification of product placements (discussed later) as subliminal (Tsai et al., 2007).

In terms of persuading people to buy products or services they do not need, this is a very value-laden perspective ignoring the simple question of who should decide on what is needed by whom. Should someone who is able to afford luxury goods or services be prevented from buying them on the basis that basic products would suffice? Is it possible, as some have claimed (Assadourian, 2010), to transform cultures from consumerism to a sustainability focus?

Think points

In your own life, what products and services have you bought for purely functional reasons? What have you purchased for more symbolic reasons, such as support of a sports team, the satisfaction of buying something you have always wanted, or the demonstration of success or achievement? Distinguish between what you needed and what you wanted. Should anyone have the right to tell you that you have made poor choices? Did you consider the environmental impact of your purchases? If so, in what way did this influence your purchase decisions? If sustainability and environmental concerns become more important in the future, how will this impact on your future purchasing behaviour?

Wasteful strategies

Criticisms in this area relate either to claims of product proliferation, with many brand variants having little meaningful differences or the expense of advertising. The reasons for the multiple variants in a category, such as toothpaste that whitens, provides fresh breath, and/or prevents cavities, will be based on market research that indicates what attributes consumers seek or which may be provided by competitive products. No organisation will market products that are not financially successful in the longer term.

While it is claimed that advertising adds to the cost of a product (Jahdi and Acikdilli, 2009), this claim is not generally correct. For most marketers, advertising is an investment (Luo and de Jong, 2012); there is no such thing as a willing advertiser – advertising is often the most efficient and economical way of raising awareness regarding a product or service and its specific attributes, thus ultimately generating sales. In the **fast moving consumer goods (FMCG)** categories such as grocery items, a specific level of advertising may be a requirement to maintain distribution and shelf space (Eagle et al., 2005).

THE RESPONSIBILITY OF BUSINESS

There is a philosophical opposition to business having any social responsibility, usually traced back to the work of Nobel Prize winning economist Milton Friedman and his frequently misreported statement that the responsibility of business is to maximise profits. As his comments are often taken out of context and reported as implying that business has no ethical responsibility, we have reproduced below Friedman's original comments on the issue, originally made in the 1970s and re-released in the 1990s:

> The view has been gaining widespread acceptance that corporate officials ... have a social responsibility that goes beyond serving the interests of their stockholders.... . This view shows a fundamental misconception of the character and nature of a free economy. In such an economy, there is one and only one social responsibility of business – to use its resources and engage in activities designed to increase its profits so long as it stays within the rules of the game, which is to say, engages in open and free competition, without deception or fraud .... Few trends could so thoroughly undermine the very foundations of our free society as the acceptance of a social responsibility other than to make as much money for their stockholders as possible. (Friedman, 2009: 133)

This view has been challenged and there is now a widespread recognition of the need to consider a wide range of stakeholders and issues related to sustainability as discussed in Chapter 1. A major criticism of the focus on a search for short-term profits is that they may be obtained at the expense of consumers who are increasingly ready to punish brands they perceive as not meeting their needs (Tadajewski and Jones, 2012). Generally, ethical brands are trusted and generate consumer loyalty (Sirgy et al., 2012a) and there are potentially severe consequences for **brand image** and the equity of unethical conduct (Leonidou et al., 2013).

While the focus on customers is widely accepted, such as via service-dominant logic discussed in Chapter 1 (Lusch and Vargo, 2006), a wider focus on other stakeholders including suppliers, has been shown to be associated with a higher marker and financial performance, reputation and employee commitment to the firm (Mitchell et al., 2010). Many firms struggle to achieve this multi-stakeholder commitment in an integrated rather than single-issue focused way (Maignan et al., 2005, 2011). CSR is a common strategy by which firms try to express their wider responsibilities.

CRITICISMS OF CORPORATE SOCIAL RESPONSIBILITY (CSR)

We discussed CSR briefly in the preceding chapter. It is a concept that is not without its critics who generally claim that it does not reflect a true commitment to any form of social responsibility on the part of an organisation, but rather a somewhat cynical attempt to make an organisation look good in the eyes of its stakeholders (Prasad and Holzinger, 2013) or to divert attention away from the negative impacts of a firm's activity (Kuznetsov et al., 2009).

While CSR is a prominent manifestation of the recognition of wider responsibility, there are significant differences in the way it is interpreted across cultures (Kuznetsov et al., 2009; Panimbang, 2013). In western cultures, there is still disagreement over its concepts and a perception that in many instances it is window dressing rather than a real commitment.

Greenwashing

Positive gains can accrue through environmentally friendly marketing strategies (Cronin et al., 2011), but insincere CSR may become **greenwashing**, i.e. tactics designed to mislead consumers regarding the pro-environmental stance of an organisation or the environmental benefits of a product or service it markets (Parguel et al., 2011). Revelations of corporate irresponsibility will lead increasingly to punishment by consumers (Sweetin et al., 2013) although cross-cultural studies indicate that different cultural groups act in different ways (Williams and Zinkin, 2008).

Think points

As an employee of a company owned by shareholders, how would you respond to the view that your only responsibility is to maximise profits? What role do you see for CSR and how do you reconcile CSR activity with profit maximisation?

Mini case study 2.1   Supply chains

Recent drives by countries such as Costa Rica to become carbon neutral, impact on companies such as the multinational fruit producer Dole and their entire supply chain, including growers, packers, transportation and warehousing facilities. Dole has limited control over some of these organisations. This raises many issues over coordination and control from the production perspective and requires a detailed analysis of the level of carbon emissions from different parts of the supply chain, together with potential strategies for emission reductions.

Given that Dole does not directly control supply chain members, issues arise of how willing and able these members are to change their business operations, whether compensation or incentives should apply, or whether alternative supply chain members can be sought.

Other issues from the consumer perspective include how consumers will perceive carbon neutral fruits relative to fruits sourced from non-carbon neutral sources, and whether they would be willing to pay a price premium for the former (Kilian et al., 2011).

Questions to consider

If Dole, having made a public commitment to carbon neutrality, is unable to achieve this throughout their supply chain, will they lose credibility or be accused of greenwashing?

Similar issues have arisen in relation to organic clothing where major brands, including retailers, have struggled to verify the organic origin of clothing materials (Baines et al., 2012; Graß, 2013).

MARKET STRUCTURES

The structure of markets can have a significant impact on the power of organisations within an industry. The more market share a company has the more potential it has for holding power within an industry. The dominance of some major firms in a market or sector may impact on ethical activity. It is claimed that people want to know about the company behind the brands they have available (Jahdi and Acikdilli, 2009). The extent of people's search for this information and the way they act on any information obtained is not clear. How much do people know about the supply chain involved in delivering their preferred products and services?

Figure 2.1 provides an illustration of the ownership concentration of FMCG products at a recent point in time. A similar diagram could be drawn for other types of products or market sectors, for example the automotive or pharmaceutical sectors.

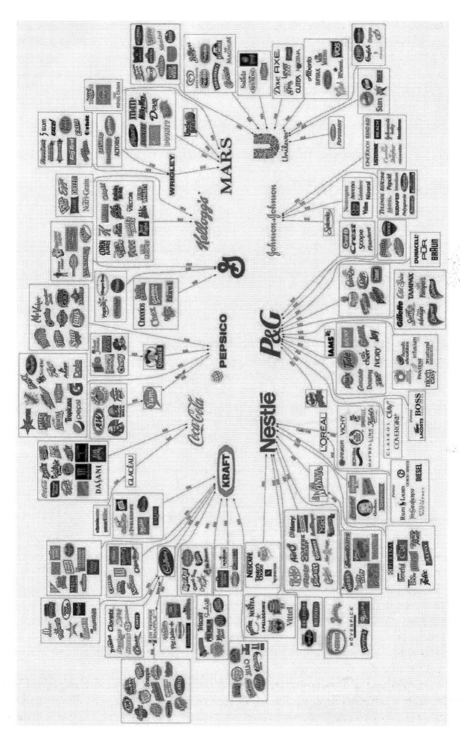

Figure 2.1 Ownership concentration of FMCG products

Source: http://davaidavai.com/

Other business strategies that have drawn criticism for poor ethical practice include the use of third world country labour to produce goods for developed markets. There have been several major exposés of poor labour practices in third world factories where goods such as electronics, clothing or shoes are made for western markets. There is no evidence of any lasting impact on brand equity and sales for organisations and their brands – often they are not revealed in news media coverage.

Additionally, several major food brands (at the time of writing this text) are owned by tobacco companies. Would it impact on people's willingness to buy these products if details of the parent organisation were more widely known?

Organisational power

Take for instance the supermarket industry in a number of countries. In America the top ten grocery retailers account for 68% of the sales (Agnese, 2010) and the top five grocery retailers in China account for 38% of the market share (Mortimer, 2013), whereas in Australia the top two grocery retailers account for 70% of the market share (IBIS World, 2014).

Supermarkets do not manufacture the products they sell, rather they resell products they have purchased from manufacturers. If we compare two extreme country concentrations (China and Australia) using Porter's (1980) seminal text on competitive structure analysis, we see that barriers to entry can be more effective if there is little market share to fight over (hence the 70% share by two firms in Australia is more of a barrier than the 62% shared amongst the smallest Chinese retailers). We also see threats of substitutes to products (such as private labels) being higher for suppliers as well as their power over the retailers being lower in the Australian market when compared to the Chinese market structure. Likewise too, the bargaining power of buyers is reduced where they only have a limited alternative to purchase food products.

The evolution of house brands, also known as private label brands (this is where the supermarket has goods manufactured on their behalf under their own label), has been criticised and blamed for the reduction of choice in markets where market power is concentrated (Geyskens et al., 2010). As Acton said in 1887:

> Power tends to corrupt, and absolute power corrupts absolutely.
>
> *Source:* http://www.phrases.org.uk/meanings/absolute-power-corrupts-absolutely.html

Some of the ethical issues involved in this are discussed in the following section.

House brands versus manufacturer brands

The growth in retailer-owned '**house brands**' that compete alongside **manufacturer brands** also warrants consideration as these brands may hold up to 20% of overall retail sales and are often in the top three brands of 70% of supermarket product categories (Sayman and Raju, 2004). Manufacturer brands are often required to provide substantial marketing communication programmes in order to retain their shelf space. House brands, often produced for the retailer by the same manufacturers against which the house brands then compete, tend to receive little promotional support and what is provided is generally price-based, with house brands positioned alongside manufacturer brands on the shelves, but sold at substantially lower prices.

Manufacturers may feel forced to enter into an agreement to produce products for a large retailer to be sold under the retailer's own brand. The choice may be that if one manufacturer does not provide the product, its main competitors may very well do so, potentially jeopardising their own long-term access to sales via the retailer. Even with some cannibalisation of a manufacturer-brand's sales by a house brand which is produced by the affected manufacturer, the additional sales generated by such a de-facto brand extension may make the combination of the two profitable, thus it may make economic sense for a manufacturer to produce a retailer's house brand to compete against its own brands.

Think points

Should consumers be made aware of the fact that house brands are produced by well-known manufacturers? Given the price differential between manufacturer and house brands, what impact might this knowledge have on the relative sales for the brands?

MARKETING STRATEGIES AND TACTICS

There are a number of ethical issues arising in relation to the traditional 4Ps of marketing (product, pricing, promotional and place), that is, distribution strategies and the market research that underpins them. The main issues are discussed in the following sections.

Market research

Criticisms directed at marketing research generally focus on deception, such as the false identification of a sponsoring organisation, or the use of claimed research as a means to sell products or services. Deception is usually classified as either active or passive. Active deception involves blatant falsehoods such as in relation to the purpose of the research. Passive deception includes withholding relevant information such as the organisation commissioning the research. Under deontology, any deception would be considered morally wrong, regardless of the consequences. It is claimed by some (Kimmel et al., 2011) that deception in research is still a widespread practice and that it is actually morally permissible in order to achieve the research objectives. Deception, however, violates participants' right to informed consent and knowledge of deception will destroy the trust between researcher and participants, potentially leading to refusals to participate further – and thus negating any initial benefits that deception might have offered.

Lesser criticisms of market research relate to breaches of privacy such as observing behaviour without consent and the lack of concern for respondents such as contacting potential respondents at inconvenient times or insensitive interviewing techniques (Ameer, 2013). As with deception, these actions will only harm the relationships with potential respondents and make the collection of valid data increasingly difficult.

Most market research is conducted by organisations and individuals who belong to industry sector organisations who have comprehensive codes of practice aimed at preventing unethical practices such as those discussed above. The efficacy of these codes in preventing unethical behaviour or in disciplining those who breach ethical provisions is unknown.

Big Data

There are now massive amounts of data available about people and their behaviours both as citizens and consumers – this is frequently referred to as being in the era of 'Big Data'. There are many ethical dilemmas relating to the use of 'Big Data'. While there is the potential to use data to help to create products and services closely aligned to people's wants and needs, there are also concerns that this will result in an invasion of privacy and invasive marketing techniques (Boyd and Crawford, 2012).

Mini case study 2.2   RFID

Radio Frequency Identification (RFID) enables consumers to be identified in the vicinity of a retail outlet and their movements within the store including their purchase behaviours can then be tracked. This tracking generally occurs without consumer knowledge. The aim is to enhance the purchase experience and to continually improve customer loyalty programmes (Bayraktar et al., 2010).

While RFID devices are usually incorporated into physical products, some recent applications have caused concern. For example, the Baja Beach Club in Spain was reported to implant (yes, via a syringe…) tiny RFID 'tag' devices under the skin of VIP club members. The intention was to enable members to access services without conventional identification, cash or credit cards. A simple surgical procedure is required to remove the tag should members wish; otherwise the tag remains active even after a guest has left the facility. Clubs in other countries are reported to be using similar 'invasive' tactics. Other organisations have opted for RFID tags to be provided via wristbands – or through mobile phones (Boeck et al., 2011).

Questions to consider

When does customer tracking become too invasive?

What data are you happy for marketers to hold regarding your past and potential future purchasing habits?

What controls currently exist regarding access to your data and how adequate do you believe those controls to be?

What are the boundaries to your own comfort with the data capture technology?

Product-related issues

Product design/safety issues and counterfeit products (including medicines) are more problematic in transitional economies than in mature economies where quality control may be more tightly regulated (Zhang et al., 2009). The availability of these products on the Internet means that substandard or even hazardous products can be accessed well beyond their country of origin even if they do not meet the standards of products produced within countries into which they may be imported.

Packaging also creates several ethical issues. The first relates to the high volume of waste generated by excessive packaging, with implications for both the resources needed to produce the packaging and packaging disposal. **Slack packaging**, that is, the practice of using large packages to visually overstate the quantity of product the package contains, for example cereals, is also held to be misleading (Ameer, 2013).

A relatively new issue is that claims made on food packaging such as 'healthy' or 'low fat' may lead consumers to infer wider positive benefits than a product actually possesses. This has been termed a 'health halo' effect which is claimed to lead to increased consumption of the product and thus to potential overeating (Chandon, 2013). Increases in serving sizes ('supersizing') and the bundling of several food items into a package deal are also claimed to be drivers of overeating.

The potential efficacy of policy decisions to counter the potential harm from packaging-based claims has been debated for some considerable time, with options including mandatory nutrition labelling, tighter regulation of health claims, education and changing the environment in which eating occurs. Despite this debate, research comparing the relative efficacy of these measures over the long term is scarce.

Segmentation and targeting-related issues

It is claimed that targeting children is inherently unfair due to their limited ability to understand the persuasive nature of marketing activity. This issue will be discussed in more detail in Chapter 7 as many of the issues involved with this segment of the population are complex.

Other criticisms of marketing targeting include criticism of the tobacco and alcohol industries for specifically targeting both low socio-economic groups (Palmer and Hedberg, 2013), and elderly groups for security products using the tactics of fear of crime (Sher, 2011). We also discussed the aggressive marketing of financial credit in Chapter 1.

Pricing-related issues

Ethical issues relating to pricing generally relate to perceptions that pricing is unfair. The impact of unfair strategies on relationships between buyers and sellers is discussed in more detail in Chapter 4. Here, we discuss only the main pricing strategies that are criticised.

Price gouging occurs when a firm sets the price of goods or services at a level that is seen as unreasonably high. Pharmaceutical companies are frequently accused of this tactic when introducing new drugs. They respond that the pricing reflects the recovery of the massive research and development investment needed to develop these drugs. This then leads to debate regarding the affordability of drugs, especially in developing countries.

Patents on new drugs expire after only a short number of years, after which competitors may enter the market, often offering generic (unbranded) versions of the original drug, but at significantly lower prices. In some countries, it is a legal requirement for patients to be offered the choice between a branded version of a drug and its generic counterpart.

Closely related to price gouging is **price skimming**, where a higher price is charged at the time a new product or service is introduced to the market. Some people, usually termed innovators, are prepared to take risks and pay higher prices for new products and services. As competitors enter the market, prices reduce. This lower pricing strategy is generally referred to as penetration pricing as all the competitors seek to attract a much wider customer base than just innovators.

Another form of pricing that causes concern is **price discrimination** which occurs when the price of goods or services is different for different groups of people or for different distribution systems, such as online versus conventional retail outlets. Finally, **price collusion** may occur when two or more firms who are dominant in a specific market collectively set and maintain prices at a higher level that would have applied if there had been free competition. This is not only unethical, but also, in many countries, illegal.

As with other forms of unethical marketing activity, perceived unethical pricing practices may be publicly exposed, both by consumer media and consumers themselves who are likely to punish the offenders by changing to other brands. It is in the interests of the long term future of a company that they are seen to use value-based pricing which is based on setting a fair price (not necessarily a cheap price) that reflects the superior value their products or services provide (Liozu et al., 2012).

Marketing communication/advertising

Like general marketing, there are a number of generic criticisms levelled at advertising and wider marketing communication activity. These focus on issues such as bad taste, irritating repetition and the use of tactics such as inappropriate humour or sexual innuendo (Shimp, 2003). Bad taste and the use of specific tactics that may offend some segments of society reflect value judgements about what is and is not acceptable. It was suggested nearly 25 years ago that advertising reflects society in a somewhat distorted mirror (Pollay and Gallagher, 1990). A scan of popular culture and mass media today would support that view; the regulations we noted earlier prevent excesses of bad taste. The interaction of law and ethics within the advertising context will be discussed in more detail in Chapter 12. We should note that marketing communication that offends those at which it is targeted will not be successful (Hoffbrand, 2008).

An additional claim is that marketing communication perpetuates stereotypes through the use of young and beautiful models, often assisted by airbrushing models and other digital editing/alterations. As noted above, this may reflect stereotypes in the wider society, but this does not excuse the industry nor does it offer any practical way to address the issue. The case study at the end of this chapter highlights the very complex issues involved here.

The ethics of new electronic media forms will be discussed in Chapter 5. One aspect of modern marketing that straddles both traditional and new media forms but which has not received much ethical focus relates to product placements. We therefore now provide a comprehensive overview of the practice and the major ethical issues it presents.

Product placement

Product placement involves the insertion of a recognisable branded product into the content or background of a range of media broadcasting formats. Placements may occur in traditional media formats such as radio, television and movies, as well as newer formats such as console-based video games, online games (advergames) and social media sites. A placement may be paid for directly, provided as part of an exchange of goods or services, or part of a joint promotional package (Karrh, 1998). In traditional media formats, such as movies and television, product placement can occur passively (the product is part of the setting but is not actually used), or actively (the product is used by an actor, with or without verbal acknowledgement, as part of the script).

Recent developments in television programmes such as reality and talent shows have provided new opportunities for product placement while product placement in popular music – particularly in rap and hip-hop genres – is endemic. In newer media formats such as console-based video games and advergames products may be peripheral or integral to the game itself. Product placement has found its way onto social media sites such as Facebook, Twitter and YouTube. The impact of this activity is poorly understood and attempts to minimise any potential harmful impacts do not reflect the realities of product placements within new media forms.

Funding from product placements has long been attractive to entertainment (movies, television and radio) producers as it provides an opportunity to offset production costs (DeLorme and Reid, 1999). One of the first recorded product placement in the movies was the featuring of Gordon's Gin in the 1951 Humphrey Bogart and Katherine Hepburn movie *The African Queen* (Balasubramanian et al., 2006).

Regulation of product placements has been inconsistent, for example product placements were permitted in the EU if contained within programme content originating from outside the EU, especially from US programming, but were not permitted within EU-originated programme content until a 2007 EU directive. With effect from February 2011, product placements have been permitted within UK-originated broadcasting, including sports programming, soaps, films and television and radio entertainment shows (O'Reilly, 2011). Placements are banned during news and children's programmes, together with religious, current affairs and consumer advice programming. The placement of items such as tobacco, alcohol, gambling, infant formula, all medicinal products, electronic or smokeless cigarettes, cigarette lighters, etc. and foods or drinks high in fat, salt and sugar is also banned (OFCOM, 2011).

Product placement in popular music – particularly in rap and hip-hop – is endemic. Music videos are, similarly, often vehicles for product placement. Lady Gaga's 9.5 minute video for her single *Telephone* includes 10 product placements and was viewed by more than 4 million people in the first 24 hours after its release (Castillo, 2010).

In newer media such as advergames – free online games that offer high quality game-play in order to promote a particular product – the product is often an integral part of the game itself. For example, the Chrysler Group created the *Island Rally Racing Series* in order to promote a new range of vehicles for their Chrysler, Jeep and Dodge brands (Moltenbrey, 2004). In console-based games product placement may be central or peripheral to the game, however, the immersive nature of game-play means that target audiences react and engage with placements differently. The repetitive exposure provided in videogames that may be played many times is also seen as an advantage for placements in newer media forms (Gunn, 2001). A particular cause for concern is the popularity of these types of games with children as how they interact with and negotiate product placement in this format is not understood. More recently, product placement has extended to social media sites with marketing companies offering cash and discount incentives to those who mention the relevant brands to their friends on social networking sites; similarly companies like Sponsored Tweets pay people for mentioning brands in their tweets (Van Buskirk, 2010). The impact of this activity is also totally unresearched.

Children's limited ability to understand the nature of persuasion knowledge and thus limited defences against persuasive communication (Moses and Baldwin, 2005) is held by lobby groups to be justification for limiting the type and amount of exposure to persuasive communication. There is, however, little specific research in this area and it remains a very difficult – and hotly contested – topic (Livingstone, 2005). International moves to deliver media literacy training to children represent attempts to increase knowledge of commercial persuasion forms and techniques and help children develop coping skills. These programmes, however, focus on overt marketing communication and not on more subtle forms of persuasive communication. There is also considerable doubt regarding the effectiveness of these programmes, particularly among younger children (O'Sullivan, 2005).

A number of general concerns have been raised in relation to the potential impact of product placement on vulnerable groups such as children if the characters using a specific brand or product type portray the product's use as 'cool' or desirable (Auty and Lewis, 2004; Sargent et al., 2001). While up to half of children do recognise the commercial intent of programme placements, 72% reported that 'seeing a favourite character using a certain brand makes them want to use that brand at least some of the time' (Kennedy, 2004: 14).

Of greater concern is the finding that the portrayal of movie stars smoking increases the likelihood of teenagers commencing smoking (Distefan et al., 2004). The incidence of smoking as portrayed in movies does not reflect its actual (lower) consumption in society. An analysis of the impact of the positive portrayal of smoking in the entertainment media indicates that non-smokers' attitudes towards smoking and smokers were affected by the exposure. This exposure appears to lead to an increased tolerance of the behaviours involved. This outcome is accounted for by Social Learning Theory, in which repeated exposure to an observed behaviour can result in actual behavioural change (Avery and Ferraro, 2000).

One study observes that 'regulators had not fully appreciated the evolution of new promotion vehicles' nor 'the industry's resourcefulness in identifying and developing these' (Hoek, 2004: 1251). This study also notes a range of promotional devices such as music and entertainment-oriented websites that are provided by tobacco companies, as well as brand stretching tactics whereby tobacco brand names are placed on products as diverse as sunglasses, clothing and retail outlets for travel and clothing.

Similar to the tobacco industry, the alcohol industry has been found to use promotional practices that circumvent advertising bans in traditional mass media (Bond et al., 2010). This includes promotions in social networks, such as Facebook, and concerns about alcohol branded merchandise and the usage of alcohol, tobacco and drugs related messages in popular music.

Regulations such as those in the UK are unlikely to have any influence on children's exposure to product placement. The National Consumer Council estimates that nearly 70% of children's viewing (up to 80% for 10–15 year olds) takes place during adult programming (Gibson and Smithers, 2006). Further, restrictions do not extend to product placement across electronic media such as video and online games. The shift to online advertising and product placement in social networking and media sharing sites such as Bebo, Facebook and YouTube are not taken into account by the restrictions. This is a significant oversight given that 16–24 year olds are estimated to spend more time online than they do watching television.

A further concern is the gap between OFCOM's restrictions on the kinds of products that can be placed and the ongoing placement of harmful products not identified by these restrictions. One example of this is the inclusion of sunbeds, in several reality-format television programmes airing in the UK despite legislation that bans the use of sunbeds by under 18s (Sunbed [Regulation] Act 2010) in recognition of sunbeds' carcinogenic properties (World Health Organisation, 2011). It would appear reasonable to expect that the intent of this legislation be reflected in regulations covering mass communication tactics such as product placements.

However, over recent years a number of popular television programmes have either directly featured the use of sunbeds and/or place an emphasis on getting a tan and being tanned. These include *Sunset Tan*, a reality series set in a tanning salon in Los Angeles which first aired on the US cable channel E! in 2007. Based on an existing tanning salon which received a great deal of media attention after it became popular with a number of high-profile celebrities (including Britney Spears, Paris Hilton and Kim Kardashian), the series ran for several seasons in the US. The show is no longer running, however video clips from the series are available to watch online (www.sunsettan.com).

Celebrity role models, such as the cast members of the shows above, who maintain year-round tans and who openly endorse the use of sunbeds, are known to influence the tanning behaviours of teenage girls (Poorsattar and Hornung, 2008), yet this is not reflected in any regulations. For example, the regulations do not address programmes whose central focus reflects unwise behaviour, such as MTV's *Jersey Shore*, a reality show that has successfully crossed over from the US to the UK and which features eight young people living and working in a number of resorts along the Jersey shoreline.

Cast members have become minor celebrities with actresses like Nicole 'Snooki' Polizzi often appearing in *Heat* magazine. A reflection of the show's popularity and influence can be seen in a recent article in the *Mirror* which cited 'the distinctly mahogany cast of MTV's *Jersey Shore*' as an inspiration for this summer's 'fashion tan', 'a deeper, ultra-luxe tan, which quickly spread to celebs like Victoria Beckham and Cheryl Cole' (Corfield-Smith, 2010).

A second example is of a UK-based reality show that has been phenomenally successful; Katie Price's ITV2 show *What Katie Did Next*. While tanning is not an explicit focus of the show, Price is a known endorser of sunbeds (Karmali, 2010) and has her own private sunbed in her home. One episode features the 'haunted sunbed' in which the sunbed alarm is triggered unexpectedly in the middle of the night.

The practice of product placements raises many legislative and ethical issues, particularly in terms of growing concerns regarding the impact of persuasive communication on vulnerable groups such as children (Auty and Lewis, 2004), for tighter regulation of products such as alcohol and outright bans on the promotion of tobacco products. The marketing of potentially harmful products such as tobacco and alcohol is discussed in more detail in Chapter 8.

PR/publicity

The ethics of public relations activity came sharply into focus in 2011 when it was revealed that Facebook had hired a PR organisation to 'bad-mouth' Google. Other ethically dubious activity subsequently revealed has included the creation of fake organisations to speak on specific issues and public relations consultants posing as journalists. Reports of '**flogs**' (fake blogs), **ghost blogging**, **ghost tweeting** (writing blog posts or tweets on behalf of the stated author without disclosing the true authorship) and '**astroturfing**' (paying people to create false grass roots support for an organisation or brand) abound (Fournier and Avery, 2011).

A number of watchdog organisation websites now exist specifically to reveal unethical corporate practices such as these (see, for example, spinwatch.com and corporatewatch.com), yet some organisations seem slow to realise that exposure of such blatant misrepresentation has potentially significant implications for brand equity. In 2013, Samsung was fined by Taiwan's Fair Trade Commission for paying people to post negative reviews of its competitor HTC. The publicity given to the fine is likely to bolster the reputation of HTC – the long-term impact on Samsung's sales has yet to be seen (Aardvark Communications, 2013).

A recent survey of US PR practitioners (Gallicano et al., 2013) found that more than half of organisational blogs were not written by the stated authors. Many high profile figures such as politicians employ speechwriters so it is perhaps not surprising that the survey participants did not find ghost blogging unacceptable, particularly if the blog comments were approved of by the stated author. Participants also viewed the process as acceptable because it was widespread. This ignores the question of whether blog members are being deceived and whether they would respond differently to blog posts if they were aware of the true authorship.

While cross cultural studies are rare in this sector, one study revealed that the majority of public relations firms in the US and in Korea do not have specific ethical parameters or ethical codes to guide practitioners' behaviour (Ki et al., 2012); what difference such guidance might have on these types of behaviours is as yet unknown.

Selling

The activity of sales staff is frequently criticised for such things as aggressive sales tactics. Sales staff in many retail environments are simply paid wages or salary, with little recognition of relative performance. Some are paid purely on commission – therefore unless they make a sale, they earn nothing. Many are also part-time, often supporting studies. It is therefore hardly surprising that some sales staff have little motivation to develop relationships with their clients and focus instead on completing the immediate transaction.

Cultural backgrounds of staff may influence how they perceive ethical issues, but more research is needed in this area. Ethical training may sensitise staff to potential ethical issues, but may not impact on whether unethical behaviour will occur or not. The overall organisational culture and working environment will influence what behaviours are seen as being ethical and what action might be taken to deal with unethical activity (McClaren, 2013).

SUMMARY

The discussion in this chapter has highlighted a wide range of issues relating to general marketing ethics. We have shown that, while many of the criticisms levelled at marketing are not correct or relate to a small amount of activity, there are a number of areas in which very real ethical challenges are evident. Many of these issues are complex, such as the evolution of Big Data and its potential implications for both positive and negative outcomes. While there is growing recognition of the responsibility of organisations beyond just the maximisation of profits, mechanisms such as CSR, if applied without genuine commitment, will have severe potential implications for organisations if their insincerity is exposed.

The activity of some specialist sectors within marketing, such as public relations, appears to lack understanding of the ethical implications of some activity, while the structure of others, such as sales forces, may create ethical challenges. By far the most visible part of marketing activity is marketing communication, and while many of the criticisms levelled at its activity are incorrect or based on value judgements, we must concur with Shimp (2003: 605) who notes that 'Advertising is not without sin, but neither does it have a monopoly on it'. The fact that marketing communication reflects wider consumer culture and stereotypes within society presents some complex challenges for which there are no ready solutions.

Case study   Skin lightening products

Skin lightening products are used medically for the treatment of a range of skin disorders, however a major market has developed in their use for cosmetic purposes, particularly in countries where darker skin tones are prevalent (Gillbro and Olsson, 2011). There are over 240 brands in India alone, with many major multinational brands represented such as Dove, Vaseline, Olay and Garnier (Goldschneider, 2012). Over 60% of Indian women reportedly use the products daily (Goldstein, 2012).

(Continued)

(Continued)

Many products currently marketed have not been subject to safety and efficacy studies and the product category appears to be poorly controlled (Draelos, 2007): while some claim to contain natural ingredients such as Vitamin B3, mercury has been found in skin lightening creams available in Mexico and other developing countries (Peregrino et al., 2011). Other potentially dangerous ingredients include hydroquinone, banned in Europe, and corticosteroids. Severe health consequences can arise as a result of prolonged use of these types of products, yet a lack of regulation means there is no consistent requirement for ingredient labelling. Further, there is evidence in some developing countries of misbranding (Olumide et al., 2008).

The marketing strategies of some products have been criticised. For example, Vaseline produced a Facebook app which allowed users to download a profile picture, drag a line across their face and digitally transform their image to a much lighter tone (Goldschneider, 2012). In Thailand, a promotion by the Unilever product range Citra appeared to offer university scholarships to students with fairer skin (Hodal, 2013).

The demand for these products is based on deeply entrenched cultural beliefs that people with paler skin are of a higher social status, or in India, a higher caste than those with darker skin, making the former more attractive and leading to better paying jobs or better marriages (Shevde, 2008). Bollywood actors are among the

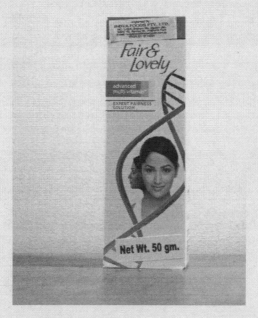

Figure 2.2 Fair & Lovely

high profile promoters of the products in India. We now examine the ethical issues involved in the marketing of the Unilever product range Fair & Lovely.

Fair & Lovely was created by Unilever's HLL Indian subsidiary. It is the largest skin whitening cream on the market, holding more than 50% of the market in India, a market valued at over US$200 million in 2006, with a 10–15% growth rate per annum. It is also marketed in other Asian countries, for example Malaysia, and in some Arabic countries such as Egypt.

The central product benefit is dramatic skin whitening within six weeks. HLL claims the product fulfils a social need, given that fair skin is valued in the country, even though dark skin is less vulnerable to skin diseases. It is not marketed as a pharmaceutical product and therefore does not have to prove efficacy – which is disputed by dermatologists on the basis of the ingredients.

Advertisements in all the countries in which Fair & Lovely is sold show product users getting better jobs, getting married or having a brighter future (and being noticeably happier) as a result of their lighter skin. Critics have claimed that the ads are socially objectionable, racist, demeaning or even 'repellent'. Two ads have been taken off air in India as a result of protests, but others are still running. HLL claims the ads promote choice and empowerment. Critics such as women's movements claim they entrench disempowerment.

The primary target market is women aged 18–35, with the poor being a significant segment. There are reports of girls aged 12–14 using the product, which is marketed in 'affordable' small packages.

Fair & Lovely is a profitable brand, but there are many ethical issues that arise in discussing the case, particularly in relation to the racist and sexist stereotypes and prejudices that exist in relation to skin colour. Additionally, a key target sector includes people who are not well educated (if at all) and who are therefore unable to understand the controversy and criticisms, or to understand that the efficacy of the product has not been verified. Use of the product by children is a further concern.

HLL claims to exercise corporate social responsibility, but its actions in the marketing strategy and tactics with Fair & Lovely have led to criticisms of hypocrisy. While HLL did not create the prejudices that underpin demand for the product, critics claim the product's marketing helps to sustain those prejudices. The company is marketing a legal product, it is not breaking any laws, and it appears to have a loyal customer base, but can it claim to be doing good while it does well out of sales of the product?

There have been calls for tighter restrictions on the sale and promotion of skin-whitening products in several countries, including proof of efficacy and safety, but to date there has been little action. Proposals in more developed countries have included a complete ban on over-the-counter sales, and a requirement for prescription-only sales (Goldschneider, 2012).

(Continued)

(Continued)

We recommend you read the full case study and also view the commercials that are available on YouTube. Also, check on the number of products that are easily available on the Internet, including on eBay and even on Amazon.

This case study is based largely on Karnani, A., 2007.

Questions to consider

Do products such as Fair & Lovely fulfil a social need?

Do they reinforce racist and sexist stereotypes and prejudices?

Do they do both?

If there was tighter regulation, what impact would this have on product demand?

At a minimum, unsafe products should be banned and clear ingredient labelling should be required. The latter, however, will be of little benefit in many markets where literacy levels are low. What other actions could and should be undertaken and by whom?

Further Reading

Sage journal articles available for free at https://study.sagepub.com/eagleanddahl include:

Assadourian, E. (2010) 'Transforming cultures: From Consumerism to Sustainability', *Journal of Macromarketing,* 30: 186–91.

Lusch, R.F. and Vargo, S.L. (2006) 'Service-dominant logic: reactions, reflections and refinements', *Marketing Theory,* 6: 281–8.

Mitchell, R.W., Wooliscroft, B. and Higham, J. (2010) 'Sustainable market orientation: A new approach to managing marketing strategy', *Journal of Macromarketing,* 30: 160–70.

Other

Bayraktar, A., Yilmaz, E. and Yamak, O. (2010) 'Implementation of RFID technology for the differentiation of loyalty programs', *Journal of Relationship Marketing,* 9: 30–42.

Chen, H. and Deterding, A. (2013) 'College-aged young consumers' interpretations of product placement in social games', *Young Consumers: Insight and Ideas for Responsible Marketers,* 14: 41–51.

Karnani, A. (2007) 'Doing well by doing good—case study: Fair & Lovely whitening cream', *Strategic Management Journal*, 28: 1351–7.

Liozu, S.M., Hinterhuber, A., Perelli, S. and Boland, R. (2012) 'Mindful pricing: Transforming organizations through value-based pricing', *Journal of Strategic Marketing*, 20: 197–209.

Redker, C., Gibson, B. and Zimmerman, I. (2013) 'Liking of movie genre alters the effectiveness of background product placements', *Basic and Applied Social Psychology*, 35: 249–55.

Shevde, N. (2008) 'All's fair in love and cream: A cultural case study of Fair & Lovely in India', *Advertising & Society Review*, 9(2).

References

Aardvark Communicatons (2013) *Samsung Unethical Marketing Highlights Possible Issues Around Company Culture*. Available at: http://newroom.aardvarkrm.com.

Agnese, J. (2010) *Industry Surveys Supermarkets & Drugstores*. New York: Standard & Poors.

Ameer, I. (2013) 'Ethical marketing decisions: Review, contribution and impact on recent research', *International Journal*, 2: 1–10.

Assadourian, E. (2010) 'Transforming cultures: From Consumerism to Sustainability', *Journal of Macromarketing*, 30: 186–91.

Auty, S. and Lewis, C. (2004) 'Exploring children's choice: The reminder effect of product placement', *Psychology & Marketing*, 21: 697–713.

Avery, R.J. and Ferraro, R. (2000) 'Verisimilitude or advertising? Brand appearances on prime-time television', *The Journal of Consumer Affairs*, 34: 217–44.

Baines, T., Brown, S., Benedettini, O. and Ball, P. (2012) 'Examining green production and its role within the competitive strategy of manufacturers', *Journal of Industrial Engineering and Management*, 5: 53–87.

Balasubramanian, S.K., Karrh, J.A. and Parwardhan, H. (2006) 'Audience response to product placement. An integrative framework and future research agenda', *Journal of Advertising*, 35: 115–41.

Bayraktar, A., Yilmaz, E. and Yamak, O. (2010) 'Implementation of RFID technology for the differentiation of loyalty programs', *Journal of Relationship Marketing*, 9: 30–42.

Boeck, H., Roy, J., Durif, F. and Grégoire, M. (2011) 'The effect of perceived intrusion on consumers' attitude towards using an RFID-based marketing program', *Procedia Computer Science*, 5: 841–8.

Bond, L., Daube, M. and Chikritzhs, T. (2010) 'Selling addictions: Similarities in approaches between Big Tobacco and Big Booze', *World Healthcare Providers*, 1.

Boyd, D. and Crawford, K. (2012) 'Critical questions for big data: Provocations for a cultural, technological, and scholarly phenomenon', *Information, Communication & Society*, 15: 662–79.

Broyles, S.J. (2006) 'Subliminal advertising and the perpetual popularity of playing to people's paranoia', *Journal of Consumer Affairs*, 40: 392–406.

Calfee, J.E. and Ringold, D.J. (1994) 'The 70% majority: Enduring consumer beliefs about advertising', *Journal of Public Policy & Marketing*, 13: 228–38.

Castillo, D. (2010) 'New PQ Media Report finds US branded entertainment spending on consumer events & product placement', *Product Placement News*.

Chandon, P. (2013) 'How package design and packaged-based marketing claims lead to overeating', *Applied Economic Perspectives and Policy*, 35: 7–31.

Cooper, J. and Cooper, G. (2002) 'Subliminal motivation: A story revisited', *Journal of Applied Social Psychology*, 32: 2213–27.

Corfield-Smith, S-J. (2010) 'Go to the dark side with your tan', *Mirror*, 20 June.

Crittenden, V., Crittenden, W., Ferrell, L., Ferrell, O.C. and Pinney, C.C. (2011) 'Market-oriented sustainability: A conceptual framework and propositions', *Journal of the Academy of Marketing Science*, 39: 71–85.

Cronin, J.J., Smith, J.S., Gleim, M.R., Ramirez, E. and Martinez, J.D. (2011)' Green marketing strategies: An examination of stakeholders and the opportunities they present', *Journal of the Academy of Marketing Science*, 39: 158–74.

DeLorme, D.E. and Reid, L.N. (1999) 'Moviegoers' experiences and interpretations of brands in films revisited', *Journal of Advertising*, 28: 71–95.

Distefan, J.M., Pierce, J.P. and Gilpin, E.A. (2004) 'Do favourite movie stars influence adolescent smoking initiation?', *American Journal of Public Health*, 94: 1239–44.

Draelos, Z.D. (2007) 'Skin lightening preparations and the hydroquinone controversy', *Dermatologic Therapy*, 20: 308–13.

Eagle, L., Rose, L. and Kitchen, P.J. (2005) 'Defending brand advertising share-of-voice: A mature market (s) perspective', *Journal of Brand Management*, 13: 65–79.

Fournier, S. and Avery, J. (2011) 'The uninvited brand', *Business Horizons*, 54: 193–207.

Friedman, M. (2009) *Capitalism and Freedom*. Chicago: University of Chicago Press.

Gallicano, T.D., Brett, K. and Hopp, T. (2013) 'Is ghost blogging like speechwriting? A survey of practitioners about the ethics of ghost blogging', *Public Relations Journal*, 7.

Geyskens, I., Gielens, K. and Gijsbrechts, E. (2010) 'Proliferating private-label portfolios: How introducing economy and premium private labels influences brand choice', *Journal of Marketing Research*, 47: 791–807.

Gibson, O. and Smithers, R. (2006) 'Junk food ad ban attacked from both sides', *The Guardian – online edition*, 18 November: 1. Available at: http://www.guardian.co.uk/media/2006/nov/18/advertising.food1.

Gillbro, J. and Olsson, M. (2011) 'The melanogenesis and mechanisms of skin-lightening agents–existing and new approaches', *International Journal of Cosmetic Science*, 33: 210–21.

Goldschneider, D. (2012) *Skin Lightening Creams, What You Need To Know*. Available at: http://www.mdhil.com.

Goldstein, R. (2012) 'Time for a reality check on skin lightening creams', *The Conversation*, online edition: 1.

Graß, T. (2013) 'H&M–a role model for organic cotton use in textile processing?', *Journal of European Management & Public Affairs Studies*, 1: 23–6.

Gunn, E. (2001) 'Product placement prize', *Advertising Age*, 72: 10.

Hodal, K. (2013) 'Thailand racism row reignited by Unilever ad for skin-whitening cream', *The Guardian*, online edition, 28 October.

Hoek, J. (2004) 'Tobacco promotion restrictions: Ironies and unintended consequences', *Journal of Business Research*, 57: 1250–7.

Hoffbrand, J. (2008) 'When does "hard-hitting" become a step too far?', *Precision Marketing*, 20: 10.

IBIS World (2014) *Competitive Landscape Market Share Concentration*. Available at: http://clients1.ibisworld.com.au/reports/au/industry/competitivelandscape.aspx?entid=1834#MSC.

Jahdi, K.S. and Acikdilli, G. (2009) 'Marketing communications and corporate social responsibility (CSR): marriage of convenience or shotgun wedding?', *Journal of Business Ethics*, 88: 103–13.

Karmali, S. (2010) 'Katie Price sparks outrage by promoting regular sunbed use', *Marie Claire*.

Karnani, A. (2007) 'Doing well by doing good – case study: "Fair & Lovely" skin whitening cream', *Strategic Management Journal*, 28: 1351–7.

Karrh, J.A. (1998) 'Brand placement: A review', *Journal of Current Issues and Research in Advertising*, 209: 31–49.

Kennedy, D.G. (2004) 'Coming of age in consumerdom', *American Demographics*, 26: 14.

Keys, W.B. (1973) *Subliminal Seduction*. New York: Signet.

Ki, E-J., Lee, J. and Choi, H-L. (2012) 'Factors affecting ethical practice of public relations professionals within public relations firms', *Asian Journal of Business Ethics*, 1: 123–41.

Kilian, B., Hettinga, J., Jiménez, G.A., Molina, S. and White, A. (2011) 'Case study on Dole's carbon-neutral fruits', *Journal of Business Research*, 65: 1800–10.

Kimmel, A.J., Smith, N.C. and Klein, J.G. (2011) 'Ethical decision making and research deception in the behavioral sciences: An application of social contract theory', *Ethics & Behavior*, 21: 222–51.

Kuznetsov, A., Kuznetsova, O. and Warren, R. (2009) 'CSR and the legitimacy of business in transition economies: The case of Russia', *Scandinavian Journal of Management*, 25: 37–45.

Leonidou, L.C., Kvasova, O., Leonidou, C.N. and Chari, S. (2013) 'Business unethicality as an impediment to consumer trust: The moderating role of demographic and cultural characteristics', *Journal of Business Ethics*, 112: 397–415.

Liozu, S.M., Hinterhuber, A., Perelli, S. and Boland, R. (2012) 'Mindful pricing: Transforming organizations through value-based pricing', *Journal of Strategic Marketing*, 20: 197–209.

Livingstone, S. (2005) 'Assessing the research base for the policy debate over the effects of food advertising to children', *International Journal of Advertising*, 24: 273–96.

Luo, X. and de Jong, P.J. (2012) 'Does advertising spending really work? The intermediate role of analysts in the impact of advertising on firm value', *Journal of the Academy of Marketing Science*, 40: 605–24.

Lusch, R.F. and Vargo, S.L. (2006) 'Service-dominant logic: Reactions, reflections and refinements', *Marketing Theory*, 6: 281–8.

Maignan, I., Ferrell, O. and Ferrell, L. (2005) 'A stakeholder model for implementing social responsibility in marketing', *European Journal of Marketing*, 39: 956–77.

Maignan, I., Gonzalez-Padron, T.L., Hult, G.T.M. and Ferrell, O.C. (2011) 'Stakeholder orientation: Development and testing of a framework for socially responsible marketing', *Journal of Strategic Marketing*, 19: 313–38.

Martin, K.D., Johnson, J.L. and French, J.J. (2011) 'Institutional pressures and marketing ethics initiatives: The focal role of organizational identity', *Journal of the Academy of Marketing Science*, 39: 574–91.

McClaren, N. (2013) 'The personal selling and sales management ethics research: Managerial implications and research directions from a comprehensive review of the empirical literature', *Journal of Business Ethics*, 112: 101–25.

Mitchell, R.W., Wooliscroft, B. and Higham, J. (2010) 'Sustainable market orientation: A new approach to managing marketing strategy', *Journal of Macromarketing*, 30: 160–70.

Moltenbrey, K. (2004) 'Adver-driving', *Computer Graphics World*, 27: 30–1.

Mortimer, G. (2013) *Factcheck: Is Our Grocery Market One of the Most Concentrated in the World?* Available at: http://theconversation.com/factcheck-is-our-grocery-market-one-of-the-most-concentrated-in-the-world-16520.

Moses, L.J. and Baldwin, D.A. (2005) 'What can the study of cognitive development reveal about childrens' ability to appreciate and cope with advertising?', *Journal of Public Policy & Marketing*, 24: 186–201.

O'Reilly, L. (2011) 'Product placement to be allowed from February', *Marketing Week*.

O'Sullivan, T. (2005) 'Advertising and children: What do the kids think?', *Qualitative Market Research*, 8: 371–84.

OFCOM (2011) *Broadcasting Code Review: Commercial References in Television Programming – Annex 1*. London: OFCOM.

Olumide, Y.M., Akinkugbe, A.O., Altraide, D., Mohammed.., Ahamefule, N., Ayanlowo, S., Onyekonwu, C. and Essen, N. (2008) 'Complications of chronic use of skin lightening cosmetics', *International Journal of Dermatology*, 47: 344–53.

Palmer, D. and Hedberg, T. (2013) 'The ethics of marketing to vulnerable populations', *Journal of Business Ethics*, 116: 403–13.

Panimbang, F. (2013) *The Reality of Corporate Social Responsibility: Experiences from China, South Korea, India and Indonesia*. Hong Kong: Asia Monitor Resource Centre.

Parguel, B., Benoît-Moreau, F. and Larceneux, F. (2011) 'How sustainability ratings might deter "greenwashing": A closer look at ethical corporate communication', *Journal of Business Ethics*, 102: 15–28.

Peregrino, C.P., Moreno, M.V., Miranda, S.V., Rubio, A.D. and Leal, L.O. (2011) 'Mercury levels in locally manufactured Mexican skin-lightening creams', *International Journal of Environmental Research and Public Health*, 8: 2516–23.

Pollay, R.W. and Gallagher, K. (1990) 'Advertising and cultural values: Reflections in the distorted mirror', *International Journal of Advertising*, 9: 359–72.

Poorsattar, S.P. and Hornung, R.L. (2008) 'Television turning more teens toward tanning', *Journal of the American Academy of Dermatology*, 58: 171–2.

Porter, M. (1980) *Competitive Strategy*. New York: Free Press.

Prasad, A. and Holzinger, I. (2013) 'Seeing through smoke and mirrors: A critical analysis of marketing CSR', *Journal of Business Research*, 66: 1915–21.

Rotfeld, H.J. and Taylor, C.R. (2009) 'The advertising regulation and self-regulation issues ripped from the headlines with (sometimes missed) opportunities for disciplined multidisciplinary research', *Journal of Advertising*, 38: 5–14.

Sargent, J.D., Tickle, J.J., Beach, M.L., Dalton, M.A., Ahrens, M.B. and Heatherton, T.F. (2001) 'Brand appearances in contemporary cinema films and contribution to global marketing of cigarettes', *The Lancet*, 357: 29–32.

Sayman, S. and Raju, J.S. (2004) 'Investigating the cross-category effects of store brands', *Review of Industrial Organization*, 24: 129–41.

She, S. (2011) 'A framework for assessing immorally manipulative marketing tactics', *Journal of Business Ethics*, 102: 97–118.

Shevde, N. (2008) 'All's fair in love and cream: A cultural case study of Fair & Lovely in India', *Advertising & Society Review*, 9.

Shimp, T.E. (2003) *Advertising, Promotion and Supplemental Aspects of IMC*. Independence, KY: Thompson Southwestern.

Sirgy, M.J., Grace, B.Y., Lee, D-J. and Huang, M.W. (2012a) 'Does marketing activity contribute to a society's well-being? The role of economic efficiency', *Journal of Business Ethics*, 107: 91–102.

Sirgy, M.J., Gurel-Atay, E., Webb, D. Cicic, M., Husic, M., Ekici, A., Herrmann, A., Hegazy, I., Lee, D.-J. and Johar, J.S. (2012b) 'Linking advertising, materialism, and life satisfaction', *Social Indicators Research*, 107: 79–101.

Svensson, G., Wood, G. and Callaghan, M. (2010) 'A corporate model of sustainable business practices: An ethical perspective', *Journal of World Business*, 45: 336–45.

Sweetin, V.H., Knowles, L.L., Summey, J.H. and McQueen, K.S. (2013) 'Willingness-to-punish the corporate brand for corporate social irresponsibility', *Journal of Business Research*, 66(10): 1822–30.

Tadajewski, M. and Jones, D.B. (2012) 'Scientific marketing management and the emergence of the ethical marketing concept', *Journal of Marketing Management*, 28: 37–61.

Tsai, M-T., Liang, W-K. and Liu, M-L. (2007) 'The effects of subliminal advertising on consumer attitudes and buying intentions', *International Journal of Management*, 24: 3–14.

Van Buskirk, E. (2010) 'Gaming the system: How marketers rig the social media machine', *Wired*, 7 July. Available at: http://www.wired.com/2010/07/gaming-the-system-how-marketers-rig-the-social-media-machine/all/.

Williams, G. and Zinkin, J. (2008) 'The effect of culture on consumers' willingness to punish irresponsible corporate behaviour: Applying Hofstede's typology to the punishment aspect of corporate social responsibility', *Business Ethics: A European Review*, 17: 210–26.

World Health Organisation (2011) *Sunbeds, Tanning and UV Exposure*, Fact Sheet No. 287. Geneva: WHO.

Zhang, J., Chiu, R. and Wei, L. (2009) 'Decision-making process of internal whistle-blowing behavior in China: Empirical evidence and implications', *Journal of Business Ethics*, 88: 25–41.

3 Contrasting Perspectives on Marketing

Stephan Dahl and Fannie Yeung

CHAPTER OVERVIEW

In this chapter we will discuss changing and contrasting perspectives towards marketing and marketing ethics. The chapter explores how marketing, and particularly marketing communication as the most visible form of marketing, can be perceived differently, and ethical challenges can arise as a consequence based on:

- Historical and societal changes
- Religious contexts
- Cross-cultural contexts

While there are a variety of reasons that can be identified as leading to changes in perceptions, such as personal experiences, political, technological or social changes and so forth, the two main avenues to allow for a discussion about marketing ethics are historical changes, and cross-cultural and religious perspectives, both of which this chapter will use to show how perceptions of marketing, and what constitutes marketing ethics, are fluid and constantly evolving together with the wider environment in which marketing operates.

HISTORICAL MARKETING AND SOCIETAL CHANGES

Some of the most pertinent examples of changes in what is considered acceptable, if not ethical, can be seen when looking at historical advertising campaigns, from hyperbolic descriptions of the effects of snake oil and other dubious remedies in the 1800s and the now notorious claims of a cigarette brand that was smoked by more doctors than any other brand, right through to blatant sexism and racism in historical marketing communications, at least for the contemporary observer. However, it is worth noting that such analysis is necessarily at the micro-level, i.e. engaged in a detailed analysis of what is considered ethical and what is not. Scholars of historical marketing suggest, when looking at more abstract principles of what is desirable, i.e. analysing marketing thought and marketing ethics at a macro level, there are both historical as well as cross-cultural similarities.

For instance, Kaufman (1987) writing about marketing thought during the Han Dynasty in China (third century BC) discusses how Confucian scholars were concerned with marketing ethics and the effects of marketing on society, including a potential rise in materialism as a result of increased market activities. Similarly, Dixon (1982) in his review of eighteenth-century views on marketing ethics points to more similarities than differences. Specifically, Dixon points out how eighteenth-century writers were highlighting the necessity of an ethical system to guide markets and marketing activity. Most of these historical concerns appear to mirror many of the concerns discussed in the previous chapter in relation to current marketing practice.

Thus, while there is agreement at the macro-level, including calls for ethical conduct, and some form of regulatory control to allow for a fair playing field, at the micro level, there are stark differences between historical and contemporary advertising. The following two examples, related to targeted groups and advertised products, highlight how perspectives on individual topics have changed. These examples show how marketing is symbiotically part of the wider societal system in which it is embedded, and thus perspectives of what is acceptable or perceived as ethical change concurrently in line with wider societal changes.

Products and claims

Chapter 1 briefly mentioned how what is ethically acceptable practice in marketing at one point in history can be considered unacceptable in another. For instance, the marketing of slaves, which occurred in the seventeenth and eighteenth century (Steen et al., 2011) is deeply repulsive in the twenty-first century. More recently, the marketing of tobacco has become an outstanding example of how society, **social norms** and marketing depend on each other. Tobacco has a long history of being cultivated and used as a recreational drug in the Americas for over 3000 years (Goodman, 2005), gaining popularity after European settlers and traders used and exported the plant worldwide. However, tobacco usage remained at the cultural periphery of society, with smoking largely an irregularly occurring activity. The systematic use of marketing techniques, particularly highly developed public relations campaigns, refashioned the product into one of the most widely used products of the earliest twentieth century, and a potent symbol of the emerging consumer and leisure culture. After gaining popularity as a male expression of status and leisure, drawing on Edwards Bernays' theories of 'engineering consent' (Bernays, 1947), marketers transformed public opinion of smoking in the late 1920s. Women's smoking was transformed from a social taboo to an expression of freedom and femininity, by equating cigarettes with 'torches of freedom' (Amos and Haglund. 2000).

Within Nazi Germany, smoking, along with Coca-Cola, some alcohol and medications, became recognised as a 'vice' blamed for laziness, as well as a poison and a drain on the German economy (Proctor, 1997). Within this context, the first credible scientific studies linking smoking to cancer emerged (Müller, 1939), although it wasn't until the 1950s, that science increasingly linked tobacco with cancer.

The industry responded, counterintuitive to some, to the emerging scientific evidence by promoting scientific discourse. Marketers seized the news agenda by promoting more scientific research and engaging in a scientific debate through the promotion of a sceptical approach to scientific results and following the scientific tradition of calling for more research (Brandt, 2012). Thus, just as a few decades earlier, marketers responded to the changing social environment, and ethical concerns with their products, by adapting their communication and marketing strategies accordingly. Pseudo-scientific messages aimed at men, and pro-feminist messages of the first half of the twentieth century, were replaced with messages of enjoyment and taste.

Think points

Take a look at other historical advertisements, for example promoting alcoholic drinks. Can you identify how the messages have changed over the years? Discuss which of the historic claims you can find would be considered ethical today.

Target groups and representation

The bidirectional nature of advertising content and wider societal norms can be seen from a variety of different perspectives, and has been examined by scholars extensively. For instance, Cui (2001) argues that academic interest on marketing to different ethnic groups has followed major policy interventions and social changes. For example, prior to the civil rights movement in the US, the number of studies addressing non-white consumers was almost non-existent, while interest rose in the years following the civil rights movement. Similarly, Cui shows how academic interest has risen following the censuses of 1990 and 1980, both of which showed large increases in the number of non-white consumers in the US. Other examples include female representation and gender role portrayal, frequently discussed in the late 1980s and 1990s (Gilly, 1988; Wiles et al., 1996), and more recently the portrayal of specifically gay men (Borgerson et al., 2006; Kates, 2004), with only cautious research (and portrayal in advertising) emerging on lesbian consumers (Mikkonen, 2010), and a practical absence of other non-heterosexual identities, such as a transsexual, bisexual or polyamorous representation. An example of the changing societal attitudes reflected in the portrayal of and marketing to a particular target group can be well documented by discussing the change in attitude of advertisers towards gay men.

Branchik (2002) explores the development of the gay market segment in the US from a historical perspective, dividing it into three distinct phases: an underground phase (pre-1941), a community building phase (1941–1970) and a mainstream phase (1971 onwards). As Branchik points out, specifically during the mainstream phase, based on increasing social acceptance, marketers started to gradually address gay men as consumers. With the emergence of studies into market size and segment attractiveness, as well as a fear of potential boycotts, gay men became increasingly the focus of marketer attention, with mainstream brands advertising to the segment by the late 1990s. This 'mainstreaming' of the open portrayal of gay consumers continues in contemporary advertising practice.

In the 1990s mainstream brands restricted advertising featuring openly gay themes mostly to media channels which were unlikely to reach a non-gay audience. During the 2000s portrayals of gay consumers in mainstream media channels became increasingly noticeable, yet these portrayals were often cautious and implied homosexuality, rather than explicitly addressing the topics. For instance, symbols associated with the gay rights movement, such as the rainbow flag, were used to imply 'gay friendliness', in a manner that would avoid alienating non-gay consumers (Um, 2012). Openly gay-themed marketing communications to a mainstream audience only emerged in the early 2010s, concurrent with the public debate on marriage equality. In the US, advertising for retailer JCPenny and clothes store Gap featured same-sex couples. And in 2012 Ray Ban advertising featured two men holding hands and the slogan 'Never Hide'. In 2013, Amazon advertised its Kindle on national television in the US by featuring a man and a woman sitting at a bar talking about their respective husbands. Similarly, in the UK, Barclays Bank used their ATM network to align itself with gay causes: customers withdrawing cash from the bank's ATMs were shown anti-homophobia advertising during the transaction. Barclays Bank

Figure 3.1 GAYTMs

in the UK and ANZ Bank (Australia) also rebranded some of their ATMs into 'GAYTMs' concurrent with pride parades in these countries in an attempt to display their support for gay rights.

However, while many minority groups have welcomed being target or represented by mainstream brands, this isn't always positive. To continue the example from above, mainstream marketers' interests in LGBT groups has been criticised as causing LGBT groups to abandon their traditional agenda of challenging social inequalities (Chasin, 2001), and instead replacing this with a culture of domesticity and consumption (Duggan, 2002). In a similar vein to 'greenwashing' (see Chapter 2), some authors have accused the deliberate display of support for purportedly progressive causes, such as gay rights, in marketing as being used to 'pinkwash' otherwise controversial organisations. The most prominent example of this was the decision by Israel to promote itself as a 'gay friendly' destination (Avraham, 2009). The term has also been applied in a different context to companies using the 'pink ribbon' as a sign of breast cancer awareness, in a very similar way to the support of LGBT (lesbian, gay, bisexual and transgender) causes, where companies display their corporate social responsibility in an attempt to appear compassionate about a cause many people associate with (Lubitow and Davis, 2011).

Further potential ethical issues arise from companies specifically targeting minority groups, particularly with products seen as unhealthy or otherwise undesirable. A notable example of this is the well documented attempt of the tobacco industry 'SCUM' – the acronym for sub-culture urban marketing – to target gay and homeless consumers (Stevens et al., 2004). Some researchers hold the view such campaigns resulted in increased smoking rates in the targeted communities and associated health problems.

Think points

Think about a particular minority group, such as ethnic, religious or other minorities. Why would these groups welcome representation and/or being targeted? Why would they not welcome this? Discuss the potentially positive and negative effects of representation of these groups in mainstream advertising.

CROSS-CULTURAL PERSPECTIVES

Normative, relative and communicative approaches

When negotiating different perspectives on ethics finding a suitable solution depends on the philosophical stance taken towards ethical problems. The approaches taken can be best categorised under three broad categories: **normative**, **relative** and **communicative** approaches.

Normative approaches are approaches that assume there is a universal, often norms- or rules-based set of ethical and moral principles. Such approaches can be illustrated briefly by referring to extreme interpretations of some religious moral principles (e.g. no consumption of certain foods, irrespective of contextual factors). A similar example, based on a normative legal principle, would be the UK Bribery Act (2010). This act outlaws **bribery** by British organisations in countries outside of the United Kingdom, thus applying UK practice and legal interpretation to the dealings of British companies abroad, i.e. assuming that the British provisions are normative.

By contrast, relativist approaches assume that there is no universal set of ethical principles, and that individual cultures or groups have their own moral guidelines and perceptions – and no framework or principles can be assumed to be superior.

In practice, both extremes are difficult to implement. Normative approaches are inflexible and can result in significant disadvantages for companies when applied globally (see also mini case study 3.1 on facilitation payments). On the other hand, relativist approaches have the potential to be upsetting for one or more of the partners in international or cross-cultural business, and may be based on incorrect information or beliefs.

Nill (2003) proposes a third alternative: a communicative approach or dialogic idealism. A communicative approach attempts to combine both normative and relativist approaches by resolving differences through dialogue. Thus, Nill's approach attempts to bring stakeholders together and find a solution that is acceptable to all parties. He gives the example of Buddy's, a low-cost, low-malt drink similar to beer, though with a higher alcohol content, marketed by Annheuser Bush in Japan. Advertising the drink as both 'strong' (in terms of alcohol content) and cheap, would be unacceptable under US marketing guidelines; however, it did not cause offence in Japan. Through a dialogic exchange, Nill suggests a consensus could be sought between the various stakeholders, such as the company, consumer organisations, other breweries and the Japanese government as to whether or not Annheuser Bush should engage in producing and marketing the drink. Such a dialogue would seek to identify risks and benefits for the involved parties and enable consumers to make informed decisions about the product.

Mini case study 3.1   Facilitation payments

Facilitation payments, also sometimes known as grease payments or expediting payments amongst other terms, are a form of payment where an organisation pays a, generally fairly small, amount of money, or gives gifts to an official in order to expedite an administrative process (Argandoña, 2005). Facilitation payments are distinct from bribery under international law if they are made not to influence the outcome of the official's decision (e.g. to grant an import license), but simply to speed up an existing process. In some jurisdictions, for instance in the US, facilitation payments are a legal form of business expense, and the Foreign Corrupt Practices Act explicitly allows for such payments, while the same act outlaws bribery anywhere else in the world. Other jurisdictions, such as, the Bribery Act in the UK, do not have a specific provision to allow for facilitating payments, and such payments are likely to be considered similar to bribes. The Serious Fraud Office describes facilitating payments as 'a type of bribe and should be seen as such' (Serious Fraud Office, 2012), leaving UK companies at a commercial disadvantage (Warin et al., 2010).

Questions to consider

Think of the positive and negative consequences of a normative approach, as taken by both the UK and US laws, to facilitation payments or bribes, both from the vantage point of a British/US company as well as from that of a recipient. Can you distinguish easily between a bribe and a facilitation payment?

Should such payments be legal or considered a bribe?

Would a communicative approach produce different results?

How can you apply normative laws in this case, for instance, in the case of a British company trying to do business in a country where facilitation payments are legal and expected?

Religious marketing perspectives

Not surprisingly, different religions have long served, and continue to serve, as sources of moral and ethical guidance in daily life, business life and also marketing in all its forms: from consumer behaviour and business practices to promotional activities. The three major monotheistic religions – Christianity, Judaism and Islam – have all inspired authors and researchers to contribute to the debate about marketing ethics. Much of this debate has been centred on typically normative ethical perspectives of these religions; however, other religious and philosophical schools of thought, some with more relativist perspectives, have also contributed, such as Buddhism and Hinduism (Darian, 1985; Gould, 1995; Watts and Loy, 1998).

Given the central and prescriptive role of either original scriptures or associated doctrines in the three major monotheistic religions, much of the writing in these areas attempts to relate marketing practice (or desired practice) with appropriate passages from the Torah, Talmud, Midrash, Bible, Koran, Hadiths or other religious scriptures or teachings. For instance, Friedman (2001) reviews a variety of business and marketing practices in relation to various Jewish teachings and scriptures. Amongst the many aspects covered in his review are some concrete examples of Jewish teachings in practice, such as the prohibition of over- and under-charging in business transactions, more general views on business, such as the view of wealth as a divine form of reward, and general duties for followers of the Jewish faith, such as the duty to help strangers, and the calling to conduct business affairs truthfully and not only following the letter, but also the spirit of the law. In a very similar manner, Laczniak and colleagues (2013) discuss marketing and consumption practices based on the third papal encyclical (*Epistula Encyclica*) issues by Pope Benedict XVI, a form of letter sent to all churches offering a papal interpretation of

Catholic doctrine. In their paper, Laczniak et al. interpret nine excerpts from the encyclical ranging from the role of markets, ethical decision making, 'stewardship' of the earth and natural resources to the duty of consumers to base decisions on ethical principles.

A particularly vibrant religiously influenced scholarly perspective is emerging around the relationship between marketing and Islam. Given the comparatively large influence of Islam on the lives of its pious followers, and more strict interpretation of scriptures and religious texts, the research field of Islamic marketing has moved rapidly beyond mere general and interpretative guidance in relation to ethics, and now embraces a wide variety of different topic areas. Facing a fast rise in a strongly consumerist mentality across the Islamic world (Varul, 2013), the Islamic marketing literature provides a large array of research with the aim of helping marketers understand Islamic consumers as well as consumers understand consumption and marketing.

A particular issue with texts relating religious principles to ethical viewpoints is the commonly normative perspective, and occasionally conceited tenor of some papers, particularly when comparing the conclusions drawn across different religious – or indeed humanist or atheist – ethical perspectives. Wilson and Grant (2013) are a laudable exception to this, taking a particularly inclusive stance in their commentary on Islamic marketing, specifically calling for the inclusion of other perspectives and arguing against a religious (and cultural) silo mentality.

Although religious guidance can serve as a moral guideline for marketers, actual interpretations of supposedly underlying religious principles in practice are often less normative, and vary from country to country. For instance, while alcohol is strictly forbidden in Islam, some countries with largely Muslim populations also produce and allow the consumption of alcohol; for instance, Efes Pilsen is a multinational brewery based in Turkey, and Morocco, Tunisia, Jordan and Algeria all have significant domestic wine production. Similarly, McDonalds operates both kosher and non-kosher restaurants in Israel, while branches in Saudi Arabia close during prayer times (Friedman, 1996).

Think points

How do you feel about religious perspectives on marketing? Identify religious guidance and discuss to what extent such guidance is adhered to where you live.

Marketing communications across cultures

Not only general marketing practices, but also marketing communications in particular across different cultures, can give rise to ethical challenges. Even though globalisation offers marketers opportunities to standardise their marketing activities and communications, care has to be taken because the differences in culture and perspectives play a vital role on how these activities, communications and products being marketed are perceived. Indeed it is not always the case that everything local remains local: it is actually more a case that everything local can be everything global. This is a problem that's very much a result of the fact that the Internet and new technologies, and especially social media, make ads and marketing messages available almost immediately around the world. For instance, an advertisement made in London for a US-based corporation like Nike once uploaded on YouTube or Twitter can go global in an instant, and be available to be seen in most countries around the world. This increases the emphasis on ethics in marketing since even though an advertisement may be considered acceptable in one country or region, it may not translate very well or be offensive in a different cultural context, and may lead to negative consequences for the advertiser.

Appeals and causing offence

Marketing Communication concepts, especially those using humour or in relation to religious, sexual or other social norms, are particularly prone to cultural misunderstandings or may cause offence. An illustration of encountering such difficulties are two very contrasting reactions to two ads with a very similar storyboard. In the early 1990s, *Expressen*, a Swedish paper, ran an ad which showed two men in sauna. Both were sitting side by side and appeared to be naked with one asleep and the other staring intently between his neighbour's legs at what seems to be that man's genitals, which are off-camera. The staring man is then seen slowly moving his head downwards towards the other man's crotch. Suddenly the sleeping man awakes and appears to be embarrassed and taken aback. He then smiles and nods as if to say it is ok. The staring man then continues moving his head and also now reaches down slowly with both hands – still off-camera. The camera then pulls back to show the neighbour was actually leaning over to read the other man's *Expressen* newspaper. More recently, the *Nairobian* – a Kenyan newspaper – ran an exact copy of the ad and just substituted the two original actors with Kenyan ones. The difference in reactions to both is remarkable and quite telling about different societal attitudes. In the case of the Swedish ad, most comments were positive with it being seen as clever, funny and interesting. In the case of the Kenyan advertisement, the commentary was primarily negative and in most cases quite openly homophobic, with many commentators seeing it as negative imagery, as can be exemplified by the following comments left on a website (*Nairobi Wire*, 2013): 'That *Nairobian* ad. If you called me to be in such an ad, I'd shoot you, burn you and shoot you again'; and 'No, offence, but I think you guys are promoting gay in that advert of yours, you should know that it's very disturbing'.

The fact that the original Swedish ad won awards including gold at the 1994 Cannes film festival whilst the Kenyan one was subject to a lot of negative, and to some vitriolic, comments just serves to show the stark difference in attitudes between a Westernised society and one in the emerging markets. It also reinforces the need for marketers to be aware that not all ad messages and communications translate well across societies and cultures.

This case is perhaps a more extreme example but one which had what are clear cut black and white divisions on attitudes held by different societies and resulting in much more hard-line attitudes towards relationships, and consequently stronger emotive responses.

Attitudes towards relationships can also be less hard-line and nuanced but nonetheless still different across cultures and countries. Take, for example, a BT broadband commercial that ran in the UK that was based around a heterosexual cohabiting couple with one of its sub-plots that of them having a child out of wedlock. This is an ad that was perfectly acceptable in the UK, a country with 2.9 million heterosexual couples living together as unmarried couples, which is roughly 16% of all the families in the UK (Office for National Statistics, 2013). While cohabitation as a living arrangement amongst couples is common-place in the West, e.g. 65% of the marriages between 1995–2002 in the US were preceded by cohabitation (Bumpass and Lu, 2000), many countries in Asia still consider marriage as the primarily acceptable family structure, with very few couples cohabiting and even fewer births outside wedlock (*The Economist*, 2011). Thus, the same BT commercial running in these countries is unlikely to find the same level of acceptability as in the UK. This might be particularly the case with countries strongly influenced by the Confucian culture (e.g. China, Japan, South Korea and Vietnam) that value the traditional family concept and promote abstinence until marriage (Gao et al., 2012). The BT advert might therefore be perceived as a further challenge to traditional and conservative family values already weakened in recent times, especially among young people in those societies, by social and cultural changes as a result of economic development and modernisation (Gao et al., 2012). Indeed, Xu and Ocker (2013) found middle-aged Chinese less accepting towards premarital cohabitation than the younger generation.

Marketers have often used sex appeal because as the cliché goes 'sex sells'. Generally though, and as can be seen from the previous two case examples, sex and relationships have an ability to evoke strong emotional responses depending on societal or cultural perspectives, and especially so in emerging markets which tend to have more conservative attitudes particularly towards sex and traditional family groupings.

Think points

Think of the portrayal of relationships in advertising. Discuss how potential issues can be avoided.

Indeed, sexual attractiveness and suggestiveness have been widely used in mainstream consumer advertising in many parts of the world although more particularly in the West (Liu et al., 2009), albeit sexism in advertising is an offensive appeal of major concern in Western literature (Boddewyn, 1991; Lin and Yeh, 2009). The use of sexism appeals tends to reinforce what are the traditionally held cultural values e.g. domestication, subservience and inequality between sexes through the use of female stereotypes as well as sexual imagery in advertisements.

Sexuality is regarded differently in different cultures (Paek and Nelson, 2007; Pollay, 1990). For example, some European countries (e.g. Italy and France) seem more accepting of this type of advertising technique than the US while most countries in Asia and the Middle East tend to be more conservative than the US and Europe in this regard (Paek and Nelson, 2007). For example, studies have found Chinese respondents to be much more negative towards sexually oriented images in advertising than their German counterparts

(Chan et al., 2007). It is therefore unsurprising that ads in China employ significantly lower degrees of sexual appeals compared to countries like France, Brazil and the US (Nelson and Paek, 2005; Paek and Nelson, 2007).

Differences in consumer responses to sexual appeal in emerging markets could arguably be due to differences in cultural values and perspectives. Several authors have used Hofstede's (1984) individualism/collectivism cultural dimension to try to explain why some cultures might find sexual appeal more acceptable while others find it offensive and unethical (see for example, Fam and Waller, 2003; Chan et al., 2007). The findings from these authors were that consumers from collective cultures like Chinese, Malaysian and South Korean found sexual appeal less acceptable than their counterparts from individualistic cultures such as the US, New Zealand and Germany (Chan et al., 2007; Fam and Waller, 2003; Ford et al., 2004; Pollay, 1990). This might be due to the fact that collective cultures highly value social harmony and respect societal norms. In such cultures, the use of sexual appeal may be perceived as a precursor to social ills that have negative impacts on the society as a whole. It is worth noting here that there is a growing trend of Chinese youth – the equivalent of millennials in the West – becoming more individualistic oriented with a consequently more liberal perception and acceptance of sexuality than their parents' generation (Moore, 2005).

Although the cross-cultural differences in how sexuality is regarded appear to indicate a East–West cultural divide, Paek and Nelson's (2007) study in fact found that sexual appeal in Thailand, a collectivist culture, is highly acceptable when compared to other countries in Asia. A possible explanation for this is that Thailand is considered to have a much higher indulgent culture than China or South Korea according to Hofstede's indulgence/constraint cultural dimension and Thai customers are therefore less straigt-laced and consider sexual appeal much more tolerable.

A marketer in China or some other emerging market should thus have an appreciation of the fact that certain societies have a lower tolerance for sexual appeal as well as reduced tolerance and high sensitivity toward female nudity. Marketers for Biotherm, a French cosmetic brand, not having this appreciation, posted a 30-metre long billboard advertisement for its body lotion product in the City of Wuhan in China (*Wuhan Morning Post*, 2007). The billboard, focusing on the upper leg of a woman in a bikini, attracted strong and heated debate among the locals with many considering it indecent and insensitive to local culture. Representatives from Biotherm, however, were baffled by the negative feedback as they believed the advert was classy and in good taste.

Gender portrayal

Since the advent of feminism, a familiar criticism of Western advertising has been its portrayal of gender roles and especially that which is interpreted as female stereotyping. In Western societies with a more established legal and societal equality agenda, there is a greater sensitivity to ads that may be seen as not conforming to equality in society – as three major supermarkets in the UK found. Over 200 official complaints were made to the UK Advertising Standards Authority in 2012 (with many more voices of protest in social media) when Asda, Tesco and Morrisons decided to take women back to the 1950s with their Christmas adverts (*The Independent,* 2012). All these adverts depicted women (the 'Mum') as miserable and exasperated in the preparation for Christmas dinner with no help from her family. The advert's implicit implication of a woman's place in the home was seen by many as a deviation from the modern viewpoints of a Western family unit and counter to women's struggle for gender equality. However, a marketer in China is unlikely to face similar issues with the same type of advertisement. For example, consumers in countries like China and South Korea, which are traditionally influenced by Confucianism, are likely to find the domesticated role of women portrayed in the advert as a positive attribute for women rather than insultingly retrograde. Under Confucian thought, women were assumed to find happiness and fulfillment by being wives and mothers (Asian Studies Center, 2013).

Portrayal of 'beauty'

Issues can still arise even when marketers appear to act especially ethically in advertising messages. Schroeder and Borgerson (2005) have suggested the term 'idealisation' in their argument that the use of idealised body images in advertisements can reinforce ideas of what is attractive in ways that result in damaged identities. The use of idealised images (whether altered using appropriate software or size zero models) – which has been the case in adverts for a long time – does play a large part in influencing what is deemed to be attractive or desirable. It is the use of such imagery and their potential negative impact on individuals that highlights some of the ethical problems with certain idealised images in advertisements as they drive people towards conformity with unrealistic or even hard to achieve body images and lifestyles.

Responding to such concerns, Dove's 'Real Beauty' campaign was highly successful in many developed economies. However, the campaign failed to engage customers in China. The constant use of idealised images in the media and adverts in China is probably the reason for the relatively poor performance. When Chinese consumers were asked to rate the Dove campaign images as either 'fat' or 'fabulous' the typical response was 'fat', with some respondents adding the word 'ugly' (Bush, 2009). Dove thus needed to explain their motivation to consumers, which they achieved by using the Chinese version of 'Ugly Betty' to sensitise consumers. After further explanations, consumers appeared to respond more positively to the arguments made by Dove, and showed greater understanding. The reactions in China to Dove's initial ad campaign are perhaps not surprising, as there has not been a public debate on the negative impact of idealistic images in adverts. Thus, it is likely that the Chinese consumers faced with Dove's 'Real Beauty' ad images experienced cognitive dissonance, due to the logical inconsistency of what they perceived to be real beauty and what the Dove campaign was telling them was real beauty (Hasan and Nasreen, 2012). As Lin and Yeh (2009) argue, low involvement and interest from consumers can come about when the imagery and appeal don't relate to products, e.g. Dove's product about beauty that didn't relate to the image presented according to the consumers.

However, Dove is owned by Unilever which also owns Fair & Lovely and Vaseline, both top-selling skin lightening products in India (see the end of chapter case study in the previous chapter). The issue of skin lightening is certainly one that has fuelled a controversial debate around the ethics of marketing such products to non-white consumers. The attraction of these products for marketers and companies like Unilever is driven by the large demand and market potential especially in the emerging markets, and one expected to be a $10bn one by 2015 (Sayeed, 2010). For example, when 'Whitenicious', a skin lightening product promoted by Cameroonian pop singer Dencia, launched, the initial supply sold out within 24 hours, with sales approaching 20,000 units after just three weeks (*Huffington Post*, 2014). The singer was accused of whitewashing and perpetuating self-hatred among women of colour, and more specifically, African women. She defended her product as one that empowered rather than disempowered women.

These two strands of arguments are often typical in any debate on the ethics of selling skin lightening products to emerging markets. On the one hand, some have argued quite strongly that skin lightening is not only disempowering but also a perpetuation of self-hate and loathing, a view associated most prominently with (white) commentators from developed economies. These commentators often raise concerns at marketers for promoting stereotypes in regions where light skin (whiteness) is seen as a signal of wealth, success and the fact that one is not of low class (Leong, 2006). Leong (2006), examining the use of 'whiteness' in China, also found that was associated this with race and ethnic identities with, for example, the 'whiter skinned' Chinese women generally perceiving themselves as higher status and 'darker skinned' Filipinos and Indonesians considered as coarse and inelegant. Sayeed (2010), for example, accuses Unilever of this in their promotion of 'Real Beauty' in the Western world whilst promoting products that whiten darker skins in emerging markets.

However, consumers in markets where these stereotypes are widely held have described the products as empowering (Hammond and Prahalad, 2004). This empowerment is not only because of the choice of affordable products available for purchase but also because, unlike her parents, the product provides access to greater control of a woman's looks (Hammond and Prahalad, 2004). Li and colleagues (2008) contend that the use of skin lightening products in four Asian countries (India, Hong Kong, Japan and Korea) serves the role of both empowering and disempowering. As the authors argue, it empowers to the extent that women using these skin lightening products now have much more control over their bodies and skin tone, but conversely it disempowers since they are still following 'the external control of a beauty standard ... and working hard to achieve social acceptance' (Li et al., 2008: 448).

Creation of unnecessary needs

As discussed in Chapter 2, marketers have been accused of creating unnecessary needs. In emerging markets, or markets with low education levels, such accusations can be further strengthened when marketers are perceived to exploit poor knowledge. Moreover, consumers in countries with lower education rates can be seen as especially vulnerable, firstly due to the lack of education as well as frequently insufficient governmental or legislative protection. Indeed, whilst Pollay (1990) argues that advertising seeks to create needs, Carrigan and colleagues (2005) assert that marketers and corporations do instead sometimes create artificial needs for unwanted products, and especially in emerging markets. Ethical misconduct is not just about the creation of artificial needs but, as Amine (1996) argues, also the creation of artificial demand for those products or services. The case of Nestlé and their baby milk formula does certainly clearly highlight some of these issues of ethics when it comes to marketing in emerging markets. The Nestlé case at the time brought into sharp focus questions on the responsibility of large global organisations when marketing in emerging markets. Nestlé, in the early 1970s, stood accused of not just creating an artificial need for infant formula in third world countries but also of pushing the product through clever marketing such that mothers living in abject poverty and squalor felt that baby formula was indispensable. Certainly the use of radio spots with jingles about milk that would make their babies 'grow and glow', as well as free samples of the product by sales girls dressed in nurses' uniforms who made unannounced hospital and home visits to new mothers, worked to get more and more babies fed the infant formula. Pressure groups like Baby Milk Action and magazines like *The New Internationalist* however argued that this caused problems like malnutrition due to a number of factors: e.g., poverty stricken mothers diluting the milk to make it last longer. In addition, with poor education and knowledge some mothers believed the nutrients were only in the bottle and thus just filled that with water. Although Nestlé put forward a spirited defence including that their milk was a better substitute to traditional and often lesser nutritional quality native weaning food, the global outcry against their practice led them to ban their mass media advertisement of infant formula.

Think points

Discuss the cases presented in the previous section using normative, relativist and communicative approaches to solving ethical issues in marketing. Compare your solutions and analyse advantages and disadvantages.

SUMMARY

The discussion in this chapter has highlighted that marketing ethics is not a static concept. Rather what is and isn't acceptable marketing practice evolves over time, and is influenced by cultural, legal and religious views. Consequently, ethical considerations are often complex, and require input from multiple sources as well as being adapted over time. Of the three potential strategies for dealing with evolving marketing ethics issues, we argue that conversational approaches are the most likely to result in a satisfactory solution being found. However, such communicative approaches require careful consideration for each participant and active seeking of, sometimes creative, solutions to allow for optimal decision making.

Case study   Flying the world

Developing products for international travellers can be a balancing act between local customs or religious laws and an international audience, requiring decisions to be made which have the potential to offend some of the clientele. An example of such decisions covers the practice of serving alcohol, a practice that is not allowed or actively discouraged by some religions and local laws. For instance, many countries in the Middle East as well as some states in India do not allow the sale or consumption of alcohol. However, for many people enjoying a glass of wine or other drink on board a plane is both enjoyment and relaxation, especially during a long flight. Likewise, many people purchase alcoholic beverages as a souvenir or in duty-free shops when travelling. The issue is further complicated, as some passengers may not follow a religion that prohibits alcohol and flights may take place above states or countries that allow alcohol sale and consumption.

Different airlines have adopted varying policies regarding both the consumption and transportation of alcohol in response to this. Some Middle Eastern airlines, such as Emirates and Qatar Airways, will only serve dishes that are prepared in accordance with halal requirements, which include not using any pork or alcohol products. However, the airlines serve alcohol routinely with meals in all travel classes, and promote their wine selection on their website. Conversely, Saudi Arabian, Kuwait, Pakistan International and Royal Brunei Airlines will not serve alcohol on board, irrespective of the destination or travel class. Some airlines will not allow passengers to carry alcoholic beverages, even in unopened containers purchased elsewhere, while other airlines will allow passengers to carry such items in checked-in baggage only.

Both approaches have been heavily criticised. For example, many international travellers regularly post about the service experience from Kuwait Airways in international travel forums online, often citing the policy of not serving alcohol as backward and unnecessarily restrictive. On the other hand, airlines such as Emirates have also been criticised for serving alcohol on flights as they are the *de facto* flag-carrier of countries where alcohol consumption is heavily restricted to non-nationals.

Questions to consider

Which policies do you think are the best ones, and why?

How should companies with a highly international clientele, such as airlines, handle this situation?

Can you think of ways to address concerns?

Further Reading

Sage journal articles available for free at https://study.sagepub.com/eagleanddahl include:

Cornwell, T.B. (2004) 'Cross-cultural consumer/consumption research: Dealing with issues emerging from globalization and fragmentation', *Journal of Macromarketing*, 24(2): 108–21.

(Continued)

(Continued)

Cui, G. (2001) 'Marketing to ethnic minority consumers: A historical journey (1932–1997)', *Journal of Macromarketing*, 21(1): 23–31.

Grein, A.F. and Gould, S.J. (2007) 'Voluntary codes of ethical conduct: Group membership salience and globally integrated marketing communications perspectives', *Journal of Macromarketing*, 27(3): 289–302.

Klein, T.A. and Laczniak, G.R. (2009) 'Applying catholic social teachings to ethical issues in marketing', *Journal of Macromarketing*, 29(3): 233–43.

Nill, A. (2003) 'Global marketing ethics: A communicative approach', *Journal of Macromarketing*, 23(2): 90–104.

References

Amine, L.S. (1996) 'The need for moral champions in global marketing', *European Journal of Marketing*, 30(5): 81–94.

Amos, A. and Haglund, M. (2000) 'From social taboo to "torch of freedom": The marketing of cigarettes to women', *Tobacco Control*, 9(1): 3–8.

Argandoña, A. (2005) 'Corruption and companies: The use of facilitating payments', *Journal of Business Ethics*, 60(3): 251–64.

Asian Studies Center (2013) *Role of Women in Modern China*. Available at: http://asia.isp.msu.edu/wbwoa/east_asia/china/culture.htm#bullet2.

Avraham, E. (2009) 'Marketing and managing nation branding during prolonged crisis: The case of Israel', *Place Branding and Public Diplomacy*, 5(3): 202–12.

Bernays, E.L. (1947) 'The engineering of consent', *The Annals of the American Academy of Political and Social Science*, 250: 113–20.

Boddewyn, J.J. (1991) 'Controlling sex and decency in advertising around the world', *Journal of Advertising*, 20(4): 25–35.

Borgerson, J.L, Schroeder, J.E., Blomberg, B. and Thorssén, E. (2006) 'The gay family in the ad: Consumer responses to non-traditional families in marketing communications', *Journal of Marketing Management*, 22(9): 955–78.

Branchik, B.J. (2002) 'Out in themarket: A history of the gay market segment in the United States', *Journal of Macromarketing*, 22 (1): 86–97.

Brandt, A.M. (2012) 'Inventing conflicts of interest: A history of tobacco industry tactics', *American Journal of Public Health*, 102(1): 63–71.

Bumpass, L. and Lu, H-H. (2000) 'Trends in cohabitation and implications for children's family contexts in the United States', *Population Studies*, 54(1): 29–41.

Bush, M. (2009) 'Festival of media case study: Dove in China's "Ugly Betty"', *Advertising Age*. Available at: http://adage.com/article/media/festival-media-case-study-dove-china-s-ugly-betty/136902/.

Carrigan, M., Marinova, S. and Szmigin, I. (2005) 'Ethics and international marketing: Research background and challenges', *International Marketing Review*, 22(5): 481–93.

Chan, K., Li, L., Diehl, S. and Terlutter, R. (2007) 'Consumers' response to offensive advertising: A cross cultural study', *International Marketing Review*, 24(5): 606–28.

Chasin, A. (2001) *Selling Out: The Gay and Lesbian Movement Goes to Market*. New York: Palgrave MacMillan.

Cui, G. (2001) 'Marketing to ethnic minority consumers: A historical journey (1932–1997)', *Journal of Macromarketing*, 21(1): 23–31.

Darian, J.C. (1985) 'Marketing and economic development: A case study from classical India', *Journal of Macromarketing*, 5(1): 14–26.

Dixon, D.F. (1982) 'The ethical component 6F marketing: An eighteenth-century view', *Journal of Macromarketing*, 2(1): 38–46.

Duggan, L. (2002) 'The new homonormativity: The sexual politics of neoliberalism', in R. Castronovo and D. Nelson (eds), *Materializing Democracy: Toward a Revitalized Cultural Politics*. Durham: Duke University Press. pp. 175–94.

Fam, K.S. and Waller, D.S. (2003) 'Advertising controversial products in the Asia Pacific: What makes them offensive?', *Journal of Business Ethics*, 48(3): 237–50.

Ford, J.B., LaTour, M.S. and Clarke, I. (2004) 'A prescriptive essay concerning sex role portrayals in international advertising contexts', *American Business Review*, 22(1): 42–55.

Friedman, H.H. (2001) 'The impact of Jewish values on marketing and business practices', *Journal of Macromarketing*, 21(1): 74–80.

Friedman, T.L. (1996) 'Foreign affairs Big Mac I', *New York Times*, 8 December: 8.

Gao, E., Zuo, X., Wang, L., Lou, C., Cheng, Y. and Zabin, L.S. (2012) 'How does traditional Confucian culture influence adolescents' sexual behavior in three Asian cities?', *Journal of Adolescent Health*, 50(3): S12–17.

Gilly, M.C. (1988) 'Sex roles in advertising: A comparison of television advertisements in Australia, Mexico, and the United States', *The Journal of Marketing*, 52(2): 75–85.

Goodman, J. (ed.) (2005) *Tobacco in History and Culture: An Encyclopedia*. Scribner Turning Points Library, Detroit: Thomson Gale.

Gould, S.J. (1995) 'The Buddhist perspective on business ethics: Experiential exercises for exploration and practice', *Journal of Business Ethics*, 14(1): 63–70.

Hammond, A.L. and Prahalad, C.K. (2004) 'Selling to the poor', *Foreign Policy*, 142: 30–7.

Hasan, U. and Nasreen, R. (2012) 'Cognitive dissonance and its impact on consumer buying behavior', *Journal of Business and Management*, 1(4): 7–12.

Hofstede, G. (1984) *Culture's Consequences: International Differences in Work-Related Values*, Vol. 5. Newbury Park, CA: Sage.

Huffington Post (2014) *Dencia Wants to Set the Record Straight on "Whitenicious" Skin Lightening Cream.* Available at: http://www.huffingtonpost.com/2014/02/03/dencia_n_4717833.html.

Kates, S.M. (2004) 'The dynamics of brand legitimacy: An interpretive study in the gay men's community', *Journal of Consumer Research*, 31(2): 455–64.

Kaufman, C.J. (1987) 'The evaluation of marketing in a society: The Han Dynasty of Ancient China', *Journal of Macromarketing*, 7(2): 52–64.

Laczniak, G.R, Klein, T.A. and Murphy, P.E. (2013) 'Caritas in Veritate: Updating Catholic social teaching for macromarketing and business strategy', *Journal of Macromarketing*, 30(3): 293–6.

Leong, S. (2006) 'Who's the fairest of them all? Television ads for skin-whitening cosmetics in Hong Kong', *Asian Ethnicity*, 7(2): 167–81.

Li, E.P.H., Min, H.J., Belk, R.W., Kimura, J. and Bahl, S. (2008) 'Skin lightening and beauty in four Asian cultures', *Advances in Consumer Research*, 35: 444–9.

Lin, C-L. and Yeh, J-T. (2009) 'Comparing society's awareness of women: Media-portrayed idealized images and physical attractiveness', *Journal of Business Ethics*, 90(1): 61–79.

Liu, F., Cheng, H. and Li, J. (2009) 'Consumer responses to sex appeal advertising: A cross-cultural study', *International Marketing Review*, 26(4/5): 501–20.

Lubitow, A. and Davis, M. (2011) "Pastel injustice: The corporate use of pinkwashing for profit', *Environmental Justice*, 4(2): 139–44.

Mikkonen, I. (2010) 'Negotiating subcultural authenticity through interpretation of mainstream advertising', *International Journal of Advertising*, 29(2): 303–26.

Moore, R.L. (2005) 'Generation Ku: Individualism and China's millennial youth', *Ethnology*, 44(4): 357–76.

Müller, F.H.. (1939) 'Tabakmissbrauch und lungencarcinom', *Zeitschrift Für Krebsforschung*, 49(1): 57–85.

Nairobi Wire (2013) *Kenyans Reaction to KTN's 'GAY' Advert for the Nairobian Newspaper, Nairobi Wire.* Available at: http://nairobiwire.com/2013/03/kenyans-reaction-to-ktns-gay-advert-for.html.

Nelson, M.R. and Paek, H-J. (2005) 'Cross-cultural differences in sexual advertising content in a transnational women's magazine', *Sex Roles*, 53(5–6): 371–83.

Nill, A. (2003) 'Global marketing ethics: A communicative approach, *Journal of Macromarketing*, 23(2): 90–104.

Office for National Statistics (2013) *Families and Households, 2013*. Available at: http://www.ons.gov.uk/ons/rel/family-demography/families-and-households/2013/stb-families.html?format=print.

Paek, H-J. and Nelson, M.R. (2007) 'A cross-cultural and cross-media comparison of female nudity in advertising', *Journal of Promotion Management*, 13(1–2): 145–67.

Pollay, R.W. (1990) 'Advertising sexism is forgiven, but not forgotten: Historical, cross-cultural and individual differences in criticism and purchase boycott intentions', *International Journal of Advertising*, 9: 319–31.

Proctor, R. (1997) 'The Nazi war on tobacco: Ideology, evidence, and possible cancer consequences', *Bulletin of the History of Medicine*, 71(3): 435–88.

Sayeed, L. (2010) *Stand up to Unilever's Hypocrisy over Skin-Lightening*. Available at: http://www.theguardian.com/commentisfree/2010/jul/16/unilever-hypocritical-promoting-skin-lightening.

Schroeder, J.E. and Borgerson, J.L. (2005) 'An ethics of representation for international marketing communication', *International Marketing Review*, 22(5): 578–600.

Serious Fraud Office (2012) *Facilitation Payments , Bribery & Corruption*, Serious Fraud Office. Available at: http://www.sfo.gov.uk/bribery--corruption/the-bribery-act/facilitation-payments.aspx.

Steen, A., Welch, D. and McCormack, D. (2011) 'Conflicting conceptualizations of human resource accounting', *Journal of Human Resource Costing & Accounting*, 15(4): 299–312.

Stevens, P., Carlson, L.M. and Hinman, J.M. (2004) 'An analysis of tobacco industry marketing to Lesbian, Gay, Bisexual, and Transgender (LGBT) populations: Strategies for mainstream tobacco control and prevention', *Health Promotion Practice*, 5(3): 129–34.

The Economist (2011) *Asian Demography: The Flight from Marriage*, 20 August. Available at: http://www.economist.com/node/21526329/.

The Independent (2012) *Mamma Mia, These Tesco, Morrisons and Asda Adverts Take Christmas back to the 1950s*, 16 November. Available at: http://www.independent.co.uk/voices/comment/mamma-mia-these-tesco-morrisons-and-asda-adverts-take-christmas-back-to-the-1950s-8323418.html.

Um, N-H. (2012) 'Seeking the Holy Grail through gay and lesbian consumers: An exploratory content analysis of ads with gay/lesbian-specific content', *Journal of Marketing Communications*, 18(2): 133–49.

Varul, M.Z. (2013) 'The Sufi ethics and the spirits of consumerism: A preliminary suggestion for further research', *Marketing Theory*, 3(4): 505–12.

Warin, F.J., Falconer, C. and Diamant, M.S. (2010) 'British are coming: Britain changes its law on foreign bribery and joins the international fight against corruption', *International Law Journal*, 46: 1–70.

Watts, J. and Loy, D. (1998) 'The religion of consumption: A Buddhist perspective', *Development-Journal of the Society for International Development-English Edition*, 1: 61–6.

Wiles, C.R., Wiles, J.A. and Tjernlund, A. (1996) 'The ideology of advertising: The United States and Sweden', *Journal of Advertising Research*, 36(3).

Wilson, J.A.J. and Grant, J. (2013) 'Islamic marketing: A challenger to the classical marketing canon?', *Journal of Islamic Marketing*, 4(1): 7–21.

Wuhan Morning Post (2007) *A Sex Appeal Billboard Ad in Central District of Wuhan Induced a Public Debate*. Available at: http://bbs.tiexue.net/post_3336272_1.html.

Xu, Y. and Ocker, B.L. (2013) 'Discrepancies in cross-cultural and cross-generational attitudes toward committed relationships in China and the United States', *Family Court Review*, 51(4): 591–604.

Ethical Issues in Marketing Relationships

Lynne Eagle and Stephan Dahl

CHAPTER OVERVIEW

In this chapter we will discuss ethical issues from a relational perspective in diverse settings ranging from:

- Marketing relationships and relationship marketing approaches, including franchising
- Retailing and personal selling
- Pharmaceutical marketing including 'detailing'
- Business to business (B2B) marketing
- Supply chain management, including:

  o Ethical challenges for Fair Trade as it moves from niche to mainstream markets
  o The ethics of payment to stock ('slotting') allowances
  o Multi-level marketing and pyramid selling

Issues that cross all sectors of marketing will also be discussed, including:

- Gifts, promotions and entertainment for certain customers
- Data mining techniques used for customer contacts
- Ethical issues with 'bait and switch' and 'loss leader' strategies
- Ethical dimensions of pricing strategies and their impact on relationships

MARKETING RELATIONSHIPS AND RELATIONSHIP MARKETING

Ethical relationship marketing

Interest in exploring the relationship between marketers and current or potential customers has evolved as a result of increased competition and increasingly 'savvy' and thus demanding consumers (Sheth et al., 2012). There is often an implicit assumption that all customers want a one-to-one relationship with suppliers of the goods and services they purchase or use. While marketing relationships can occur at any stage and in any part of the purchase process, relationship marketing has a more focused definition, i.e.:

> Relationship Marketing is the ongoing process of engaging in collaborative activities and programs with immediate and end-user customers to create or enhance mutual economic, social and psychological value, profitably. (Sheth et al., 2012: 7)

There is an implicit assumption in the literature that businesses operate on the basis of honesty, fairness and transparency (Finkle and Mallin, 2011), but there are numerous examples where the assumed business principles are violated. These frequently occur at the sales or personal selling point.

The 'ideal' **relationship-based sales** encounter focuses on generating customer satisfaction, trust and long-term commitment which in turn leads to both repeat and potential new business as a result of positive word-of-mouth from satisfied customers (Mulki and Jaramillo, 2011). The dimensions of ethical relationship marketing are shown in Figure 4.1.

Think points

Study Figure 4.1. Is it just a statement of good intent or can it be operationalised in managing relationship marketing? If the latter, how might this be achieved?

Franchising

A problem for many brand owners is that their retail activity is based on **franchising**. This is a business arrangement where an organisation (the franchisor) contracts with other

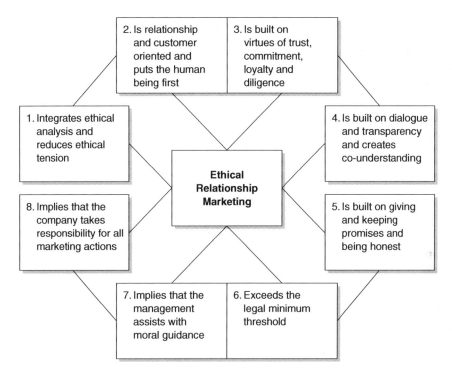

Figure 4.1 Fundamentals of ethical relationship marketing

firms, individuals or groups (franchisees) to offer products and services under its brand names. For example, many McDonald's outlets are franchises.

Each party, i.e. franchisor and franchisee, is vulnerable to negative impacts by the other party. If franchisees do not deliver on the contracted quality of offerings, it is the franchisor's brand reputation that will suffer. If a franchisor does not provide the level of support agreed to, franchisees may struggle to deliver the outputs expected (Cicala et al., 2014). These issues can be examined using agency theory, which applies to a wide range of marketing situations including a marketer–communications agency relationship where trust is an essential element in assessing initial and ongoing competencies and the quality of future service provision (Tate et al., 2010).

RETAILING AND PERSONAL SELLING

Many criticisms of unethical marketing activity stem from retailing or personal selling encounters. This should not be surprising as the selling function is where the customer most frequently interacts with the company, either through the company's own sales force or via a retailer over which the company may have limited control, if any. This encounter may in fact be the only contact point – the sales staff therefore become the *de facto* 'face' or representative of the company.

There is a range of different channels where this interaction may occur. What these have in common is that, while the company's focus may be on building long-term positive relationships with customers, they are reliant on sales staff to take a strategic role in developing and maintaining those relationships. Sales staff however may have a different perspective and must balance short-term sales level targets against relationship building (Roche, 2013). This may result in **transaction-based sales** situations. Here the emphasis is on completing a specific transaction with no consideration of the implications for future sales opportunities (Sharma, 2007).

Different sectors place different emphasis on short-term transactions versus long-term relationship building. For example, banks and other financial institutions focus on customer retention and loyalty based on continuous transactions (Alrubaiee, 2012). Many sectors of retailing rely on part-time 'casual' sales staff who have little motivation to build a long-term relationship with customers. Thus a bad encounter at a retail outlet or via phone, Internet or email contact may lead to negative perceptions about the organisation and the brands on offer, coupled with an increased likelihood of considering other brands or outlets.

The sales function also offers more direct opportunities for unethical activities due to managerial pressures to meet sales or financial targets, coupled with low levels of supervision and a lack of training, particularly for part-time staff (Pettijohn et al., 2011). Examples of unethical behaviours due to pressure to make sales targets abound, such as where sales force remuneration is based primarily on commission from sales (Valentine and Bateman, 2011). In the insurance sector, overselling to high-risk customers without disclosing the risk magnitude to management has been noted (Tseng and Kang, 2014).

Ethical lapses may in turn impact negatively on customer perceptions of the firm as a whole, or in extreme cases in the demise of the entire organisation. There have been examples of deliberate training of sales staff to engage in fraudulent selling, such as the US-based Alliance for Mature Americans which was prosecuted for using deception and misrepresentation in selling living trusts and annuities to older age groups (DeLiema et al., 2014). This moves the sales function beyond unethical to illegal and results in appropriate penalties. Fortunately, this type of blatant criminality is comparatively rare.

Think points

What are the ethical issues involved in promoting products and services that have no function other than to make people feel better about themselves?

Implications for sales management

There are obvious issues relating to role clarity and clear expectations regarding ethical standards, but also sales management issues such as how sales performance is measured, levels of supervision and, importantly, how ethical standards are not only communicated, but also enforced (Cicala et al., 2014). Modelling of appropriate behaviours by senior staff and by management is obviously important in communicating and reinforcing expectations (Li and Murphy, 2012).

The overall organisational culture is obviously important here, but management needs to recognise the existence – and implications – of potential sub-cultures that may be at odds with the overall organisation's culture (McClaren, 2013).

A particular challenge relates to the management of sales teams across national and cultural boundaries. One of the most commonly discussed challenges relates to what is acceptable business practice across cultures. For example, what might be perceived as bribery in western countries may be perceived as acceptable in other cultures (see mini case study 3.1 on facilitation payments in the previous chapter for example). Bribery may be perceived as necessary in order to enter a foreign market. There is an extensive body of literature in this area (for example, Holtbrügge and Baron, 2013) and we discuss the topic in more detail later in the chapter in the context of gifts and incentives.

Mini case study 4.1   Student workers

A US study of ethical dilemmas faced by undergraduate students working at least part time in low-level, primarily retail, organisations revealed the following:

> The types of ethical dilemmas that entry-level working students most frequently encountered dealt with the value of honesty. More than one third of the respondents in the study indicated that they witnessed, were told to, or told customers themselves something that was false or left out enough details to render the encounter truthful but not honest. Most accounts detail how the dishonesty, if detected, is covered with a well-rehearsed script, non-apparent scapegoat, or simple excuse. Some examples include the following: not telling the customer the whole truth, padding the bill in areas where customers typically do not notice, failing to provide the downside while embellishing the upside of a product, and skirting around the issue of poor product quality. (Bush et al., 2013: 111)

Analyse this description – what are the causes of the ethical dilemmas reported by the respondents and how might these be addressed?

ETHICAL ISSUES IN SPECIFIC SALES SECTORS

Pharmaceutical marketing – detailing

> The pharmaceutical industry spends more than $5.5 billion to promote drugs to doctors
> each year – more than what all U.S. medical schools spend to educate medical students.
> (Waxman, 2005: 2576)

Detailing is the direct marketing or promotion of pharmaceutical products to doctors or other medical professionals. Sales representatives visit medical professionals, primarily doctors, provide free product samples and gifts, and explain the 'details' of drugs in their portfolio including results from drug trials (Hoffman, 2012), with the aim of reinforcing prescribing choices or persuading doctors to switch to the company's brand.

Ethical issues involve overstating the advantages of a medication compared to other options or the suppression of negative information, an example of which is provided in the end of chapter case study. The impact of this activity on prescribing behaviours and potential increases in expenditure on medication due to prescribing branded drugs versus cheaper generic alternatives is vigorously debated in the academic and practitioner literature, with widely divergent views and contradictory evidence evident (see for example, Bala and Bhardwaj, 2010; Huddle, 2010; Manchanda and Honka, 2013).

Direct to consumer advertising of prescription medications

This activity will be discussed in more detail in Chapter 9, but a brief overview has been provided here to complement the discussion of pharmaceutical marketing overall as interactions between detailing and **direct-to-consumer advertising** (DTCA) of medication have been identified (Bala and Bhardwaj, 2010). DTCA (often shown as DTC to reflect activity beyond conventional advertising) involves the promotion of medication direct to the consumer through mass media, including television, radio, newspaper and consumer magazines, and through personalised communication (such as direct mail) with individual patients, and, increasingly, through both advertising and the 'editorial' content of Internet sites (Dens et al., 2008: 45). In terms of mass media, branded advertising of prescription medications is only technically legal in the United States, where the law was changed to permit it, and in New Zealand, where the American actions led to the identification of a loophole in prevailing legislation. The Internet and related technologies however enable the promotion of branded drugs across national borders (Brennan et al., 2010).

The main concern in the context of relationship marketing is whether, and in what way, DTCA changes the nature of patient–doctor relationships.

Business-to-business marketing (B2B)

While the ethical issues discussed so far have relevance to the **business-to-business (B2B) marketing** sector, there are some additional characteristics in the sector that warrant examination. B2B sales staff will deal with individuals or groups of individuals from the 'buyer' firm with sales being of high value and repeat business being the seller's aim. The relationship between the two parties may develop into social settings, where close personal relationships may develop, with the potential for inappropriate behaviour noted (Fisher, 2007).

One strategy to minimise the potential negative effects from this has been to propose a splitting of functional sales, increasingly using various levels of automation, and ongoing relationship development and maintenance of commitment to the relationship (Davies et al., 2010b) although there is no evidence of this having been widely accepted – or minimising rather than transferring the potential for unethical behaviour from sales to relationship development staff.

Think points

Do you think the role splitting recommended by Davies is likely to be effective or not? What other strategies might be considered?

ETHICAL ISSUES IN SUPPLY CHAIN MANAGEMENT RELATIONSHIPS

Supply chains are, very simply, the various producers and distributors involved from the point of production of raw materials through all stages of conversion to a final product available for purchase by consumers. For example, fruit growers may sell to a cooperative packing organisation that will grade, pack and arrange transport for produce to retail stores for sale as fresh fruit, to factories for canning or conversion into jams etc. Included in the supply chain are all transport, warehousing and distribution facilities.

There is an increasing focus on Environmentally Conscious Supply Chain Management (ECSCM) where all the environmental effects of products and production processes are tightly controlled to minimise any adverse environmental effects such as the disposal of waste (Beamon, 2005).

Ideally, the organisations at each point in the chain will add value to the evolving product, hence the term 'value chain' now being used interchangeably with 'supply chain' (Closs et al., 2011). Also ideally, knowledge transfer will occur between all parties in the chain, leading to high levels of understanding of each other's roles, efficiency and innovation. We discussed some of the challenges relating to coordination and control issues in Chapter 2 where no one organisation has control over other members but wishes them to adopt specific practices. Ethical issues may also arise when there is a significant power imbalance between channel members. This can be illustrated by the way the changing balance of power between manufacturers and large retail chains has shifted in recent years – but not in all markets – as discussed in Chapter 2. We now discuss the impact of dominant organisations on relationships with their suppliers and customers.

Retailer dominance

Supermarket **own-label brands** (also referred to as **house brands**) compete directly with manufacturer brands, often with preferential shelf positioning and lower relative prices. Supermarket retail chains are frequently criticised for aggressive negotiations with suppliers to drive purchase prices down and to thus generate greater profits for themselves. While some suppliers, such as farmers, have been able to form large marketing cooperatives or strategic alliances in order to provide themselves with market negotiating power, this is not always an effective option if there is a high risk of being blocked from supplying products to the chains.

Farmers and food producers have been increasingly vocal in many countries regarding dominant supermarket chains, complaining of abuse of power, including driving prices paid to suppliers down below the cost of production, together with other tactics such as 'delayed payment times for goods supplied; retrospective reductions in prices paid to suppliers; and requiring suppliers to contribute to marketing costs (including bearing the cost of "special" offers)' (Burch et al., 2013: 263). These problems are not just restricted to food retailers, but also apply to other sectors with dominant organisations within the supply chain.

Calls for greater regulation and control to reduce supermarket abuses of supplier relationships have revealed the ineffectiveness of current voluntary codes of practice, mediation and other regulatory processes across several countries, with some authors referring to the current structures as a 'toothless Chihuahua' (Richards et al., 2012: 230).

Slotting and promotional allowances

Slotting allowances are lump sum payments made by manufacturers to retailers, especially, but not restricted to, the **fast moving consumer goods (FMCG)** sector in return for shelf space ('slots') (Innes and Hamilton, 2013). They are commonly used for new product introductions, in effect sharing the risk of failure between producer and retailer.

Ethical issues arise in relation to the use of slotting to restrict access by competitor products. Some manufacturers cannot afford to pay the slotting fees demanded by dominant retailers, even if their product offers a competitive advantage over competitor offerings. It is also argued that slotting fees drive up prices for the consumer as the manufacturer seeks to recover the costs (Aalberts and Jennings, 1999). It is claimed that Walmart, the world's largest retailer, and owner of the Asda supermarket chain in the UK, is one of the few dominant retail organisations that neither demands nor accepts slotting fees (Kaikati and Kaikati, 2006).

Closely related to slotting is the equally controversial practice of promotional allowances where marketers offer, or are forced by dominant retailers to provide, funds to cover advertising costs or price discounting (Kaikati and Kaikati, 2006). Again, consumers do not benefit from this as the costs of the activity are passed on to them; some brands may lose shelf space if competitors offer more lucrative promotional allowances to retailers, thereby potentially reducing consumer choice.

Think points

What do you believe would be an effective mechanism whereby supermarket abuse of relationships with their suppliers might be stopped and why?

Multi-level marketing and pyramid selling

Multi-level marketing

Multi-level marketing (MLM) evolved from door-to-door selling approaches that were common until the middle of the twentieth century. It is a strategy whereby products or services are distributed or sold through a number of different supply chain levels. Agents at a high level in MLM distribute products to lower level agents in return for commission or other forms of payment. Payment is also made for recruiting other agents. Examples of companies using MLM include Avon, Amway and Tupperware. Ethical issues arise in relation to the cost of purchasing stock at different levels within the structure and the level of fees or commission agents may be required to provide; other issues relate to the use of personal home environments into which the home occupier's friends are invited to meet the selling agent and to view and try the products, potentially leading to feelings of obligation on the part of friends to make purchases (Koehn, 2001).

As western-based MLM organisations have expanded globally into potentially lucrative markets such as China, they have faced significant legal restrictions on their MLM operations and have been forced to adopt more traditional supply-chain strategies including establishing retail stores (Keep and Vander Nat, 2014).

Think points

Have you ever taken part in an MLM selling event in a person's home? Did you feel any sense of obligation to make a purchase because of your friendship with the host? How did that make you feel about the selling organisation? How should ethical issues such as these be addressed?

A distinction needs to be made between the usually legal activities of MLM schemes and the fraudulent investment schemes that are variously described as Pyramid or Ponzi schemes.

Pyramid selling

Pyramid selling is unethical and in many countries illegal. It involves people making a financial investment in return for a license to recruit others to the scheme, with the promise of high financial returns. These recruits in turn recruit others to the scheme, with each tier of the pyramid being paid for each person they recruit, and for those recruited by those they introduced to the scheme. Payments are made to those who invested early using revenue from new recruits. Those who invest early in a scheme's establishment may gain good initial returns – those at the bottom of the recruitment chain will make very little if anything. These schemes rely on continuous recruitment to generate funds to keep rewarding those already in the system. Closely related are **Ponzi schemes**, illegal investment schemes named after Charles Ponzi who used a scheme in the 1920s; more recent prosecutions include that of Bernard Madoff in the USA in 2008 (Hurt, 2010). In these, no action is required from the investor beyond handing over money – they are not required to recruit additional scheme members.

Fair Trade

The origins and intentions of the Fair Trade movement

The **Fair Trade** movement was established in order to offer better trading conditions for small producers and workers in developing countries. It is recognised as providing a new supply chain model (Nicholls, 2010) although the evolution of Fair Trade from niche to mainstream marketing is presenting several challenges to the original concept.

What we now know as Fair Trade started in the 1960s with the importation of handicrafts from under-developed countries to be sold in charity and specialist shops or via mail-order catalogues. Fair Trade commodity products such as coffee, tea and sugar began to appear in the late 1980s. A Fair Trade trademark (see Figure 4.2. below) was established in 1991 with organisations set up in several countries to oversee the awarding of the trademark and to monitor the standards set for achieving it (Davies et al., 2010a).

The key principles of Fair Trade are shown in Table 4.1. These principles align to Distributive Justice as discussed in Chapter 1 (for a detailed discussion of the application of Distributive Justice to Fair Trade see Beji-Becheur et al., 2008). Of note are the following: a guaranteed minimum price is paid to producers to cover the cost of sustainable production and to provide a living, with advance payments being available before a crop is harvested. A social premium, usually 10% of the net price, is paid to allow producers to invest in community infrastructures such as drilling water wells (Doherty et al., 2013). Three quarters of the world's coffee is produced by small, family-owned farms who have in the past been marginalised in the supply chain, and were faced with volatile markets and thus wide fluctuations in prices obtained, compounded by the need to sell products through often lengthy chains of brokers and other middlemen who each added fees to the eventual sales price (Davies et al., 2010a).

The principles on which the Fair Trade movement was established have been challenged with the entry of large mainstream organisations into the Fair Trade arena. For example, in 2005, Walmart, Nestlé and Tesco obtained licences to place the Fair Trade Mark on some of their house brands. Other major companies followed over the next few years, gaining Fair Trade certification for major established brands, as did some supermarkets with own-label products. Moving to the mainstream rather than just retailing through niche specialist stores has expanded sales enormously – estimated in the UK alone to be £1.32 billion in 2011 compared to less than £100 million in 2003 (Doherty et al., 2013).

Table 4.1 Fair Trade principles and implementation expectations

Principle	Implementation
Direct trade	Direct purchase. Provides direct access to the market for producers' products avoiding, to the greatest possible extent, middlemen and speculators
Fair price	A price that covers the costs of more sustainable production and living, with a social premium to allow producers to invest in development
Long-term commitment	Stable business partnerships established with producers via long-term contracts that facilitate long-term production planning and sustainable production practices
Credit	Pre-financing to provide producers with the necessary resources to complete an order without falling into debt
Labour standards	Producers must uphold basic labour standards involving rights to association, collective bargaining, freedom from discrimination and unequal pay, no forced or child labour, minimum social and labour conditions and working conditions
Environment	Producers must uphold basic environmental goals, encouraging biodiversity, preventing soil erosion and water pollution, controlling pesticide and fertilizer use, and reducing waste
Capacity development and information	Alternative trade organisations (ATOs) assist marginalised producers to build up management and production efficiency to enable them eventually to access mainstream export markets. ATOs provide information to producers on design, demand, regulations and prices

Fair Trade extension into mainstreaming: potential ethical issues with dominant retailers

Big retailers such as McDonald's and Walmart have leveraged off the Fair Trade and wider sustainability activity in high volume, high profit lines such as coffee. Their buying power means that these retailers are becoming increasingly powerful forces in coffee production as well as consumption, i.e. influencing every stage of the supply chain. McDonald's is now the largest buyer – and seller – of sustainably produced coffee in the UK (Elder et al., 2014), a strategy designed to build brand reputation and consumer trust.

There are a number of emerging concerns regarding the potential impact of mainstreaming. The first is the potential for **fairwashing** where retailers 'convey a (sometimes false) image of the company as a responsible purchaser' (Doherty et al., 2013: 174) and thus oversell their commitment to Fair Trade principles. A second issue is the behaviour of some supermarket chains who are reported to behave towards Fair Trade suppliers as they do to other suppliers (see the section on retailer dominance above), without considering Fair Trade principles (Smith, 2010). A third concern is that the social premiums do not always filter back to the communities in which the producers live (Blowfield and Dolan, 2010).

While companies such as Walmart support coffee growers to obtain sustainability and Fair Trade certification, there is concern that the poorest producers will be unable to meet the strict criteria, resulting in their becoming worse off. Indeed, there is evidence of some farms having increased production costs in order to produce certified sustainable coffee but not being able to recover the full production costs (Smith, 2010).

Until these issues are resolved for all members of the supply chain, there is the potential for reputational damage to the Fair Trade brand – and for negative economic impacts on producers. Whether the Fair Trade movement and its various administration structures throughout the world will be strong enough to counter potentially negative impacts and uphold the movement's founding principles – or revisions to them that are acceptable to all stakeholders – remains to be seen.

Think points

There is evidence that while they continue to support the notion of Fair Trade, consumers become increasingly price sensitive and decrease their actual purchasing of Fair Trade products during economic downturns (Bondy and Talwar, 2011). What do you recommend the Fair Trade movement does to counter this?

CONTROVERSIAL TACTICS

Gifts and incentives

Returning to the pharmaceutical sector as an example, this sector has a long history, particularly but not restricted to the US, of making large cash payments and providing expensive gifts such as free holidays to prescribers such as doctors. These tactics were common until the late twentieth century when US Congressional hearings led to the adoption of maximum values of payments and gifts (Katz et al., 2010).

This is not the only market sector in which payments and gifts have frequently been used. In the medical sector, it is still debatable as to whether even small gifts such as pens and notepads that contain branded medication names are mere reminders that promote positive relationships between the pharmaceutical sales representatives and doctors or whether they have a stronger influence on actual prescribing. The influence of these tactics on purchase behaviours in other sectors such as B2B is un-researched. More controversial still is the provision of free meals or other forms of hospitality such as free tickets to sporting or cultural events (Fisher, 2007).

The issue with all corporate gifts is whether their impact is just to strengthen relationships and the creation of goodwill. If they also promote sales of a company's products or services, which is an obvious objective of the selling company, are the end customers' interests best served?

A related issue is whether and at what point gift giving becomes bribery. While gifts may be a means of rewarding past business, they are also an inducement to continue the business relationship, i.e. the gift recipient feels obliged or even pressured into future purchases. Some countries such as the UK provide controls on the practice by stipulating a threshold for gift values (£100 including **sales tax**, i.e. VAT). Income tax must be paid on gifts above this value (Fan, 2006).

When a gift becomes a bribe remains a contested area, particularly in relation to cultural perceptions of acceptable practice. Bribery implies payment for an act (such as a purchase) that would not have occurred without the bribe, resulting in an action that is actually or potentially detrimental to the interests of an employee's firm or ultimately to its customers. This may lead to conflicts of interest which will ultimately undermine long-term relationships (Fisher, 2007).

Ethical issues with 'bait and switch' and loss leader tactics

Bait and switch tactics

Bait and switch tactics are said to have been used when a specific product is offered at a low price, but when potential buyers try to make a purchase, the advertised product is not available and they are offered more expensive alternatives instead. These tactics attempt to deter potential purchasers from conducting a detailed price comparison that would include competitors' products and other retailers (Lindsey-Mullikin and Petty, 2011). Comparisons become more difficult of potential purchasers when separate products are bundled together into a single package that is cheaper overall than if the individual products or components were purchased individually. For example, a package may include a computer, plus a printer, plus a guarantee with potential bonus items such as printer cartridges or paper being offered 'free' with a purchase – or even a free tablet computer with a package worth over a specific amount.

Online bait and switch tactics are a relatively new phenomenon. Consumers making Internet searches for a specific brand name or company are presented with promotional material for a competitor (Rosso and Jansen, 2010).

Loss leader tactics

Loss leader practices involve selling a specific product at or below cost price in order to draw in customers who will purchase other full price products. This may seem a non-controversial tactic – unless you are the supplier of the products being sold as a loss leader and you are expected to lower your own selling price to 'compensate'.

Additional issues arise in terms of the types of products used as loss leaders, such as alcohol. We will discuss a range of issues relating to alcohol marketing in more detail in Chapter 8 – here we focus only on the impact of loss leader strategies. Alcohol abuse is recognised as the third leading cause of preventable and premature disease and disability globally (Coltart and Gilmore, 2012). Alcohol is causally linked to cancer, cardiovascular disease, liver disease, diabetes and several other serious diseases (Parry et al., 2011) as well as injury and communicable diseases such as HIV and TB (Parry et al., 2009). Despite considerable evidence of a direct link between pricing levels and alcohol consumption levels (Lhachimi et al., 2012), alcohol is frequently sold at below cost price in the expectation, particularly in countries where it is sold alongside groceries, that people buying the alcohol will then buy other full price grocery products. Retailers have attempted (unsuccessfully) to claim sales tax (VAT) for these offers on the basis of their being classed by the retailer as advertising (Chick, 2010).

The industry's response to criticisms has frequently been to stress that they are involved in alcohol moderation programmes and voluntarily include moderation messages within their brand advertising. First, there is ambiguity in brand-specific messages containing moderation messages, with the conflict of interest being noted by consumers; where advertiser motives are inferred as self-serving, attitudes towards the brand are negative, potentially impacting on brand purchase intentions (Atkin et al., 2008).

It is suggested that current anti-drink interventions centred on mass media are not only ineffective but may also actually be reinforcing current unwise alcohol consumption-related behaviour by accidentally reinforcing the pride taken by some segments of the population in drunken antics (Hackley, 2008). Being able to purchase alcohol at extremely low prices is claimed to exacerbate existing alcohol abuse problems, resulting in calls in many countries for minimum pricing levels to be set (Holmes et al., 2014).

Think points

In some countries such as Germany, coffee is frequently used as a loss leader (Langen and Adenaeuer, 2013), potentially placing pressures on the Fair Trade value chain as discussed. What actions might be taken and by whom to counter any negative impacts from this?

DATA MINING

We provided an overview of 'Big Data' in Chapter 2. We now focus on ethical issues as they relate to the use of data for marketing purposes. Obvious concerns relate to privacy and data security, such as when data have been stored with a third party, e.g. with the increasingly popular **cloud computing** facility. Not only is there a chance of unauthorised access to, and use of data, there is also at least one instance where a cloud computing service provider withdrew service provision and access to the stored electronic information (Ratten, 2013).

Both traditional retail and online retailers maintain sophisticated customer purchase analysis programs, enabling customer shopping activity to be tracked and analysed. The aim is to help the retailer better understand their customers and determine how well their needs are being met. This enables future promotional activity to be tailored to individuals or specific groups of customers (Chen et al., 2012).

Ethical problems can arise if the profiling of purchase activity results in discrimination such as on the basis of ethnicity, gender, religion or sexual preference. Individuals may be judged, often by an automated process, by the characteristics of groups that they don't individually possess (Schermer, 2011), such as being associated with a particular location that has a higher than average crime rate, or refusing to provide credit or a loan on the basis that members of a particular ethnic group have higher than average default payment levels.

Mini case study 4.2   Personal Data

Different countries have very different legislative provisions regarding what personal data can be sold to third parties without an individual's consent. Consider the following: the on-selling of prescribing data, minus patient names and other forms of identification, but containing prescriber names, drugs prescribed and their dosage and prescribing frequency, is permitted in some USA states. Other states, and many other countries, have prohibited this practice. The data purchasers are usually pharmaceutical companies who use the data to inform their marketing activity (Petersen et al., 2013).

While we have once again highlighted a pharmaceutical marketing practice, the ethical issues it raises apply to other business sectors as well. What do you believe the main ethical issues are in relation to this practice?

PRICING STRATEGIES

We discussed pricing strategies in Chapter 2, but return to these now in the context of the potential impact of perceived unfair pricing on relationships. We all have beliefs, however vague, about a 'fair' price or price range for products and services. This may be based on previous purchasing, web searches or word of mouth. Fairness perceptions can be explained by theories about distributive justice (refer to Chapter 1), i.e. that there should be fair assignments of benefits and burdens between parties. This explains why some consumers are willing to pay higher prices – but only to a set level – for environmentally friendly/green products, organic products and Fair Trade products in the expectation that these products do offer some form of superior value compared to those from other competitors (Dekhili and Achabou, 2013).

When prices increase above the expected level, the perceived motive of the firm – such as taking advantage of consumers or buyers in the B2B sector in order to increase profits – may lead to negative reactions. These may at times be sufficiently strong that potential purchasers will avoid making future purchases from offending firms (Campbell, 2007). This revenge-seeking behaviour may result in the purchase of less than optimal choices from competitor products rather than purchasing from the organisation – manufacturer or retailer – that is perceived to have transgressed. These aggrieved former customers may also spread negative word of mouth (Xia et al., 2004).

There are obvious implications for the management of relationships between the firm and customers, from sales staff actions through to ways of communicating value for money and a range of relationship management strategies.

Think points

Assume your organisation has been accused of unfair pricing strategies and it is evident that you have lost customers as a result. What strategies might you consider in attempting to redress the issue?

Think points

Pricing is an important component of food choices. Given increasing concerns worldwide about rising obesity levels and unhealthy diets, there have been two distinct calls for action relating to pricing. Some call for discounts or reduced taxes on healthy food (see, for example, Steenhuis et al., 2011); others advocate placing taxes on unhealthy foods (see, for example, Mytton et al., 2012).

What ethical issues might arise from either of these potential strategies?

SUMMARY

The discussion in this chapter has highlighted the complexity of relationships and their management within marketing. The range of issues discussed within the chapter highlights a short-term transaction focus rather than long-term relationship building as a consistent theme underlying ethical issues.

Evolving supply chain challenges including the impact of dominant organisations such as large retailers present significant challenges across a broad range of marketing sectors, with particular implications for the suppliers of goods such as commodity food items.

Some of the issues we have discussed have no simple solution as they have context and cultural dimensions that make their resolution difficult, with the consequence that the principles of ethical relationship marketing remain an ideal rather than routinised practice, in spite of a substantial body of evidence regarding the benefits of the approach.

Case study   Ethical issues in withholding information – lessons from Vioxx

This case focuses on the marketing (and eventual withdrawal) of Vioxx, a non-steroidal anti-inflammatory drug (NSAID) in the mid-2000s, the largest prescription drug withdrawal in US history (Jain et al., 2005). There is a growing body of literature detailing the circumstances leading up to the drug's eventual withdrawal from the market, examining marketing ethics and also legal aspects of the case. Some of these papers have been included in the list of further reading which follows this case study. While the focus of this case is on pharmaceutical marketing tactics, the issues relating to selective presentation of information apply to much wider product categories.

Vioxx (also called rofecoxib) was introduced by Merck Sharp & Dohme in 1999 as an effective and safer alternative to other NSAID drugs already on the market. The primary use was for the treatment of pain in conditions such as osteoarthritis. In a large-scale trial of Vioxx – Vioxx Gastrointestinal Outcomes Research study, also known as VIGOR – its gastro-intestinal safety relative to existing medications was proven. However, these trials raised concerns about increased risk of 'cardiovascular events' such as heart attacks, strokes, blood clots and unstable angina (Rotthoff, 2010). Information regarding the latter aspect of Vioxx was not communicated to prescribing doctors or their patients (Dieppe et al., 2004).

After a 2001 committee meeting for the US Food and Drug Administration (FDA) at which the VIGOR study – and cardiovascular risks – were discussed, Merck instructed its 3000+ sales force to not discuss the FDA meeting or the VIGOR study itself when talking to medical professionals. A pamphlet which provided selective information and thus a misleading picture of effectiveness and risk factors was provided by Merck's marketing department for distribution to doctors (Waxman, 2005).

Vioxx was withdrawn from the market in September 2004 at the FDA's request. A second trial confirmed an increased risk of cardiovascular events, particularly in patients who had been taking the drug for longer than 18 months (Jain et al., 2005). At the time of its withdrawal, over two million people were taking the drug and sales were estimated to be in the vicinity of US$2.5 billion per year. As at 2007, Merck faced legal claims from nearly 30,000 people who had 'cardiovascular events' while taking Vioxx. While the company announced intentions to vigorously defend itself, its reputation suffered, as did its share price (Krumholz et al., 2007).

Documentation subsequently obtained as part of litigation against Merck indicates that wording in a report on the study was changed at Merck's request in order to obscure risk data. Nearly one million copies of the report were distributed to health professionals.

An 'expression of concern' was published in *The New England Journal of Medicine* in 2005 and reaffirmed in 2006 (Curfman et al., 2005; Curfman et al., 2006), which included allegations that critical data on cardiovascular toxicity had been withheld in reports of the VIGOR trial. For example, an article published in *The New England Journal of Medicine* (Bombardier et al., 2000) and one in the *Annals of Internal Medicine* (Lisse et al., 2003) compared differences between Vioxx and a competitor focusing on gastrointestinal tolerance and effectiveness but minimised or did not discuss cardiovascular risk. These articles, and articles in other journals, were subsequently claimed to have been ghostwritten by Merck staff, leading the journal to subsequently publish a full correction (Krumholz et al., 2007).

An author of the 2003 study admitted to a journalist that:

> Merck designed the trial, paid for the trial, ran the trial … . Merck came to me after the study was completed and said, 'We want your help to work on the paper. The initial paper was written at Merck, and was then sent to me for editing'. (Laine and Mulrow, 2005: 611)

(Continued)

(Continued)

Drugwatch.com, an organisation that helps people who have been harmed by prescription drugs that have harmful side effects and medical devices that cause damage, notes the following:

> To resolve the consumer claims quickly and quietly, Merck set up a $4.85 billion settlement fund and paid nearly 35,000 complaints. The varied financial settlements to injured patients allowed for compensation in accord with injuries. Of the original 59,365 claims, about 25,000 resulted in no payment. The remaining claimants received a sliding-scale settlement based on individual injuries. Of the 20,591 heart-attack claims, which included 2,878 deaths, payments ranged from $18,000 to $1.79 million. For the 12,447 valid stroke claims, including 590 related deaths, settlements ranged from $5,000 to $820,000.

Civil lawsuits were also commenced. Drugwatch.com also notes that, in the US:

> Although Merck agreed to pay $950 million and plead guilty to a federal misdemeanour related to its marketing practices, many were outraged by the settlement because the company still gleaned billions of dollars in Vioxx profits and was hardly reprimanded for the related deaths. The company did pay a $321 million criminal fine, $426 million to the federal government and $202 million to 48 states and the District of Columbia to settle civil claims that Merck's illegal marketing influenced doctors to prescribe a drug they would not have otherwise prescribed. (Drugwatch.com, 2014)

Subsequently, in late 2004, Pfizer announced that a clinical study on its NSAID Celebrex revealed an elevated risk of heart attacks. In 2005, the FDA asked Pfizer to remove its painkiller Bextra from the market, and called for stronger warnings on the Celebrex label (Epstein, 2013; Smith, 2005), raising questions about the safety of all drugs in the class and leading to an FDA directive *'that all prescription and over-the–counter NSAIDs include specific information regarding potential cardiovascular, gastrointestinal and other risks'* (Cotter and Wooltorton, 2005: 1299).

This case study presents numerous issues ranging from the process by which approval of new drugs is given through to what disclosures of safety and risk information must be provided by marketers – and not just for pharmaceutical products. It also raises the question of ghost writing – which is not confirmed to the medical industry: the tobacco industry has been accused of ghostwriting reports for the International Advertising Association (Davis, 2008).

Of concern is a recent content analysis of efficacy descriptions of material from pharmaceutical websites. This study shows that less than 5% of drugs featured on the websites studied provided 'a complete, specific and numerical description of drug efficacy' (Davis, 2012: 211), while almost 80% used vague and general terms, potentially leading to over-estimates of efficacy.

Questions to consider

Given the criticisms of PR and publicity tactics such as ghost blogging reviewed in Chapter 2, critique the apparent ghost writing involved in this case.

What are the ethical responsibilities of academic authors who appear as the apparent authors of research studies such as the ones reviewed here?

What is the responsibility of the journals in which these papers appear to ensure accurate attribution of authorship?

Further Reading

Sage journal articles available for free at https://study.sagepub.com/eagleanddahl include:

Beji-Becheur, A., Pedregal, V.D. and Ozcaglar-Toulouse, N. (2008) 'Fair Trade—just how "fair" are the exchanges?', *Journal of Macromarketing*, 28: 44–52.

Brennan R., Eagle, L. and Rice, D. (2010) 'Medicalization and marketing', *Journal of Macromarketing,* 30: 8–22.

Bush, V.D., Smith, R.K. and Bush, A.J. (2013) 'Ethical dilemmas and emergent values encountered by working college students: Implications for marketing educators, *Journal of Marketing Education*, 35: 107–18.

Elder, S.D., Lister, J. and Dauvergne, P. (2014) 'Big retail and sustainable coffee: A new development studies research agenda', *Progress in Development Studies*, 14: 77–90.

Golding, K.M. (2009) 'Fair Trade's dual aspect: The communications challenge of Fair Trade marketing', *Journal of Macromarketing*, 29: 160–71.

Other

Davies, I.A., Doherty, B. and Knox, S. (2010) 'The rise and stall of a fair trade pioneer: The Cafédirect story', *Journal of Business Ethics*, 92: 127–47.

Li, L. (2011) 'Performing bribery in China: Guanxi-practice, corruption with a human face', *Journal of Contemporary China*, 20: 1–20.

(Continued)

(Continued)

Lyon, A. and Mirivel, J.C. (2011) 'Reconstructing Merck's practical theory of communication: The ethics of pharmaceutical sales representative–physician encounters', *Communication Monographs*, 78: 53–72.

Nichols, A. and Opal, C. (2005) *Fair Trade: Market-driven Ethical Consumption*. London: SAGE.

Reid, D.A., Pullins, E.B., Plank, R.E. and Buehrer, R.E. (2004) 'Measuring buyers' perceptions of conflict in business-to-business sales interactions', *Journal of Business & Industrial Marketing*, 19: 236–49.

Tate, W.L., Ellram, L.M., Bals, L., Hartmann, E. and van der Valk, W. (2010) 'An Agency Theory perspective on the purchase of marketing services', *Industrial Marketing Management*, 39: 806–19.

References

Aalberts, R.J. and Jennings, M.M. (1999) 'The ethics of slotting: Is this bribery, facilitation marketing or just plain competition?', *Journal of Business Ethics*, 20: 207–15.

Alrubaiee, L. (2012) 'Exploring the relationship between ethical sales behavior, relationship quality, and customer loyalty', *International Journal of Marketing Studies*, 4.

Atkin, J.L., McCardle, M. and Newell, S.J. (2008) 'The role of advertiser motives in consumer evaluations of "responsibility" messages from the alcohol industry', *Journal of Marketing Communications*, 14: 315–35.

Bala, R. and Bhardwaj, P. (2010) 'Detailing vs. direct-to-consumer advertising in the prescription pharmaceutical industry', *Management Science*, 56: 148–60.

Beamon, B.M. (2005) 'Environmental and sustainability ethics in supply chain management', *Science and Engineering Ethics*, 11: 221–34.

Beji-Becheur, A., Pedregal, V.D. and Ozcaglar-Toulouse, N. (2008) 'Fair Trade—Just how "fair" are the exchanges?', *Journal of Macromarketing*, 28: 44–52.

Blowfield, M.E. and Dolan, C. (2010) 'Fairtrade facts and fancies: What Kenyan Fairtrade tea tells us about business' role as development agent', *Journal of Business Ethics*, 93: 143–62.

Bombardier, C., Laine, L., Reicin, A., Shapiro, D., Burgos-Vargas, R., Davis, B., Day, R., Ferraz, M.B., Hawkey, C.J., Hochberg, M.C., Kvien, T.K. and Schnitzer, T.J. (2000) 'Comparison of upper gastrointestinal toxicity of rofecoxib and naproxen in patients with rheumatoid arthritis', *New England Journal of Medicine*, 343: 1520–8.

Bondy, T. and Talwar, V. (2011) 'Through thick and thin: How fair trade consumers have reacted to the global economic recession', *Journal of Business Ethics,* 101: 365–83.

Brennan, R., Eagle, L. and Rice, D. (2010) 'Medicalization and marketing', *Journal of Macromarketing*, 30: 8–22.

Burch, D., Lawrence, G. and Hattersley, L. (2013) 'Watchdogs and ombudsmen: Monitoring the abuse of supermarket power', *Agriculture and Human Values*, 30: 259–70.

Bush, V.D., Smith, R.K. and Bush, A.J. (2013) 'Ethical dilemmas and emergent values encountered by working college students: Implications for marketing educators', *Journal of Marketing Education*, 35: 107–18.

Campbell, M.C. (2007) '"Says who?!" How the source of price information and affect influence perceived price (un) fairness', *Journal of Marketing Research*, 44: 261–71.

Chen, D., Sain, S.L. and Guo, K. (2012) 'Data mining for the online retail industry: A case study of RFM model-based customer segmentation using data mining', *Journal of Database Marketing & Customer Strategy Management*, 19: 197–208.

Chick, J. (2010) 'What price for an extra-ordinary commodity?' *Alcohol and Alcoholism*, 45: 401–2.

Cicala, J.E., Bush, A.J., Sherrell, D.L. and Deitz, G.D. (2014) 'Does transparency influence the ethical behavior of salespeople?', *Journal of Business Research*, 67: 1787–95.

Closs, D.J., Speier, C. and Meacham, N. (2011) 'Sustainability to support end-to-end value chains: The role of supply chain management', *Journal of the Academy of Marketing Science*, 39: 101–16.

Coltart, C.E. and Gilmore, I.T. (2012) 'The need for a global alcohol strategy: Upscaling the issue in a downstreaming environment', *Clinical Medicine*, 12: 29–34.

Cotter, J. and Wooltorton, E. (2005) 'New restrictions on celecoxib (Celebrex) use and the withdrawal of valdecoxib (Bextra)', *Canadian Medical Association Journal*, 172: 1299.

Curfman, G.D., Morrissey, S. and Drazen, J.M. (2005) 'Expression of concern: Bombardier et al., "Comparison of upper gastrointestinal toxicity of rofecoxib and naproxen in patients with rheumatoid arthritis", *New England Journal of Medicine* 2000, 343: 1520–8', *New England Journal of Medicine*, 353: 2813–14.

Curfman, G.D., Morrissey, S. and Drazen, J.M. (2006) 'Expression of concern reaffirmed', *New England Journal of Medicine*, 354: 1193.

Davies, I.A., Doherty, B. and Knox, S. (2010a) 'The rise and stall of a fair trade pioneer: The Cafédirect story', *Journal of Business Ethics*, 92: 127–47.

Davies, I.A., Ryals, L.J. and Holt, S. (2010b) 'Relationship management: A sales role, or a state of mind?: An investigation of functions and attitudes across a business-to-business sales force', *Industrial Marketing Management*, 39: 1049–62.

Davis, J.J. (2012) 'Content analysis of efficacy descriptions on branded pharmaceutical websites', *Journal of Medical Marketing: Device, Diagnostic and Pharmaceutical Marketing*, 12: 211–20.

Davis, R.M. (2008) 'British American Tobacco ghost-wrote reports on tobacco advertising bans by the International Advertising Association and JJ Boddewyn', *Tobacco Control*, 17: 211–14.

Dekhili, S. and Achabou, M.A. (2013) 'Price fairness in the case of green products: Enterprises' policies and consumers' perceptions', *Business Strategy and the Environment*, 22: 547–60.

DeLiema, M., Yon, Y. and Wilber, K.H. (2014) 'Tricks of the trade: Motivating sales agents to con older adults', *The Gerontologist*, May: 1–11.

Dens, N., Eagle, L.C. and De Pelsmacker, P. (2008) 'Attitudes and self-reported behavior of patients, doctors, and pharmacists in New Zealand and Belgium toward direct-to-consumer advertising of medication', *Health Communication*, 23: 45–61.

Dieppe, P.A., Ebrahim, S., Martin, R.M. and Juni, P. (2004) 'Lessons from the withdrawal of rofecoxib: Patients would be safer if drug companies disclosed adverse events before licensing', *BMJ: British Medical Journal*, 329: 867.

Doherty, B., Davies, I.A. and Tranchell, S. (2013) 'Where now for fair trade?', *Business History*, 55: 161–89.

Drugwatch.com. (2014) *Vioxx Lawsuit*. Available at: http://www.drugwatch.com/vioxx/lawsuit/.

Elder, S.D., Lister, J. and Dauvergne, P. (2014) 'Big retail and sustainable coffee: A new development studies research agenda', *Progress in Development Studies*, 14: 77–90.

Epstein, R.A. (2013) 'Regulatory paternalism in the market for drugs: Lessons from Vioxx and Celebrex', *Yale Journal of Health Policy, Law, and Ethics*, 5: 741–70.

Fan, Y. (2006) 'Promoting business with corporate gifts–major issues and empirical evidence', *Corporate Communications: An International Journal*, 11: 43–55.

Finkle, T.A. and Mallin, M.L. (2011) 'Ethical considerations of sales channel selection in the field of entrepreneurship', *Journal of Ethics and Entrepreneurship*, 1: 27–40.

Fisher, J. (2007) 'Business marketing and the ethics of gift giving', *Industrial Marketing Management*, 36: 99–108.

Golding, K.M. (2009) 'Fair Trade's dual aspect: The communications challenge of Fair Trade marketing', *Journal of Macromarketing*, 29: 160–71.

Hackley, C. (2008) 'UK alcohol policy and market research: Media debates and methodological differences', *International Journal of Market Research*, 50: 429–31.

Hoffman, M N. (2012) 'Pharmaceutical detailing is not for everyone: Side effects may include sub-optimal prescribing decisions, compromised patient health, and increased prescription drug spending', *Journal of Legal Medicine*, 33: 381–97.

Holmes, J., Meng, Y., Meier, P.S., Brennan, A., Angus, C., Campbell-Burton, A., Guo, Y., Hill-McManus, D. and Purshouse, R.C. (2014) 'Effects of minimum unit pricing for alcohol on different income and socioeconomic groups: A modelling study', *The Lancet*, 383: 1655–64.

Holtbrügge, D. and Baron, A. (2013) 'Market entry strategies in emerging markets: An institutional study in the BRIC countries', *Thunderbird International Business Review*, 55: 237–52.

Huddle, T.S. (2010) 'The pitfalls of deducing ethics from behavioral economics: Why the Association of American Medical Colleges is wrong about pharmaceutical detailing', *The American Journal of Bioethics*, 10: 1–8.

Hurt, C. (2010) 'Evil has a new name (and a new narrative): Bernard Madoff', *Michigan Law Review*, Winter (4): 947–87.

Innes, R. and Hamilton, S.F. (2013) 'Slotting allowances under supermarket oligopoly', *American Journal of Agricultural Economics*, 95: 1216–22.

Jain, A., Atreja, A., Harris, C.M., Lehmann, M., Burns, J. and Young, J. (2005) 'Responding to the rofecoxib withdrawal crisis: A new model for notifying patients at risk and their health care providers', *Annals of Internal Medicine*, 142: 182–6.

Kaikati, J.G. and Kaikati, A.M. (2006) 'Slotting and promotional allowances: Red flags in the supply chain', *Supply Chain Management: An International Journal*, 11: 140–7.

Katz, D., Caplan, A.L. and Merz, J.F. (2010) 'All gifts large and small: Toward an understanding of the ethics of pharmaceutical industry gift-giving', *The American Journal of Bioethics*, 10: 11–17.

Keep, W.W. and Vander Nat, P.J. (2014) 'Multilevel marketing and pyramid schemes in the United States: An historical analysis', *Journal of Historical Research in Marketing*, 6: 188–210.

Koehn, D. (2001) 'Ethical issues connected with multi-level marketing schemes', *Journal of Business Ethics*, 29: 153–60.

Krumholz, H.M., Ross, J.S., Presler, A.H. and Egilman, D.S. (2007) 'What have we learnt from Vioxx?', *BMJ*, 334: 120–3.

Laine, C. and Mulrow, C.D. (2005) 'Exorcising ghosts and unwelcome guests', *Annals of Internal Medicine*, 143: 611–12.

Langen, N. and Adenaeuer, L. (2013) 'Where does the Fair Trade price premium go? Confronting consumers' request with reality', *Social Enterprise Journal*, 9: 293–314.

Lhachimi, S.K., Cole, K.J., Nusselder, W.J., Smit, H.A., Baili, P., Bennett, K., Pomerleau, J., McKee, M., Charlesworth, K., Kulik, M.C., Mackenbach, J.P. and Boshuizen, H. (2012) 'Health impacts of increasing alcohol prices in the European Union: A dynamic projection', *Preventive Medicine*, 55: 237–43.

Li, N. and Murphy, W.H. (2012) 'A three-country study of unethical sales behaviors', *Journal of Business Ethics*, 111: 219–35.

Lindsey-Mullikin, J. and Petty, R.D. (2011) 'Marketing tactics discouraging price search: Deception and competition', *Journal of Business Research*, 64: 67–73.

Lisse, J.R., Perlman, M., Johansson, G.,Shoemaker, J.R., Schechtman, J., Skalky, C.S. et al. (2003) 'Gastrointestinal tolerability and effectiveness of Rofecoxib versus Naproxen in the treatment of osteoarthritis: A randomized, controlled trial', *Annals of Internal Medicine*, 139: 539–46.

Manchanda, P. and Honka, E. (2013) 'The effects and role of direct-to-physician marketing in the pharmaceutical industry: An integrative review', *Yale Journal of Health Policy, Law, and Ethics*, 5: 785–822.

McClaren, N. (2013) 'The personal selling and sales management ethics research: Managerial implications and research directions from a comprehensive review of the empirical literature', *Journal of Business Ethics*, 112: 101–25.

Mulki, J.P. and Jaramillo, F. (2011) 'Ethical reputation and value received: Customer perceptions', *International Journal of Bank Marketing*, 29: 358–72.

Mytton, O.T., Clarke, D. and Rayner, M. (2012) 'Taxing unhealthy food and drinks to improve health', *BMJ*, 344: e2931.

Nicholls, A. (2010) 'Fair Trade: Towards an economics of virtue', *Journal of Business Ethics*, 92: 241–55.

Parry, C.D., Rehm, J., Poznyak, V. and Room, R. (2009) 'Alcohol and infectious diseases: An overlooked causal linkage?', *Addiction*, 104: 331–2.

Parry, C.D., Patra, J. and Rehm, J. (2011) 'Alcohol consumption and non-communicable diseases: Epidemiology and policy implications', *Addiction*, 106: 1718–24.

Perret, J. and Holmlund, M. (2013) 'Ethics and responsibility in relationship marketing: The business school and the next generation of managers', *Marketing Intelligence & Planning*, 31: 746–63.

Petersen, C., DeMuro, P., Goodman, K.W. and Kaplan, B. (2013) 'Sorrell v. IMS Health: Issues and opportunities for informaticians', *Journal of the American Medical Informatics Association*, 20: 35–7.

Pettijohn, C.E., Keith, N.K. and Burnett, M.S. (2011) 'Managerial and peer influence on ethical behavioral intentions in a personal selling context', *Journal of Promotion Management*, 17: 133–47.

Ratten, V. (2013) 'Cloud computing: A social cognitive perspective of ethics, entrepreneurship, technology marketing, computer self-efficacy and outcome expectancy on behavioural intentions', *Australasian Marketing Journal (AMJ)*, 21: 137–46.

Richards, C., Lawrence, G., Loong, M. and Burch, D. (2012) 'A toothless Chihuahua? The Australian competition and consumer commission, neoliberalism and supermarket power in Australia', *Rural Society*, 21: 250–63.

Roche, D. (2013) 'Ethical decision-making in private enterprise: A study of its antecedents in the sales sector', *Journal of Private Enterprise*, 28: 97–109.

Rosso, M.A. and Jansen, B.J. (2010) 'Smart marketing or bait & switch: Competitors' brands as keywords in online advertising', *Proceedings of the 4th Workshop on Information Credibility*, ACM: 27–34.

Rotthoff, K.W. (2010) 'Product liability litigation: An issue of Merck and lawsuits over Vioxx', *Applied Financial Economics*, 20: 1867–78.

Schermer, B.W. (2011) 'The limits of privacy in automated profiling and data mining', *Computer Law & Security Review*, 27: 45–52.

Sharma, A. (2007) 'The metrics of relationships', *Journal of Relationship Marketing*, 6: 33–50.

Sheth, J., Parvatiyar, A. and Sinha, M. (2012) 'The conceptual foundations of relationship marketing: Review and synthesis', *Economic Sociology—the European Electronic News Letter*, 13: 4–26.

Smith, A. (2005) *Pfizer pulls Bextra off the Market*. Available at: http://money.cnn.com/2005/04/07/news/fortune500/bextra/.

Smith, S. (2010) 'For love or money? Fairtrade business models in the UK supermarket sector', *Journal of Business Ethics*, 92: 257–66.

Steenhuis, I., Waterlander, W.E. and de Mul, A. (2011) 'Consumer food choices: The role of price and pricing strategies', *Public Health Nutr*, 14: 2220–6.

Tate, W.L., Ellram, L.M., Bals, L., Hartmann, E. and van der Valk, W. (2010) 'An Agency Theory perspective on the purchase of marketing services', *Industrial Marketing Management*, 39: 806–19.

Tseng, L-M. and Kang, Y-M. (2014) 'The influences of sales compensations, management stringency and ethical evaluations on product recommendations made by insurance brokers', *Journal of Financial Regulation and Compliance*, 22: 26–42.

Valentine, S.R. and Bateman, C.R. (2011) 'The impact of ethical ideologies, moral intensity, and social context on sales-based ethical reasoning', *Journal of Business Ethics*, 102: 155–68.

Waxman, H.A. (2005) 'The lessons of Vioxx—drug safety and sales', *New England Journal of Medicine*, 352: 2576–8.

Xia, L., Monroe, K.B. and Cox, J.L. (2004) 'The price is unfair! A conceptual framework of price fairness perceptions', *Journal of Marketing*, 68: 1–15.

5 Ethics in New Media

Stephan Dahl

CHAPTER OVERVIEW

In this chapter we will discuss:

- The impact of new and evolving media forms on marketing communications
- Disclosure and oblique marketing techniques
- Anthropomorphic marketing and branding in new media
- Concepts of privacy and data collection, storage and usage
- Marketing-related technologies, such as behaviourally targeted advertising
- Ethics in online sales and the 'sharing economy'

New media technologies have substantially enriched the way many products are marketed in recent years. New media marketing tools allow an ever-increasing possibility of reaching consumers in more sophisticated ways and an increasing variety of contexts: new technologies allow personalised communication about brands to be delivered while a consumer is playing a video game, suggesting purchases to consumers browsing on websites, and tailoring messages to the specific current location and previous shopping habits of consumers on mobile phones. While many of the criticisms of marketing, including the ethical concerns raised in other chapters, are applicable to both new and traditional media forms and the rise of a multitude of 'online' marketing possibilities, ethical concerns regarding the use of new media can be broadly categorised into three areas:

1. Firstly, concerns related to a specific type of new media, social media. In social media, the main focus is on interaction within an existing social network: for example amongst friends on Facebook. Naturally, as with a conversation amongst friends, social networks are also places where consumption and brand-related information are shared amongst users. However, in their early history, social media's distinguishing feature was the emphasis on content that was created exclusively by its human users; for example, Facebook did not allow brands to create profiles until 2007 (Hof, 2007), three and a half years after Facebook was founded. Thus, brand-related information on the social network was restricted to content created exclusively by humans, and therefore outside the scope of marketing regulations. With increasing popularity, marketers were seeking to engage with consumers directly through these channels, and marketers were increasingly courted by social media networks seeking to monetise their business models and captive audiences. From Facebook pages and company-run Twitter accounts, to corporate blogs, marketers engaged increasingly actively using social media with their audiences during the second half the 2000s. Many of these interactions required marketers to re-imagine ways to engage people, as the medium was fundamentally different, and used differently, from many traditional advertising platforms, presenting new ethical challenges.

2. The second category of ethical concerns is related to the way consumer activity can, and is, tracked across many new media platforms. There is a general perception that many online activities are anonymous. Yet, any activity involving transmitting data across networks, from visiting a website, paying for purchases with a mobile phone-based app, or even watching a TV programme on an Internet-enabled satellite receiver, becomes at least potentially traceable and in many cases identifiable. These data can then be combined with other data, resulting in an increasingly sophisticated way of tracking individual consumers and their behaviours, something that often gets referred to under the nebulous term of 'Big Data'. Should these data be available to marketers? Will this result in more targeted and relevant communication for the individual? Or will it result in intrusion into customer privacy?

3. Finally, the third category of potential ethical issues is related to the use of fairly traditional marketing techniques using new media channels; for instance, product placement in games or advertising on traditional websites.

The remainder of the chapter will consider each of these areas in turn. However, before considering these issues it is important to briefly discuss what is meant by the term 'new media', including defining associated terms such as social media, advergames, etc.

NEW MEDIA DIVERSITY

New media, also sometimes referred to as 'non-traditional media' (Wilson and Till, 2012), refers to a wide variety of relatively recently developed communication tools, the majority of which are reliant on technology and/or computer-mediated communication to reach consumers. While the term has been used to describe placing standard advertising messages in non-conventional places – for example, the use of **guerrilla marketing** techniques such as placing advertising messages on zebra crossings, parking lots or projecting advertising messages onto buildings using projectors – this chapter will focus on new media forms relying on computer-mediated communication.

Thus, the main focus of this chapter will be on a variety of different media vehicles, which can be broadly classified into five broad categories:

1. Games-based media
2. Traditional web-based media
3. Social media
4. Location-based media
5. A combination of the above (hybrid media)

Games-based media encompass promotional messages as part of computer-based games. This can be in the form of specifically and obviously branded games, released by companies purposely to engage customers and potential customers (also called advergames); for example, Fanta Fruit Slam, a Fanta-branded game for the iPhone. However, brand communication within games is not only restricted to branded 'advergames', but can also appear in the form of advertising (or product placement) within the context of a game which is not itself brand-related – it is then called **in-game advertising** or IGA. For example, the video game FIFA International Soccer contains advertising screens that display messages by Adidas and Panasonic.

Traditional online, or more correctly web-based, media are media forms that make use of mostly static webpages, including text, images, video and audio files. A particular distinguishing feature between traditional web-based media and 'social media' is that the former are normally hosted on a server owned or operated by the advertising company, for example a company web page.

In contrast, engaging with customers through social media relies nearly always on **third-party** 'social media' websites or apps to reach customers – Facebook, YouTube or Twitter, for example. A critical distinguishing factor is not only the use of a third-party owned and operated site, but also the motivation for visitors. In a social media context, users typically seek to primarily engage with their social network through the consumption of content created by other users (or social actors). This social network may include brands as social actors, though it is traditionally seen as consisting mostly of humans. Conversely, in traditional web-based media contexts, users visit websites predominantly specifically for the content created by the website owners; for example, to read the news on the website of a news organisation or find out more about a company (in the case of a company website).

Newly emerging technologies are location-based media, such as iBeacon clients. Using technologies, such as **near-field communication**, **Bluetooth** or **GPS**, **location-based media** enable the delivery of **push-notifications** to mobile devices when the device is in a specified area; for instance, special sales promotions can be pushed to mobile phones in supermarkets when a customer enters a specified aisle.

Finally, there is a multitude of hybrid media vehicles which use different technologies: for instance, Foursquare, the location-based social network platform, combines social networking features with location-based information in a games-like content. Similarly, traditional web-based media can contain links or have embedded social media features, or can contain advergames or other online games.

The above classification is not intended to be exhaustive, but rather serves to demonstrate the diversity of different media forms available to modern marketers. What all these media forms have in common is that they are regarded as highly efficient in delivering advertising messages by marketers. In particular, many marketers feel that new media tools are superior in achieving successful campaigns based on the two central theoretical ideas of advertising practitioners, identified by Nyilasy and Reid (2009) in their review of practitioners' views on advertising as 'break through and engage' and the 'mutation of effects'. The practitioner view of 'break through and engage' describes two simple steps of effective advertising. Firstly, it reaches consumers and catches their attention, for example by exposing an unsuspecting consumer to a commercial message in an new environment, such as a computer game. This is then followed by some form of emotional or behavioural engagement with the message, such as liking the message, skipping the advert playing before a YouTube video, etc.

This is complemented by the second practitioner view of 'mutation of effects', which suggests that consumers learn over time to resist advertising, especially any messages using a specific media channel. Thus, the effectiveness of a message channel effectively 'mutates', resulting in a loss of effectiveness. This in turn bears a notable similarity to the Persuasion Knowledge Model (Friestad and Wright, 1994), which postulates that over time consumers learn coping strategies in response to persuasion attempts by marketers, although Friestad and Wright explicitly state that activated Persuasion Knowledge does not always result in negative or defensive reactions (in fact, they argue it can result in positive reactions). Notwithstanding this assertion, most advertising practicioners assume that consumers will react negatively when a persuasion attempt is detected, and will therefore try and minimise persuasion knowledge (see Nyilasy and Reid, 2009 for a more extensive review of practitioners' views). New media, by offering constantly changing opportunities of engaging with consumers using different types of channels, clearly manage to minimise the chances of a 'mutation of effects'.

Having characterised the main areas of new media, we now review some of the specific areas of potential ethical issues created by these new media channels.

SOCIAL MEDIA

Social media can be defined as 'a group of Internet-based applications that build on the ideological and technological foundations of Web 2.0, and that allow the creation and exchange of **user-generated content**' (Kaplan and Haenlein, 2010). Focusing on user-generated content, social media encompass a sheer uncountable number of different applications and websites, from highly specialised **wikis** and small online **brand communities** to large social networking sites like Facebook. While the terminology surrounding social media is not uncontroversial – and in fact, some argue that social media, and particularly the philosophical bases, Web 2.0, started well before the Internet gained popularity (see Dahl, 2014 for a discussion of these arguments) – sites commonly referred to as social media sites gained popularity as marketing tools around the turn of the millennium. The main obstacle during the early years of the social media boom was, however, that social media content relied almost exclusively on the creation of content by individuals, and that commercial organisations were both cautious as well as slow to embrace this media form. There were only limited tools available to marketers to engage with customers using social media platforms, other than by trying to encourage individual social media users and content creators specifically to speak up on the behalf of marketers.

Clearly, in an environment where content is expected to be representing individual views, a multitude of potential ethical issues arise where content is generated not by brands but by users talking about products. For example, when an individual fashion blogger posts about products they have received as samples – or when they have been paid to write about in their blog.

These sponsored posts, which occur not only in blogs but also on other social networking websites such as Twitter, raise serious ethical concerns regarding the disclosure of commercial interests or sponsorships. So serious were these concerns, that the Federal Trade Commission in the US established specific guidelines regarding the sponsorship of seemingly independently created, user-generated content, such as blog posts and other sponsored social media activity (Paul, 2009). These guidelines threatened bloggers, other posters of sponsored updates and companies not disclosing fully any commercial interests, with severe penalties (see Sprague and Wells, 2010, for a legal interpretation of the regulation and need for regulation).

The concerns from the FTC came as a result of a series of revelations where seemingly independent bloggers accepted rewards for reviewing products, or, in some cases, even marketers were appearing as independent bloggers. Early examples of this practice emerged in 2003, when Dr Pepper paid bloggers to write about a new product line, the Raging Cow milk drink (Goddard, 2003). Protests in the blogsphere against the commercial intrusion were so intense that a Raging Cow boycott was organised by irritated bloggers (www.bloggerheads.com/raging_cow/), and the brand itself was quietly discontinued. There were several other well-documented cases in the following years, including the frequently cited scandal of Jim and Laura's 'Wal-marting Across America' blog, which was probably the first such scandal to be featured on primetime news across the US. In essence, the blog was a travel blog, apparently written by a couple, Jim and Laura, travelling across the US. In their blog, they frequently reviewed Walmart stores, praising local employees and the offers available in stores they visited. However, the blog's authors did not disclose that they were funded by a front group called 'Working Families for Walmart', meaning that in effect Walmart was sponsoring the adventures they reported about (see Gogoi, 2006, for more details).

In other cases companies themselves, or marketing agencies acting on behalf of their clients, have been identified as the authors of seemingly independent social media posts, a practice also known as flogging (short for fake blogging). For instance, Sony had to apologise after it was revealed that a blog entitled 'All I want for Xmas is a PSP', allegedly written by a teenager desperate to get the new games console, was in fact created by a **viral marketing** agency and was a marketing 'stunt' created on behalf of the electronics company (Megagames, 2006).

Think points

Using the examples above, discuss the positive and negative points of using social media marketing techniques which closely mirror personal experiences. How can you distinguish between brand characters, brand spokespersons and marketer-generated social media in such an environment?

As companies embraced new media tools, many quickly realised that they needed to adopt their promotional strategies to avoid becoming 'the univinvited brand' (Fournier and Avery, 2011), especially as in the context of social media, which was essentially 'made for people, not brands' (Fournier and Avery, 2011: 193). Social media are not only more people focused, they are also an environment where companies and brands have to relinquish control and engage with their customers on an equal footing, i.e. as equal 'social actors' in a 'social space'. Fearing a negative backlash from users, particularly if the company messages were perceived to be deceptive, such as those discussed in the previous paragraph, companies had to adopt a different strategy to engage successfully in this emerging 'social space'. Simply providing information in a similar way to conventional advertising through social media is, in most cases, boring for followers, nor reflective of the space in which the communication occurs. Thus, many organisations turned to **anthropomorphic marketing**, where brands or brands spokes-characters appeared as independent social actors within social media environments, making the communication effectively more human-like.

Anthropomorphic marketing is, in itself, not a new concept. For over a hundred years brands have attempted to attach human values to brands by using brand characters, cartoons and spokespersons, such as the Michelin Man or the Cream of Wheat Chef (Garretson and Niedrich, 2004). Initially such spokes-characters were restrained by the limits of promotional media, e.g. they could appear in print ads, or usually only relatively briefly, in television or cinema advertising spots. Consequently, it was difficult for such characters to develop a permanent and durable relationship with consumers, let alone interact and reach out to consumers on a personal basis. However, in a social media environment, where much of the emphasis is on relationships and the interaction between users, this restriction no longer applied. Using social media, consumers can interact with spokes-characters and find out daily about what the character is 'up to', leading to herewith unimaginable intimacies between the them and consumers. So Mr Peanut, brand mascot for Planters, can talk to his followers about working out, his leisurely lunches in the park or how much he enjoys reading nature essays to beautiful women on Facebook.

Many brands use social media to expand the conventional anthropomorphism seen in traditional marketing, by developing their spokes-characters as main interaction points between the brand and the consumer. However, countering the adage of the famous 1990s 'On the Internet, nobody knows you're a dog cartoon' (Steiner, 1993) cartoon, which insinuated two dogs at a desk with a computer using the Internet to interact with humans, new media marketing techniques increasingly allow customers to forget that they are interacting with a human marketer. A brand can interact with fans on social networks like Facebook 'as the brand itself', liking updates by fans, being tagged in followers' pictures or posts and commenting on activities by followers.

Despite the relative lack of research into anthropomorphic marketing, the persuasiveness of this technique has long been recognised. From a practitioner perspective, Baldwin (1982) talks about the persuasive effect of non-human spokes-characters in television advertising as achieving a 'suspension of disbelief' in the audience. Academics have confirmed that perceiving a product as human-like, for example as a result of anthropomorphic marketing techniques, leads to a stronger and more positive evaluation of brand attributes (Aggarwal and McGill, 2007), a decrease in risk perception (Kim and McGill, 2011) and that overall, anthropomorphic messages result in a stronger emotional response than conventional product-focused messages (Delbaere et al., 2011). Dahl and Desrochers (2013) have further argued that anthropomorphic brand activities create increased brand liking, a clearer and more varied attribution of brand personality, and are likely to lead to increased purchase intention.

The persuasiveness of social media interactions is likely to be the result of an environment where the persuasion knowledge of consumers is relatively low, particularly when companies refrain from engaging in overt sales talk – and will instead focus on updates and interactions which are human-like and subtle. This practice is relatively common. Dahl and Desrochers, for example, show that amongst alcohol companies, a majority (60%) of updates on Facebook do not mention the brand name at all. Further, many companies share stories which are unrelated to the product. A typical example is a Foster's update sharing a 'Heads Up From Down Under: That's going to be an almighty big smoothy! That's going to be an almighty big smoothy!', linking to a news story about the world's largest mango being harvested in Australia.

Current regulation is based largely on what can be said specifically about products. For instance, alcoholic drinks cannot be portrayed as enhancing social abilities. In an environment where brands are actively not making any product-related statements, but rather focus on providing at best subtle clues related to their brand personality (see, for example, the Foster's update above), regulation is unlikely to be effective. Consequently, new models of regulation may have to be developed to deal with the more subtle, human-like interactions of consumers and marketers.

SOCIAL MEDIA AS DATA SOURCES

A different set of potential ethical issues arises from the way data derived from social media, or other new media sites, are used in market research to create increasingly sophisticated images of consumer sentiment and other related marketing data. '**Big Data**' has become a buzzword in marketing in recent years; however, the term has so far escaped a commonly agreed definition, and in fact has been criticised as being a poor characterisation of the actual phenomenon it seeks to describe (Manovich, 2011). A specific challenge when defining 'Big Data' is the question of what constitutes 'small' or 'normal' data. Traditionally, the term was reserved for extensive data sets surpassing average computing power to analyse, and thus requiring the use of a super computer. However, this definition has become largely meaningless when considering that the average smartphone has more computing power than an early generation supercomputer.

Similarly, quoting the example of all Twitter messages relating to a particular topic, Boyd and Crawford (2012) point out that some data sets considered 'Big Data' are in fact smaller than data sets which traditionally have not been considered large enough to merit being called Big Data, such as census data. Boyd and Crawford define Big Data therefore as a cultural, technological and scholarly phenomenon (2012: 663) which combines three essential components: technology, analysis and mythology. The technological component highlights the use of computing power relying on increasingly complex algorithms to 'gather, link and compare large data sets' (2012: 663). The analysis component refers to the identification of patterns within these data sets to allow, specifically marketers, to draw sophisticated conclusions about relevant economic, technological and social patterns. Finally, Boyd and Crawford point out that Big Data are often characterised as a mythological tool, credited with creating 'insights that were previously impossible, with the aura of truth, objectivity and accuracy' (2012: 663).

Directly linked to data derived from Big Data is the question of ownership of the data. Market research conventionally assumes that consent is sought from the participants before researchers collect data about them. However, in numerous Big Data derived data sets, the creators of the data have no knowledge that their updates or other material posted or shared are being used for the creation of market insights. For instance, if all Twitter messages concerning a specific brand get analysed, is it fair to assume that everyone posting about the brand has given their consent for the data to be used?

TRADITIONAL USES OF NEW MEDIA CHANNELS

In addition to the novel functionality, and associated potential ethical issues, marketing and specifically marketing communication are also being used in traditional ways within new media context. That is to say, such promotional activity is similar in its execution and appearance to promotional activity found in traditional media environments. For example, product placement can be found in online games – or in movies, with similar ethical concerns. However, there are two areas in which new media differs from traditional media as an environment in which to conduct promotional campaigns. Firstly, in most countries new media face much less regulatory restrictions than traditional media. Secondly, new media functionality can enhance the targeting and segmenting of communication, leading to potential ethical concerns discussed in detail below.

Product placements

The concept of product placement is, of course, by no means restricted to online or even new media. Rather, early examples of product placement date back to the late 1800s

(Al-Kadi, 2013). Product placement has been popular in early radio serials, movies, music videos and pop music lyrics (see Eagle et al., 2012, for an in-depth discussion of product placement). Product placement has, as a technique, been criticised for being inherently deceptive (Banerjee, 2004), while marketers have argued that it is a reflection of real life, where brands are omnipresent.

Despite some contradictory evidence as to the effectiveness of product placement (Balasubramanian et al., 2006; Homer, 2009), there is some evidence that brand exposure, including length of exposure, has a positive effect on purchase intentions (Chang et al., 2010). These effects are, however, likely to be common to product placements in both new and traditional media. It is therefore useful to consider how product placements differ in new media. To discuss these issues, it is useful to consider two types of product placements in a new media context: advergames (and other online games) and online soaps.

Advergames

Advergames are branded games, in which often a product or brand is an integral part of the game itself. Originally these games were popular as website additions, for example, many food manufacturers used advergames on their website (c.f. Dahl et al., 2009), often circumventing the regulation of other marketing communication channels, such as television advertising.

Increasingly, advergames have evolved to become cross-platform games, that is, games that can be played on a multitude of different devices; for example, Fanta's King of the Park can be played online, on Facebook, and on mobile devices such as the iPad or iPhone (Johnson, 2012). Particular ethical concerns with advergames arise because of the immersive nature of the games, time spent playing, the increasing sophistication of game-play, the social nature of some games and the potential targeting of under-age consumers. For instance, many mobile games offer enhanced game-play options when the user connects with friends using social networks. One mobile consultancy reported that users spend on average around 40 minutes a day playing games on their mobile (Flurry, 2013), allowing for repeated exposure to products placed in those games. These issues raise some important concerns, especially as there are some regarding awareness of the commercial nature of advergames, particularly in the key target group of teenagers and children (Owen et al., 2013).

Online soaps

A more conventional form of product placement involving social media platforms has been the use of product placement in online content, notably to circumvent regulation or indeed the prohibition of product placement. Mobile operator Orange, Proctor & Gamble, Microsoft and Paramount had placed products in online content prior to the practice becoming legal in the UK (Hodge, 2009). Such promotions would be banned under product placement rules. For example, Cadbury featured its Crème Egg, a product high in sugar and therefore banned from product placement in the UK, in the online soap *Kate Modern*, which was produced in the UK and screened on the social networking website Bebo (Palmer and Koenig-Lewis, 2009).

It is unlikely that, at least for product placement similar to the Crème Egg example, the media context would be significantly different if the soap opera would be primarily screened using traditional media. Thus, the concerns and ethical considerations from a media channel perspective are likely to be the same as for traditional media. However, the example illustrates that in the absence of appropriate regulation, it is likely that some brands will try to circumvent regulation, even if they should be fully aware that this action complies with the letter but not the spirit of the law.

While the two examples above show that ethical issues can result from the use of new media channels to circumvent existing regulation, a different set of potential ethical concerns can arise from the perfectly legal, and arguably primarily ethical, 'mashing-up' of old and new technology. Two examples can illustrate this: Behaviourally Targeted Advertising, which combines Big Data and behavioural data with traditional display advertising, and location-based marketing, which combines location-specific information and traditional forms of promotions.

Behaviourally targeted advertising

Behaviourally targeted advertising (or **BTA**) is advertising displayed based on previously captured behavioural data about the user, for example, by displaying advertising related to recent searches on websites or items looked at in an online shop. Within social networks specifically, BTAs can be based on demographic and psychographic information about the user based on profile information or friend activity. In other words, BTA is a **mash-up** of traditional, web-based display advertising and Big Data derived data merging. At least hypothetically, BTA has the potential to offset the more limited but targeted reach of social media in relation to traditional media, by minimising exposure to advertising that is irrelevant to the viewer.

In practice, there are serious privacy concerns related to BTA. For instance, given the technical possibilities of BTA, which data should be used to target advertising? Should such advertisers be permitted to collect and distribute BTA content based on sensitive topics, such as finances, health, political affiliation, ethnicity or sexual orientation? Who collects this information and how is it shared?

In the European Union, and Australia, the industry has responded to political and consumer concerns by setting up websites where consumers can 'opt out' of receiving BTAs from specific companies. The Australian Digital Advertising Alliance offers consumers the ability to opt out of being tracked by 11 companies by visiting http://www.youronlinechoices.com.au/. The European Interactive Digital Advertising Alliance offers a site that is both similar in appearance, name and content (http://www.your onlinechoices.com/), though it allows Internet users to opt out of behaviourally targeted communication from currently 89 companies operating in the EU. While such industry efforts are no doubt laudable, the different number of companies a user can opt out of also illustrate that global communication networks are hard to regulate with regional or national regulation. To effectively 'opt out' of all behaviourally targeted advertising, a user would have to visit all of the sites in all jurisdictions across the world, including in areas where no such regulation or functionality exists.

Location-based marketing

A further emerging phenomenon in targeted marketing communications is location-specific marketing communication, either as standalone activity (e.g. iBeacon) or synergistically combining other new media functionality with location-specific data, for example in the case of augmented reality software or location-based social networking (e.g. FourSquare).

The rise of location aware, ubiquitously connected mobile devices, and particularly smartphones, tablets and wearable technology, enables the constant delivery of updates and a mix of paid-for and non-commercial information. For instance, through location social networking applications such as FourSquare (and the sister-software Swarm), users can be informed about friend activities nearby: they receive notifications if their friends are close, and are able to join them. However, the communication is not limited to real-time updates. The software further 'suggests' places it considers the user may like, reckoned on calculations based in part on Big Data technologies and in part on previous check-ins by friends nearby. For instance, if a user is in a foreign city, the software will suggest restaurants and shops based on the history of check-ins by the user, the user's friends and other users of the software. In addition, restaurants (or other businesses) can be recommended in return for payment to FourSquare or by participating in 'reward specials'. Examples of such specials include the American Express Sync cash back offers, where users are required to register their American Express card with FourSquare and then check in at specific locations, such as restaurants, and pay with their registered card to receive a cash back reward.

SHARING ECONOMY

Apart from the use of social media platforms for marketing communications and promotional activities, an increasingly important product of ubiquitous connectivity and social media presence is the rise of the '**sharing economy**'. A sharing economy is based on the sharing of human and physical resources, largely facilitated through social media platforms. Prominent examples include the 'peer-to-peer' room-rental platform AirBnB, and ad-hoc taxi and lift-share services like Lyft or Uber. The basic idea behind these platforms is that, based on the use of peer-to-peer-sharing of resources and technology-enabled low transaction costs, users can 'share' their ownership for a fee, making use of otherwise potentially unused or underused resources. For example, Lyft users share rides with other people, thus potentially lessening waste, not having to purchase their own cars and reducing the ecological impact of driving themselves. While there are many different business models, ranging from collaborative ownership of products, such as a 'car club', to exclusively peer-to-peer transaction-based business, such as AirBnB, sharing economy platforms raises a multitude of ethical issues, while at the same time addressing other ethical issues of ownership and individual (versus collective) consumption.

The ethical dimensions can be exemplified by discussing ride-share platforms. The average privately owned car is unused a substantial proportion of its time, with some estimates putting the figure at approximately 92% (Atcheson and Green, 2012). Through partaking in a sharing economy social website, car owners can decrease the idle time by turning this into potentially profitable usage of the car they own. Clearly, apart from security issues, such business models face three larger categories of potential issues. The first category of issues arises out of the relationship between the 'sharers'; the second potential issue concerns the effect of utilising previously unused resources on the wider economy; and the third issue relates to the business practices of the transaction enablers.

1. In terms of the first set of potential issues, a fundamental principle of the sharing economy is the reviewing of the sharing by both sides, e.g. both the driver and the rider on the ride-share platform Lyft review each other, and future transactions often depend on these reviews. For example, if one of them rates the other lower than a given score, they will not be matched again. Similarly, the scores are open for other people to see, for example, before giving another ride. On the one side such practices contribute greatly to openness and transparency; on the other side, all reviews are necessarily subjective and based on subjective biases.

2. The second category of issues relates to the release of previously unused resources into the economy. For instance, a survey based on hotel bookings in Texas estimated that a 1% rise in listings on the sharing economy website AirBnB resulted in a 0.05% drop in quarterly hotel revenues. While this number appears relatively small at first, it is nevertheless significant based on both the dramatic rise of listings as well as the potential for an ongoing reduction in hotel revenues (Byers et al., 2013). While no study to date has evaluated the effect of ride-sharing, potential benefits, such as lower cost for the sharers, incremental income for the drivers and increased usage of the resource, are potentially offset by a loss of earning for other, related or competing sectors. Moreover, considering the ride-share example, it is also important to note that not necessarily all sharers will avoid other, private means of transport. However, because of the lower cost, some sharers may choose ride-share over public transport, resulting in potential environmentally less optimal use of resources.

3. The third category of issues arises from the business models of the transaction enablers themselves, falling into two broad groups: taxation and regulation. On one side, there is little incentive for transaction enablers, such as the website owners, whose primary objective is to facilitate transactions between peers, including the lowest possible transaction cost, to operate under a presence model in many markets, which would result in a substantially increased tax burden. Higher taxation would inevitably result in higher fees from the providers, as well as potentially direct taxation on the remuneration for people offering rides. Thus, for instance, the car-sharing service Uber has been criticised for 'opting out' of the UK tax regime by channelling payments made for rides in the UK through Dutch subsidiaries (Houlder, 2014). Similarly, while traditional taxi companies face extensive checks on their drivers, training and certification before operation, many ride-shares are substantially less regulated. Thus it can be argued that part of the cost-reduction between ride-shares and traditional taxi services is due to circumventing or avoiding the traditional regulation associated with other transport options.

Therefore, the social media reliant sharing economy presents a particular conundrum for ethical business and marketing practices. On the one side, the business model clearly addresses the shortcomings of more hierarchical, traditional and property-ownership based models. At the same time, the rise of the peer-to-peer economy raises other potential issues and potentially unintended consequences.

Think points

Debate the pros and cons of shared economy models. How do you think negative unintended consequences can be overcome?

SUMMARY

New media have significantly contributed to the convergence of entertainment and commercial messages, something that in traditional media was mostly separated. Because of the variety of different marketing communication vehicles available, regulation has been slow to catch up. The effect of this has been that marketers have been caught out as behaving less than exemplary in a variety of new media forms. While they have, mostly, not been directly contravening regulation, there are plenty of examples where marketers have circumvented existing regulation. Some of these practices have caused significant damage to the brands concerned once discovered; however, the possibility of enduring potential regulation may be even stronger, particularly for goods targeting young consumers, or those goods which are considered detrimental to the **social good** (such as alcohol).

A different effect of the rise of social media, with the potential for ethical issues arising, is the rise of the sharing economy. This social media enabled, peer-to-peer based economy has on the one side the ability to address many of the negative consequences of traditional economic models; however, in doing so also it opens up the possibility of unintended and negative consequences arising.

Case study   Facebook Beacon project

Facebook Beacon was an early project by Facebook, similar to the later Facebook Connect, allowing user data from external websites to be sent back to Facebook. These data could then be used to share activity on third party websites amongst friends on Facebook. For example, if a user posted a review on TripAdvisor, one of the Beacon partner sites, the activity could be shared with friends on Facebook. Moreover, collecting data about activity on external websites allowed the Facebook advertising network to target users with behaviourally targeted advertising based on activities on other websites. Beacon used a technical bug to operate, based on placing a small image on the third party website. When the image was loaded, the Beacon technology would then allow looking for an active Facebook account and session of the user by examining the user's cookies. If an active cookie was found, the user activity was published, such as making a purchase, originally without requiring the user to explicitly give permission on his or her timeline.

The Beacon system sparked considerable controversy because of privacy concerns. Even though Facebook quickly changed the Beacon system to require user permission before posting about activities on third party websites, doubts remained over which information was being exchanged between the websites and Facebook (for example, if Facebook received data about declined purchases).

Following several lawsuits, and a class action settlement, Facebook terminated the controversial project, which gained much attention at the time, including the high profile withdrawal of some advertisers/Beacon users, such as Coca Cola. However, despite the termination of the programme, many people remained distrustful towards social networks such as Facebook. Although Facebook-founder Mark Zuckerberg characterised Beacon as a 'high profile mistake' (Zuckerberg, 2011), future activities by the company have stirred enormous controversy and raised privacy concerns. On the other hand, despite these concerns, many users have remained largely loyal to Facebook, and a significant proportion of users make use of Facebook Connect. Facebook Connect allows for similar interactions between Facebook and third party websites; however, it relies on an explicit opt-in by the user.

Questions to consider

Explain why Beacon was marred by controversy while many users readily accepted Facebook Connect. What lessons can be learned from comparing these?

How would you ethically guide marketers in the use of social media?

Further Reading

Books discussing social media marketing ethics include:

Dahl, S. (2014) *Social Media Marketing: Theories and Applications*. London: Sage.

DiStaso, M.W. and Bortree, D.S. (eds) (2014) *Ethical Practice of Social Media in Public Relations*, Routledge Research in Public Relations. Routledge: New York.

Sage journal articles available for free at https://study.sagepub.com/eagleanddahl include:

Cohen, B. and Kietzmann, J. (2014) 'Ride on! Mobility business models for the sharing economy', *Organization & Environment*, 27(3): 279–96.

(Continued)

(Continued)

Huang, E. and Dunbar, C.L. (2013) 'Connecting to patients via social media: A hype or a reality?', *Journal of Medical Marketing: Device, Diagnostic and Pharmaceutical Marketing*, 13: 14–23.

Jacobson, W.S. and Tufts, S.H. (2013) 'To post or not to post: Employee rights and social media', *Review of Public Personnel Administration*, 33: 84–107.

Khan, G.F., Swar, B. and Lee, S.K. (2014) 'Social media risks and benefits: A public sector perspective', *Social Science Computer Review*, 28: 24–44.

References

Aggarwal, P. and McGill, A.L. (2007) 'Is that car smiling at me? Schema congruity as a basis for evaluating anthropomorphized products', *Journal of Consumer Research* 34(4): 468–79.

Al-Kadi, T. (2013) 'Product placement: A booming industry in search of appropriate regulation', *Journal of Marketing Research & Case Studies*, 2013: 72.

Atcheson, J. and Green, L. (2012) 'Car sharing and pooling: Reducing car over-population and collaborative consumption', *Stamford Energy Seminar*, 9 April. Available at: http://energyseminar.stanford.edu/node/425.

Balasubramanian, S.K., Karrh, J.A. and Patwardhan, H. (2006) 'Audience response to product placements: An integrative framework and future research agenda', *Journal of Advertising*, 35(3): 115–41.

Baldwin, H. (1982) *Creating Effective TV Commercials*. New York: Crain Books.

Banerjee, S. (2004) 'Playing games', *Billboard*, 116(20): 3–4.

Boyd, D. and Crawford, K. (2012) "Critical questions for Big Data: Provocations for a cultural, technological, and scholarly phenomenon', *Information, Communication & Society*, 15(5): 662–79.

Byers, J., Proserpio, D. and Zervas, G. (2013) 'The rise of the sharing economy: Estimating the impact of Airbnb on the hotel industry', *SSRN Electronic Journal*. Available at: http://ssrn.com/abstract=2366898.

Chang, Y., Yan, J., Zhang, J. and Luo, J. (2010) 'Online in-game advertising effect: Examining the influence of a match between games and advertising', *Journal of Interactive Advertising*, 11(1): 63–73.

Dahl, S. (2014) *Social Media Marketing: Theories and Applications*. London: Sage.

Dahl, S. and Desrocher, D. (2013) My Friend Bud: Alcohol promotion across social media, European Marketing Academy, Istanbul, 4–7 June.

Dahl, S., Eagle, L.E. and Baez, C. (2009) 'Analyzing advergames: Active diversions or actually deception. An exploratory study of online advergames content', *Young Consumers*, 10(1): 46–59.

Delbaere, M., McQuarrie, E.F. and Phillips, B.J. (2011) 'Personification in advertising: Using a visual metaphor to trigger anthropomorphism', *Journal of Advertising*, 40(1): 121–30.

Eagle, L., Dahl, S. and Morrey, Y (2012) 'Subtle sophistry or savvy strategy: Ethical and effectiveness issues regarding product placements in mass media', in T. Langner, S. Okazaki and M. Eisend (eds), *Advances in Advertising Research* (Vol. III). Wiesbaden: Gabler.

Flurry (2013) *Flurry Five-year Report: It's an App World. The Web Just Lives in It*, 3 April. Available at: http://www.flurry.com/bid/95723/Flurry-Five-Year-Report-It-s-an-App-World-The-Web-Just-Lives-in-It#.U7BrIo1dV7Q.

Fournier, S. and Avery, J. (2011) 'The uninvited brand', *Business Horizons*, 54(3): 193–207.

Friestad, M. and Wright, P. (1994) 'The persuasion knowledge model: How people cope with persuasion attempts', *Journal of Consumer Research*, 21(1): 1.

Garretson, J.A. and Niedrich, R.W. (2004) 'Spokes-characters: Creating character trust and positive brand attitudes', *Journal of Advertising*, 33(2): 25–36.

Goddard, C. (2003) 'Jive Bunny – Nestle is pushing its Nesquik Brand with an £8 million campaign', *BrandRepublic*, 1 May. Available at: http://www.brandrepublic.com/news/179080/.

Gogoi, P. (2006) 'Wal-Mart vs. the Blogosphere', *Msnbc.com*, 18 October. Available at: http://www.nbcnews.com/id/15319926/ns/business-us_business/t/wal-mart-vs-blogosphere/.

Hodge, N. (2009) 'Misleading advertising rules', *In-House Persp.*, 5: 15.

Hof, R. (2007) 'Facebook declares new era for advertising', *Bloomberg Business Week*, 6 November. Available at: http://www.businessweek.com/the_thread/techbeat/archives/2007/11/facebook_declar.html.

Homer, P.M. (2009) 'Product placements', *Journal of Advertising*, 38(3): 21–32.

Houlder, V. (2014) 'MP criticises Uber for "opting out" of UK tax regime – FT.com', *Financial Times*, 1 August. Available at: http://www.ft.com/cms/s/0/c63f9500-1965-11e4-9745-00144feabdc0.html#axzz3JQiNiu2a.

Johnson, L. (2012) 'Coca-Cola's Fanta mixes social and mobile with iPhone app – gaming – mobile marketer', *Mobile Marketer*, 13 January. Available at: http://www.mobilemarketer.com/cms/news/gaming/11889.html.

Kaplan, A.M. and Haenlein, M. (2010) 'Users of the world, unite! The challenges and opportunities of social media', *Business Horizons*, 53(1): 59–68.

Kim, S. and McGill, A.L. (2011) 'Gaming with Mr. Slot or gaming the slot machine? Power, anthropomorphism, and risk perception', *Journal of Consumer Research*, 38(1): 94–107.

Manovich, L. (2011) *Trending: The Promises and the Challenges of Big Social Data*. Available at: http://manovich.net/index.php/projects/trending-the-promises-and-the-challenges-of-big-social-data.

Megagames (2006) *Sony Fake PSP Blog Busted*. Available at: http://megagames.com/news/sony-fake-psp-blog-busted (accessed 23 August 2013).

Nyilasy, G. and Reid, L.N. (2009) 'Agency practitioner theories of how advertising works', *Journal of Advertising*, 38(3): 81–96.

Owen, L., Lewis, C., Auty, S. and Buijzen, M. (2013) 'Is children's understanding of non-traditional advertising comparable to their understanding of television advertising?', *Journal of Public Policy & Marketing*, 32(2): 195–206.

Palmer, A. and Koenig-Lewis, N. (2009) 'An experiential, social network-based approach to direct marketing', *Direct Marketing: An International Journal*, 3(3): 162–76.

Paul, I. (2009) 'New FTC blogging regulations: Forcing transparency on a culture of full disclosure', *Huffington Post The Blog*, 6 October. Available at: http://www.huffingtonpost.com/ian-paul/new-ftc-blogging-regulati_b_311851.html.

Sprague, R. and Wells, M.E. (2010) 'Regulating online buzz marketing: Untangling a web of deceit', *American Business Law Journal*, 47(3): 415–54.

Steiner, P. (1993) 'On the internet, nobody knows you're a dog', *The New Yorker*, 69(20): 61.

Wilson, R.T. and Till, B.D. ((2012) 'Managing non-traditional advertising: A message processing framework', in S. Rodgers and E. Thorson (eds), *Advertising Theory*, Routledge Communication Series. New York: Routledge.

Zuckerberg, M. (2011) '(1) Our commitment to the Facebook community', *Facebook Blog*, 29 November. Available at: https://www.facebook.com/notes/facebook/our-commitment-to-the-facebook-community/10150378701937131.

 # Ethical Consumption

Stephan Dahl and Nadine Waehning-Orga

CHAPTER OVERVIEW

This chapter discusses ethics from the perspective of the consumer, examining how consumption ethics and marketing ethics are linked from that perspective. To examine this topic, the chapter focuses on:

- The different motives consumers can have to make choices based on particular ethical guidelines
- The consumption practices used to guide these ethical guidelines
- The theoretical models used to explain ethical consumption behaviour
- The consistency and spillover of ethical consumption

INTRODUCTION

We may think of marketing as spanning, and operating at the interface of, the production and consumption of goods and services. According to marketing doctrine, consumers are the most powerful force in the market exchange as they – through purchasing – hold the ultimate power over what is produced (and by extension marketed). Yet, as far as marketing ethics is concerned, the largest amount of burden is placed on the producers of goods, services and marketing (communications in particular) to behave ethically, while much less emphasis is placed on the opposite party in the exchange: the consumer. This focus is also evident in research, policies (e.g. regulation focuses on marketers and marketing practices – not consumers), and indeed in the structure of this book.

TYPOLOGY AND MOTIVES

To better understand what drives some consumers to behave in ethical ways, it is first important to explore the motives of ethical consumers. As ethical consumption behaviour is far-reaching and can entail different types of behaviours, this discussion is necessarily restrictive and over-generalised. Nevertheless, it is important to identify the major motivators for perceived ethical behaviour.

A number of different motivations of consumers to engage in 'ethical' consumption have been identified. These challenge the economic assumption that consumers always try to obtain the 'best deal'. Rather, ethical behaviour frequently means placing societal needs before individual ones. for example, by purchasing more expensive organic produce or abstaining from **conspicuous consumption**.

Peattie (2012) offers a typology of seven major reasons and motivators for consumers to consume in unselfish ways. The motivators suggested by Peattie are **pious, patriotic, green, socially conscious, responsible, citizenship-based and mindful consumption**. Although these classifications are not exhaustive, nor the categories mutually exclusive, they provide a practical basis for considering different, and sometimes conflicting, reasons for consumers to avoid engaging in purely selfish consumption practices. Ordered roughly chronologically, we now briefly review each of these motives/reasons.

Pious consumption

Major religious works have prescribed consumption behaviour for thousands of years. The most obvious examples include the consumption of certain food items, such as pork and alcohol or meat during certain times. Chapter 3 describes some of the major pious consumption principles, including the study of religiously inspired marketing ethics. Peattie (2012) argues that religiously inspired consumption practices are different from other ethical consumption practices in two ways:

1. Firstly they are reliant on a desire to adhere to a given principle, and avoidance of potential negative consequences resultant from non adherence (e.g. becoming 'unclean', requiring forgiveness, damnation, etc.). Traditional ethical consumption practices, in contrast, are based

on seeming external environmental and/or social consequences, such as those resulting from damages to the environment based on food-miles.

2. Secondly, religious consumption principles are frequently ingrained in the consumer to such an extent that, even in a life-threatening situation, such as a famine, deviation from those principles becomes inconceivable or at least difficult to perform. Generally, other consumption practices, Peattie argues, are less deeply ingrained and are potentially more transient in nature.

Patriotic consumption

Consumption based on patriotic or ethnocentric principles has long been recognised. Ethnocentrism has been widely discussed in the marketing literature (Shimp and Sharma, 1987). Shimp and Sharma themselves credit sociologist William Graham Sumner (1906) with the designation of the term. Peattie (2012) observes that such consumption practices predate the academic debate significantly, citing the purchasing of war bonds as a patriotic consumption choice, and drawing particular attention to the fact that these bonds offered lower rates of return than were generally available in the market at the time (e.g. requiring a sacrifice of interest based on patriotic motives).

Green consumption

The 'green consumer' emerged as a consumer response to growing concerns about the limits of natural resources and concerns about the environmental impact of consumption practices. Green consumption typically places an emphasis on sustainable and environmentally friendly consumption practices, largely aiming for an overall consumption reduction: for example, using recycled materials, biodegradable cleaning products where necessary, complemented by a reduction of consumption, especially, but not limited to, products which are perceived to have a negative impact on the natural environment. Academic and practitioner interest developed in researching from the early 1970s, including theory building on this emergent 'responsible consumption' (Fisk, 1973).

Socially conscious consumption

Emerging concurrently with the principally environmentally concerned 'green consumer', and an example of the potential overlap of some of the motives and consumers, the socially conscious consumer can be traced back to mass boycotts organised in support of social causes. Socially motivated consumption practices gained increasing prevalence in the early and mid-1970s (although large-scale boycotts significantly predate this decade). Different from green consumption, socially concious consumption practice is, however, not predominantly focused on consumption reduction. Rather, socially concious supportive consumption practices are sometimes actively encouraged, e.g. purchasing Fair Trade goods.

Responsible consumption

Peattie (2012) uses the term responsible consumers for consumers who combine social and environmental motives, based on the characterisation provided by Fisk (1974).

Responsible consumers consequently base their consumption choices on an individual evaluation of the socio-environmental behaviour of a company, and adjust their consumption accordingly (e.g. boycotting certain companies, actively purchasing from others, etc.).

Citizenship-based consumption

During the 1990s, the term citizen consumers emerged to describe socially connected socio-environmentally aware consumers. The emphasis for citizen consumers is on reaching out to other consumers, i.e. focusing less on individual consumption practices, but with a 'motivation linked to social solidarity rather than simply principle based individualism' (Peattie, 2012: 210). Thus, rather than focusing on their own consumption practices, citizen consumers will join together with similar consumers in an attempt to utilise collective power to achieve socio-environmental outcomes. Technological advancements, especially social media, have nurtured the growth in citizen consumers. Calls for action have rapidly spread amongst social networks and this helps to identify other citizen consumers and as a potential result provides access to community resources where needed.

Mindful (integrated) consumption

The most recent form of consumer type to emerge is that of the 'mindful consumer'. A 'mindful consumer' is motivated by a 'mindset of caring for self, for community, and for nature, that translates behaviourally into tempering the self-defeating excesses associated with acquisitive, repetitive and aspirational consumption' (Sheth et al., 2011: 21). Thus, mindful consumers are less single-minded in their consumption approaches than previous consumption practices and focus on the reduction of unethical consumption behaviour rather than total avoidance. For instance, mindful consumers may strive to avoid meat rather than focus exclusively on vegetarian consumption. Similarly, mindful consumers may give preference to organic or fair-traded products where available, but are likely to balance their consumption with other considerations, such as price, availability and product attributes. Peattie (2012) points out the narrow definition of mindful consumers as primarily tempering consumption, rather than focusing on the wider aspects of consumption. Nevertheless, Peattie also points towards publication of an article related to mindful consumerism in the *Journal of the Academy of Marketing Sciences* as a sign of the relative importance and growth of ethical consumption behaviour. He argues that the publication in a mainstream, commercially focused publication demonstrates that the concept of unselfish consumer behaviour is gaining recognition in the mainstream marketing literature, and thus moving beyond fringe publications.

A tabular overview of Peattie's consumer typology based on the research foci within the marketing literature is given in Table 6.1. As can be seen, there are considerable overlaps between distinct consumer types, e.g. a mix of both social and environmental factors motivates responsible, mindful and citizen consumers, resulting in a significant overlap.

Table 6.1 Peattie's consumer typology

Name	Emergence in the literature	Motive	Behaviour	Focus
Pious	1970s	Religious	Non-consumption	External principle
Patriotic		Ethnocentric	Consumption reduction or encouragement	Nationalistic
Green		Environmental only	Consumption reduction	
Socially conscious		Social only	Consumption reduction or encouragement	
Responsible		Mixed social and environmental	Consumption reduction or encouragement	
Citizenship-based	1990s			Individual and collective
Mindful	2010s		Consumption temperance	Individual ethical evaluation

Think points

Using the typology above, discuss the implications for encouraging ethical consumption. What do you think marketers can do to encourage more people to consume ethically?

BEHAVIOUR

It is important to recognise that consumption extends beyond the mere purchasing of products and services. Although there are different definitions of consumption, many rely on the juxtaposition of consumption vs. production, and a multistage consumption process consisting of three core stages: acquisition (purchase) of goods or services, their use, and the disposal of these.

Purchase behaviour

Some of the motives described in the previous paragraph are often linked to one type and stage of behaviour (e.g. a religious motivation to the non-consumption of prescribed food items relate to both non-acquisition and a resultant behaviour), and are generally focused on

Figure 6.1 Rationing posters from the US and the UK during WWII, and the encouragement of patriotic buying during the 1930s

a specific behavioural outcome. Other motives and associated reasons can be used both for consumption reduction and encouragement. For instance, the 'Buy British' campaign, an example of patriotic consumption during WWII, is clearly linked with encouraging the consumption of nationally produced products for patriotic reasons. Yet patriotic appeals have also been used during crisis times, for example during WWII, to reduce the consumption of goods that were scarce, such as food items (see Figure 6.1).

Thus, the behavioural expression of ethical consumption behaviour can be typified by a continuum ranging from strict anti-consumption to active encouragement of consumption, some of which can occur at the same time.

Anti-consumption

Strict **anti-consumption** of all products – i.e. no consumption – is, of course, relatively rare and impractical. More commonly found are fairly restrictive and wide-ranging anti-consumption behaviours, for example as a result of political or religious principles. Nevertheless, there are examples of far-reaching, albeit not complete, anti-consumption practices and ideologies. For example, Noam Chomsky, as a spokesperson of the Occupy movement, discourages all forms of consumption for political reasons: 'Consumption distracts people. You cannot control your own population by force, but it can be distracted by consumption. The business press has been quite explicit about this goal' (Chomsky, 2008).

Non-consumption/consumption temperance

Owing to the impracticalities of comprehensive anti-consumption, less restrictive forms of consumption reduction, i.e. **non-consumption** movements, are often more practical and popular. Similar to anti-consumption movements, non-consumption or consumption temperance is habitually linked to political, social or environmental ideologies. Such non-consumption can take the form of abstinence or the reduction of purchases from a specific product category, or can take the form of temporal reductions of consumption, for example, Buy Nothing Day (BND) – www.adbusters.org/campaigns/bnd – initiated by former marketing manager-cum-political activist and editor of *Adbuster Magazine*, Kalle Lasn. Somewhat paradoxically, BND is using the same principles successfully used in many pro-consumption marketing techniques, such as advertising and branding in magazines, posters and on social media. According to Lasn, the aim of the campaign is to create 'an economy and a culture in which it eventually becomes cool to consume less' (Revkin, 2011).

Consumption restraints, e.g. non-consumption and anti-consumption, are ideologies drawing upon socio-political and/or religious beliefs. In contrast to more fundamental political movements, religious perspectives generally restrict themselves to critiquing overt materialism, thus calling for mindful consumption practices. Conspicuous consumption practices are frequently criticised, and religion rarely explicitly advocates anti-consumerist or non-consumerist views. Although there is some disagreement as to the virtue of relative materialism, e.g. the interpretation of material wealth as a sign of good (Turner, 1991), the general and more contemporary view of most religious scholars appears to support consumption reduction. For instance, Pope Benedict XVI warned his followers of the 'tyranny of materialism' (Vatican News Service, 2012), and Buddhist views on materialism are not only traditionally negative, but some have also suggested that following Buddhism reduces materialism (Pace, 2013).

More outspoken advocacy of wide-ranging consumption temperance comes from social activist groups, particularly **anti-** and **alter-globalisation** movements during the early years of the 2000s, and since 2011 Occupy movements following the global financial crisis.

Boycotts

Boycotts involve consumers voluntarily refusing to purchase or consume goods from a particular person, company or country. Thus, boycotts are specifically targeted in comparison to anti-consumption or non-consumption practices. Similar to other forms of consumption temperance or avoidance, boycotts tend be based around a social or political objective. An early example of a relatively organised appeal for abstaining from consumption of specific goods as a way to achieve social change can be traced back to the late eighteenth century. At the time, British anti-slavery campaigners called for a refusal to buy sugar produced by slaves (Midgley, 1996), although the tactic had certainly been used prior to this.

While calls for boycotts are popular tools for many social movements, there is a distinctly mixed record for boycott effectiveness. While some boycotts have been highly successful, an analysis of 63 Internet-based boycotts showed they were ineffective in causing economic harm (Koku, 2012). Nevertheless, consumer boycotts can cause reputational harm to companies, which has been argued to affect companies in more subtle and long-term ways, and to result in often significant increases of other pro-social claims by the targeted companies (McDonnell and King, 2013).

Buycotts

The flipside to boycotts are **buycotts**, or specific campaigns encouraging purchase and consumption from a particular person, company or country (Friedman, 1996) – sometimes to counter or complement an ongoing boycott. For instance, following the emergence of eighteenth century anti-slavery boycotts, so called 'free produce' stores opened to encourage people to purchase goods not produced by slaves, concurrently with the ongoing boycott of slave-produced products (Glickman, 2004). A contemporary example of positive buycotts can be found in the activities organised via the Carrotmob social networking site, which organises **flashmobs** of shoppers to reward the pro-social or environmentally responsible behaviour of generally small businesses (Hoffmann and Hutter, 2012). Buycotts can also try to counter boycotts of opposing groups. For example, BuycottIsrael is a website that alerts subscribers of boycott calls against Israel, so that followers can counter these boycotts by specifically purchasing goods that are being boycotted.

Table 6.2 gives a summary of the purchase-associated responses to ethical concerns. Despite reservations regarding the overall effectiveness of such responses to create actual economic harm, with the exception of buycotting, all responses are threatening negative economic consequences.

Table 6.2 Purchase-associated responses to ethical concerns

Name	Target	Economic Effect
Anti-consumption	All, or all non-essential, goods and services	Negative
Non-consumption	Specific categories of goods or for a defined time	Negative
Boycott	Non-purchasing of products from specific organisations/countries	Potentially negative
Buycott	Explicit purchasing of products from specific organisations/countries	Potentially positive

Much of the literature is concerned with the first two stages of consumer behaviour, e.g. purchase and consumption. Much less attention is being paid to the disposal of goods (Peattie, 2012), despite this now triggering another stage of selling and consumption for many, for example, private eBay sellers and second-hand or 'vintage' fashion. Yet, amongst second-hand fashion followers, pro-social or behaviours based on ethical considerations have been found to constitute merely a secondary motivation. The desire to be unique and frugal was common among women purchasing 'vintage' fashion (Cervellon et al., 2012). Thus there is a need for further research to explore the last stage of how products are transformed or passed on and then re-consumed.

THEORETICAL MODELS

The previous section reviewed behaviours associated with ethical consumption decisions. We now briefly discuss theoretical models aiming to explain consumption behaviour.

Economic rational models

Traditional economic models often assume that people make choices based on relatively rational considerations, aiming to maximise their own satisfaction. Maximising satisfaction does, of course, not necessarily mean paying the least amount of money. Rather, it can also be seen as maximising prestige gained through admiration from others who observe the consumption, or a combination of price and the perceived prestige gain. An example of such a rationalist view can be found in Miller's (2001) 'dialectics of shopping'. Miller argues that shopping often results in an innate contradiction between saving money and ethical decisions. Saving money benefits the shopper or immediate family. Conversely, while making ethical decisions, such as buying more expensive, but ethically produced items, the benefit is transferred to distant others. One way to overcome this contradiction is by engaging in socially responsible conspicuous consumption. When engaging in socially responsible conspicuous consumption, essentially self-interested motives such as prestige, promise of better health or taste compensate for the higher price paid. Thus, the higher price becomes 'justifiable' as non-price advantages are gained by the consumer, and the monetary benefit transferred to the distant producer is converted into immediate benefits for the consumer. Corporate Social Responsibility (CSR) initiatives and branded ethical products pander to such a rationalist view, for example, by evoking improved prestige appeals. Richey and Ponte (2011), for example, in their book *Brand Aid* argue that branding ethical products, such as the Product(Red) initiative, is a potential way of satisfying both prestige and price desires by offering specifically (Red)-branded products at the same price as regular products, while also donating funds to HIV/AIDS charities. However, they also criticise that these products mark a shift in consumer culture away from compassionate consumption and towards a consumption culture where affluent consumers can purchase a feeling of superiority while creating an illusion of proximity to the most disadvantaged.

While rational economic models have a wide ranging appeal, they have also been criticised as needlessly rationalist, and denying the existence of altruism (Peattie, 2012). Using the example of *LiveAid*, Peattie argues that altruism can be found in everyday life, and that is inconceivable that consumption choices are unaffected by altruistic motives. Thus purely altruistic factors, without the gain of prestige or other non-monetary values, should also be considered.

Think points

Think about ethical decisions you are making. List the advantages and disadvantages of one ethical and one unethical choice you have recently made. Can you explain these using rational models? Which role did altruism play in your decision making?

Norms and beliefs

Other theoretical frameworks have questioned purely rational motives for behaviour, and place greater emphasis on underlying values and norms. For instance, the **Value-Belief-Norm theory** (Stern et al., 1999) explains participation in pro-environmental causes on the basis of personal values (such as environmental conservation). Focused largely on environmental causes, the theory explains that where individuals recognise that their personal values (or something they individually value) are under threat, and if the individual holds the belief that their actions can help to restore these values, then they will engage in actions to restore the threatened personal values, driven by personal norms.

A similar model, the **Norm-activation model** had been previously developed by social psychologists Schwartz and Howard (1981) specifically in relation to altruistic behaviour.

Both theories place a strong emphasis on personal norms and values as the main, or only, determinants of ethical decision-making and behaviour. While both theories are relatively straightforward and self-explanatory, the placement of the sole responsibility for ethical decision making onto the individual has been subject to criticism. While individual motives and underlying values are undeniably an important part of ethical decision making, other factors, such as social and societal factors are likely to also play a considerable role.

A different perspective on the decision making of consumer behaviour is, apart from personal norms and attitudes, the sense of identity and personality, in the form of a complex interaction of (perceived) social norms and an individual desire to adhere to these. An interesting, if somewhat extreme, argument is made by Halperin (2012). He contends that a 'gay' identity, irrespective of actual sexual orientation or activity, can be achieved by engaging in essentially 'gay' consumption behaviour. Through the consumption of stereotypical, classical movies, someone (anyone) can learn 'How to be gay'. Of course, Halperin's observations are somewhat tongue in cheek, and an admiration of, to take the example given by Halperin, Judy Garland movies is unlikely to lead to a 'gay identity', but it raises an important point neglected by a focus on purely individual values or attitudes, specifically the importance of social norms, desires to adhere to social norms and other social influences.

Mixed models

Eventually, when trying to model ethical consumer behaviour, both personal factors, such as identities and personal values, and shared social or cultural norms, are likely to influence behaviour. Thus it is essential to consider both when trying to model, predict or explain observed behaviour. The **Theory of Planned Behaviour** (Ajzen, 1985), itself an extension of the Theory of Reasoned Action (Fishbein, 1979), can be a useful theoretical model when understanding ethical consumer behaviour as a result of both social and individual influences. The theory is shown in Figure 6.2.

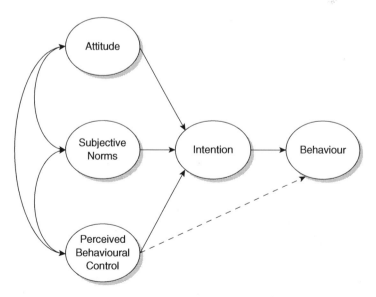

Figure 6.2   Theory of Planned Behaviour (Ajzen, 1985)

Using the Theory of Planned Behaviour (TPB), rather than singularly focusing on personal beliefs and norms, can be more powerful when explaining behaviour. For instance, Kaiser and colleagues (2005) found that, while Stern's Value-Belief-Norms theory (see above) can successfully predict pro-environmental behaviour, using the TPB covered the behavioural intentions more fully, and was more powerful to predict actual behaviour. A similar result was obtained by Bamberg and Schmidt (2003) who compared the TPB with the Norm-activation model. Thus, the role of social and factors other than individual norms is an important aspect when considering altruistic or ethical behaviour, and a sole reliance on individual norms is likely to be less effective.

The TPB is by no means limited to ethical consumer behaviour, but has been used to explain consumer behaviour in a wide variety of contexts, including commercial marketing contexts and health behaviours. Specifically in the context of social marketing, the TPB has been further developed into the Integrative Model of Behavioural Prediction and Change (Fishbein and Cappella, 2006). The Integrative Model adds salient background influences, such as past behaviours, cultural and demographic factors and exposure to previous health or social marketing campaigns or related messages. It further acknowledges the overlap between 'perceived behavioural control' in the original model and the more widely used term 'self-efficacy'.

A further noteworthy advancement of the Integrative Model is the identification of two variables capable of influencing the 'gap' between intention and actual behaviour: environmental factors, and skills and abilities. It is important to recognise that many people have good intentions, yet for one reason or another fail to carry those intentions through into actual behaviour. For instance, 87% of consumers have been found to be concerned about the environmental impact the products they purchase have, yet only 33% of these consumers indicated they made specific purchases to reduce the environmental impact (Bonini and Oppenheim, 2008), a paradox sometimes referred to as the 'green gap' in relation to environmental issues (Black, 2010), or more generally, the attitude–behaviour gap or intention–behaviour gap.

The addition of these two variables suggests the importance of considering both as effective ways to narrow the attitude–behaviour or intention–behaviour gap.

Based on the basic premise of the TPB, Bagozzi's **Comprehensive Model of Consumer Action** aims to further refine the predictive power of theoretical models related to ethical consumption.

However, while Bagozzi's model claims to increase the predictive power of the theoretical model, it does so at the expense of simplicity and testability, and it has been criticised as too complex to be useful (Peattie, 2012).

While there is growing research, including theory building, to explain consumer behaviour, a potential flaw in much of the research on ethical consumption is the focus on consumer attitudes and behaviours related to specific products or product categories. The consumer perspectives and potential responses are explored in the next section.

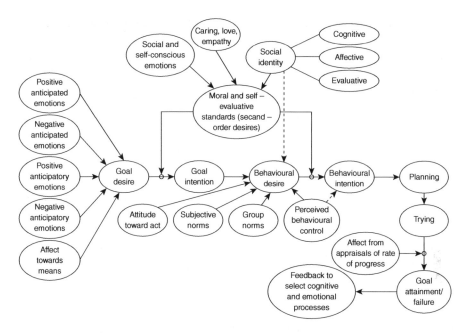

Figure 6.3 Bagozzi's Comprehensive Model of Consumer Action

CONCERNS AND ETHICAL DILEMMAS

While on the one hand marketing may have the possibility and tools to persuade more consumers to behave ethically, such attempts are not uncontroversial. The first part of this section will focus on concerns in relation to marketing efforts to encourage more ethical consumption that have been raised, covering both marketing's role in encouraging consumption as well as the effect on specific consumption behaviours (e.g. ethical consumption of a specific category of products, or behaviour following ethical consumption). The second part will try to identify the behavioural consequences of ethical consumption behaviour, before the chapter concludes by discussing the specific roles marketing can play.

Marketing and consumption as causes

A foremost ethical problem in relation to ethical consumption behaviour, and the relationship with marketing, is the role that marketing itself plays (see also the discussion in Chapter 2). In fact a major cause of damage to the environment, and arguably other unethical business practices, is the high levels of consumption fuelled by marketing activities. As such marketing itself has been harshly condemned as a major cause of environmental problems (c.f. Kilbourne et al., 1997), and cost-cutting measures, for example resulting from low-cost pricing strategies, have been linked to low-wage production and modern slavery (Crane, 2013).

In addition to contributing to specific social and environmental problems, marketing's core function has been criticised as promoting a culture of consumption, which itself is necessarily unsustainable. Witkowski (2010: 108), for example, urged asking 'deep and sometimes disturbing questions' about the role of marketing and consumer culture and the effect on sustainability. The solutions offered by marketers have been criticised as paradoxical. Essentially, the solution proposed by marketing is a shifting of consumption from 'unsustainable' to 'more sustainable' products. However, such an approach often emphasises increasing sales over actually sustainable policies and strategies. Thus, the emphasis is on increasing consumption, although of individually more ethical or sustainable goods, rather than decreasing consumption as a whole. This leads Varey (2010: 114) to conclude that 'It is self-evidently pointless – stupid even – to consume more (…) in an attempt to fix the problems caused by consuming more!'.

Consumers, on the other hand, can easily shift attention onto marketers rather than engaging in more considered consumption behaviours. While consumers largely recognise that overconsumption exists, they also largely ignore environmental problems as a consequence. Moreover, they tend not to perceive their own actions as powerful enough to make a significant change. Rather, consumers rely on blaming marketers for stimulating demand and creating consumption (Pereira Heath and Chatzidakis, 2012). Thus for many consumers environmental concerns are essentially created by the supply side of the consumption process, and are removed from the demand side.

Spillover

Marketing, for example as a result of a social marketing programme or because a product is highlighting particular ethical credentials, can create ethical consumption behaviour. However, a single behaviour is unlikely to have a significant impact. It is therefore important to consider behaviours not only in the context of what motivates them (as done in the preceding part of this chapter), but also in what follows ethically inspired behaviour.

An area with conflicting and contradictory results focuses on the effects of individual actions, such as engaging in recycling, on other pro-environment or ethical consumption practices on following actions. These so-called behavioural **spillover effects**, such as where a campaign or intervention in one area results in subsequently changed behaviour in other areas, remain critically understudied, and the studies that have been published often give contradictory results. In the area of pro-environmental behaviour, some studies have supported a positive spillover effect, for example, customers engaging in recycling have also been found to avoid excess packaging (Thøgersen, 1999). However, in other areas a negative spillover effect was observed. For instance, where people purchased sustainably produced energy voluntarily, they subsequently also used more energy (Jacobsen et al., 2012). In a similar vein, following a successful social marketing campaign to reduce water consumption, it was found that consumers increased energy consumption (Tiefenbeck et al., 2013). Even more alarmingly, consumers who act highly environmentally aware in everyday life frequently use the most environmentally damaging modes of transport to go on (long-haul) holidays (Barr et al., 2010). In other words, positive behaviour in one domain resulted in significantly more damaging behaviour in another domain.

While it is tempting to seek the answer to these behavioural paradoxes in the relative closeness of these behaviours, such a view has not been validated. For example, a person is not more likely to display congruently pro-environmental behaviour in areas that are relatively closely associated, such as energy production and energy conservation (Jacobsen et al., 2012). Indeed, in some instances, studies have found evidence of a positive spillover occurring in relatively dissimilar domains. For instance, engaging in recycling has been found to have a positive spillover onto other domains, ranging from cognitively relatively close areas such as composting and using reusable bags, to more different areas such as energy and water conservation (Berger, 1997). Thus the answer to consistent behaviour is unlikely to be connected to the actions performed, but rather to the initial motivations for engaging in the behaviour or behaviours.

Two psychological effects appear to support the view that motivations are key to consistent behaviour across different domains, e.g. a positive spillover occurring.

The first one is **consistency theory**. It has long been recognised that individuals prefer to behave in consistent ways (Festinger, 1962). Consistency in behaviour is particularly important for individuals in areas where a public commitment to a particular behavioural norm has been made. For example, public commitment has a positive effect on energy reduction (Abrahamse et al., 2005) and towel reuse by hotel guests (Baca-Motes et al., 2013). The latter study is particularly insightful, as it found that those hotel guests who made a public commitment to towel reuse also engaged in energy reduction during their hotel stay. Therefore underlying motives, and the desire to act consistently with these, can be one factor not only for a positive behaviour change but also for a positive spillover.

Social identity has been suggested as a second, though connected, explanation for positive spillover (Truelove et al., 2014). Consistent with the Theory of Planned Behaviour, perceived social norms are seen as powerful motivational factors in eliciting desired behaviour, especially where individuals identify with the reference group from which they draw the perceived social norms. Consequently, where individuals hold relevant and consistent views about their role, behaviour and identity in life, they are more likely to act consistently with their views as held by others or expected of them.

Studies have shown that 'cueing', i.e. making individuals believe that they are environmentally responsible, results in further and more varied pro-environmental behaviours in different domains (Cornelissen et al., 2013). Even small cues, such as making people pay for plastic bags, appear to have a positive effect. People in Wales, for example, where a government levy for plastic bags was introduced prior to the UK, were shown to perceive themselves as more environmentally conscious than their English counterparts (Poortinga et al., 2013).

Three different explanatory perspectives have been offered for the phenomenon of negative spillover: **rebound effects**, **moral licensing** and **single action bias** (Truelove et al., 2014). Economists have long studied rebound effects. For example, the Jevons paradox is based on the observation of coal-use during industrialisation; following efficiency improvements in coal-use, the consumption of coal increased, rather than decreased as would have been expected (Polimeni, 2008). The Jevons paradox can thus be used to explain findings where households insulating their homes better have been found to subsequently increase the heating temperature setting, leading to a reduction in savings (Hirst et al., 1985).

Moral licensing effects offer an alternative explanation of negative spillover. Licensing effects explain that in scenarios where a consumer has made a choice to increase their self-image, for example through purchasing ethical products, subsequent choices may be more self-indulgent or hedonic rather than ethically driven. Moral licensing is by no means restricted to socially responsible consumption; through a series of different experiments Khan and Dhar (2006), for example, show the licensing effect at work in different domains of consumption. They show, amongst other, that participants in their research following a charitable action are more likely to purchase a hedonic product (designer jeans) than a utilitarian product (vacuum cleaner). In a different study, Khan and Dhar show that participants who helped someone were subsequently less likely to donate to charity. Thus, engaging in acts which are likely to be self-affirmative, such as ethical choices or abstention from consumption, may result in consumers attributing themselves with a moral licence to perform a hedonic action.

The final potential explanation for negative spillover is single action bias (Weber, 1997). Single action bias shows that some people, in situations of uncertainty and risk, tend to simplify their decision making and focus on a single action. Thus, consumers responding to a threat, such as potential environmental damage or negative social impact, are likely to focus on a single action, irrespective of whether the action taken is the most effective option – or would benefit from further actions being taken. The failure to engage in further or other actions is likely to occur as a result of the success of the first action. As the first action is removing the cognitive dissonance or worry experienced, following actions are no longer needed to restore cognitive balance. In other words, individuals following single action bias may feel as if they are doing enough, and are thus foregoing other actions that would be beneficial. For example, individuals may switch to energy efficient light bulbs in their home, and feel that this single action suffices (Wagner and Zeckhauser, 2012).

Spillover-related research is mostly confined to pro-environmental consumer behaviour. Research into other areas, such as socially conscious research, has however produced remarkably similar results. For instance, Carrigan and Attalla (2001) ended their study into pro-social consumer behaviour with the sobering conclusion that most consumers pay little attention to ethical considerations when making purchases, even speculating that 'One might conclude from this evidence that the current emphasis on social responsibility and marketing ethics by academics and practitioners is both misplaced and misguided' (2001: 574).

The role of marketing in fostering ethical consumption is therefore complex. On the one hand, marketing itself has been implemented in creating unethical and unsustainable consumption practices. On the other hand, simple marketing of sustainable consumption practices on its own is unlikely to be sufficient for two reasons. Firstly, it attempts to eliminate the ills caused by unsustainable consumption with more consumption. Secondly, where marketing succeeds in creating sustainable consumption, there is the danger of negative spillover effects occurring.

MARKETING (AND OTHER) WAYS FORWARD

As many consumers place greater weight on price, quality and value rather than the ethical or environmentally sound behaviour of suppliers (Carrigan and Attalla, 2001), and tend to see problems caused by overconsumption from the supply and not from the demand side (Pereira Heath and Chatzidakis, 2012), encouraging pro-social and pro-environmental ethical consumption practices is no easy task. Potential solutions are therefore complex and require advanced marketing skill. However, there is evidence that ethical consumer behaviour can be fostered and nurtured through skilled marketing interventions. Potential, marketing-based solutions come from a number of different directions, ranging from increasing information provision and choice editing to social marketing and demarketing.

Information provision/labelling

Better and more consistent information has been highlighted as a potential way to encourage consumers to make ethical consumption choices. For general (pro-social) ethical behaviour of companies, consumers are often uninformed and only possess limited knowledge about the ethical conduct or otherwise of companies. In relation to pro-social behaviour, information must therefore become clearer, avoiding the confusion and alienation of consumers and must be able to convince consumers that their purchases contribute to making a difference rather than remaining abstract contributions (Carrigan and Attalla, 2001).

For pro-social issues, lessons may be drawn from pro-environmental behaviour, where the use of (relatively) effective labelling initiatives is more established. Despite occasional claims of confusion, consumers appear to trust eco-labelling and labelling products accordingly has a positive influence on brand perception as well as actual purchase behaviour (Rahbar and Abdul Wahid, 2011).

Choice editing

Choice editing is the process of limiting consumers' choices of undesirable products, for example by imposing taxation or making certain choices unavailable. For instance, supermarkets can choose to no longer stock products that are seen as environmentally damaging or are produced under socially undesirable conditions, thus effectively removing such choices from consideration by consumers.

Three different types of influencing consumer choice from a supply perspective can be distinguished (in order of severity): choice provision, architecture and editing:

1. Choice provision assumes that retailers actively provide choices alongside conventional, harmful products. Choice provision thus relies on the consumer to swap to a more desirable product.
2. Choice architecture refers to practices where retailers take a more active role in influencing consumer choice, creating an environment that nudges consumers towards more ethical consumption choices.

3. Pure choice editing is the most severe form of choice influencing, where retailers influence consumers' choice making actively by reducing the choices available. For example, retailers can choose not to make energy wasting incandescent light bulbs available to consumers, and instead rely on exclusively stocking energy efficient forms of light bulbs. Choice editing is, however, not uncontroversial. Consumers see choice as a means of expressing their identities and position themselves vis-à-vis other consumers in the market, and consumer choice is often conflated with individual sovereignty in consumers' minds (Schwartz, 2004). Thus removing choice can be seen as essentially undemocratic and limiting consumer sovereignty.

Social marketing

Social marketing is discussed in detail in Chapter 11. However, it is useful to point out at this stage that social marketing has been successfully applied to a range of environmental issues, such as recycling (Cole and Fieselman, 2013), and in creating sustainable communities where suppliers and consumers engage in sustainable practices (Carrigan et al., 2011).

The particular contribution of social marketing to pro-social and pro-environmental consumer behaviour is the prominence it places on understanding and overcoming the barriers perceived by consumers. And while social marketing may involve choice provision and occasionally choice architecture-based interventions, voluntary behaviour change is a central component of social marketing.

Despite this, there are potential ethical issues connected to social marketing-based approaches. These are discussed in detail in Chapter 11, and thus are not reiterated at this stage.

Demarketing

Demarketing as a concept was first discussed in the 1970s (Kotler and Levy, 1971). The claim put forward by Kotler and Levy is that marketing can not only be used to increase consumption, but also that it can be used more universally to shape and eventually dampen the consumption of particular goods and services. In other words, demarketing is marketing in reverse, involving traditional marketing elements, but with a focus on reducing consumption.

So far demarketing has been largely employed by government organisations, for instance, in the health sector as a means to reduce smoking (Shiu et al., 2009). However, Kotler and Levy (1971) had originally suggested that demarketing could also be used by commercial companies to reduce demand for their products, for example in times of shortages or to avoid consumption by 'undesirable segments' (1971: 78).

Demarketing thus operates in a manner similar to that of social marketing (in reverse), and faces many similar ethical issues. However, it is noteworthy that governmental demarketing efforts are perceived as largely ineffective by their target audiences (Wall, 2007). Thus, demarketing is by no means a fast and easy solution to some pressing problems.

Case study   Fair and unionised? The case of Theo Chocolates

Theo Chocolates is a high-end chocolate manufacturer, based in Seattle, Washington. It was the US's first chocolatier to achieve Fair Trade and organic certification for its products. The certification clearly suggests that the chocolate is made with ingredients sourced according to high ethical standards, including sustainable farming practices, marketing and fair treatment of workers, such as the right to form unions and to bargain collectively.

Theo Chocolates operates in a market segment marred by controversies about unsustainable sourcing of raw ingredients and human rights of workers, predominantly in developing countries. Other chocolate manufacturers have been accused of unethical business practices including child labour (Stevens, 2012) and large-scale deforestation (Tabacek, 2010). As a premium product, Theo Chocolates places great emphasis on convincing consumers that it is sustainable and ethical in its business practices, which include prominently displaying logos of both the company's 'Fair for Life' and organic certification on their products.

However, in 2009 workers at the Seattle plant of the chocolate maker walked out in a dispute over safety and bad working conditions. What followed were attempts to establish a trade union in the American part of the business. As a response, Theo Chocolates hired a company claiming to be a specialist in 'union avoidance strategies'. Further attempts by the management to undermine unionisation at the plant followed, while some of the workers and trade union officials attempted to form a union.

After nearly a year, the trade unions appealed to the certifying body for the company's Fair Trade certification. Fair Trade explicitly encourages unionisation in countries where the raw material is produced, and the trade unions assumed that the certifying organisation would uphold these workers' rights in the US. However, the Institute for Market Ecology, the certifying body for Theo's Chocolates, did not rule in favour of the trade union, and decided to maintain their accreditation.

For an extensive report with more details of the dispute, see the International Labour Organisation report, available from http://laborrights.org/sites/default/files/publications/IMO_Report.pdf.

Questions to consider

How do you evaluate the failure to unionise?

What role did certification bodies, such as the IMO, play in this dispute? What influences might this case have on consumers?

What lessons can be learned from this case?

Further Reading

Carrigan, M. and Attalla, A. (2001) 'The myth of the ethical consumer: Do ethics matter in purchase behaviour?', *Journal of Consumer Marketing*, 18(7): 560–78.

Kotler, P. and Levy, S.J. (1971) 'Demarketing, yes, demarketing', *Harvard Business Review*, 49(6): 74.

Peattie, K. (2012) 'Researching the unselfish consumer', in V.K. Wells and G.R. Foxall (eds), *Handbook of Developments in Consumer Behaviour*. Cheltenham, UK: Edward Elgar.

References

Abrahamse, W., Steg, L., Vlek, C. and Rothengatter, T. (2005) 'A review of intervention studies aimed at household energy conservation', *Journal of Environmental Psychology*, 25(3): 273–91.

Ajzen, I. (1985) *From Intentions to Actions: A Theory of Planned Behavior*. Berlin: Springer.

Baca-Motes, K., Brown, A., Gneezy, A., Keenan, E.A. and Nelson, L.D. (2013) 'Commitment and behavior change: Evidence from the field', *Journal of Consumer Research*, 39(5): 1070–84.

Bamberg, S. and Schmidt, P. (2003) 'Incentives, morality, or habit?: Predicting students' car use for university routes with the models of Ajzen, Schwartz, and Triandis', *Environment & Behavior*, 35(2): 264–85.

Barr, S., Shaw, G., Coles, T. and Prillwitz, J. (2010) '"A holiday is a holiday": Practicing sustainability, home and away', *Journal of Transport Geography*, 18(3): 474–81.

Berger, I.E. (1997) 'The demographics of recycling and the structure of environmental behavior', *Environment and Behavior*, 29(4): 515–31.

Black, I. (2010) 'Sustainability through anti-consumption', *Journal of Consumer Behaviour*, 9(6): 403–11.

Bonini, S. and Oppenheim, J. (2008) 'Cultivating the green consumer', *Stanford Social Innovation Review*. Available at: http://www.ssireview.org/articles/entry/cultivating_the_green_consumer.

Carrigan, M. and Attalla, A. (2001) 'The myth of the ethical consumer: Do ethics matter in purchase behaviour?', *Journal of Consumer Marketing*, 18(7): 560–78.

Carrigan, M., Moraes, C. and Leek, S. (2011) 'Fostering responsible communities: A community social marketing approach to sustainable living', *Journal of Business Ethics*, 100(3): 515–34.

Cervellon, M-C., Carey, L. and Harms, T. (2012) 'Something old, something used: Determinants of women's purchase of vintage fashion vs second-hand fashion', *International Journal of Retail & Distribution Management*, 40(12): 956–74.

Chomsky, N. (2008) 'Interview with Noam Chomsky: "The United States Has Essentially a One-Party System"', *Der Spiegel Online*, 10 October. Available at: http://www.spiegel.de/international/world/interview-with-noam-chomsky-the-united-states-has-essentially-a-one-party-system-a-583454.html.

Cole, E.J. and Fieselman, L. (2013) 'A community-based social marketing campaign at Pacific University Oregon: Recycling, paper reduction, and environmentally preferable purchasing', *International Journal of Sustainability in Higher Education*, 14(2): 176–95.

Cornelissen, G., Bashshur, M.R., Rode, J. and Le Menestrel, M. (2013) 'Rules or consequences? The role of ethical mind-sets in moral dynamics', *Psychological Science*, 24(4): 482–8.

Crane, A. (2013) 'Modern slavery as a management practice: Exploring the conditions and capabilities for human exploitation', *Academy of Management Review*, 38(1): 49–69.

Festinger, L. (1962) *A Theory of Cognitive Dissonance*, Vol. 2. Stanford: Stanford University Press.

Fishbein, M. (1979) 'A Theory of Reasoned Action: Some applications and implications', in H. Howe and M. Page (eds), *Nebraska Symposium on Motivation*. Lincoln: University of Nebraska Press. pp. 65–116.

Fishbein, M. and Cappella, J.N. (2006) 'The role of theory in developing effective health communications', *Journal of Communication*, 56: S1–17.

Fisk, G. (1973) 'Criteria for a Theory of Responsible Consumption', *The Journal of Marketing*, 37(2): 24–31.

Fisk, G. (1974) *Marketing and the Ecological Crisis*, Perspectives on Marketing Series. New York: Harper & Row.

Friedman, M. (1996) 'A positive approach to organized consumer action: The "buycott" as an alternative to the boycott', *Journal of Consumer Policy*, 19(4): 439–51.

Glickman, L.B. (2004) '"Buy for the sake of the slave": Abolitionism and the origins of American consumer activism', *American Quarterly*, 56(4): 889–912.

Halperin, D.M. (2012) *How to Be Gay*. Cambridge, MA: Belknap Press of Harvard University Press.

Hirst, E., White, D. and Goeltz, R (1985) 'Indoor temperature changes in retrofit homes', *Energy*, 10(7): 861–70.

Hoffmann, S. and Hutter, K. (2012) 'Carrotmob as a new form of ethical consumption. The nature of the concept and avenues for future research', *Journal of Consumer Policy*, 35(2): 215–36.

Jacobsen, G.D., Kotchen, M.J. and Vandenbergh, M.P. (2012) 'The behavioral response to voluntary provision of an environmental public good: Evidence from residential electricity demand', *European Economic Review*, 56(5): 946–60.

Kaiser, F.G., Hubner, G. and Bogner, F.X. (2005) 'Contrasting the Theory of Planned Behavior with the Value-Belief-Norm model in explaining conservation behavior', *Journal of Applied Social Psychology*, 35(10): 2150–70.

Khan, U. and Dhar, R. (2006) 'Licensing effect in consumer choice', *Journal of Marketing Research*, 43(2): 259–66.

Kilbourne, W., McDonagh, P. and Prothero, A. (1997) 'Sustainable consumption and the quality of life: A macromarketing challenge to the dominant social paradigm', *Journal of Macromarketing*, 17(1): 4–24.

Koku, P.S. (2012) 'On the effectiveness of consumer boycotts organized through the Internet: The market model', *Journal of Services Marketing*, 26(1): 20–26.

Kotler, P. and Levy, S.J. (1971) 'Demarketing, yes, demarketing', *Harvard Business Review*, 49(6): 74.

McDonnell, M.-H. and King, B. (2013) 'Keeping up appearances: Reputational threat and impression management after social movement boycotts', *Administrative Science Quarterly*, 58(3): 387–419.

Midgley, C. (1996) 'Slave sugar boycotts, female activism and the domestic base of British anti-slavery culture', *Slavery & Abolition*, 17(3): 137–62.

Miller, D. (2001) *The Dialectics of Shopping*, The Lewis Henry Morgan Lectures 1998. Chicago: University of Chicago Press.

Pace, S. (2013) 'Does religion affect the materialism of consumers? An empirical investigation of Buddhist ethics and the resistance of the self', *Journal of Business Ethics*, 112(1): 25–46.

Peattie, K. (2012) 'Researching the unselfish consumer', in V.K. Wells and G.R. Foxal (eds), *Handbook of Developments in Consumer Behaviour*. Cheltenham, UK: Edward Elgar.

Pereira Heath, M.T. and Chatzidakis, A. (2012) '"Blame it on marketing": Consumers' views on unsustainable consumption', *International Journal of Consumer Studies*, 36(6): 656–67.

Polimeni, J.M. (ed.) (2008) *The Jevons Paradox and the Myth of Resource Efficiency Improvements*, Earthscan Research Editions. London/Sterling, VA: Earthscan.

Poortinga, W., Whitmarsh, L. and Suffolk, C. (2013) 'The introduction of a single-use carrier bag charge in Wales: Attitude change and behavioural spillover effects', *Journal of Environmental Psychology*, 36: 240–7.

Rahbar, E. and Abdul Wahid, N. (2011) 'Investigation of green marketing tools' effect on consumers' purchase behavior', *Business Strategy Series*, 12(2): 73–83.

Revkin, A. (2011) 'The ad man behind Occupy Wall Street, and "Buy Nothing Day"', *New York Times*, 25 November. Available at: http://dotearth.blogs.nytimes.com/2011/11/25/on-black-friday-a-look-at-the-occupy-movement-and-buy-nothing-day/?_php=true&_type=blogs&_php=true&_type=blogs&_r=1.

Richey, L.A. and Ponte, S. (2011) *Brand Aid: Shopping Well to Save the World*. Minneapolis, MN: University of Minnesota Press.

Schwartz, B. (2004) *The Paradox of Choice: Why More is Less*. New York: Ecco.

Schwartz, S.H. and Howard, J.A. (1981) 'A normative decision-making model of altruism', in J.P. Rushton and R.M. Sorrentino (eds), *Altruism and Helping Behavior*. Hillsdale, NJ: Lawrence Erlbaum Associates. pp.189–211.

Sheth, J.N., Sethia, N.K. and Srinivas, S. (2011) 'Mindful consumption: A customer-centric approach to sustainability', *Journal of the Academy of Marketing Science*, 39(1): 21–39.

Shimp, T.A. and Sharma, S. (1987) 'Consumer ethnocentrism: Construction and validation of the CETSCALE', *Journal of Marketing Research*, 24(8): 280–9.

Shiu, E., Hassan, L.M. and Walsh, G. (2009) 'Demarketing tobacco through governmental policies – the 4Ps revisited', *Journal of Business Research*, 62(2): 269–78.

Stern, P.C., Dietz, T., Abel, T., Guagnano, G.A. and Kalof, L. (1999) 'A Value-Belief-Norm Theory of support for social movements: The case of environmentalism', *Human Ecology Review*, 6(2): 81–98.

Stevens, H. (2012) 'Child labor concerns across Hershey's supply chain prove it pays to be proactive', *GreenBiz*, 19 October. Available at: http://www.greenbiz.com/blog/2012/10/18/child-labor-concerns-hershey-supply-chain.

Sumner, W.G. (1906) *Folkways: A Study of the Sociological Importance of Usages, Manners, Customs, Mores, and Morals*. Boston, MA: Ginn.

Tabacek, K. (2010) 'Nestlé stars in smear campaign over indonesian palm oil | guardian sustainable business', *The Guardian*, March 18. Available at: http://www.theguardian.com/sustainable-business/nestle-indonesian-palm-oil.

Thøgersen, J. (1999) 'Spillover processes in the development of a sustainable consumption pattern', *Journal of Economic Psychology*, 20(1): 53–81.

Tiefenbeck, V., Staake, T., Roth, K. and Sachs, O. (2013) 'For better or for worse? Empirical evidence of moral licensing in a behavioral energy conservation campaign', *Energy Policy*, 57: 160–71.

Truelove, H.B., Carrico, A.R., Weber, E.U., Raimi, K.T. and Vandenbergh, M.P. (2014) 'Positive and negative spillover of pro-environmental behavior: An integrative review and theoretical framework', *Global Environmental Change*, 29: 127–38.

Turner, B.S. (1991) *Religion and Social Theory*, 2nd edn. London: Sage.

Varey, R.J. (2010) 'Marketing means and ends for a sustainable society: A welfare agenda for transformative change', *Journal of Macromarketing*, 30(2): 112–26.

Vatican News Service (2012) 'Pope Benedict XVI urged to reject the tyranny of materialism', *Vatican News Service*. Available at: http://www.vaticans.org/index.php?/archives/1254-Pope-Benedict-XVI-urged-to-reject-the-Tyranny-of-Materialism.html.

Wagner, G. and Zeckhauser, R.J. (2012) 'Climate policy: Hard problem, soft thinking', *Climatic Change*, 110 (3–4): 507–21.

Wall, A.P. (2007) 'Government "demarketing" as viewed by its target audience', *Marketing Intelligence & Planning*, 25(2): 123–35.

Weber, E.U. (1997) 'Perception and expectation of climate change', in M. Bazerman, D. Messick, A. Tenbrunsel and K. Wade-Benzoni (eds), *Psychological and Ethical Perspectives to Environmental and Ethical Issues in Management*. San Francisco, CA: Jossey-Bass. pp. 314–41.

Witkowski, T.H. (2010) 'In this issue', *Journal of Macromarketing*, 30(2): 108.

7 Marketing to Young and Vulnerable Consumer Groups

Stephan Dahl and Lynne Eagle

CHAPTER OVERVIEW

In this chapter we will discuss:

- the impact of marketing to young age groups, within the context of non-traditional media forms such as advergames
- current concerns about such activity
- the effectiveness of industry self-regulation
- media literacy effects
- the effects and effectiveness of commercial media literacy programmes
- marketing to other vulnerable groups such as the elderly, those with low literacy levels and those with low income levels

NON-TRADITIONAL MEDIA FORMS

In the last decade the ways in which young people socialise have been complemented by an upsurge in new technologies, moving beyond traditional media and computer-based Internet access. Mobile phones in particular have found their way into the everyday life of young people (Davie et al., 2004), and the increasing penetration of mobile Internet and smartphones allows these devices to become portable 'virtual leisure spaces' where a wide range of applications and websites can be nearly universally accessed free from adult oversight. Further, our own observational research indicates that children are often allowed to play games on adults' mobile phones, potentially exposing them to advergames, and, while these 'apps' and games are often accessing and making connections online (e.g. by posting to the Facebook profiles of the players), they fall outside the remit of regulators. For example, the Advertising Standards Authority in the UK only covers 'non-paid-for space online under [the advertiser's] control', which includes 'advertiser-controlled pages on social networking websites' but not, for example, the pages and profiles of other users (Committee of Advertising Practice, 2010). In spite of the 'initiatives' noted earlier, the Australian Advertising Standards Bureau is completely silent on the issue. A challenge for effective regulation is that 'digital marketing in many ways evades national boundaries' (Clarke and Svanaes, 2012: 28).

Non-traditional media forms are becoming increasingly popular, particularly among younger age groups who seek customised entertainment forms. **Advergames**, i.e. computer-based games containing embedded advertising, are a rapidly growing and controversial form of marketing communication (Dahl et al., 2008). In spite of more than a decade of literature, there is still a lack of understanding and also a lack of integrated theoretically grounded research regarding the effects and effectiveness of advergames, yet there are calls for regulation or restriction on the activity (Coleman, 2012; Garde, 2011). The field is growing rapidly but while Internet-based games have been subject to study, advergames accessed via mobile phone 'apps' have so far received relatively little attention.

Advergame brand 'impact'

While there are numerous claims about the potential negative effects of exposure to brands and advertisements embedded in advergames (van Reijmersdal et al., 2012), evidence of actual impact on brand purchase appears to be elusive. Advergames, and by extension apps, are situated in the context of wider marketing communication activity, particularly product placements (Cowley and Barron, 2008; Winkler and Buckner, 2006), covert and viral strategies (see, for example Cruz and Fill, 2008; Milne et al., 2008), and therefore some form of measurement of return on investment measurement should be evident within the extant body of research.

Part of the appeal of advergames for advertisers is the prolonged brand exposure opportunities that the gaming environment offers. Children have been reported as playing one game over one hundred times (Gunn, 2001). Directly comparable data for adults are not available, however adults may spend 30 hours or more playing one specific game, creating different experiences each time the game is played (Nelson et al., 2004). Early research into the activity suggested that the repeated use of specific games does seem to have an impact on the recall for sponsors' advertising; 30% of in-game ads are recalled in the short term and 18% in the longer term (Grigorovici and Constantin, 2004). Conversely, more recent research suggests that more than 10% of game players claim to have not noticed the advertisements at all (Chang et al., 2010). There may be wear-out issues that result in negative attitudes towards brands featured in games played multiple times (Cauberghe and De Pelsmacker, 2010). The difference in brand impact, let alone actual purchase decisions across type of game and media, has not yet been studied.

Current concerns

There is concern regarding the potential negative effects of advergames, particularly in relation to their impact on children. The main concern is the possible negative influence of food-sponsored advergames on diet. Food marketers have long been criticised for contributing to childhood obesity (Boyland and Halford, 2012) and for causing domestic conflict when children pester their parents for advertised products (Marshall et al., 2007). The strength of the link between exposure to persuasive messages and unhealthy lifestyles is small relative to wider factors such as socio-economic status, family and cultural influences (Livingstone, 2006); however, the fact that there is some influence raises the issue of marketer responsibility and potential regulation of activity. A further concern is that children's **cognitive abilities** are not yet fully developed and that they are influenced by advertising in different ways from adults and thus may warrant 'special protection' (Eagle, 2007). Further concerns are evident from research that indicates children are less able to distinguish advertisements on web pages than on television (Ali et al., 2009).

Brand preferences are evident from a young age (John, 1999) and brand knowledge may be a part of socialisation and 'playground cool' (Ritson and Elliott, 1999), but studies such as these have been conducted with traditional mass media forms and do not extend to actual brand purchase influences. Concerns are evident that children may be highly susceptible to persuasion such as that delivered in advergames, due to their immersive nature (Mallinckrodt and Mizerski, 2007). For mobile marketing, the reduction in time between exposure to persuasive messages and potential impulse purchasing is an additional concern (Calvert, 2008). There is, however, a lack of empirical evidence regarding the impact advergames may have on children's relationships with brands and their purchase behaviours. These issues require further study in the context of the ever-changing media environment in order to enable testing of potential revised theoretical models' guides and discussion on how any potential detrimental effects should be addressed through regulation or legislation.

Think points

What ethical issues do you believe are presented by advergames? Are they the same or different for apps? What actions, if any, do you believe should be taken by whom to address these issues?

Self-regulatory effectiveness

The industry has responded to concerns about the impact of their activity by claiming to self-regulate advergame content (and other marketing activity) directed at children, and to engage in the provision of healthy dietary or lifestyle options (Council of Better Business Bureaus, 2010), for example through the US-based Children's Food and Beverage Advertising Initiative (CFBAI), which includes 17 of the largest food advertisers, including Mars, PepsiCo, Kraft, Kellogg's and Nestlé. Their website states:

> The Initiative is a voluntary self-regulation program comprising many of the nation's largest food and beverage companies. The Initiative is designed to shift the mix of foods advertised to children under 12 to encourage healthier dietary choices and healthy lifestyles. (www.bbb.org/us/childrens-food-and-beverage-advertising-initiative/)

Similar initiatives exist in other countries, such as Australia's Responsible Children's Marketing Initiative and Quick Service Restaurant Initiative (Australian Food and Grocery Council, 2011), or the 123 Healthy Balance Initiative by British manufacturer United Biscuits (www.123healthybalance.com/).

The value of these initiatives is debatable. A comparative content analysis found that companies signing up to the CFBAI initiative were actually more likely to include greater amounts of unhealthy foods in their Internet-based advergames than food marketers who had not signed up to the initiative (Quilliam et al., 2011). This is consistent with later findings of significant differences between Internet-based advergame content and the content that would be permitted in more strictly regulated media.

Communication theory and advergame effects

Existing communications theories are increasingly noted as being inadequate to explain new media communications forms (Brown et al., 2007; Kozinets et al., 2010). While there is a considerable amount of rhetoric regarding the possible impact of advergames on players, the mechanism by which any effects can be explained or predicted is less clear. Part of the reason for this is that traditional communication theories and models such as the **Hierarchy of Effects model** – that suggested people pass through clearly defined stages of response to advertising messages (e.g. AIDA, i.e. *A*wareness, *I*nterest, *D*esire and *A*ction) and was originally developed a century ago in the personal selling domain (Barry, 1987) – and DAGMAR (Defining Advertising Goals for Measured Advertising Response) (Colley, 1962), do not provide analytical or predictive explanations of the actual way brand information is received and processed by advergame players.

These traditional models were predicated on marketer originated and controlled, one-way information flow and became prominent during an era in which mass media were dominant and the prevailing belief, particularly in the USA, was that advertising was a strongly persuasive force and people passive recipients of communication messages. These became the prevailing wisdom, if not dominant paradigms, in spite of considerable evidence that, even before the Web 2.0 era, they were not universally applicable (Barnard and Ehrenberg, 1997; Jones, 1990).

Subliminal or low involvement processing effects

Advergames have also been claimed to provide subliminal messages (Dias and Agante, 2011; Jain, 2010). We pointed out the lack of evidence regarding subliminal advertising effects in Chapter 2. As advertising content in advergames is overt, albeit subtle, it is questionable if the subliminal literature offers a useful explanation of any real-world advergames effects. However, low involvement processing of information may represent an avenue to be explored in future research. Most advertising is processed using low involvement, with few cognitive/rational decision choices. **Low involvement processing** is not a subconscious or unconscious process, even though very little cognitive processing occurs (Heath, 2001). As such, it may link to **mere exposure effects** first noted in the 1960s (Zajonc, 1968) and more recent studies (Grimes, 2009). These studies suggest that preference can be created by simply repeating message exposure with no active cognitive processing of messages. However, this fails to consider real-world social and competitive competing forces (Lee, 2002) and is another area that warrants more detailed examination.

Think points

How do you think low involvement processing works in the context of non-traditional media such as advergames? What ethical issues might this raise and how should these be resolved?

Policy implications

While mobile advergames, i.e. those played on mobile devices such as smartphones, are still a relatively new phenomenon, currently available games successfully enhance conventional video-gaming by using social networking features and virtual reality/augmented reality features – making these games more engaging, personal and interactive than tradition 'standalone' games and many advergames. While there are still relatively few advergames available for both the iPhone and Android phones, these are rapidly increasing in terms of numbers and in popularity for both advertisers and users, with both platforms recording record 'app downloads' (BBC News, 2011). Greater understanding of their effects and effectiveness is needed to determine whether regulatory or legislative intervention is needed to protect vulnerable groups such as children, and what forms this might take.

Although current regulatory codes promised to extend beyond traditional media, and provide a framework for digital media, these codes fail to encompass the new and constantly evolving media forms. For example, the emerging 'branded play-scape' is a blurring of the boundary not only between entertainment and commerce, but also between interpersonal and commercial communication, the potentially symbiotic effects of which have so far not been studied.

Self-regulation of the industry seems so far not to hold pace with these developments and both the spirit and substance of advertising codes seem to be interpreted inconsistently, both across advertisers and within brands owned by the same parent company. Unfortunately, some advertisers ignore some or all of the current codes, or industry initiatives – at least for some brands. For example, both CFBAI signatories Kellogg and PepsiCo developed games that require purchases for full access (Quavers and Krave). Both games also require age verification by entering a date of birth when playing the game for the first time, but not thereafter. Moreover, the separate (and low) age rating for the game by Apple and Google avoids these games being blocked by parental access controls on the phone, i.e. even if parents activate the phone's build-in age restrictions, and then these games will remain accessible for children (unlike applications with a higher age rating).

The effectiveness of voluntary agreements was criticised in a recent UK House of Lords report (Science and Technology Select Committee, 2011) with a specific recommendation made (Section 5.26: 41) that: *'Voluntary agreements should be rigorously and independently evaluated against measurable and time-limited outcome'*. However, it is not only the industry that is making enforcement of the codes difficult or inconsistent. Distributors of these games, i.e. Apple and Google, should consider revising their guidance as to the age requirements for these applications, as the present advice is confusing. For example, all but one of the games reviewed in a recent study for iPhone is rated suitable for ages 4 and above in Apple's App store (or 'everyone'/'low maturity' in the Google market). However, for example, in the case of Krave, the game (rated 4+ in the App store) asks for age verification when first launching, requiring the player to enter an age of 18 and above once. On the other hand, games that encourage health behaviours, such as NHS Football Fan Challenges, a game that encourages healthy eating, exercise and smoking cessation, are rated 17+ in the app store – and can therefore be permanently blocked by using parental controls on the iPhone (Dahl et al., 2013).

As has been noted in the wider context of advergames, given the current climate of increased attention being paid to the link between advertising and obesity, coupled with sustained calls for advertising restrictions (Hawkes et al., 2011), it seems surprising that some sectors of the industry seem to view a less than totally responsible approach in unregulated areas as unproblematic. Failure of the industry to ensure exemplary behaviour from its members may lead to the imposition of greater restrictions on marketing communication for all members of the industry. The absence of definite, empirical evidence regarding negative impacts from food promotion is suggested as potentially resulting in future regulatory measures being based on 'a judgement of probable influence' (Livingstone, 2005: 278). Implementation of the House of Lords recommendation noted above may hasten this.

It is in the interests of both industry and academia to participate in an integrated, collaborative research programme in order to systematically evaluate the wider issues this paper has identified. Calls have been made for well over 20 years for a collaborative research agenda between industry and academia, yet 'few advertisers have supported research to both understand how advertising affects children or to examine ways to protect the interests of child viewers' (Armstrong and Brucks, 1988: 105). The academic community must also bear some of the burden of responsibility in this regard.

Earlier commentary suggested researchers lacked confidence about what advertising actually was in the Internet age – we would suggest that the question is becoming increasingly complex as new media forms evolve. A lack of agreed methodology and common concepts is hindering progress.

Future research programmes should enable explanations and predictions of actual behaviours across different cultures and population segments. Findings should then inform public policy decisions about whether there is a need for the protection of vulnerable groups such as children from the intended and unintended effects of persuasive communication and give direction as to the type of protection that is likely to be effective.

MEDIA LITERACY

Media literacy received a large amount of attention in the late 1990s and early years of the twenty-first century. While interest appears to have waned in recent years, the issues involved are important for ethical marketing activity and we therefore provide an overview of the key elements in the debate regarding both general media literacy and **commercial media literacy**.

Media literacy is a wide research area, broadly defined as the 'ability to access, analyze, evaluate and communicate messages in a wide variety of forms' (Aufderheide, 1993: 16).

Specifically in relation to marketing and other commercial communication, commercial literacy is defined as an 'understanding of the persuasive intent behind advertising' (Austin and Johnson, 1997: 21).

The theoretical foundation of media literacy programmes is **inoculation theory** (McGuire, 1961). Inoculation theory assumes that media exposure is pathological in nature – and consequently it is possible to 'immunise' people against the pressures generated via media content and advertising. Following on from this, the key notion of media literacy and programmes to enhance media literacy for both adults and children is that individuals can be 'forewarned' of the persuasive intent of certain communications, and thus activate cognitive defences against the persuasive effect (Wright et al., 2005). The aim is consequently to make individuals more critical and sceptical of commercial messages in the hope that this may lead to better decision-making about products and purchases.

Other theoretical foundations have been largely ignored. For instance, enjoyment as a major driver of media use remains largely under-researched (Nabi and Krcmar, 2004). Following the notion that media usage is not necessarily passive and pathological, but driven by enjoyment, **disposition theory** suggests that enjoyment of media often results in strong feelings, or affective disposition which may be positive or negative regarding specific characters or situations portrayed (Raney, 2004). The exact mechanisms by which these effects occur are not well understood. While early studies suggested that television can passively aid in mood elevation 'as a kind of valium' (Lee and Lee, 1995: 19), others posit a more active role where individuals become absorbed into the narrative world portrayed (Green and Brock, 2000). The application of disposition theory could be extended: while children may accept that advertisements represent 'fantasies about brands', such scepticism does not prevent positive attitudes towards the brands advertised.

The interaction between media consumer and the media itself is undoubtedly complex. Critics suggest that approaches taken by both educators and policy makers with regard to media literacy education are overly simplistic (Worth, 2004) and ignore the complex relationship consumers have with their chosen media.

It is important to note that persuasive communication is not necessarily intentionally deceptive, rather that some individuals, for example children who have lesser developed cognitive skills to recognise the deceptive nature of communication, are at greater risk of being misled by persuasive communication than others. Based on this reasoning, media literacy education has been proposed as a crucial intervention in order to protect vulnerable consumers, especially children, from the negative impact of persuasive communication (Kennedy, 2004). The result of this is that substantial media literacy campaigns have been developed, including campaigns by organisations affiliated to, or with input from, the marketing industry.

Industry-sponsored media literacy campaigns are not uncontroversial: critics have argued that the motivation is simply to be seen to address a problem created by the industry itself, that is, the negative social impacts to which marketing activity has contributed. Programme organisers have responded by pointing out that these programmes were developed voluntarily and some were created before issues such as childhood obesity arose, such as a campaign in Canada that has operated for over 15 years. Thus the marketing industry is positioning itself as being part of the solution. Moreover, some sectors of the industry have openly acknowledged that they need to be seen to be taking positive action to avoid further restrictions on promotions and marketing communication activity (Cincotta, 2005).

Think points

What are the ethical responsibilities of marketers in regard to ensuring that target markets are able to understand the persuasive intent behind marketing communication? Is there a role for tighter regulation in this area? Do marketers have an ethical responsibility to participate in commercial media literacy initiatives? If so, how should the effectiveness of these be evaluated and by whom?

Commercially-sponsored media literacy interventions: evidence regarding effects and effectiveness

In the late 1980s, there were calls for regulators and the advertising industry to work together to create effective programmes to counterbalance product promotions and advertising to children (Armstrong and Brucks, 1988). However, despite these calls there has been little progress in terms of a joined-up approach between policy makers, regulators and the industry. The result is that policy makers have largely relied on the industry to develop, set and evaluate the aims, outcomes and effectiveness measures of media literacy programmes. These are reviewed briefly in the next section in order to evaluate their usefulness.

The Canadian programme run by 'Companies Committed to Kids', a non-profit organisation including Coca-Cola, McDonald's, Kellogg's and Nestlé, has run extensive programmes addressing diverse issues ranging from drug use to bullying as well as media literacy programmes. In relation to media literacy programmes, CCK has commissioned a number of studies aiming to measure their efficiency. Measures have shown overall high recall rates of the CCK programmes, both among parents and children; 74% of children and 50% of parents agreed that the CCK adverts helped them to better understand television advertising. However, these measures of effectiveness have been criticised as largely relying on recall, and not measuring attitudinal or behavioural change (Eagle, 2007).

In the UK and other European countries, MediaSmart has run media literacy-focused programmes with the aim of developing children's ability to critically engage with media communication. Some of the material used by MediaSmart draws directly from the CCK campaigns run in Canada. Similar to the Canadian results, MediaSmart claims positive results.

Reports stated that the response from teachers using MediaSmart as part of the curriculum had been extremely positive, with 98% intending to use it in the future and 86% of these teachers rating it 'extremely valuable or very useful'. A closer examination of feedback from teachers who have used the material indicates somewhat mixed results (Media Smart, 2005). Much of the data indicate little more than high content recall levels. Evidence of movement beyond that does not appear promising, as the following quotes from teachers indicate:

> It was quite difficult for the children to grasp this.

> The children's understanding in this area didn't really change.

> The theory was there in the resource although I'm not sure if the children got it in practice – still voting with their hearts and not their heads.

> It was good for the more able students – but the less able just became more confused.

Such comments may reflect the various stages of **cognitive development** among the children (Moses and Baldwin, 2005; Neeley and Schumann, 2004) and an underlying expectation of a greater change in children's perceptions than their developmental stage will allow. Additionally, critics suggest that the programme is not as helpful as claimed, noting that nutrition is not included, nor are 'increasingly-used health-related claims made in adverts' (*Which?* Magazine, 2003: 19). This latter strategy appears to be an attempt 'to stress whatever healthy ingredients their products contain (contains fibre), or to desperately add something they think will make their brand seem healthier (now with Vitamin C)' (Preston, 2004: 368).

Similarly, a study carried out using the Portuguese version of MediaSmart found no evidence for effectiveness. However, the study's author cautioned that this may be because the children did not have enough time to absorb the entire campaign (Magalhães, 2010). Other campaigns have no accessible data of effectiveness, for example, Willy Munchright in New Zealand. The New Zealand campaign is based on a campaign devised by McDonald's

Restaurants and used in the USA since 1992. However, the New Zealand version contains no McDonald's identification and has audio with local accents (Drinnan, 2004). The campaign does not provide additional resources for schools beyond the adverts on television, and a complete lack of specific objectives for the programme has been noted, with only very general aims cited, such as, 'to provide straightforward information to young people in a cartoon form which will encourage healthy eating and actions' (New Zealand Television Broadcasters' Council, 2004). Opponents have criticised the campaign as nothing more than a public relations campaign on behalf of the food industry because there has been no attempt to empirically measure the effects of the programme (Cincotta, 2005).

Think points

Given the material reviewed in the preceding sections, what value do you believe current commercial media literacy programmes have in teaching young children about the commercial intent of marketing communications? What actions do you believe should be taken to improve the efficacy of such programmes and by whom should this action be taken?

OTHER VULNERABLE GROUPS

Much of the emphasis for researchers, policy makers and the advertising industry is on communication and marketing directed at children. However, it is important to note that other groups are also vulnerable and research and policy need to address potential ethical issues when marketing is directed at these groups.

Elderly

There is a lot of anecdotal material relating to elderly people being 'ripped off' by aggressive direct marketing tactics such as in the areas of home security and home maintenance. Actual evidence of the extent of this activity is difficult to determine (Yoon et al., 2009). One of the problems in this regard is the tendency to treat all elderly people as an homogeneous group – which is far from correct.

There may be issues with declining abilities to read 'fine print' information, including leaflets and packaging – with potentially serious implications for products such as medications (Moschis et al., 2011) – however older people may also be able to draw on past knowledge and experience to compensate for changes in their abilities and resources (Yoon et al., 2009).

Low literate groups

Up to 20% of people in most developed countries have significant literacy challenges, and a further 20% have less severe challenges (Kemp and Eagle, 2008), yet the needs of these large sectors of the population are largely ignored by marketers. Consumers with low literacy levels use a range of coping strategies to acquire information but may face challenges in understanding consumer rights, or making complaints, let alone understanding 'fine print' details as discussed in the previous section (Adkins and Ozanne, 2005).

When marketers are heavily dependent on written information, including brochures, leaflets or on-pack information, to differentiate their products and services from those of competitors, the needs of the low-literate sectors should be taken into account, but there is little evidence of this actually occurring. In the case of medications, including those that may be intended for children of low-literate parents, the ethical obligations of marketers are clear.

Low income groups/'bottom of the pyramid'

The wants and needs of those living in poverty have received considerable focus, often framed in terms of 'Bottom of the (economic) Pyramid' or 'Base of the Pyramid' (BOP). It is estimated that some 2.7 billion people live on less than US$2 per day (Davidson, 2009); others estimate the number to be as high as 4 billion (Sama and Casselman, 2013). Their limited financial resources mean they have, until recently, been largely ignored by marketers. While improving the lives of these people may be a laudable aim, there is a growing amount of cynicism evident in regard to attempts to improve people's living standards by selling new (branded) products and services that are expensive substitutes for locally produced products, resulting in claims of exploitation and manipulation (Arora and Romijn, 2012). Further, criticism of the marketing tactics of tobacco and alcohol marketers in targeting the BOP sector has focused on the implications of prioritising these products over essential goods such as food, clothing and adequate shelter (Davidson, 2009).

Another aspect of marketing to the BOP that has received considerable recent criticism is **microfinancing** loans, usually less than US$100, which are provided to enable people, often women, to set up small businesses (Adams and Raymond, 2008). There are increasing numbers of reports of abuses of the microfinancing systems, including 'loan sharking' (charging excessive interest rates) and the lack of sustainability of many schemes – partially because of the lack of basic business knowledge and expertise of those obtaining loans (Lewis, 2008).

SUMMARY

The discussion in this chapter focused on the complexities associated with communicating and marketing to children as well as other, under-researched and frequently overlooked vulnerable groups. Using the example of advergames, the chapter highlighted the challenges for regulation as well as the problems caused by some industry players behaving contrary to the spirit of the regulations.

The main answer brought forward by industry, and tacitly agreed to by regulators and policy makers, appears to be media literacy programmes. These programmes often feature substantial involvement by the industry, and we showed that evaluation is focused largely on recall, with little evidence of effectiveness. While the stated intentions behind such programmes are laudable, the absence of measureable objectives and proof of effectiveness opens avenues for critics to argue that such programmes are little more than public relations programmes, designed to avert further, more stringent regulation of advertising and marketing communications.

Case study Krave cereal

Krave is a highly sugary breakfast cereal manufactured by Kellogg's. Kellogg's engages in an extensive advertising campaign using Facebook, as well as mobile apps, online games and television advertising, to promote their product range. In 2011, Krave introduced a game on Facebook featuring a Krave piece dressed as a superhero.

This campaign was challenged over the promotion of unhealthy eating habits. In their response, Kellogg's maintained that they directed the game exclusively to young adults, based on the information they provided on their Facebook account. Thus, only adults over the age of 17 were allowed to access and play the game.

In its ruling, the Advertising Standards Authority accepted the argument by Kellogg's that the game was not aimed at children, and did not encourage poor nutritional habits in children. They accepted that using the safeguarding mechanism of Facebook profile information was sufficient to avoid exposure to children.

Since then Krave has continued to develop their gaming platforms, with later offerings including a mobile app. On the mobile app, players were prompted to enter their age when first launching the app, but not again afterwards. The launch of the game was heavily advertised on television and using other promotional tools costing around £1.7 million (Miller, 2011). An important aspect was the integration of consumption and game experience – the player could enhance the game and unlock new levels by purchasing Krave packets and entering codes.

Kellogg's continues to promote the 'Chocovore' brand experience for allegedly young adults only by continuing to launch new games, such as the PittFall!Krave game in 2014. The game tied in with a promotional campaign run across Europe and in association with MTV – a 'key teen brand' (West, 2014). The promotion in 2014 cumulated in Krave and MTV staging a 'real world event' in Malta, including a £10,000 prize for the Chocovore Idol.

Questions to consider

Take a look at the Krave games and website and evaluate the ethical issues involved. Discuss why the behaviour should, or should not, be different for a highly sugary cereal – or a healthy snack.

What do you think could be the potential ramifications of continuing to heavily promote unhealthy cereals for the industry?

Further Reading

Sage journal articles available for free at https://study.sagepub.com/eagleanddahl:

Arora, S. and Romijn, H. (2012) 'The empty rhetoric of poverty reduction at the base of the pyramid', *Organization*, 19: 481–505.

Epstein, M.J. and Yuthas, K. (2010) 'Mission impossible: Diffusion and drift in the microfinance industry', *Sustainability Accounting, Management and Policy Journal*, 1: 201–21.

Other

Hernandez, M.D. (2011) 'A model of flow experience as determinant of positive attitudes toward online advergames', *Journal of Promotion Management*, 17: 315–26.

Panic, K., Cauberghe, V. and De Pelsmacker, P. (2013) 'Comparing TV ads and advergames targeting children: The impact of persuasion knowledge on behavioral responses', *Journal of Advertising*, 42: 264–73.

Waiguny, M.K., Nelson, M.R. and Terlutter, R. (2013) 'The relationship of persuasion knowledge, identification of commercial intent and persuasion outcomes in advergames—the role of media context and presence', *Journal of Consumer Policy*, 37: 1–21.

Waiguny, M.K.J., Terlutter, R. and Zaglia, M.E. (2011) 'The influence of advergames on consumers' attitudes and behaviour: An empirical study among young consumers', *International Journal of Entrepreneurial Venturing*, 3: 231–47.

References

Adams, J. and Raymond, F. (2008) 'Did Yunus deserve the Nobel Peace Prize: Microfinance or macrofarce?', *Journal of Economic Issues*, 42(2): 435–43.

Adkins, N.R. and Ozanne, J.L. (2005) 'The low literate consumer', *Journal of Consumer Research*, 32: 93–105.

Ali, M., Blades, M., Oates, C. and Blumberg, F. (2009) 'Young children's ability to recognize advertisements in web page designs', *British Journal of Developmental Psychology*, 27: 71–83.

Armstrong, G.M. and Brucks, M. (1988) 'Dealing with children's advertising: Public policy issues and alternatives', *Journal of Public Policy & Marketing*, 7: 98–113.

Arora, S. and Romijn, H. (2012) 'The empty rhetoric of poverty reduction at the base of the pyramid', *Organization*, 19: 481–505.

Aufderheide P. (1993) 'Media literacy: A report of the National Leadership Conference on Media Literacy, ERIC Document Reproduction Service No. ED 365 294, cited in R. Hobbs (1998), 'The seven great debates in the media literacy movement', *Journal of Communication*, 48: 16–32.

Austin, E.W. and Johnson, K.K. (1997) 'Effects of general and alcohol-specific media literacy training on children's decision making about alcohol', *Journal of Health Communication*, 2: 17–42.

Australian Food and Grocery Council (2011) Available at: www.afgc.org.au/our-expertise/industry-codes/advertising-to-children and www.communicationscouncil.org.au/public/content/viewcategory.aspx?id=890.

Barnard, N. and Ehrenberg, A.S.C. (1997) 'Advertising: Strongly persuasive or nudging?', *Journal of Advertising Research*, 37: 21–31.

Barry, T.E. (1987) 'The development of the Hierarchy of Effects: A historical perspective', *Current Issues and Research in Advertising*, 10: 251–95.

BBC News (2011) *Google's Android Racks up its 10 Billionth App Download*. Available at: http://www.bbc.co.uk/news/technology-16054945.

Boyland, E.J. and Halford, J.C.G. (2012) 'Television advertising and branding. Effects on eating behaviour and food preferences in children', *Appetite*, 62: 236–41.

Brown, J., Broderick, A.J. and Lee, N. (2007) 'Word of mouth communication within online communities: Conceptualizing the online social network', *Journal of Interactive Marketing (formerly Journal of Direct Marketing)*, 21: 2–20.

Calvert, S.L. (2008) 'Children as consumers: Advertising and marketing', *The Future of Children*, 18: 205–34.

Cauberghe, V. and De Pelsmacker, P. (2010) 'Advergames. The impact of brand prominence and game repetition on brand responses', *Journal of Advertising*, 39: 5–18.

Chang, Y., Yan, J., Zhang, J. and Luo, J. (2010) 'Online in-game advertising effect: Examining the influence of a match between games and advertising', *Journal of Interactive Advertising*, 11: 63–73.

Cincotta, K. (2005) *Accord Gets Kids to Munch Right*. Available at: www.bandt.com.au.

Clarke, B. and Svanaes, S. (2012) *Digital Marketing and Advertising to Children: A Literature Review*. London: Advertising Education Forum.

Coleman, M. (2012) *The Challenges of Regulating New Media Technologies for Children and Young People*. Adelaide: University of Adelaide.

Colley, R.H. (1962) 'Squeezing the waste out of advertising', *Harvard Business Review*, July–August: 76–88.

Committee of Advertising Practice (2010) *Landmark Agreement Extends ASA's Digital Remit – Committee of Advertising Practice*. Available at: http://www.cap.org.uk/Media-Centre/2010/Extending-the-Digital-remit-of-the-CAP-Code.aspx.

Council of Better Business Bureaus (2010) *The Children's Food & Beverage Advertising Initiative in Action: A Report on Compliance and Implementation During 2009*. Available at: http://www.bbb.org/us/storage/0/Shared%20Documents/BBBwithlinks.pdf.

Cowley, E. and Barron, C. (2008) 'When product placement goes wrong: The effects of program liking and placement prominence', *Journal of Advertising*, 37: 89–98.

Cruz, D. and Fill, C. (2008) 'Evaluating viral marketing: Isolating the key criteria', *Marketing Intelligence & Planning*, 26: 743–58.

Dahl, S., Eagle, L. and Baez, C. (2008) 'Analyzing advergames: Active diversions or actual deception. An exploratory study of online advergame content', *Young Consumers*, 10: 17–34.

Dahl, S., Eagle, L. and Low, D. (2013) 'Not quite playing the game? Mobile applications for healthier lifestyles', In proceedings of the Academy of Marketing Science presented at the World Marketing Congress Melbourne, pp. 335–345.

Davidson, K. (2009) 'Ethical concerns at the bottom of the pyramid: Where CSR meets BOP', *Journal of International Business Ethics*, 2: 22–33.

Davie, R., Panting, C. and Charlton, T. (2004) 'Mobile phone ownership and usage among pre-adolescents', *Telematics and Informatics*, 21: 359–73.

Dias, M. and Agante, L. (2011) 'Can advergames boost children's healthier eating habits? A comparison between healthy and non-healthy food', *Journal of Consumer Behaviour*, 10: 152–60.

Drinnan, J. (2004) 'Health and nutrition claims get advertising go-ahead', *The National Business Review*, 3 September: 34.

Eagle, L. (2007) 'Commercial media literacy: What does it do, to whom—and does it matter?', *Journal of Advertising*, 36(2): 101–10.

Garde, A. (2011) 'Advertising regulation and the protection of children-consumers in the European Union: In the best interests of... commercial operators?', *The International Journal of Children's Rights*, 19: 523–45.

Green, M.C. and Brock, T.C. (2000) 'The role of transportation in the persuasiveness of public narratives', *Journal of Personality and Social Psychology*, 79: 401–21.

Grigorovici, D.M. and Constantin, C.D. (2004) 'Experiencing interactive advertising beyond rich media. Impacts of ad type and presence on brand effectiveness in 3D gaming immersive virtual environments', *Journal of Interactive Advertising*, 4: 1–26.

Grimes, D.A. (2009) 'Forgettable contraception', *Contraception*, 80: 497–9.

Gunn, E. (2001) 'Product placement prize', *Advertising Age*, 72: 10.

Hawkes, C., Lobstein, T. and The Polmark Consortium (2011) 'Regulating the commercial promotion of food to children: A survey of actions worldwide', *International Journal of Pediatric Obesity*, 6: 83–94.

Heath, R. (2001) 'Low involvement processing – a new model of brand communication', *Journal of Marketing Communications*, 7: 27–33.

Jain, A. (2010) 'Temptations in cyberspace: New battlefields in childhood obesity', *Health Affairs*, 29: 425–9.

John, D.R. (1999) 'Consumer socialization of children: A retrospective look at twenty-five years of research', *Journal of Consumer Research*, 26: 183–213.

Jones, J.P. (1990) 'Advertising: Strong force or weak force? Two views an ocean apart', *International Journal of Advertising*, 9: 233–46.

Kemp, G. and Eagle, L. (2008) 'Shared meanings or missed opportunities? The implications of functional health literacy for social marketing interventions', *International Review on Public and Nonprofit Marketing*, 5: 117–28.

Kennedy, D.G. (2004) 'Coming of age in consumerdom', *American Demographics*, 26: 14.

Kozinets, R.V., de Valck, K., Wojnicki, A.C. and Wilner, S.J.S. (2010) 'Networked narratives: Understanding word-of-mouth marketing in online communities', *Journal of Marketing*, 74: 71–89.

Lee, A.Y. (2002) 'Effects of implicit memory on memory-based versus stimulus-based brand choice', *Journal of Marketing Research (JMR)*, 39: 440–54.

Lee, B. and Lee, R. (1995) 'How and why people watch TV. Implications for the future of interactive television', *Journal of Advertising Research*, 35: 9–18.

Lewis, J.C. (2008) 'Microloan sharks', *Stanford Social Innovation Review*, 6: 54.

Livingstone, S. (2005) 'Assessing the research base for the policy debate over the effects of food advertising to children', *International Journal of Advertising*, 24: 273–96.

Livingstone, S. (2006) 'Does TV advertising make children fat?', *Public Policy Research*, 13: 54–61.

Magalhães, A.F.V. de (2010) *The Effectiveness of the Media Smart Program on Promoting the Critical Thinking of Children Towards the Use of Celebrities in Television Advertising*. Universitade Nova, Lisbon.

Mallinckrodt, V. and Mizerski, D. (2007) 'The effects of playing and advergame on young children's perceptions, preferences and requests', *Journal of Advertising*, 36: 87–100.

Marshall, D., O'Donohoe, S. and Kline, S. (2007) 'Families, food, and pester power: Beyond the blame game?', *Journal of Consumer Behaviour*, 6: 164–181.

McGuire, W.J. (1961) 'The effectiveness of supportive and refutational defenses in immunizing and restoring beliefs against persuasion', *Sociometry*, 24: 184–97.

Media Smart (2005) *Be Advise*, Teacher and Pupil Evaluation Report. London: Media Smart.

Miller, M.J. (2011) *Kellogg's UK Shows How to Krave Social and Mobile Connections*. Available at: http://www.brandchannel.com/home/post/2011/09/06/Kelloggs-Krave-UK-Digital-Marketing.aspx (accessed 11 December 2014).

Milne, G.R., Bahl, S. and Rohm, A. (2008) 'Toward a framework for assessing covert marketing practices', *Journal of Public Policy & Marketing*, 27: 57–62.

Moschis, G,P,, Mosteller, J. and Fatt, C.K. (2011) 'Research frontiers on older consumers' vulnerability', *Journal of Consumer Affairs*, 45: 467–91.

Moses, L.J. and Baldwin, D.A. (2005) 'What can the study of cognitive development reveal about childrens' ability to appreciate and cope with advertising?', *Journal of Public Policy & Marketing*, 24: 186–201.

Nabi, R.L. and Krcmar, M. (2004) 'Conceptualizing media enjoyment as attitude. Implications for mass media effects research', *Communication Theory*, 14: 288–310.

Neeley, S.M. and Schumann, D.W. (2004) 'Using animated spokes-characters in advertising to young children', *Journal of Advertising*, 33: 7–23.

Nelson, M.R., Heejo, K. and Yaros, R.A. (2004) 'Advertainment or advercreep? Game players' attitudes towards advertising and product placement in computer games', *Journal of Interactive Advertising*, 4: 1–30.

New Zealand Television Broadcasters' Council (2004) *Food Industry Accord Launched*. Available at: http://www.nztbc.co.nz/news/story.html?story_020904.inc.

Preston, C. (2004) 'Children's advertising: The ethics of economic socialisation', *International Journal of Consumer Studies*, 28: 364–70.

Quilliam, E.T., Lee, M., Cole, R.T. and Mikyoung, K. (2011) 'The impetus for (and limited power of) business self-regulation: The example of advergames', *Journal of Consumer Affairs*, 45: 224–47.

Raney, A.A. (2004) 'Expanding disposition theory: Reconnecting character liking, moral evaluations and enjoyment', *Communication Theory*, 17: 38–53.

Ritson, M. and Elliott, R. (1999) 'The social uses of advertising: An ethnographic study of adolescent advertising audiences', *Journal of Consumer Research*, 26: 260–77.

Sama, L.M. and Casselman, R.M. (2013) 'Profiting from poverty: Ethics of microfinance in BOP', *South Asian Journal of Global Business Research*, 2: 82–103.

Science and Technology Select Committee (2011) *Behaviour Change*. London: House of Lords.

van Reijmersdal, E.A., Rozendaal, E. and Buijzen, M. (2012)'Effects of prominence, involvement, and persuasion knowledge on children's cognitive and affective responses to advergames', *Journal of Interactive Marketing*, 26: 33–42.

West, G. (2014) 'Kellogg's targets youth market with "The Quest for the Chocovore Idol" integrated campaign for Krave cereal', *The Drum*. Available at: http://www.thedrum.com/

news/2014/02/11/kelloggs-targets-youth-market-quest-chocovore-idol-integrated-campaign-krave-cereal (accessed 11 December 2014).

Which? Magazine (2003) 'Marketing food to kids', *Which?* Magazine, August: 18–21.

Winkler, T. and Buckner, K. (2006) 'Receptiveness of gamers to embedded brand messages in advergames: Attitudes towards product placement', *Journal of Interactive Advertising*, 7: 37–46.

Worth, P. (2004) *Evaluating the Effectiveness of School-Based Media Literacy Curricula.* Available at: ldt.stanford.edu/~pworth/ papers/effectiveness_medialit.doc.

Wright, P., Friestad, M. and Boush, D.M. (2005) 'The development of marketplace persuasion knowledge in children, adolescents, and young adults', *Journal of Public Policy & Marketing*, 24(2): 222–33.

Yoon, C., Cole, C.A. and Lee, M.P. (2009) 'Consumer decision making and aging: Current knowledge and future directions', *Journal of Consumer Psychology*, 19: 2–16.

Zajonc, R.B. (1968) 'Attitudinal effects of mere exposure', *Journal of Personality and Social Psychology*, 9: 1–27.

8   Promotion of Harmful Products

Lynne Eagle, Debra M. Desrochers, Stephan Dahl, Tracey Mahony and David R. Low

CHAPTER OVERVIEW

In this chapter we will discuss:

- Alcohol and tobacco as two examples of products considered to be harmful
- Evidence of harm created by excess alcohol consumption and tobacco use
- Promotions used within these two sectors, particularly in relation to electronic media forms
- Recent research relevant to these products
- Legal and ethical issues relating to these categories

WHICH PRODUCTS CAN BE CLASSIFIED AS HARMFUL?

Any product that is misused can be harmful. A review of popular media will reveal concerns about excess consumption of foods, particularly those deemed to be low in nutritional value or high in fat, salt and sugar. There are also warnings about overuse of electronic devices and many other products that are not in themselves harmful but whose use may lead to harm. However, a greater concern is when a product is harmful when used as intended.

Unlike other products that attract no attention when using strategies to increase market share, many of these potentially harmful products attract criticism from concerned members of society and often governments when their markets increase (Buchanan et al., 2009). In this chapter, we focus on two main products, tobacco and alcohol, with a particular focus on the use of electronic media forms of promotion. In the closing case study, these concepts can be extended to gambling.

While the consequences of the promotion of harmful products are worldwide, we use examples from the UK, USA and Australia to illustrate the magnitude of several of the key problems and issues facing policy makers and regulators. We begin with a review of the extant literature regarding the impact of tobacco and excess alcohol consumption, then turn to the current regulatory activity and research regarding its efficacy, with a particular focus on the alcohol promotions that do not yet face the same level of restrictions (in terms of marketing communication and advertising) as tobacco. Finally, we will review emerging concerns in the promotion of harmful products.

TOBACCO AND ITS ADVERSE EFFECTS

It is widely recognised that tobacco use in any form is dangerous and is the single most preventable cause of death (Erisksen et al., 2012). The World Health Organisation (WHO) estimates that tobacco kills nearly six million people a year; that more than five million of those deaths are the result of direct tobacco use while more than 600,000 are the result of non-smokers being exposed to second-hand smoke; that approximately one person dies every six seconds due to tobacco, accounting for one in 10 adult deaths; and that nearly 80% of the more than one billion smokers worldwide live in low and middle income countries, where the burden of tobacco-related illness and death is heaviest (World Health Organisation, 2014).

The most popular use of tobacco is smoking, which can lead to a multitude of diseases. According to a recent US government report, smoking causes 87% of lung cancer deaths, 32% of coronary heart disease deaths, and 79% of all cases of chronic obstructive pulmonary disease (COPD) (US Department of Health and Human Services, 2014). One out of three cancer deaths is caused by smoking; smoking causes colorectal and liver cancer and increases the failure rate of treatment for all cancers; smoking causes diabetes mellitus, rheumatoid arthritis and immune system weakness, increases the risk for tuberculosis disease and death, ectopic (tubal) pregnancy and impaired fertility, cleft lip and cleft palates in babies of women who smoke during early pregnancy, erectile dysfunction, and age-related macular degeneration (US Department of Health and Human Services, 2014).

One differentiating feature regarding tobacco usage is that there is a lag of several years between when people start using the product and when their health suffers.

Therefore, future health consequences are based on today's tobacco usage. The World Health Organisation reveals that tobacco caused 100 million deaths in the twentieth century and, if this trend continues, it may cause one billion deaths in the twenty-first century. Furthermore, unchecked tobacco-related deaths will increase to more than eight million per year by 2030 and more than 80% of those deaths will be in low and middle income countries (World Health Organisation, 2014).

Tobacco users who die prematurely deprive their families of income, raise the cost of health care prior to death, and hinder economic development since large investments are made into addressing preventable diseases rather than needs in transportation, education, public safety and rural development (World Health Organisation, 2014). Ten years ago, the American Cancer Society cited estimates that $96 billion dollars were spent on tobacco-related health care costs in the United States from 2000 to 2004; $16.6 billion dollars were spent in France; $9.5 billion dollars in the United Kingdom; $6.2 billion dollars in China; and $2.8 billion dollars were spent on tobacco-related health care costs in Canada (American Cancer Society, 2014). Based on more recent data, tobacco use costs the United States more than $289 billion a year, of which at least $133 billion is in direct medical care for adults and more than $156 billion is in lost productivity. In addition, $5.6 billion a year (2006 data) accrues due to lost productivity from exposure to second-hand smoke (US Department of Health and Human Services, 2014).

ALCOHOL AND ITS ADVERSE EFFECTS

Alcohol is not only the 'drug of choice' among young people (Mart, 2011: 889), it is also integrated into social life (Wettlaufer et al., 2012). However, alcohol misuse accounts for approximately 2.5 million deaths worldwide per year, including over 300,000 young people between 15 and 29 years of age (World Health Organisation, 2010). It also contributes 4.5% of total measured disability-adjusted life years, higher than tobacco at 3.7% and **illicit drugs** at 0.9% (Donovan et al., 2011), leading to claims that alcohol is more dangerous than heroin (Lee and Forsythe, 2011). Alcohol misuse imposes significant costs on society through factors such as reduced workplace productivity and the impact of alcohol-fuelled violence (Manning et al., 2013).

Alcohol is recognised as the third leading cause of preventable and premature disease and disability globally (Coltart and Gilmore, 2012). Alcohol is causally linked to cancer, cardiovascular disease, liver disease, diabetes and several other serious diseases (Parry et al., 2011) as well as injury and communicable diseases such as HIV and TB (Parry et al., 2009).

Young people are claimed to be particularly vulnerable to the harmful effects of excess alcohol consumption (Anderson et al., 2009) as up to 90% of underage drinking occurs in **binge drinking** episodes (Fournier et al., 2013). Heavy alcohol consumption during adolescence can permanently impair brain development; there is also an association between drinking levels within this age group and road traffic accidents, depression, suicide and a range of sexually transmitted diseases (Anderson, 2009). Children who start drinking before the age of 13 are claimed to have a 40% higher risk of becoming dependent on alcohol later in life than those who start to drink at older ages (van Amsterdam and van den Brink, 2013).

Perceived drinking behaviour and perceived approval of drinking are strong predictors of how much college students drink (Fournier and Clarke, 2011) even though perceived **normative behaviour** may be inaccurate. For example, a Swiss study found 45% of young males overestimated drinking by others and 35% underestimated it (Bertholet et al., 2011). Perceived social norms regarding desirable behaviours will outweigh education and information-based interventions which have been found to be ineffective in reducing alcohol-related harm (Anderson et al., 2009). Attempts to alter **social norms** will be countered by the pro-consumption messages of the alcohol industry (Pettigrew et al., 2012).

In 2010 the direct costs of alcohol misuse in Australia alone were estimated as being in excess of AU$14.4 billion per annum (Manning et al., 2013), with a further AU$6.8billion in indirect costs from the negative impacts of another person's drinking (Laslett et al., 2010). The breakdown of the direct costs is shown in Table 8.1 below. In the USA, the estimated total economic cost of excessive drinking was $223.5 billion in 2006. Of the total cost, $161.3 billion (72.2%) came from lost productivity; $24.6 billion (11.0%) came from increased health care costs; $21.0 billion (9.4%) came from criminal justice costs; and $16.7 billion (7.5%) came from other effects, including fire losses, crime victim property damage, and special education on foetal alcohol syndrome (Bouchery et al., 2011).

Table 8.1　Breakdown of estimated direct costs of alcohol misuse (Manning et al., 2013)

	Estimated cost AU$	Costs converted to US$	% of total cost
1a. Direct costs Australia and extrapolated indicative costs for UK and USA			
Criminal justice system	2.958 billion	2.788 billion	20.6
Health system	1.686 billion	1.589 billion	11.7
Loss of productivity	6.046 billion	5.698 billion	42.1
Traffic accidents	3.662 billion	3.451 billion	25.5
Total direct costs	**14.35 billion**	**13.53 billion**	**100%**

Equivalent direct health system costs UK and USA, based on a straight extrapolation of Australian direct costs above on the basis of population:

UK: AU$38.61 billion (£21.2 billion/US$36.8 billion)

USA: AU$191.68 billion (£109.04 billion/US$186.68 billion

1b. Comparison of costs of alcohol misuse to Australian, UK and USA economies

	Australia (population 23.5 million)	UK (population 63.23 million)	USA (population 313.9 million)
Estimated % of GDP spent on treating alcohol misuse (Mohapatra et al., 2010)	0.42%	1.06%	1.0%
Estimated cost based on % of GDP (World Bank, 2014)	US$6.39 billion	US$25.81 billion	US$156.8 billion

Think points

Controls on alcohol production, marketing and consumption have been imposed for many reasons. Historically, public health considerations have played a relatively small role in alcohol controls (Room, 1990). Government agricultural policies, such as providing subsidies to farmers, and as a basis for tax generation are two other reasons to implement controls in the alcohol industry. Alcohol taxes are an important source of revenues and were particularly important prior to the advent of the income tax (Room, 1990).

Against the evidence of harms it should be noted that alcohol sales generated **tax revenue** of AU$7.1 billion in 2010 (Manning et al., 2013), of which over AU$100 million is estimated to be derived from under-age drinkers (Donovan et al., 2011). In total in the US, alcohol and tobacco sales generate $24 billion in tax revenues (Alcohol and Tobacco Tax and Trade Bureau, 2012). What are the implications for any future government policy?

PROMOTION OF HARMFUL PRODUCTS

Marketing communication has long been held to reflect culture through a distorted mirror (Pollay and Gallagher, 1990). Therefore portrayals of the use of harmful products have to be seen within the context of established cultures.

Tobacco promotion expenditures

In 2008, $9.9 billion was spent on cigarette advertising and promotion in the US alone, which equated to more than $34 being spent on tobacco marketing for every man, woman and child in the US that year (Eriksen et al., 2012). By 2011, cigarette company marketing expenditures was reduced, but still totalled approximately $8.4 billion, such that trade promotion was 94.3%, traditional media was 0.3%, sponsorships was 1.6%, online and digital was 0.3%, outdoor and **transit media** was 0%, and other expenditures was 3.6% (Federal Trade Commission, 2013).

Alcohol promotion expenditures

The alcohol industry is estimated to have spent more than $6 billion on advertising and promotion in 2005 (Mart, 2011) and over AU$125 million in Australia alone in 2007 on traditional media advertising, with two or three times that amount estimated to be spent on sponsorship and point of sale (Australian Chronic Disease Prevention Alliance, n.d.). In the US, total advertising spending by the alcohol industry was $3.45 billion in 2011, such that trade promotion was 33%, traditional media was 32%, sponsorships was 18%, online and digital was 8%, outdoor and transit was 7%, and other expenditures was 2% (Federal Trade Commission, 2014). The amount invested across the various digital technologies such as mobile phones, online video channels, interactive games, and social networks such as Facebook and Twitter is unknown; there is a small body of literature relating to its potential effects. However, although there is a substantial amount of controversy, especially regarding the alcohol industry circumventing advertising restrictions (Hastings et al., 2010), there is, to date, little evidence of social media marketing effectiveness.

Impact of tobacco promotion

In spite of lengthy debate, evidence of direct causal effects of exposure to tobacco advertising and smoking imagery has been difficult to identify (DiFranza et al., 2006). Strong associative effects have been found in numerous studies, for example exposure to smoking imagery in movies during early adolescence has been found to be a significant predictor of progression to smoking through observational learning and pro-smoking reinforcement messages (Dalton et al., 2009). Some authors are more definite in their stances. For example, a systematic literature review suggests that there is now 'considerable evidence for a causal link' between pro-smoking imagery and smoking commencement (Wellman et al., 2006: 1293).

A growing body of research also shows that even anti-smoking advertising can, inadvertently, encourage youth smoking. For example, a study of more than 1000 adolescents found that, overall, the more the students were exposed to anti-smoking messages, the more inclined they were to smoke. The exception occurred only among students who said their friends listened to and were influenced by the anti-smoking messages (Paek and Gunther, 2007).

Impact of alcohol promotion

Alcohol advertising shapes attitudes and behaviours, normalising and encouraging drinking and potentially unsafe amounts (Dobson, 2010; Pettigrew et al., 2012). Significant associations have been found between involvement with alcohol marketing and both current drinking behaviours and future drinking intentions, and between movie alcohol use exposure and binge drinking (Gordon et al., 2011; Hanewinkel et al., 2012). We should stress that association does not imply cause and effect; however there is sufficient evidence to warrant concern.

Engaging with web-based alcohol marketing is claimed to increase the odds of being a drinker by 98%; engagement with traditional marketing forms increases the odds by 51% (Lin et al., 2012). Given this evidence, it may be concerning that a third of UK 11–18 year olds are estimated to be exposed to online alcohol advertising daily (Atkinson et al., 2011). Furthermore, it is claimed that social networks contribute to pro-alcohol environments and thus encourage drinking as they blur brand-specific promotional activity and user-generated content, integrating real-world and online activity which both normalise and promote drinking occasions (McCreanor et al., 2013).

Think points

What ethical responsibilities do alcohol marketers have in regard to social media sites they sponsor?

ADVERTISING RESTRICTIONS

Tobacco

The tobacco industry has faced increasing restrictions on promotion, especially advertising, since the 1960s as concerns about the health impacts of smoking and the impact of tobacco promotion on young people's decisions to commence smoking have been accepted by legislators (Brown and Moodie, 2009; Moodie et al., 2008). The industry, however, has a long history of denial, firstly of adverse health impacts, then of the impact of their promotional activity on primary demand among young people (Hoek, 2004).

While mass media tobacco advertising is banned in many countries, the industry responded to restrictions by developing other marketing techniques to attract and retain smokers that evade the restrictions placed on traditional mass media (Braverman and Aarø, 2004; Elkin et al., 2010). One example is the sponsorship of high profile sporting events until countries began to restrict, and then ban, this activity (Sparks, 1997). In other examples, these methods include advertisements at the point of sale, promotional allowances paid to retailers to facilitate product placement, promotions such as 'buy one get one free' ('BOGOF') and price discounts. In fact, in the US in 2008, price discounts, **coupons**, and retail **value-added promotions** accounted for 83% of all tobacco marketing expenditures (Eriksen et al., 2012).

The WHO's Framework Convention on Tobacco Control (FCTC) was introduced in 2005 (World Health Organisation, 2005) and banned all forms of tobacco advertising, promotion and sponsorship within its 168 signatory countries (Thomson et al., 2012). The USA is not a signatory due to the existence of the Master Settlement Agreement (MSA) between the major tobacco companies and most but not all of the individual US states (National Association of Attorneys General, 1998). The MSA included provisions for restricting advertising and promotional activity but stipulated that coverage of the MSA applied 'within any Settling State' (1998: 18). It also fails to provide explicitly for non-standard advertising; for example, the only mention of video games is within the context of video game arcades.

Unfortunately, only 5% of the world's population live in countries in which tobacco advertising, promotion and sponsorship restrictions apply (Freeman and Chapman, 2009), with evidence of aggressive promotional activity in developing countries (Sebrié and Glantz, 2006).

Alcohol

Actual regulation of alcohol advertising is currently a mix between self-regulation and statutory frameworks, depending on the country or state. In the UK, for example, the industry-sponsored Portman Group developed a voluntary code of practice in 1996. This code is complementary to the ASA's two advertising codes for broadcast or non-broadcast media, which also includes specific regulations for alcohol advertising. In the US, the regulatory framework is more complex, with both local/state regulation and federal-level regulation and self-regulation. In the self-regulatory domain, several beverage sectors themselves developed their own codes of practice (Federal Trade Commission, 1999). In fact, the Distilled Spirits Council (DISCUS), the Beer Institute and the Wine Institute all have codes of practice regarding their marketing communications that its member companies commit to accommodate.

Across the European Union (EU) there is also a mixture of statutory and non-statutory regulation (self-regulation) regarding the marketing of alcohol within and between member states. The only EU Directive that contains explicit regulation on the marketing of alcoholic beverages is the 'Television without Frontiers Directive' and this is the foundation for future recommendations (STAP, 2007).

Two common standards across the UK, US and EU regulations pertain to age and appropriate drinking behaviour. First, all regulatory entities emphasise the industry's responsibility for making marketing communications accessible to people of legal purchasing age (or above) only. Second, across all these governing bodies, marketing communications should not encourage immoderate, irresponsible or anti-social drinking (e.g. Beer Institute, n.d.; Distilled Spirits Council, 2011). Furthermore, some standards specifically state that advertising should not imply that the consumption of these beverages would lead to success, popularity or achievement (e.g. The Portman Group, 2009; The Wine Institute, 2011).

Regarding digital communications, guidance pertains to producer-sponsored websites and any third party website where the producer installs product placements. In all cases, again, the member is to ensure that materials are consistent with the provisions of the appropriate standard regarding age of the viewer and depiction of drinking activities.

In many countries, including Australia and the UK, the self-regulatory systems have been criticised as ineffective (Jones and Gordon, 2013). With this growing concern and potential for further scrutiny, it appears that the alcohol industry is taking steps to avoid the restrictions that the tobacco industry now faces. Analysis of tobacco industry document archives indicates that the alcohol and tobacco industries have worked together and used similar arguments to prevent or delay restrictions on marketing activities (Bond, 2010).

Potential impact of further alcohol advertising restrictions

Changing excess consumption habits is difficult. While marketing communication is only one of a multitude of influences on alcohol use, with parental and peer influences also impacting on decisions (Kinard and Webster, 2010), partial or complete bans on alcohol advertising have been estimated to yield benefits of at least AU$2.45 billion and AU$3.86 billion respectively in Australia alone (Collins and Lapsley, 2008). These figures, coupled with the estimated costs of alcohol-related harm noted above, have led to frequent calls for a ban on all alcohol advertising (Mart, 2011; Nicholls, 2012). Recent proposals to ban all alcohol advertising in South Africa (Jernigan, 2013) will no doubt be followed with interest.

Some writers stress the difficulty of effective enforcement of bans (Nicholls, 2012). This is, in part, due to a lack of a precise definition of what constitutes advertising or marketing communication: there are frequent references to alcohol consumption in popular music (Primack et al., 2012), and a study of popular movies found alcohol content in 83%, including 36% of G/PG-rated movies (Dal Cin et al., 2008), although this study does not report on whether responsible or irresponsible drinking was portrayed. Similarly,

75% of top rating US TV shows featured alcohol use (Brown and Bobkowski, 2011). While advertising in children's programmes is not permitted, approximately half of alcohol television advertisements appear during times when children are likely to be watching (Pettigrew et al., 2012).

Think points

We note calls, such as those from the WHO, to ensure that those who chose not to drink alcohol are supported and protected from pressure to drink (Hellman, 2011). We suggest that this, while a laudable principle, is extremely difficult to implement. What practical measures might be taken and what ethical dimensions might there be in these measures?

Mini case study 8.1   Industry-sponsored alcohol moderation campaigns

There are a number of factors that impact on the potential effectiveness of mass-media based **alcohol moderation campaigns**. First, there is ambiguity in brand-specific messages containing moderation messages, with the **conflict of interest** being noted by consumers; where advertiser motives are inferred as self-serving, attitudes towards the brand are negative, potentially impacting on brand purchase intentions. This effect has also been identified in broader corporate social responsibility (CSR) activity when such activity is seen as not congruent with perceptions of the company or brand image (Sen and Bhattacharya, 2001).

Additional issues relate to the nature of the creative platform around which advertisements are developed. Many 'responsible drinking' messages have been criticised firstly for the portrayal of non-drinkers as less fun than, or different from, the norm, and secondly for messages that are inconsistent with mainstream brand promotions. It is suggested that current anti-drink interventions centred on mass media are not only ineffective but may also actually be reinforcing current unwise alcohol consumption-related behaviour by accidentally reinforcing the pride taken by some segments of the population in drunken antics. Being seen to be behaving badly may become a badge of honour in the same way that the coverage of ASBOs has led some individuals into perpetuating their **anti-social behaviour** because of the attention it brings (Griffin et al., 2008).

Questions to consider

What ethical questions does the mini case study raise?

What action should be taken and by whom?

RECENT CONCERNS

Much of the regulatory framework regarding the marketing of harmful products is built around traditional mass media, and remains woefully inadequate for a modern communication age. As Hoek (2004) observes, regulators failed to appreciate the impact of new promotion vehicles. For example, until 2011, the British Advertising Standards Authority (ASA) only dealt with paid for advertising on the Internet, while all other forms of endorsement, including claims made on an advertiser's website, fell outside of their remit (Doherty and Terry, 2010), although the extended remit has already been criticised before it came into force as difficult to enforce and inadequate (Palomba, 2010).

Many industries, including those for harmful products, have expanded communications activities into Internet-based social media channels including Facebook and YouTube (Freeman and Chapman, 2010; Ribisl and Jo, 2012). The potential impact of such exposure may be stronger for social media and apps-based exposure due to the amount of control users have over what messages to attend to, how long to do so and how often they return to the material.

It has been suggested that there is a policy vacuum regarding Internet-based promotional activity that should be addressed to ensure that the intent of the WHO's FCTC and other legislation is applied to all communications channels (Elkin et al., 2010). We suggest that this policy vacuum is much wider than just the Internet, as we will now illustrate.

An upsurge of new technologies in the last decade has impacted on the ways in which young people socialise. Increasing penetration of mobile Internet and smartphones allow these devices to become portable 'virtual leisure spaces' where a wide range of applications and websites can be accessed free from adult oversight (Kim et al., 2013). Further, our own observational research indicates that children are often allowed to play games on adults' mobile phones, potentially exposing them to the marketing of age-inappropriate or harmful products. Furthermore, while these 'apps' and games are often accessing and making connections online (e.g. by posting to the Facebook profiles of the players), they fall outside the remit of regulators.

For example, regarding tobacco, there is considerable evidence that 'if smoking behaviour does not commence in the teenage years, it is unlikely to occur later in life' (Coombs et al., 2011: 655). First, it is suggested that sites with the highest appeal are 'devoted to smoking

Think points

Drawing on evidence from other sectors it is reported that children will choose foods advertised in games (Dias and Agante, 2011). Self-reported liking for non-healthy foods significantly increased when exposed to them in game content. Conversely, children playing healthier games selected more healthy snacks (Pempek and Calvert, 2009). Those with a less positive brand attitude have been found to show increases in the attitude towards a brand after playing games where the brand is placed (Mackay et al., 2009). We can thus assume that similar effects may be encountered when young people are exposed to messages regarding harmful products.

as part of culture, often with interactive features designed to create online discussion and pro-smoking communities' (Jenssen et al., 2009: 181). Furthermore, popular apps may thus become social currency in the way that conventional advertising has long been known to operate (Ritson and Elliott, 1999). High attention level is given to smartphone apps when in use, which may be for 80 minutes or more per day. Together, the evidence of the use of communication channels popular with young age groups where a harmful product is showcased, such as social media sites, electronic games, and phone apps, must be of concern.

Appeal of social media

There is a need to determine the extent, nature and potential impact of harmful product promotion, including those using new media channels not explicitly covered by current regulation. There is also a need to determine whether self-regulation by the marketing industry of promotional activity is adequate or whether additional regulation is warranted and if so what form it should take. In reducing risk the vulnerabilities of young people should be recognised, but in conjunction the rights of individuals to be active partici-pants in media culture and the wider society should also be recognised (Livingstone and Brake, 2010).

With regard to alcohol promotions, theoretical concepts are used to explain young people's involvement with alcohol promotional activity, particularly in social media. Self-identity is important to adolescents and young adults and alcohol is a key component of identity exploration (Ridout et al., 2012) and friendship practice (Niland et al., 2013). Adolescents and young adults frequently display alcohol content or references on social networking sites in order to appear 'cool' (Moreno et al., 2009) or to create a distinct identity for themselves (Sashittal et al., 2012). The potential for the creation of 'intoxigenic social identities' (Griffiths and Casswell, 2010: 525) gives rise to concern, as do claims that the alcohol industry leverages off self-identity formation to normalise daily alcohol consumption (Nicholls, 2012). This is of particular concern given reports of children lying about their ages in order to be able to access social media services (O'Keeffe and Clarke-Pearson, 2011).

In the longer term, those posting photos of excess alcohol consumption may have cause to regret their actions as some employers are searching social network sites of potential employees before making their final hiring decisions (Brown and Vaughn, 2011). Young women are noted as showing regret after posting or featuring in a posting by others of images of binge drinking occasions (Brown and Gregg, 2012). However, there is also some evidence that the perceived positive social effects outweigh any potential negative consequences (Niland et al., 2013), thus potentially negating any impact of risk-based alcohol harm interventions.

Use of cartoon characters

The use of cartoon figures to promote smoking in traditional media has been condemned due to their intrinsic appeal to younger age groups (Forsyth and Malone, 2010). While there has been no specific investigation of the effects of cartoon-based electronic games and phone apps, evidence from earlier campaigns raises cause for concern. The cartoon-based 'Joe Camel' campaign for Camel cigarettes which ran from 1988–1997 increased market share among both adolescents and under-aged smokers until growing criticism forced the parent company, RJR Nabisco, to discontinue it (Arnett and Terhanian, 1998). The MSA bans the use of cartoons 'in the advertising, promoting, packaging and labelling of tobacco products' (NAAG, 1998: 19). One cartoon-based app called Puff Puff Pass (also in Figure 2.1) depicts smoking as a fun activity to do with friends, going as far as translating this activity into a game-based activity.

Think points

Does the use of cartoon characters present specific ethical issues compared to other creative approaches?

Games and apps

In recent research, we focused on mobile phone applications ('apps') to assess the amount and nature of apps-based activity and to analyse its potential effects against the somewhat fragmented extant literature. This sector has received very little attention relative to other electronic platforms such as Facebook (Fournier and Clarke, 2011) in spite of high penetration. Smartphone penetration is high in most developed countries: 65% in Australia, 62% in the UK – higher than the USA at 56%, with all three countries expected to achieve approximately 80% penetration by 2017. Penetration among teenagers is estimated at more than 75% (O'Keeffe and Clarke-Pearson, 2011). One of the few studies of alcohol smartphone apps simply focused on the correctness of the blood alcohol concentration data provided in the apps (Weaver et al., 2013).

Satisfaction with the use of an electronic game or app does not necessarily result in behaviour change (Trautmann and Kröner-Herwig, 2008) and potential **boomerang effects** – whereby an electronic game or app may be enjoyable but result in reinforcement of existing behaviours – have also been noted (David et al., 2006). Simply presenting material in a game-like setting is insufficient to motivate their use (Forsyth and Malone, 2010) and there is evidence that enthusiasm for video games wanes in a short time period (Baranowski et al., 2012). However, one could argue that there is sufficient evidence of potential negative impact, i.e. encouragement of smoking, to warrant concern regarding pro-smoking app effects.

Recently, the use of mobile phone apps to promote a variety of pro-smoking apps has been criticised (Wakefield et al., 2003). It should be noted that there are also a variety of anti-smoking and smoking cessation apps available. Like social media, this medium also lacks explicit regulation, and due to its relative recency its effects and effectiveness as a positive or negative behaviour change vehicle have not yet been examined.

It cannot be assumed that the tobacco industry is directly involved in the production of the pro-smoking apps or other user-generated activity such as YouTube; new electronic media forms make it easy to hide the identities and affiliations of content providers (Sprague and Wells, 2010). However, previous studies have provided evidence of unofficial support. For example, employees of British American Tobacco (BAT) were found to be 'energetically promoting BAT and BAT brands on Facebook' (Freeman and Chapman, 2010: e8).

It is possible that some apps represent examples of designer ability as there are no messages within the apps. The Virtual Zippo Lighter app, for example, opens by swiping across the lid and lights with a turn of your thumb and the 'windproof' flame stays upright, no matter how the phone is moved. The app has attracted more than 15 million users and is credited with leading to a US$2.6 million investment in the designer, Skyrockit, to 'enhance what it calls its Mobile Entertainment Studio' (Kelly, 2011: 1).

While this app appears to indirectly promote smoking, it is also promoted by Zippo on the Internet (PR Newswire, 2013) as an alternative to the use of real lighters by fans at live concerts who hold them aloft and wave them during favourite songs or 'power ballads' (Metzer, 2012). The app was extended in 2013 to include a premium version which provides links and alerts regarding local concerts and performances (Google Play, 2013). The Zippo innovation was joined by a similar Bic Virtual lighter product in 2010 (Elliott, 2010), with a concert mode feature that allows the flame to be magnified (Jackson, 2010). We can only speculate on what impact this type of app might have on smoking-related behaviours.

Other more crude apps may be the work of design students hoping to attract the eye of future employers. For example, some apps allow users to smoke a virtual cigarette by holding the phone near their mouth. Others allow users to set cigarette brands or images as their phone wallpaper, and show a burning cigarette on their phone screen.

A motive for both app designers and downloaders/users may relate to the concept of 'forbidden fruit' whereby involvement with a product that many would regard as undesirable leads to excitement and pleasure (Sussman et al., 2010). A second motive related to the concept of forbidden fruit may be reactance. The theory of psychological reactance posits that perceived threats to personal freedom, such as being told not to engage in behaviours like smoking, may be resisted; individuals may be motivated to assert their freedom to make their own decisions (Ringold, 2002). This may result in the behaviour itself becoming more attractive and engaging and the undesirable behaviour becoming a means of re-establishing this freedom (Rummel et al., 2000).

Reactance effects explain not only why some anti-smoking interventions may not only be ineffective, but may also produce effects contrary to those intended; being advised not to smoke may have the opposite effect as young people seek to assert their independence from authority figures by smoking (Buller et al., 1998). This effect may be further reinforced by tobacco industry youth smoking prevention programmes that purport to delay decisions regarding smoking commencement until adulthood (Wakefield et al., 2006). Children and adolescents using these apps may thus perceive the use of pro-smoking apps as adult behaviour.

In recent studies (Eagle et al., 2013), we found that there was a surprisingly high number of pro-alcohol and pro-smoking apps available, particularly for Android devices, as shown in Tables 8.2 and 8.3.

Table 8.2   Availability and stance of Android and Apple iPhone alcohol apps

Stance	Android		Apple iPhone		Total	
	n	%	n	%	n	%
Anti-consumption/consumption reduction	47	22	14	21	61	22
Pro-consumption	168	78	53	79	221	78
Total	**215**	**100**	**67**	**100**	**282**	**100**

Table 8.3   Availability and stance of Android and Apple iPhone tobacco apps

Stance	Android		Apple iPhone		Total	
	n	%	n	%	n	%
Anti-smoking	156	47	37	77	193	51
Pro-smoking	137	42	9	19	146	39
Neutral	37	11	2	4	39	10
Total	**330**	**100**	**48**	**100**	**378**	**100**

Taking just the example of the tobacco apps, we compared the design principles advocated for persuasive strategy (Andrew et al., 2007) to compare pro- and anti-smoking apps. The key difference is in the use of conditioning to reinforce behaviour by pro-smoking apps, which would appear to be in breach of the spirit, if not the letter, of existing regulations. Both the quantity of pro-smoking apps and the extent of the use of conditioning strategies in pro-smoking apps to reinforce smoking behaviour are concerning. The precautionary principle noted earlier, coupled with evidence of the impact of smoking imagery in more traditional media, would appear to give grounds for tighter regulation of this type of activity. The mechanisms for this to occur appear to exist in the WHO's FCTC but support from countries not currently signatories and effective action by those that are already signatories has already been signalled as needed (Thomson et al., 2012). As will be discussed later, we would also include in this a review of the status of both Google and Apple as being more than passive carriers of these apps.

There is also a need for transdisciplinary and transcultural approaches to the development of appropriate future research programmes. These programmes should include investigation of which theory or combination of theories can be used to explain and predict the effects of both pro- and anti-smoking apps and other electronic media-based activity and whether, and in what way, demographic factors impact on the way this activity is used and its influence relative to other forms of communication (Watson et al., 2010).

CONTEXT-MULTIPLE INFLUENCES

Exposure to pro-smoking (or anti-smoking) messages via media channels needs to be seen in the context of other potential influences, such as family, friends and peer groups; where smoking is seen as normal and important to social identity, people are likely to smoke (Amos et al., 2006). Any attempt to use the same media channels to discourage smoking will be hampered by conflicting messages (Bernthal et al., 2006). Additionally, it has been recognised for more than two decades that, when there is a perceived conflict between injunctive norms (portrayal of what people ought to do) and descriptive norms (what people actually do), message effectiveness will also be hampered (Cialdini and Goldstein, 2004).

A range of potential pro- and anti-influences on behaviour is shown in Figure 8.1. Thus we would expect that using a pro-smoking app when family and social networks and possibly anti-smoking social marketing activity convey anti-smoking messages may not have a strong smoking initiation effect. Conversely, the use of a pro-smoking app may reinforce family and social perceptions of smoking being normal, i.e. social encouragement to start smoking or social discouragement to attempt to stop smoking. Thus future research into the impact of app-based pro-smoking messages should control for as many of these factors as possible.

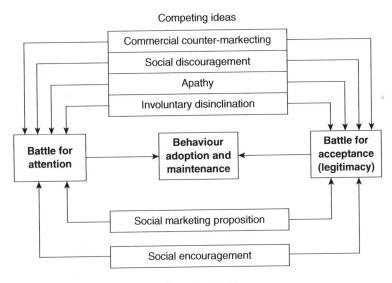

Figure 8.1   Competing ideas (Peattie and Peattie, 2003)

PRECAUTIONARY PRINCIPLE, LEGAL AND ETHICAL LIABILITIES

The Rio Declaration on Environment and Development suggests, under the 'Precautionary Principle', that 'regulatory policy should seek to prevent harm before it occurs, and that it should reject the insistence of regulatory targets that a never-ending quest for improved information should indefinitely postpone sensible regulatory measures' (Liberman and Heyward, 2008). And yet, there is sufficient evidence of potential harm to warrant action to be taken to restrict pro-tobacco phone apps and those that promote excess alcohol consumption.

If this type of activity constitutes stealth marketing via sponsored product endorsement of any kind, issues of industry and individual liability may arise. However, to date in the USA:

> Courts have regarded the Internet as being more like a 'common carrier,' such as a telephone company, rather than a medium, such as newspaper or television ... Legal challenges in the United States have been largely ineffective due to Section 230 of the Communications Decency Act, which states that 'No provider or user of an interactive computer service shall be treated as the publisher or speaker of any information provided by another information content provider,' thus effectively immunizing providers of interactive Web sites, such as YouTube from liability for third party postings. (Forsyth and Malone, 2010: 814)

Similar provisions apply in the EU, for example, Directive 2000/31/ Section 4 which 'shields intermediaries from liability unless they have notice of infringing content and fail to act on such notice' (George and Scerri, 2007: 10).

One may query whether Google and Apple can be regarded as mere passive carriers/ publishers of material created by others or whether an implied contract exists where apps are purchased.

Ethical dimensions

Both Google and Apple claim high ethical standards in their activity. For example, Google's Code of Conduct:

> ... is one of the ways we put 'Don't be evil' into practice. It's built around the recognition that everything we do in connection with our work at Google will be, and should be, measured against the highest possible standards of ethical business conduct. (Google, 2013)

Similarly, Apple's *Business Conduct: The Way We Do Business Worldwide* (2012) states:

> Apple conducts business ethically, honestly, and in full compliance with all laws and regulations. This applies to every business decision in every area of the company worldwide.

Apple's Principles of Business Conduct include: 'Honesty. Demonstrate honesty and high ethical standards in all business dealings'.

While they make these claims, their actions in accepting pro-smoking apps – and, in many instances, accepting payment for them – appear to be at variance with their claimed stance. Indeed, it has been asked 'Can an industry be socially responsible if its products harm consumers?' (Yani-de-Soriano et al., 2012).

Drawing on the ethics coverage in Chapter 1, under 'Deontological reasoning', the two organisations would have a duty to society to not knowingly take any action that might cause harm. Under 'Teleological reasoning', the consequences of actions, even if there was no intent to cause harm, should result in the two organisations revising their policies regarding which products to host via their apps stores.

Given the discussion above, it is necessary to assess the amount and nature of apps-based activity and to analyse their potential effects against the somewhat fragmented extant literature. From this, decisions regarding potentially effective strategies to combat negative influences, and strategies for the use of apps for positive rather than negative behaviour influence, can be made.

Targeting vulnerable consumers

The alcohol industry's marketing efforts have been characterised as 'exploiting youth and young adults through its niche marketing' (Mart et al., 2009: 1) and failing to stipulate the risks involved in alcohol consumption. Meanwhile, although direct advertising of tobacco products is now banned in many countries, concerns continue regarding the impact of smoking portrayals in entertainment media such as movies on young people (Dalton et al., 2009). These portrayals are seen as normalising tobacco use and portraying smoking as aspirational behaviour (Chapman, 2008).

Think points

Do the producers of television programmes or movies in which smoking is portrayed as normal behaviour have any ethical responsibilities? If so, what are they? Should this activity be regulated?

Table 8.4   Types of targeting strategies[1]

| | | PRODUCT | |
		Less harmful	More harmful
TARGET	Low vulnerability	e.g., Low-fat hamburgers to above-average income consumer target	e.g., High-interest rate credit card to suburban consumer target
	High vulnerability	e.g., Low-nicotine cigarettes to black consumer target[2]	e.g., High-alcohol content malt liquor to less than high-school educated consumer target

[1] References to product harmfulness and target vulnerability are to the perceptions of these factors. Also, both in reality could be conceived as having a continuum; however, for our purposes, each is divided into two categories.

[2] Some people would never consider cigarettes to be in a less harmful category because of the strong evidence of the harmful nature of smoking. However, we note that cigarettes can differ in their levels of harm (e.g., through a reduction in benzo(a)pyrene, the cancerous compound in tobacco smoke) and hence some types can be considered 'less harmful'.

Table 8.4 presents the conceptual framework developed to inform the understanding of the controversy over targeting (Smith and Cooper-Martin, 1997). These authors note that while it is true that there is concern about the marketing of harmful products to select segments of consumers, the criticism is exacerbated when targeting also involves 'vulnerable' consumers. Furthermore, the authors define vulnerability as a susceptibility to injury or to being taken advantage of by another person.

SUMMARY

In this chapter, we have discussed the adverse effects of harmful products, using the specific examples of tobacco use and of excess alcohol consumption. We have highlighted the inadequacies of existing regulation of marketing activity and the tendency of both the tobacco and alcohol industries to circumvent the intention of regulations by moving marketing communication activity into newer electronic media forms that are, as yet, largely unregulated.

We have also highlighted the appeal of social media for young people and the activity of alcohol marketers in particular in these spaces. Similarly, games containing overt or implicit embedded persuasive messages are widely used to convey both pro-alcohol consumption and pro-smoking messages, with the dominant strategy being to reinforce behaviour as acceptable.

Ethical issues relate not just to the industries who exploit these communication channels to reach young people, but also to providers of the apps such as Google and Apple.

Clearly, existing regulatory provisions are inadequate in minimising exposure to persuasive communication relating to potentially harmful products and, in relation to tobacco products, not in keeping with ongoing efforts to reduce smoking rates. For example, Thomas and Gostin (2013: 55) suggest an 'Endgame Strategy', that is, a strategy to reduce 'smoking prevalence to near zero levels' that could be used as a legal and ethical trade-off to increase public health and economic productivity. They suggest this may be achieved through placing a generational ban on tobacco use, and thereby nullifying discussions on the rights and wrongs of promoting tobacco products in apps; restricting tobacco content in products below an addictive threshold; and economic measures to reduce the supply or demand of tobacco products. While these courses of action are extreme, it is worth noting that some countries such as Australia may have a political environment suiting more forceful change than other countries, having already banned tobacco industry donations to political parties in addition to having a long-standing ban on tobacco promotion.

Case study   Gambling addiction and advertising

Problem gambling has a negative effect on the life of the gambler or the people close to him or her, including parents, friends, brothers and sisters, boyfriends or girlfriends, and others. It might be that someone's gambling is causing them to be unhappy, have less energy, fall behind at school, underperform at work, stress about money, or have arguments with family members and friends. If someone's gambling is causing any of these effects, it is considered to be problem gambling.

According to the UK's National Health Service (NHS), there may be as many as 450,000 problem gamblers in Great Britain. The anticipation and thrill of gambling create a natural high that can become addictive. The Internet has made gambling more accessible, allowing more and more people to do it from home. This is thought to be one of the reasons for the increase in the number of women gamblers (NHS, 2014).

There's also a link between gambling and alcohol abuse. Many gambling addicts are also addicted to alcohol. Rates of depression and attempted suicide among gambling addicts are around double the national average. Gambling addicts are also more likely to go to prison as a result of criminal activity. This is almost entirely theft and fraud.

Gambleaware.co.uk, a UK organisation that aims to promote responsibility in gambling, states that anyone can develop a gambling problem. Two of the things that seem to put young people at risk of developing a problem are a history of gambling in their family and the age they started gambling themselves. The earlier people start, the more likely they are to experience gambling-related problems later on.

In November 2013, Ofcom published a report on the volume, scheduling, frequency, and exposure of gambling advertising on British television. The report showed that there had been a 600% increase in gambling advertising in the UK in 2012 compared to 2006 – more specifically there were 1.39 million adverts on television in 2012 compared to 152,000 adverts in 2006. In 2005, the number of televised gambling adverts was 90,000 and rose to 234,000 by 2007, and 537,000 in 2008 (Ofcom, 2013).

The responsibility for overseeing that advertising of all products, including gambling, is appropriate falls to the UK's Advertising Standards Authority (ASA). According to the ASA, betting and gaming companies have been permitted to advertise across all media, but the introduction of strict content rules has ensured that they can only do so in a socially responsible way (ASA, 2014).

Among the key clauses, the rules state that advertisements for gambling must not:

1   portray, condone or encourage gambling behaviour that is socially irresponsible or could lead to financial, social or emotional harm;
2   be likely to be of particular appeal to under 18s, especially by reflecting or being associated with youth culture;
3   suggest that gambling can be a solution to financial concerns, an alternative to employment or a way to achieve financial security;
4   exploit the susceptibilities, aspirations, credulity, inexperience or lack of knowledge of children, young persons or other vulnerable persons;
5   link gambling to seduction, sexual success or enhanced attractiveness.

(Continued)

(Continued)

Despite the potentially harmful effects of gambling, a UK organisation has been established to raise funds through gaming operations to boost the revenue needed to promote various health and welfare issues of critical importance to the quality of life for British citizens. (The idea is based on Finland's Slot Machine Association whose goal is to raise funds through gaming operations to promote Finnish health and welfare – see RAY, 2014.)

The British Organisation for Gambling Online (BOGO) developed its online operations to offer entertaining and exciting games and services in a responsible manner. BOGO's entire proceeds are used for supporting British health and social welfare organisations as well as for the benefit of the country's war veterans. The aim is to continue to achieve excellent results in a highly responsible manner and thus secure funding for innumerable important projects and ventures. Around 800 organisations receive funding each year from BOGO.

Professor Mark Griffiths, of Nottingham Trent University, UK, argues that one of the possible reasons for this statistically significant increase in problem gambling could well have been the increased exposure to gambling adverts on television (Griffiths, 2013).

Questions to consider

How is this situation similar or dissimilar to those of alcohol or tobacco discussed in the chapter?

Which segments of consumers may be most vulnerable to BOGO's advertising?

Which segments of citizens may be most vulnerable if BOGO's advertising is restricted and the participation in its operations declines?

What are the major advertising and promotion issues to be resolved or monitored?

What are the policy implications regarding BOGO?

Further Reading

Anderson, P., Chisholm, D. and Fuhr, D.C. (2009) 'Effectiveness and cost-effectiveness of policies and programmes to reduce the harm caused by alcohol', *The Lancet*, 373(9682): 2234–46.

Borland, R. (2013) 'Minimising the harm from nicotine use: Finding the right regulatory framework', *Tobacco Control*, 22(suppl 1): i6–i9.

Burton, S., Dadich, A. and Soboleva, A. (2013) 'Competing voices: Marketing and counter-marketing alcohol on Twitter', *Journal of Nonprofit & Public Sector Marketing*, 25(2): 186–209.

Coombs, J., Bond, L., Van, V. and Daube, M. (2011) '"Below the Line": The tobacco industry and youth smoking', *The Australasian Medical Journal*, 4(12): 655–73.

Engels, R.C. and Koordeman, R. (2011) 'Do alcohol portrayals in movies and commercials directly affect consumption?', *Addiction*, 106(3): 472–3.

Fournier, A.K., Hall, E., Ricke, P. and Storey, B. (2013) 'Alcohol and the social network: Online social networking sites and college students' perceived drinking norms', *Psychology of Popular Media Culture*, 2(2): 86.

Freeman, B. (2010) 'British American Tobacco on Facebook: Undermining article 13 of the global World Health Organization Framework Convention on Tobacco Control', *Tobacco Control*, 19(3): e1–e9.

Thomas, B.P. and Gostin, L.O. (2013) 'Tobacco endgame strategies: Challenges in ethics and law', *Tobacco Control*, 22(supplement 1): i55–i57.

Wakefield, M.A., McLeod, K. and Perry, C.L. (2006) '"Stay away from them until you're old enough to make a decision": Tobacco company testimony about youth smoking initiation', *Tobacco Control*, 15(supplement 4): iv44–iv53.

Wakefield, M.A., Germain, D. and Durkin, S.J. (2008) 'How does increasingly plainer cigarette packaging influence adult smokers' perceptions about brand image? An experimental study', *Tobacco Control*, 17(6): 416–21.

References

Alcohol and Tobacco Tax and Trade Bureau (2012) *Program Summary and Budget Activity*. Washington DC: Department of the Treasury.

ASA (2014) *Gambling*. Available at: http://www.asa.org.uk/News-resources/Hot-Topics/New-gambling-advertising-rules.aspx#.U8fl55RdV8E (accessed 17 July 2014).

American Cancer Society (2014) *The True Cost of Smoking*. American Cancer Society.

Amos, A., Wiltshire, S., Haw, S. and McNeill, A. (2006) 'Ambivalence and uncertainty: Experiences of and attitudes towards addiction and smoking cessation in the mid-to-late teens', *Health Education Research*, 21: 181–91.

Anderson, P. (2009) 'Is it time to ban alcohol advertising?', *Clinical Medicine*, 9: 121–4.

Anderson, P., Chisholm, D. and Fuhr, D.C. (2009) 'Effectiveness and cost-effectiveness of policies and programmes to reduce the harm caused by alcohol', *The Lancet*, 373: 2234–46.

Andrew, A., Borriello, G. and Fogarty, J. (2007) 'Toward a systematic understanding of suggestion tactics in persuasive technologies', *Persuasive Technology*, 4744: 259–70.

Apple (2012) *Business Conduct Policy: The Way We Do Business Worldwide*. Available at: http://files.shareholder.com/downloads/AAPL/2524777024x0x443008/5f38b1e6-2f9c-4518-b691-13a29ac90501/business_conduct_policy.pdf.

Arnett, J.J. and Terhanian, G. (1998) 'Adolescents' responses to cigarette advertisements: Links between exposure, liking, and the appeal of smoking', *Tobacco Control*, 7: 129–33.

Atkinson, A., Elliott, G., Bellis, M. and Sumnall, H.R. (2011) *Young People, Alcohol and the Media*. York: Joseph Rowntree.

Australian Chronic Disease Prevention Alliance (n.d.) *Marketing and Promotion of Alcohol. Position Statement*. Available at: http://www.cancer.org.au/content/pdf/ACDPA/110930-Final-ACDPA-PS-Alcohol-advertising.pdf.

Baranowski, T., Baranowski, J., O'Connor, T., Lu, S.A. and Thompson, D. (2012) 'Is enhanced physical activity possible using active videogames?', *Games for Health Journal*, 1: 228–32.

Beer Institute (n.d.) *Beer Institute Advertising and Marketing Code*. Washington, DC: Beer Institute.

Bernthal, M.J., Rose, R.L. and Kaufman, P. (2006) 'When norms collide: Normative conflict in the processing of public service announcements', *Journal of Nonprofit & Public Sector Marketing*, 16: 21–39.

Bertholet, N., Gaume, J., Faouzi, M., Daeppen, J-B. and Gmel, G. (2011) 'Perception of the amount of drinking by others in a sample of 20-year-old men: The more I think you drink, the more I drink', *Alcohol and Alcoholism*, 46: 83–7.

Bond, L. (2010) 'Selling addictions: Similarities in approaches between Big Tobacco and Big Booze', *World Healthcare Providers*, 1.

Bouchery, E.E., Harwood, H.J., Sacks, J.J., Simon, C.J. and Brewer, R.D. (2011) 'Economic costs of excessive alcohol consumption in the US, 2006', *American Journal of Preventative Medicine*, 41: 516–24.

Braverman, M.T. and Aarø, L.E. (2004) 'Adolescent smoking and exposure to tobacco marketing under a tobacco advertising ban: Findings from two Norwegian national samples', *Journal Information*, 94: 1230–8.

Brown, A. and Moodie, C. (2009) 'The influence of tobacco marketing on adolescent smoking intentions via normative beliefs', *Health Education Research*, 24: 721–33.

Brown, J.D. and Bobkowski, P.S. (2011) 'Older and newer media: Patterns of use and effects on adolescents' health and well-being', *Journal of Research on Adolescence*, 21: 95–113.

Brown, R. and Gregg, M. (2012) 'The pedagogy of regret: Facebook, binge drinking and young women', *Continuum*, 26: 357–69.

Brown, V.R. and Vaughn, E.D. (2011) 'The writing on the (Facebook) wall: The use of social networking sites in hiring decisions', *Journal of Business and Psychology*, 26: 219–25.

Buchanan, J., Elliott, G. and Johnson, L.W. (2009) 'The marketing of legal but potentially harmful products and corporate social responsibility: The gaming industry view', *International Journal of Interdisciplinary Social Sciences*, 4: 81–97.

Buller, D.B., Borland, R. and Burgon, M. (1998) 'Impact of behavioral intention on effectiveness of message features: Evidence from the Family Sun Safety Project', *Human Communication Research*, 24: 433–53.

Chapman, S. (2008) 'What should be done about smoking in movies?', *Tobacco Control*, 17: 363–7.

Cialdini, R.B. and Goldstein, N.J. (2004) 'Social influence: Compliance and conformity', *Annual Review of Psychology*, 55: 591–621.

Collins, D.J. and Lapsley, H.M. (2008) *The Costs of Tobacco, Alcohol and Illicit Drug Abuse to Australian Society in 2004/05*. Canberra: Department of Health and Ageing.

Coltart, C.E. and Gilmore, I.T. (2012) 'The need for a global alcohol strategy: "upscaling the issue in a downstreaming environment"', *Clinical Medicine*, 12: 29–34.

Coombs, J., Bond, L., Van V. and Daube, M. (2011) '"Below the line": The tobacco industry and youth smoking', *The Australasian Medical Journal*, 4: 655–73.

Dal Cin, S., Worth, K.A., Dalton, M.A. and Sargent, J.D. (2008) 'Youth exposure to alcohol use and brand appearances in popular contemporary movies', *Addiction*, 103: 1925–32.

Dalton, M.A., Beach, M.L., Adachi-Mejia, A.M., Longacre, M.R., Matzkin, A.L., Sargent, J.D., Heatherton, T.F. and Titus-Ernstoff, L. (2009) 'Early exposure to movie smoking predicts established smoking by older teens and young adults', *Pediatrics*, 123: e551–8.

David, C., Cappella, J.N. and Fishbein, M. (2006) 'The social diffusion of influence among adolescents: Group interaction in a chat room environment about antidrug advertisements', *Communication Theory*, 16: 118–40.

Dias, M. and Agante, L. (2011) 'Can advergames boost children's healthier eating habits? A comparison between healthy and non-healthy food', *Journal of Consumer Behaviour*, 10: 152–60.

DiFranza, J.R., Wellman, R.J., Sargent, J.D., Weitzman, M., Hipple, B.J. and Winickoff, J.P. (2006) 'Tobacco promotion and the initiation of tobacco use: Assessing the evidence for causality', *Pediatrics*, 117: e1237–48.

Distilled Spirits Council (2011) *Code of Responsible Practices for Beverage Alcohol Advertising*. Washington, DC: DISCUS.

Dobson, C. (2010) *Alcohol Marketing and Young People: Time for a New Policy Agenda*. Canberra: Australian Medical Association.

Doherty, S. and Terry, A. (2010) 'Extension to the CAP Code - 1 March 2011', *Journal of Brand Management*, 18: 238–40.

Donovan, R.J., Fielder, L. and Jalleh, G. (2011) 'Alcohol advertising advocacy research no match for corporate dollars: The case of Bundy R Bear', *Journal of Research for Consumers*, 20: 1–13.

Eagle, L., Dahl, S., Low, D. and Mahoney, T. (2013) 'Troubling thoughts about tobacco promotion in the on-line environment', Academy of Marketing Science World Marketing Congress, Monash University, Melbourne, 17–20 July.

Elkin, L., Thomson, G. and Wilson, N. (2010)' Connecting world youth with tobacco brands: YouTube and the internet policy vacuum on Web 2.0', *Tobacco Control*, 19: 361–6.

Elliott, A-M. (2010) *BIC Lighter iPhone App Joins Innumerous Others on App Store*. Available at: http://www.pocket-lint.com/news/102230-bic-lighter-iphone-app-joins-innu-merous-others.

Eriksen, M., Mackay, J. and Ross, H. (2012) *The Tobacco Atlas,* 4th edn. Atlanta, GA: American Cancer Society.

Federal Trade Commission (1999) *Self-regulation in the Alcohol Industry: A Review of Industry Efforts to Avoid Promoting Alcohol to Underage Consumers*, Washington, DC. Available at: https://www.ftc.gov/reports/self-regulation-alcohol-industry-federal-trade-commission-report-congress (accessed 6 March 2015).

Federal Trade Commission (2013) *Cigarette Report for 2011*. Washington, DC: Federal Trade Commission.

Federal Trade Commission (2014) *Responsible Marketing of Alcoholic Drinks in Digital Media*. Washington, DC: Federal Trade Commission.

Forsyth, S.R. and Malone, R.E. (2010) '"I'll be your cigarette—Light me up and get on with it": Examining smoking imagery on YouTube', *Nicotine & Tobacco Research*, 12: 810–16.

Fournier, A.K. and Clarke. S.W. (2011) 'Do college students use Facebook to communicate about alcohol? An analysis of student profile pages', *Cyberpsychology: Journal of Psychosocial Research on Cyberspace*, 5(2).

Fournier, A.K., Hall, E., Ricke, P. and Storey, B. (2013) 'Alcohol and the social network: Online social networking sites and college students' perceived drinking norms', *Psychology of Popular Media Culture*, 2: 86.

Freeman, B. and Chapman, S. (2009) 'Open source marketing: Camel cigarette brand marketing in the "Web 2.0" world', *Tobacco Control*,18: 212–17.

Freeman, B. and Chapman, S. (2010) 'British American Tobacco on Facebook: Undermining Article 13 of the global World Health Organization Framework Convention on Tobacco Control', *Tobacco Control*, 19: e1–9.

George, C. and Scerri, J. (2007) 'Web 2.0 and user-generated content: Legal challenges in the new frontier', *Journal of Information, Law and Technology*, 2.

Google (2013) *Investor Relations. Code of Conduct*. Available at: http://investor.google.com/corporate/code-of-conduct.html.

Google Play (2013) *Virtual Zippo Lighter*. Available at: https://play.google.com/store/apps/details?id=com.moderati.zippo2&hl=en.

Gordon, R., Harris, F., Marie Mackintosh, A. and Moodie, C. (2011) 'Assessing the cumulative impact of alcohol marketing on young people's drinking: Cross-sectional data findings', *Addiction Research & Theory*, 19: 66–75.

Griffin, C., Szmigin, I., Hackley, C., Mistral, W., Bengrey-Howell, A., Clark, D. and Weale, L. (2008) 'Branded consumption and social identification: Young people and alcohol', ESRC End of Award Report, RES-148-25-0021. Swindon: ESRC.

Griffiths, M. (2013) *Expert Opinion: Has Gambling Advertising Helped Increase Problem Gambling in the UK?* Available at: http://www.ntu.ac.uk/apps/news/150964-15/Expert_opinion_Has_gambling_advertising_helped_increase_problem_gambling_i.aspx (accessed 17 July 2014).

Griffiths, R. and Casswell, S. (2010)' Intoxigenic digital spaces? Youth, social networking sites and alcohol marketing', *Drug and Alcohol Review*, 29: 525–30.

Hanewinkel, R., Sargent, J.D., Poelen, E.A., Scholte, R., Florek, E., Sweeting, H., Hunt, K., Karlsdottir, S., Jonsson, S.H., Mathis, F., Faggiano, F. and Morgenstern, M. (2012) 'Alcohol consumption in movies and adolescent binge drinking in 6 European countries', *Pediatrics*, 129: 709–20.

Hastings, G., Brooks, O., Stead, M., Angus, K., Anker, T., and Farrell, T. (2010) 'Failure of self regulation of UK alcohol advertising'. *BMJ, 340*: b5650.

Hellman, M. (2011) 'Studying young recipients of alcohol marketing-Two research paradigms and their possible consolidation', *Nordic Studies on Alcohol and Drugs*, 28: 415–31.

Hoek, J. (2004) 'Tobacco promotion restrictions: Ironies and unintended consequences', *Journal of Business Research*, 57: 1250–7.

Jackson, R. (2010) *BIC Lighter App Gives Concert Fans Flames Without Fluid*. Available at: http://phandroid.com/2010/03/04/bic-lighter-app-gives-concert-fans-flames-without-fluid/.

Jenssen, B.P., Klein, J.D., Salazar, L.F., Daluga, N.A. and DiClemente, R.J. (2009) 'Exposure to tobacco on the Internet: Content analysis of adolescents' internet use', *Pediatrics*, 124: e180–6.

Jernigan, D. (2013) 'Why South Africa's proposed advertising ban matters', *Addiction*, 108(7): 1183–5.

Jones, S.C. and Gordon, R. (2013) 'Regulation of alcohol advertising: Policy options for Australia', *Evidence Base*: 1–37.

Kelly, M. (2011) *Maker of Virtual Zippo Lighter Grabs $2.6M*. Available at: http://venture-beat.com/2011/07/11/skyrockit-zippo-funding/.

Kim, E., Lin, J-S. and Sung, Y. (2013) 'To app or not to app: Engaging consumers via branded mobile apps', *Journal of Interactive Advertising*, 13: 53–65.

Kinard, B.R. and Webster, C. (2010) 'The effects of advertising, social influences, and self-efficacy on adolescent tobacco use and alcohol consumption', *Journal of Consumer Affairs*, 44: 24–43.

Laslett, A-M., Catalano, P., Chikritzhs, Y., Dale, C., Doran, C., Ferris, J., Jainullabudeen, T., Livingston, M., Matthews, S., Mugavin, J., Room, R., Schlotterlein, M. and Wilkinson, C. (2010) *The Range and Magnitude of Alcohol's Harm to Others*. Fitzroy, Victoria: AER Centre for Alcohol Policy Research, Turning Point Alcohol and Drug Centre, Eastern Health.

Lee, G.A. and Forsythe, M. (2011) 'Is alcohol more dangerous than heroin? The physical, social and financial costs of alcohol', *International Emergency Nursing*, 19: 141–5.

Liberman, J. and Heyward, M. (2008) 'Use of the precautionary principle in the debate about emissions limits: A cautionary note', *Tobacco Control*, 17: 286–7.

Lin, E-Y., Caswell, S., You, R.Q. and Huckle, T. (2012) 'Engagement with alcohol market-ing and early brand allegiance in relation to early years of drinking', *Addiction Research & Theory*, 20: 329–38.

Livingstone, S. and Brake, D.R. (2010) 'On the rapid rise of social networking sites: New findings and policy implications', *Children & Society*, 24: 75–83.

Mackay, T., Ewing, M., Newton, F. and Windisch, L. (2009) 'The effect of product placement in computer games on brand attitude and recall', *International Journal of Advertising*, 28: 423–38.

Manning, M., Smith, C. and Mazerolle, P. (2013) 'The societal costs of alcohol misuse in Australia', *Trends and Issues in Crime and Criminal Justice*: Item 454.

Mart, S.M. (2011) 'Alcohol marketing in the 21st century: New methods, old problems', *Substance Use & Misuse*, 46: 889–92.

Mart, S., Mergendoller, J. and Simon, M. (2009) 'Alcohol promotion on Facebook', *The Journal of Global Drug Policy and Practice*, 3: 1–8.

McCreanor, T., Lyons, A., Griffin, C., Goodwin, I., Barnes, H.M., Borell, S. and Hutton, F. (2013) 'Youth drinking cultures, social networking and alcohol marketing: implications for public health', *Critical Public Health*, 23: 110–20.

Metzer, D. (2012) 'The power ballad', *Popular Music*, 31: 437–59.

Mohapatra, S., Patra, J., Popova, S., et al. (2010) 'Social cost of heavy drinking and alco-hol dependence in high-income countries', *International Journal of Public Health*, 55: 149–57.

Moodie, C., MacKintosh, A.M., Brown, A. and Hastings, G. (2008) 'Tobacco marketing awareness on youth smoking susceptibility and perceived prevalence before and after an advertising ban', *European Journal of Public Health*, 18: 484–90.

Moreno, M.A., Briner, L.R., Williams, A., Walker, L. and Christakis, D.A. (2009) 'Real use or "real cool": Adolescents speak out about displayed alcohol references on social networking websites', *Journal of Adolescent Health*, 45: 420–2.

National Association of Attorneys General (1998) *Master Settlement Agreement*. Washington, DC: National Association of Attorneys General.

NHS (2014) *Gambling Addiction*. Available at: http://www.nhs.uk/Livewell/addiction/Pages/gamblingaddiction.aspx (accessed 17 July 2014).

Nicholls, J. (2012) 'Everyday, everywhere: Alcohol marketing and social media—current trends', *Alcohol and Alcoholism*, 47: 486–93.

Niland, P., Lyons, A.C., Goodwin, I. and Hutton, F. (2013) "Everyone can loosen up and get a bit of a buzz on": Young adults, alcohol and friendship practices. *International Journal of Drug Policy*, 24: 530–7.

Ofcom (2013) *Trends in Advertising Activity – Gambling*. Available at: http://stakeholders.ofcom.org.uk/binaries/research/tv-research/Trends_in_Ad_Activity_Gambling.pdf (accessed 17 July 2014).

O'Keeffe, G.S. and Clarke-Pearson, K. (2011) 'The impact of social media on children, adolescents, and families', *Pediatrics*, 127: 800–4.

Paek, H-J. and Gunther, A. (2007) 'How peer proximity moderates indirect media influence on adolescent smoking', *Communications Research*, 34: 407–32.

Palomba, M. (2010) 'Think BR: The extended 'self-regulation' remit could spell trouble for advertisers and the ASA', *PR Week*, 18 October.

Parry, C.D., Patra, J. and Rehm, J. (2011) 'Alcohol consumption and non-communicable diseases: Epidemiology and policy implications', *Addiction*, 106: 1718–24.

Parry, C.D., Rehm, J., Poznyak, V. and Room, R. (2009) 'Alcohol and infectious diseases: An overlooked causal linkage?', *Addiction*, 104(3): 331–2.

Peattie, K. and Peattie, S. (2003) 'Ready to fly solo? Reducing social marketing's dependence on commercial marketing theory', *Marketing Theory*, 3: 365–85.

Pempek, T.A. and Calvert, S.L. (2009) 'Tipping the balance: Use of advergames to promote consumption of nutritious foods and beverages by low-income african american children', *Archives of Pediatrics & Adolescent Medicine*, 163: 633–7.

Pettigrew, S., Roberts, M., Pescud, M., Chapman, K., Quester, P. and Miller, C. (2012) 'The extent and nature of alcohol advertising on Australian television', *Drug and Alcohol Review*, 31: 797–802.

Pollay, R.W. and Gallagher, K. (1990) 'Advertising and cultural values: Reflections in the distorted mirror', *International Journal of Advertising*, 9: 359–72.

Portman Group, The (2009) *Responsible Marketing of Alcoholic Drinks in Digital Media.* Available at: http://www.portmangroup.org.uk/codes/alcohol-marketing/advice-and-guidance (accessed 6 March 2015).

PR Newswire. (2013) *Virtual Zippo Lighter Marks 10 Million Downloads With Launch of Premium Version* Available at: http://www.prnewswire.com/news-releases/virtual-zippo-lighter-marks-10-million-downloads-with-launch-of-premium-version-94098354.html.

Primack, B.A., Nuzzo, E., Rice, K.R. and Sargent, J.D. (2012) 'Alcohol brand appearances in US popular music', *Addiction*, 107: 557–66.

RAY (2014) Available at: http://www2.ray.fi/en (accessed 17 July 2014).

Ribisl, K.M. and Jo, C. (2012) 'Tobacco control is losing ground in the Web 2.0 era: invited commentary', *Tobacco Control*, 21: 145–6.

Ridout, B., Campbell, A. and Ellis, L. (2012) '"Off your Face (book)": Alcohol in online social identity construction and its relation to problem drinking in university students', *Drug and Alcohol Review*, 31: 20–6.

Ringold, D.J. (2002) 'Boomerang effect in response to public health interventions: Some unintended consequences in the alcoholic beverage market', *Journal of Consumer Policy*, 25: 27–63.

Ritson, M. and Elliott, R. (1999) 'The social uses of advertising: An ethnographic study of adolescent advertising audiences', *Journal of Consumer Research*, 26: 260–77.

Room, R. (1990) 'Thinking about alcohol controls', in R.C. Engs (ed.), *Controversies in the Addiction's Field.* Dubuque, IA: Kendall-Hunt. pp. 68–75.

Rummel, A., Howard, J., Swinton, J.M. and Seymour, D.B. (2000) 'You can't have that! A study of reactance effects and children's consumer behavior', *Journal of Marketing Theory and Practice*, 8: 38–44.

Sashittal, H.C., Sriramachandramurthy, R. and Hodis, M. (2012) 'Targeting college students on Facebook? How to stop wasting your money', *Business Horizons*, 55: 495–507.

Sebrié, E. and Glantz, S.A. (2006) 'The tobacco industry in developing countries has forestalled legislation on tobacco control', *BMJ: British Medical Journal*, 332: 313–14.

Sen, S. and Bhattacharya, C.B. (2001) 'Does doing good always lead to doing better? Consumer reactions to corporate social responsibility', *Journal of Marketing Research*, 38(2): 225–43.

Smith, N.C. and Cooper-Martin, E. (1997) 'Ethics and target marketing: The role of product harm and consumer vulnerability', *Journal of Marketing*, 61: 1–20.

Sparks, R. (1997) 'Tobacco-control legislation, public health and sport sponsorship', *Asia-Australia Marketing Journal*, 5: 59–70.

Sprague, R. and Wells, M.E. (2010) 'Regulating online buzz marketing: Untangling a web of deceit', *American Business Law Journal*, 47: 415–54.

STAP (2007) *Regulation of Alcohol Marketing in Europe*. Utrecht: National Foundation for Alcohol Prevention in the Netherlands.

Sussman, S., Grana, R., Pokhrel, P., Rohrbach, L. and Sun, P. (2010) 'Forbidden fruit and the prediction of cigarette smoking', *Substance Use & Misuse*, 45: 1683–93.

Thomas, B. and Gostin, L.O. (2013) 'Tackling the global NCD crisis: Innovations in law and governance', *The Journal of Law, Medicine & Ethics*, 41(1): 16–27.

Thomson, G., Wilson, N. and Hoek, J. (2012) 'Pro-tobacco content in social media: The devil does not have all the best tunes', *Journal of Adolescent Health*, 50: 319–20.

Trautmann, E. and Kröner-Herwig, B. (2008) 'Internet-based self-help training for children and adolescents with recurrent headache: A pilot study', *Behavioural and Cognitive Psychotherapy*, 36: 241–5.

US Department of Health and Human Services (2014) *The Health Consequences of Smoking—50 Years of Progress: A Report of the Surgeon General*. Atlanta, GA: US Department of Health and Human Services.

van Amsterdam, J. and van den Brink, W. (2013) 'The high harm score of alcohol. Time for drug policy to be revisited?', *Journal of Psychopharmacology*, 27: 248–55.

Wakefield, M.A., Flay, B., Nichter, M. and Giovino, G. (2003) 'Effects of anti-smoking advertising on youth smoking: A review', *Journal of Health Communication*, 8: 229–47.

Wakefield, M.A., McLeod, K. and Perry, C.L. (2006) '"Stay away from them until you're old enough to make a decision": Tobacco company testimony about youth smoking initiation', *Tobacco Control*, 15: iv44–53.

Watson, S.E.J., Vannini, N., Woods, S., Dautenhahn, K., Sapouna, M., Enz, S., Schneider, W., Wolke, D., Hall, L., Paiva, A. and André, E.. (2010) 'Inter-cultural differences in response to a computer-based anti-bullying intervention', *Educational Research*, 52: 61–80.

Weaver, E.R., Horyniak, D.R., Jenkinson, R., Dietze, P. and Lim, M.S.C. (2013) '"Let's get Wasted!" and other apps: Characteristics, acceptability, and use of alcohol-related smartphone applications', *JMIR Mhealth and Uhealth* 1(1): e9.

Wellman, R.J., Sugarman, D.B., DiFranza, J.R. and Winickoff, J.P. (2006) 'The extent to which tobacco marketing and tobacco use in films contribute to children's use of tobacco: A meta-analysis', *Archives of Pediatrics & Adolescent Medicine*, 160: 1285–96.

Wettlaufer, A., Cukier, S., Giesbrecht, N. and Greenfield, T.K. (2012) 'The marketing of responsible drinking: Competing voices and interests', *Drug and Alcohol Review*, 31: 231–9.

Wine Institute (2011) *Code of Advertising Standards*. Washington, DC: Wine Institute.

World Bank (2014) *GDP (Current US$) by Country*. Available at: http://data.worldbank.org/indicator/NY.GDP.MKTP.CD.

World Health Organisation (2005) *Framework Convention on Tobacco Control (FCTC)*. Available at: http://whqlibdoc.who.int/publications/2003/9241591013.pdf.

World Health Organisation (2010) *Global Strategy to Reduce Harmful Use of Alcohol*. Geneva: World Health Organisation.

World Health Organisation (2014) *Facts Sheet*. Geneva: World Health Organisation.

Yani-de-Soriano, M., Javed, U. and Yousafzai, S. (2012) 'Can an industry be socially responsible if its products harm consumers? The case of online gambling', *Journal of Business Ethics*, 110: 481–97.

9 Lifestyle, Health and Pharmaceutical Marketing

Mustafa Ebrahimjee, Stephan Dahl and Lynne Eagle

CHAPTER OVERVIEW

Lifestyle and pharmaceutical products, including both over-the-counter and prescription medication, present further potentially challenging issues to marketers and consumers. Using marketing of prescription drugs as a starting point, this chapter explores:

- ethical issues related to and effects of direct-to-consumer advertising
- drivers and effects of medicalisation of society
- lifestyle drugs, cosmetic surgery and medical tourism as effects of medicalisation

INTRODUCTION

Advertising and marketing of pharmaceutical products is a growing and important market. A range of medical products is routinely advertised and marketed. Frequently advertised products include dental and cosmetic surgery, alternative therapies and products such as vitamins and minerals. Advertising also extends to over-the-counter medication, and where allowed, advertising of prescription medication. It is thus not surprising that pharmaceutical companies spend a large amount of money marketing their products. In fact, the expenditure for marketing medicines surpasses the expenditure for research into new medicines (Brezis, 2008; Sufrin and Ross, 2008). In the United States in 2005 approximately $29.9 billion was spent on pharmaceutical marketing (Sufrin and Ross, 2008). While most of the expenditure was on free samples (56%) and on pharmaceutical sales representatives promoting the drugs directly to the physicians (25%), around 12.5% was direct-to-consumer (Barfett et al., 2004).

Promotion of medical products can be seen on a continuum, ranging from advertising related to invasive and potentially harmful products and procedures, such as prescription medication and cosmetic surgery, to products less likely to cause harm, such as alternative treatments and over-the-counter medication. Academic attention and public debate have been overwhelmingly paid to the marketing of serious medical products, especially the effects of direct-to-consumer advertising of prescription medication. The marketing of non-prescription drugs is less well researched, and subject to lesser public debate. However, it should be noted that alternative therapies and over-the-counter medication can also cause serious harm.

The remainder of the chapter first focuses specifically on advertising of prescription drugs and the evidence and arguments for and against this form of advertising. It then extends the debate to other types of medical products, including medicines used to treat non-urgent medical issues related largely to lifestyle, discussing the effects of pharmaceutical marketing and the evidence for a claimed '**medicalisation**' of society before concluding by raising issues connected to health tourism.

DTC ADVERTISING

Direct-to-consumer advertising (DTCA) of prescription drugs is only permitted in the US and New Zealand. In the US and New Zealand, advertising of prescription drugs is heavily regulated in an attempt to counteract some of the claimed negative effects of DTCA. Regulatory organisations in other countries have not permitted advertising of prescription drugs because of concerns related to the impact on public health, despite claims that DTCA has several positive public health functions.

It is important to note that the end user cannot freely purchase the advertised product in the case of prescription advertising. Rather, the purchase has to be approved by a gatekeeper, i.e. the prescribing doctor or health care professional. Moreover, prescription drugs are often complex, can have significant side effects, and may only be effective in specific circumstances.

Prescription medication thus presents a particular product group with a host of different potential ethical challenges. Table 9.1 gives an overview of the claimed benefits and disadvantages of DTC advertising.

Table 9.1   Benefits and disadvantages of DTC advertising

Advantages	Disadvantages
Education	Diminished time per patient
Informed discussion with patients	Unnecessary prescription of drugs
Increased diagnosis	Withholding information
Increased compliance	Misinformation

Education

The pharmaceutical industry has put forward the argument that DTCA performs a significant public health function through the education of patients. However, this view is not shared by the majority of medical professionals, who have been found to be more sceptical about the educational effects of DTCA. A larger proportion, yet only around 44%, of patients consider DTCA educational (Bozic et al., 2007).

A contested claim is that DTCA educates specifically minority populations, which are frequently underserved and have been associated with poorer health outcomes. While in a survey of doctors, a majority of them claimed that DTCA performs this function (Morris et al., 2007), other research indicates that ethnic minorities were less likely to be exposed to DTCA (Lee and Begley, 2010). Ethnic minorities were, however, more likely to be influenced by DTCA seeking formation and requesting the advertised medications, though numerous requests were then refused by the health care providers, raising issues of potential influence on the health care provider relationship with patients and/or health literacy and the clarity of advertising claims where requests were made for unsuitable medication. A similar result was obtained in a later study focusing on lower-income patients (Joseph et al., 2008). The study found people from a lower-income background were more likely to be persuaded by DTCA, more likely to make requests to doctors, and more likely to prefer being prescribed branded, rather than equally effective but cheaper, generic medications.

Several researchers have linked DTCA with patients seeking consultations, including empowering patients to seek help for embarrassing or rarely discussed conditions (Deshpande et al., 2004). However, this positive effect must be counterbalanced by the potential for oversubscribing.

Informed discussion

Proponents of DTCA have argued that because DTCA encourages information seeking by patients and discussion with health care providers, such discussions tend to be more informed and therefore medically more useful. However, it should be noted that discussions with health care providers typically focus on patients making specific requests, e.g. for the brand of medicines they saw advertised, or the broader category of medicine advertised (Parker and Pettijohn, 2003).

Increases in diagnosis

A further argument for DTCA is that it encourages patients to seek help for under-diagnosed conditions. One survey found that around 25% of patients who sought clinical advice following exposure to DTCA received a new diagnosis (Weissman et al., 2003). Some of these patients were found to suffer from conditions such as diabetes and high cholesterol, which require urgent treatment or where early treatment allows for a better prognosis and cost-savings for the health sector over a longer term.

Increased compliance

A further claim by proponents of DTCA is that it increases compliance rates amongst patients, a claim based on industry studies (*Prevention Magazine*, 1998). Noncompliance with prescribed medical regimens is a cause of unnecessary hospitalisations as well as representing a significant loss of pharmaceutical sales. However, the widely stated positive effect of DTCA has been challenged in an academic study investigating compliance to a drugs regimen to treat an asymptomatic chronic medical condition (high cholesterol) (Wosinska, 2005). Although the study found some evidence for compliance for the advertised brand, patients were also more compliant if they were treated with a competing brand. Thus, there was a spillover effect from the advertised brand to competing brands. However, overall the effects of the increase in compliance were found to be minimal, and the study suggests that a targeted unbranded compliance campaign may be more effective.

Diminished time per patient

Following patient requests for specific drugs where an advertised brand was unsuitable for the patient, health providers frequently have to spend a significant time of the allotted appointment time discussing why a particular drug may be unsuitable. This time can then not be spent discussing the underlying condition and other treatment options, thus resulting in a diminished length of time available during the allocated appointment time. A survey of health care providers found that many report spending significant time on rectifying overly optimistic marketing messages or explaining potential side-effects (Robinson et al., 2004).

Unnecessary prescription of drugs

A significant criticism of DTCA relates to unnecessary prescriptions or tests for conditions as a direct result of patient requests following exposure to DTCA. Wastage may result because of two factors. Firstly, requests not justified medically, and secondly, requests for branded medication rather than cheaper alternatives.

Results from studies regarding the first reason for unnecessary expenditure are surprising. One study amongst doctors found that nearly half the requests made by patients were unsuitable, but even more surprising 69% of these requests were granted, despite the doctor considering the request clinically inappropriate (Murray et al., 2003).

Similarly, an overwhelming majority (66%) of doctors reported that DTCA resulted in patients requesting and preferring branded medication over cheaper, generic medications (Friedman and Gould, 2007). This effect was more pronounced with people from lower economic backgrounds (Joseph et al., 2008). These findings raise serious concerns regarding the influence of DTCA on spending of medical budgets, and the potential for advertised medications being allocated more budget resources based on patient requests, with fewer resources available for treating other potentially more serious conditions.

Withholding information

Because of the desire of patients being prescribed the requested medication, some doctors fear that patients may resort to withholding information from their health care providers in order to get them to agree the need for a specific medication (Chaar and Kwong, 2010). Moreover, combined with over-the-counter medication being available and advertised, there are concerns that patients may attempt to self-medicate leading to sub-optimal outcomes. Of particular note in this category may be the availability of DTCA advertised medication via Internet sites, where patients are remotely diagnosed by a doctor and prescribed drugs. To date, no reliable studies have evaluated the impact of such sites and a potential connection with advertised drugs or the effects of this.

Misinformation

The final, but potentially most important point, relates to the information contained in the adverts. DTCA, as with most advertising, has been accused of an overly positive depiction of medical conditions and the role medication can play in alleviating an illness. A content analysis of DTCA found that the bulk contained false or misleading information. Based on a sample of 164 adverts for prescription and non-prescription drugs, 57% were potentially misleading and 10% were false – and only 33% contained factually accurate information (Faerber and Kreling, 2014). The same study did however point out that prescription drug advertising contained somewhat less potentially misleading (55%) and false claims (2%) than the less regulated non-prescription drug advertising examined (61% potentially misleading and 7% false).

Other forms of promotion

DTCA in relation to traditional media has been widely researched, not least because of the ethical and professional issues it raises as pointed out above. Specific concerns have been raised in relation to interactive and Internet-based advertising, for which there are fewer, or in some countries no, regulations.

Pharmaceutical companies have been reported to invest heavily in digital marketing (Hobson, 2010). As Internet-based media transcend boundaries, this raises the concern that online advertising aimed at a specific market, e.g. the US or New Zealand, will be accessible to a global audience. Moreover, drug companies have been reported to make extensive use of social media (Liang, 2011), with internationally accessible Facebook pages, Twitter accounts and YouTube channels.

Even in markets where there is strict regulation against the advertising of drugs to patients, companies have used alternative means to communicate with target groups. For instance,

Gilead, MSD, ViiV and Janssen Pharmaceuticals sponsor the 'Saving Lives' Charity in the UK (Saving Lives, n.d.). The charity is seeking to increase testing for HIV treatment – which is developed and marketed by the sponsoring companies.

In addition to reaching out to the consumers, the pharmaceutical industry has also long been a supporter of industry sponsored medical research. Concerns have been raised about the ethics of the relationship between research and commercial interests. In a recent review of independent versus industry sponsored studies, the review found that industry sponsored studies consistently find more positive results for treatment efficiency, reported fewer occasions of evidence of harm, and presented overall more positive conclusions (Bero, 2013).

Pricing

A specific area of concern has been pricing strategies used by pharmaceutical companies. This has been extensively debated in relation to the pricing of HIV drugs, but also includes other drugs for potentially life-threatening diseases such as malaria and other infectious diseases readily treatable in developed countries.

The issue of access to affordable medicine remains the subject of significant controversy. *Fire in the Blood*, a film released in 2013, raised the issue specifically in relation to HIV medication. The film reveals the efforts undertaken by pharmaceutical companies and governments to avoid making cheaper, **generic drugs** available to millions suffering from HIV in sub-Saharan Africa who are unable to afford expensive but lifesaving medication. Although substantial progress has been made in making treatments available in recent years (WHO, 2010), there is still a significant imbalance between people who can, privately or through medical cover, access lifesaving treatments, and for those unable to access medicines, and who, as a consequence of these pricing strategies, are predestined to die.

Think points

Discuss if direct-to-consumer advertising of prescription-only medicines should be allowed in your country. What are the likely effects on the health system? Do you think it is generally performing a beneficial role? Or should prescription-only medicines only be allowed to be marketed to intermediaries, e.g. doctors rather than consumers?

OTC DRUGS

Relatively less research is available on the effects of promotion of **over-the-counter (OTC)** medications, i.e. prescription-free drugs and alternative therapies. This dearth of research is somewhat surprising, given that OTC medications and alternative therapies are by no means necessarily harmless and can have serious medical consequences. Alternative and herbal medicines can interfere with a range of prescription medicines for serious conditions. For example, garlic supplementation can interfere with a range of medicines, for instance, by reducing the effectiveness of medicines used to treat blood clotting, tuberculosis and HIV as well as certain birth control pills (WebMD, n.d.). Moreover, the market for OTC medications is a large and growing one, worth an estimated $106.3 billion in 2017 (Visograin, 2013). Vitamins and dietary supplements are worth $23 billion in the US alone (Ng and Rockoff, 2013).

For OTC medications there is often small but limited evidence of efficacy available. As OTC medications have fewer regulatory guidelines and are frequently not subject to stringent medical tests, the lack of evidence of both benefit and potential harm is a potential issue.

Marketing for OTC medications is, however, relatively tightly controlled in many countries, for instance by the MHRA codes of practice in the UK (the so called 'Blue Book'), covering both traditional as well as online marketing communications.

Vitamins, 'health foods' and supplements on the other hand face fewer regulations, and advertising is less regulated. In the UK, the Advertising Standards Authority made several rulings in the past few years in which it upheld or partially upheld claims made by supplement and health food advertisers (see mini case study below).

While the EU has relatively strict guidelines regarding health claims made for supplements, many of these can still be considered misleading or can be misinterpreted. For instance, evidence from Canada suggests that many supplements use misleading claims, such as 'rich in antioxidants' (Temple, 2013), and many have a weak evidence base for the claims made. Similarly, in the US, an investigation into the claims made by health food supplements found that a 'large part of [their] marketing is based on claims that are blatantly dishonest' (Temple, 2010: 803).

It is noteworthy that claims of efficiency, or perceptions of efficiency, are not always restricted to marketing claims in advertising messages. Rather, brand names of medicines and supplements can also convey essential messages for consumers and subtly imply efficiency – although these are not regulated by the codes governing advertising. A study by Tasso and colleagues (2014) found that consumers attributed efficacy and had a reduced risk perception of medicines whose brand name suggested expected treatment outcomes (e.g. Dermosan for 'san' = healthy and 'dermo' = skin).

Mini case study 9.1   Vitabiotics menopause formula

Vitabiotics is a leading manufacturer of vitamins and health supplements in the UK. The company specialised in 'branded' vitamin sales, such as Cardioace, WellMan, PregnaCare, etc. In 2014 Vitabiotics ran a national advertising campaign for its menopause formulation. The advert stated:

> MENOPAUSE? This is not HRT. Many thousands of women have discovered the comprehensive daily support of Menopace micronutrients. Specially formulated by experts, it is ideal whether or not you are on HRT and can be taken for as long as required.

(Continued)

(Continued)

Following a complaint, the Advertising Standards Authority evaluated whether or not the advertisement breached advertising guidelines by firstly making a health claim that was not authorised under EU law, and secondly by implying efficacy through claiming the product was the 'UK's No.1 Menopause formula' and 'Voted No. 1 for the menopause'.

Following consultation, the ASA ruled that the advert did breach EU regulations for unauthorised health claims, especially by implying that the formula regulated or helped to regulate hormonal activity.

The second claim was not upheld, as the company provided data to back up the claims: the brand was the number one selling vitamin formula specifically designed for menopause support, and secondly, it was voted as the top supplement in a poll of Boots customers, and displayed this information graphically.

Questions to consider

Do you think it was right to partially uphold the complaint? Which arguments would you bring forward for a different decision?

Obtain a copy of the EC Regulation 1924/2006 – Nutrition and health claims made on foods – which was used in this case. Evaluate claims made by other companies in terms of how far they are likely to be confusing or misleading.

Visit the website for Vitabiotics and discuss the branding of the vitamin formulations based on evidence from the study Tasso et al. (2014).

MEDICALISATION

In addition to the specific ethical issues arising from the marketing of pharmaceutical companies, there is wider concern regarding the broad social effect pharmaceutical marketing activity has.

Specifically, it has been suggested that pervasive marketing of medications encourages the medicalisation of formerly non-medical conditions, while simultaneously diverting attention from non-drug options to achieve desired results. For example, medical marketing may encourage the use of medicines and alternative health products in an attempt to fight obesity, rather than encouraging dietary and lifestyle changes.

Medicalisation is the process through which previously non-medical human conditions and problems become defined, diagnosed, studied and treated as medical conditions. Obvious examples which have become heavily treated using drugs and surgery in recent years include obesity and erectile dysfunction, but may also include anxiety, depression and other minor mental health problems, as well as largely cosmetic and age-related conditions such as baldness and the menopause (Montagne, 1992).

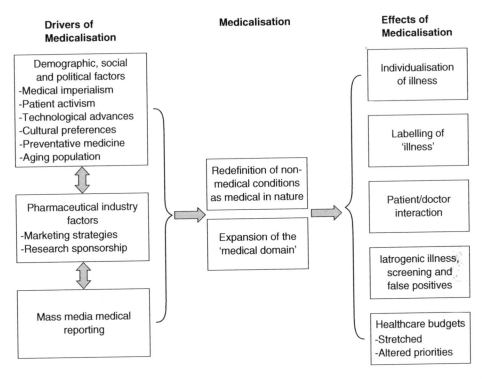

Drivers of Medicalisation

Demographic, social and political factors
-Medical imperialism
-Patient activism
-Technological advances
-Cultural preferences
-Preventative medicine
-Aging population

Pharmaceutical industry factors
-Marketing strategies
-Research sponsorship

Mass media medical reporting

Medicalisation

Redefinition of non-medical conditions as medical in nature

Expansion of the 'medical domain'

Effects of Medicalisation

Individualisation of illness

Labelling of 'illness'

Patient/doctor interaction

Iatrogenic illness, screening and false positives

Healthcare budgets
-Stretched
-Altered priorities

Figure 9.1   Interaction between pharmaceutical marketing and medicalisation (Brennan et al., 2010)

Mechanisms of medicalisation

Expansion of the medical realm, or medicalisation, occurs in two ways. Firstly, through the redefinition of previously non-medical conditions as medical in nature, as discussed in the previous paragraph. Secondly, medicalisation can occur by expanding the definitions and limits of medical conditions, covering a larger number of individuals classed as diseased or 'at risk', and thus necessitating treatment. For example, mild forms of irritable bowel syndrome have traditionally not been regarded as necessitating treatment (Moynihan et al., 2002). However, the pharmaceutical company GlaxoSmithKline engaged in an extensive marketing campaign, classed as a 'medical education programme', to 'create a new perception of irritable bowel syndrome as a "credible, common and concrete disease"' (2002: 325). Thus, marketing activity was specifically designed to expand a previously non-treated nor necessitating treatment condition to become perceived as a serious medical condition.

Drivers of medicalisation

In addition to the two processes through which medicalisation operates, Figure 9.1 gives an outline of the drivers and effects of medicalisation. As can be seen from the above, there are three main drivers of medicalisation: general societal factors, pharmaceutical industry factors and mass media medical reporting.

Medical marketing activity targets, and supports, all three of the driving factors:

1. *Pharmaceutical marketing* often specifically targets patient activism through marketing activities. This activity is widespread, and often disguised as 'patient education' programmes (Elliott, 2004). For example, Moynihan (1998) describes how drug companies targeted and funded patient groups in order to encourage uptake of osteoporosis treatment, despite limited evidence of its efficacy. More recently, pharmaceutical companies have been accused of engaging in 'astroturfing' (*New Scientist*, 2007). **Astroturfing** is the highly contentious public relations practice of artificially creating an organisation in order to give the impression of a grass-roots campaign, such as a patient activist group.

2. *Mass media reports,* such as popular health reports in magazines, on radio and online websites, are further important influencers of public opinion about health and well-being (MacKendrick, 2010). Extensive criticism has been levelled at media reporting and its influence on medicalisation. Media reporting has been criticised as dramatised and sensationalised, and creating fear of medical conditions. This sensationalised reporting is frequently followed by presenting an often one-sided 'miracle cure', with little or no discussion of side effects (Seale, 2003). Much of the media work has been linked to public relations activities by pharmaceutical companies, which included supplying expert opinion by scientists with financial ties to the discussed drugs or medication (Sweet, 2002).

3. *Direct pharmaceutical industry marketing strategies* are the third important driver of medicalisation. Seven strategies have been directly linked to pharmaceutical marketing, in addition to DTCA discussed above. The majority of these target doctors, though some of these strategies involve doctors passing on information or products to patients. **Physician-targeted marketing** involves visits from personal sales reps, free lunches and paying for travel expenses amongst other directly targeted measures (Brennan et al., 2010). **Detailing** involves providing explicit details about treatments and specifically spelling out the usefulness of medicines to doctors in the hope that they will prescribe the marketed products. Studies support the notion that detailing as a messaging strategy increases the chances of doctors prescribing drugs across a variety of different conditions. This includes relatively costly traditional forms of detailing through sales visits and information materials, as well as electronic forms of detailing (Gönül and Carter, 2010). The accuracy and balance of information presented to doctors by sales reps and in the information provided by pharmaceutical companies have been widely questioned (Brennan et al., 2010). A third marketing strategy used is that of **sampling**. Through sampling, medication samples are given to doctors to give to patients. There is evidence that sampling increases the likelihood of prescribing the sampled medication (Gönül et al., 2001). The fourth strategy used involves giving relatively minor gifts, such as cups, pens, free lunches or textbooks to students and medical practitioners. This practice has been widely criticised, and has been subject to policy scrutiny and regulation (Löfgren, 2013). **Educational events** supported by drug companies constitute a further means of marketing products to doctors and other stakeholders. These often involve inviting doctors or health care workers to specific presentations, often accompanied by hospitality, in order to present how drugs can be used to treat specific conditions. While funding for these events

has increased steadily, there is however some evidence that public policy interventions have started to limit the engagement and influence industry has on these events. Nevertheless, these continuing education events have been harshly criticised as essentially drug promotion events (Steinman and Baron, 2007). Medical professionals have, however, been found to deny being directly influenced as a result of attending such events (Steinman et al., 2010). A substantial marketing expenditure is connected with conducting and publishing medical research. Concerns about a positive bias of industry funded research have previously been noted (Bero, 2013). Moreover, pharmaceutical companies have been known to employ ghost writers and communication agencies unacknowledged to assist in the publication of medical research (Logdberg, 2011). Actual named writers, i.e. the scientists appearing to have written the research reports, have complained that they had little or no input into the study design, no access to data and only limited participation during the writing stage (Davidoff et al., 2001). The final strategy routinely used by pharmaceutical companies involves sponsorship in various forms. For instance, Sanofi Pateur MSD, manufacturer of an HPV vaccine, has sponsored advertising and patient information material relating to vaccination in the UK under the label '123 Against HPV'. The accompanying website presents HPV vaccinations as an effective means to prevent '70% of cervical cancers' and '90% of genital warts' (123 Against HPV, n.d), however it makes no reference to evidence that HPV vaccines are not cost effective in countries with comprehensive pap screening programmes (Wilyman, 2013).

Effects of medicalisation

The effects of medicalisation include individualisation of illness, labelling, a change of the doctor–patient relationship, the potential for **'false positives'** and increased demands on the health care budgets. These effects are thus largely consistent with those discussed in the previous section of this chapter relating to DTC.

Not surprisingly then, medicalisation has not been universally condemned. Rather, it has been argued that, similar to DTC, medicalisation gives more autonomy to the patients, specifically involving the individual with looking after their health and becoming more responsible (Verweij, 1999).

In a similar manner, labelling can be problematic when applied to non-medical conditions being labelled as medical conditions necessitating treatment. On the other hand it can also reduce the frustration and also uncertainty associated with a condition and bring hope of a medical solution to the problem (Montagne, 1992).

Similar to DTC, medicalisation can increase awareness, decrease stigma and encourage people to seek treatment and testing. However, such demands need to be balanced with over-assessments, unnecessary screening and creating illnesses or conditions through over-examination (e.g. false positives) or as a side effect of potentially unnecessary treatments (Moynihan et al., 2013). For example, mass screening procedures carry risks of significant false positives; for example, while it is possible to screen for prostate cancer using a blood test (PSA test), this test is highly unreliable, and mass screening would, most likely, produce large numbers of false positives. However, despite this medical evidence, the PSA test was presented in a flagship current affairs programme as a 'cheap and effective' way to screen for prostate cancer (McCartney, 2013).

LIFESTYLE DRUGS AND HEALTH TOURISM

A relatively novel aspect of increasing medicalisation is the emergence of widespread **medical tourism**. Cosmetic surgery and related medical tourism can be understood as an extension of lifestyle-based medical interventions offering relatively affordable medical solutions for conditions not normally considered a medical necessity.

Convergence of drugs and surgery

Following aggressive medicalisation of society, and a popularised notion of 'a pill for every ill', medication, and even surgical interventions, are increasingly seen as part of maintaining a healthy lifestyle (Busfield, 2010). For example, taking alternative treatments, such as vitamin or herbal supplements, is commonly associated with leading a healthy lifestyle, rather than being seen as resulting from malnutrition.

A notable form of this trend is so-called '**lifestyle drugs**'. Lifestyle drugs are medications used to treat non-medical conditions, often because conditions for these drugs have been medicalised. For example, the erectile dysfunction drug Viagra was originally limited to be used in cases of major dysfunction as a result of medical conditions, such as following prostate surgery. Contrary to the original indication, it is now also used for mild and temporary dysfunctions, such as age-related erectile dysfunction or simple nervousness, and it is also used as an enhancement drug during sexual intercourse (Conrad and Potter, 2004).

Increasingly the trend of lifestyle-related medical products also extends to smaller surgical procedures, especially cosmetic surgery. Traditionally surgical procedures were carried out based on medical necessity and expected health outcomes. In cosmetic surgery one's health may or may not be one of the factors taken into consideration when making the decision to undergo a particular procedure (Sullivan, 2001). Between 1992 and 2005 cosmetic surgery procedures carried out in the US increased by 725% (Liu and Miller, 2008), and continue to grow steadily (American Association of Plastic Surgeons, 2014). There is evidence that cosmetic surgery is increasingly being seen as an extension of health related practice, merged with commercial considerations. Consumers are increasingly evaluating the perceived return on investment of cosmetic surgery, such as perceived better career prospects. Thus the role of the cosmetic surgeon is changing into the role of a medical entrepreneur (Adams, 2013), selling an increasingly idolised and idealised body image.

Health tourism

In order to get the best value for money a growing number of people resort to seeking medical treatment, especially lifestyle related and cosmetic surgery, abroad (Connell, 2013). Reasons for seeking treatments abroad can range from easier access to certain medications as well as cost savings of private medical interventions performed abroad when compared to the home country, to availability of, or easier access to, certain procedures.

However, interventions specifically when performed abroad can be problematic. Many cosmetic interventions are not always uniformly regulated and so it is often difficult to assess the effectiveness or the safety of the interventions. This is particularly important as some of these interventions are being aggressively marketed with no mentioning of downsides, including marketing on social networks (Wong and Gupta, 2011). Of course, this is not restricted to surgery or interventions carried out abroad; for example, a recent review of the regulations of cosmetic interventions performed in the UK labelled one procedure as 'a crisis waiting to happen' (Department of Health, 2013: 5).

Moreover, countries like Malaysia and Thailand have become major hubs for medical tourism (Connell, 2013). Investment in state of the art facilities for medical tourists poses a potential ethical concern, as often even basic facilities are not made available to local (non-paying) citizens, raising serious concerns about uneven access to health resources. Furthermore, **health tourism** raises the medical concern of disrupting continuity of care. For instance, it may become necessary to have follow-up procedures in the home country, and medical tourists may experience side effects or later problems which cannot be easily dealt with during their stay abroad (Snyder et al., 2011).

SUMMARY

This chapter has highlighted the complexities involved in medical-related marketing. DTC advertising, for example, can both empower patients and misinform, it can both increase and decrease consultation times with doctors and so forth. In a similar way, non-prescription drug advertising and marketing of nutritional supplements has similar issues as DTC advertising of prescription-only drugs – from the potential to mislead to the potentially useful effects.

The wider social impact of medical advertising has further been linked to medicalisation, encouraging using drugs or supplements of formerly non-medical conditions, while diverting attention from non-drug options to treat these conditions. Medicalisation includes turning to surgical procedures, with significant issues especially in the case of medical tourism.

Case study   PrEP – medicalisation or prevention?

Modern HIV medications have transformed HIV infection from a death sentence to a chronic condition that is largely treatable. However, despite years of efforts to curb new infection rates, new infections are at an all-time high in many countries around the world. The rise in new infections is largely attributed to the message of persistent condom use becoming increasingly stale and largely ignored.

In the late 2000s, scientists started to speculate that potent medication given to treat patients infected with HIV could also be used to prevent infection. A series of human studies confirmed that taking a combination of two anti-HIV medications regularly largely prevented HIV infection. In fact, two European trails were so effective that they

(Continued)

(Continued)

were stopped early. Those that had previously been given a placebo were also offered the real medication, because results showed the efficacy of the intervention.

PrEP has been lauded that it 'could play a major role in bringing the HIV/AIDS epidemic to a close' (Nogrady, n.d.), and widely praised by the media and HIV prevention organisations. But some activists have voiced concerns. For example, writer and HIV prevention activist, Al Cunningham, argued that more targeted social marketing campaigns were better suited to address the HIV pandemic, especially considering the high cost of the PrEP. He further added that there is still inadequate access to medically necessary HIV treatment for those who need it in the US (and other parts of the world), and questioned how available PrEP would become for example in prisons and the military, where condoms are rarely made available. Moreover, he pointed out that condoms protect not only from HIV, but also a range of other sexually transmitted infections and pregnancy (Cunningham, 2014).

Veteran AIDS activist Sean Strub also voiced a similar, more critical view. In an interview with *The Huffington Post*, he commented that people 'like something that seems easy, something we can buy' (Shapiro, 2014). Moreover, new infections are highest in communities where people are less open about their sexuality, and so the argument goes, less likely to ask their doctor to prescribe preventive drugs, even if they can afford these.

Questions to consider

What do you think about PrEP: is it a viable prevention method? Or is it medicalisation?

Evaluate PrEP, considering the cost aspect of approximately US$30 per day, against other intervention methods, such as social marketing-based interventions. Which intervention methods should a government focus on?

Further Reading

Sage journal articles available for free at https://study.sagepub.com/eagleand-dahl include:

Brennan, R., Eagle, L. and Rice, D. (2010) 'Medicalization and marketing', *Journal of Macromarketing*, 30(1): 8–22.

Civaner, M., Sarikaya, O., Alici, S.U. and Bozkurt, G. (2008) 'Exposing nursing students to the marketing methods of pharmaceutical companies', *Nursing Ethics*, 15(3): 396–410.

Davis, J.J. and Meader, A. (2009) 'Beyond content analysis: Assessing fair balance in DTC pharmaceutical advertising', *Journal of Medical Marketing*, 9(1): 57–66.

Furr, L.A. (2004) 'Medicalization in Nepal: A study of the influence of westernization on defining deviant and illness behavior in a developing country', *International Journal of Comparative Sociology*, 45(1–2): 131–42.

Williams, S.J., Seale, C., Boden, S., Lowe, P. and Steinberg, D.L. (2008) 'Medicalization and beyond: The social construction of insomnia and snoring in the news', *Health*, 12(2): 251–68.

Wong, W.W. and Gupta, S.C. (2011) 'Plastic surgery marketing in a generation of "tweeting"', *Aesthetic Surgery Journal*, 31(8): 972–6.

References

123 Against HPV (n.d.) *123 Against HPV/About HPV Vaccination/What does HPV Vaccination Protect Against?* Available at: http://www.123againsthpv.co.uk/about-hpv-vaccination/what-does-hpv-vaccination-protect-against.html (accessed 4 December 2014).

Adams, J. (2013) 'Medicalization and the market economy: Constructing cosmetic surgery as consumable health care', *Sociological Spectrum*, 33(4): 374–89.

American Association of Plastic Surgeons (2014) *Plastic Surgery Procedures Continue Steady Growth in U.S.* Available at: http://www.plasticsurgery.org/news/past-press-releases/2014-archives/plastic-surgery-procedures-continue-steady-growth-in-us.html (accessed 4 December 2014).

Barfett, J., Lanting, B., Lee, J., Lee, M., Ng, V. and Simkhovitch, P. (2004) 'Pharmaceutical marketing to medical students: The student perspective', *McGill J Med*, 8(1): 21–7.

Bero, L. (2013) 'Industry sponsorship and research outcome: A Cochrane review', *JAMA Internal Medicine*, 173(7): 580.

Bozic, K.J., Smith, A.R., Hariri, S., Adeoye, S., Gourville, J., Maloney, W.J. and Rubash, H.E. (2007) 'The 2007 ABJS Marshall Urist Award: The impact of direct-to-consumer advertising in orthopaedics', *Clinical Orthopaedics and Related Research*, 458: 202–19.

Brennan, R., Eagle, L. and Rice, D. (2010) 'Medicalization and marketing', *Journal of Macromarketing*, 30(1): 8–22.

Brezis, M. (2008) 'Big pharma and health care: Unsolvable conflict of interests between private enterprise and public health', *Israel Journal of Psychiatry and Related Sciences*, 45(2): 83.

Busfield, J. (2010) '"A pill for every ill": Explaining the expansion in medicine use', *Social Science & Medicine*, 70(6): 934–41.

Chaar, B. and Kwong, K. (2010) 'Direct-to-consumer advertising: Australian pharmacists' experiences with non-prescription medicines', *International Journal of Pharmacy Practice*, 18(1): 43–50.

Connell, J. (2013) 'Contemporary medical tourism: Conceptualisation, culture and commodification', *Tourism Management*, 34: 1–13.

Conrad, P. and Potter, D. (2004) 'Human growth hormone and the temptations of biomedical enhancement', *Sociology of Health & Illness*, 26(2): 184–215.

Cunningham, A. (2014) *Viewpoint: No PrEP For Me!* Available at: http://www.pridesource.com/article.html?article=67428.

Davidoff, F., DeAngelis, C.D., Drazen, J M., Nicholls, M.G., Hoey, J., Højgaard, L. Horton, R., Kotzin, S., Nylenna, M., Overbeke, A., Sox, H.C., Weyden, M. and Wilkes, M.S. (2001) 'Sponsorship, authorship and accountability', *Canadian Medical Association Journal*, 165(6): 786–8.

Department of Health (2013) *Review of the Regulation of Cosmetic Interventions*. London: Department of Health.

Deshpande, A., Menon, A., Perri III, M. and Zinkhan, G. (2004) 'Direct-to-consumer advertising and its utility in health care decision making: A consumer perspective', *Journal of Health Communication*, 9(6): 499–513.

Elliott, C. (2004) 'Pharma goes to the laundry: Public relations and the business of medical education', *The Hastings Center Report*, 34(5): 18.

Faerber, A. and Kreling, D. (2014) 'Content Analysis of false and misleading claims in television advertising for prescription and nonprescription drugs', *Journal of General Internal Medicine*, 29(1): 110–18.

Friedman, M. and Gould, J. (2007) 'Physicians' attitudes toward direct-to-consumer prescription drug marketing', *Journal of Medical Marketing*, 7(1): 33–44.

Gönül, F.F. and Carter, F.J. (2010) 'Impact of e-detailing on the number of new prescriptions', *Health Care Management Science*, 13(2): 101–11.

Gönül, F.F., Carter, F., Petrova, E. and Srinivasan, K. (2001) 'Promotion of prescription drugs and its impact on physicians' choice behavior', *Journal of Marketing*, 65(3): 79–90.

Hobson, K. (2010, August 26). *Report: Pharma Digital Spending Growing — But Slowly – Health Blog – WSJ*. Available at: http://blogs.wsj.com/health/2010/08/26/report-pharma-digital-spending-growing-but-slowly/ (accessed 3 December 2014).

Joseph, M., Spake, D.F. and Finney, Z. (2008) 'Consumer attitudes toward pharmaceutical direct-to-consumer advertising: An empirical study and the role of income', *International Journal of Pharmaceutical and Healthcare Marketing*, 2(2): 117–33.

Lee, D. and Begley, C.E. (2010) 'Racial and ethnic disparities in response to direct-to-consumer advertising', *American Journal of Health-System Pharmacy*, 67(14): 1185–90.

Liang, B.A. (2011) 'Direct-to-consumer advertising with interactive internet media: Global regulation and public health issues', *JAMA*, 305(8): 824.

Liu, T.S. and Miller, T.A. (2008) 'Economic analysis of the future growth of cosmetic surgery procedures', *Plastic and Reconstructive Surgery*, 121(6): 404e–412e.

Löfgren, H. (2013) 'Drug promotion in Australia: Policy contestation and the tightening of regulation', *Australian Review of Public Affairs*, 11(2): 19–41.

Logdberg, L. (2011) 'Being the ghost in the machine: A medical ghostwriter's personal view', *PLoS Medicine*, 8(8): e1001071.

MacKendrick, N.A. (2010) 'Media framing of body burdens: Precautionary consumption and the individualization of risk', *Sociological Inquiry*, 80(1): 126–49.

McCartney, M. (2013) 'Screening propaganda: The television shows that gave harms second billing', *BMJ*, 347: f7643.

Montagne, M. (1992) 'The promotion of medications for personal and social problems', *Journal of Drug Issues*, 22(2): 389–405.

Morris Jr, A.W., Gadson, S.L. and Burroughs, V. (2007) '"For the good of the patient": Survey of the physicians of the National Medical Association regarding perceptions of DTC advertising, Part II', *Journal of the National Medical Association*, 99(3): 287.

Moynihan, R. (1998) *Too Much Medicine? The Business of Health and its Risks for you*. Sydney: ABC Books.

Moynihan, R., Heath, I. and Henry, D. (2002) 'Selling sickness: The pharmaceutical industry and disease mongering – Commentary: Medicalisation of risk factors', *BMJ*, 324(7342): 886–91.

Moynihan, R., Glasziou, P., Woloshin, S., Schwartz, L., Santa, J. and Godlee, F. (2013) 'Winding back the harms of too much medicine', *BMJ*, 346: f1271.

Murray, E., Lo, B., Pollack, L., Donelan, K. and Lee, K. (2003) 'Direct-to-consumer advertising: Physicians' views of its effects on quality of care and the doctor-patient relationship', *Journal of the American Board of Family Practice*, 16(6): 513–24.

New Scientist (2007) 'Astroturfing', *New Scientist*, 193(2590): 48.

Ng, S. and Rockoff, J. (2013) *Vitamins Become Growing Business for Consumer-Product Companies – WSJ*. Available at: http://online.wsj.com/articles/SB10001424127887324392 8045783620736243344816 (accessed 3 December 2014).

Nogrady, B. (n.d.) *PrEP: The New "Little Blue Pill" – Health & Wellbeing* Available at: http://www.abc.net.au/health/thepulse/stories/2014/11/27/4137351.htm (accessed 6 December 2014).

Parker, R.S. and Pettijohn, C.E. (2003) 'Ethical considerations in the use of direct-to-consumer advertising and pharmaceutical promotions: The impact on pharmaceutical sales and physicians', *Journal of Business Ethics*, 48(3): 279–90.

Prevention Magazine (1998) 'National survey of consumer reactions to direct-to-consumer advertising', *Prevention Magazine*.

Robinson, A.R., Hohmann, K.B., Rifkin, J.I., Topp, D., Gilroy, C.M., Pickard, J.A., and Anderson, R.J. (2004) 'Direct-to-consumer pharmaceutical advertising: Physician and public opinion and potential effects on the physician-patient relationship', *Archives of Internal Medicine*, 164(4): 427–32.

Saving Lives (n.d.) *Supporters/ Saving Lives*. Available at: http://www.savinglivesuk. com/?page_id=1855%22 (accessed 3 December 2014).

Seale, C. (2003) 'Health and media: An overview', *Sociology of Health & Illness*, 25(6): 513–31.

Shapiro, L. (2014, December 1) 'The most celebrated, mistrusted little pill in the world', *Huffington Post*, 1 December. Available at: http://www.huffingtonpost.com/2014/12/01/ prep-hiv-truvada_n_6185028.html (accessed 6 December 2014).

Snyder, J., Crooks, V. and Turner, L. (2011) 'Issues and challenges in research on the ethics of medical tourism: Reflections from a conference', *Journal of Bioethical Inquiry*, 8(1): 3–6.

Steinman, M.A. and Baron, R.B. (2007) 'Is continuing medical education a drug-promotion tool?: YES', *Canadian Family Physician [Medecin De Famille Canadien]*, 53(10): 1650–7.

Steinman, M.A., Boscardin, C.K., Aguayo, L. and Baron, R.B. (2010) 'Commercial influence and learner-perceived bias in continuing medical education', *Academic Medicine: Journal of the Association of American Medical Colleges*, 85(1): 74.

Sufrin, C B. and Ross, J.S. (2008) 'Pharmaceutical industry marketing: Understanding its impact on women's health', *Obstetrical & Gynecological Survey*, 63(9): 585–96.

Sullivan, D.A. (2001) *Cosmetic Surgery: The Cutting Edge of Commercial Medicine in America*. New York: Rutgers University Press.

Sweet, M. (2002) 'Press: How medicine sells the media', *BMJ*, 324(7342): 924.

Tasso, A., Gavaruzzi, T. and Lotto, L. (2014) 'What is in a name? Drug names convey implicit information about their riskiness and efficacy: Implicit information of drug names', *Applied Cognitive Psychology*, 28(4): 539–44.

Temple, N.J. (2010) 'The marketing of dietary supplements in North America: The emperor is (almost) naked', *Journal of Alternative and Complementary Medicine*, 16(7): 803–6.

Temple, N.J. (2013) 'The marketing of dietary supplements: A Canadian perspective', *Current Nutrition Reports*, 2(4): 167–73.

Verweij, M. (1999) 'Medicalization as a moral problem for preventive medicine', *Bioethics*, 13(2): 89–113.

Visograin (2013) *World OTC Pharmaceutical Market 2013–2023*. London: Visograin Research.

WebMD (n.d.) *Garlic: Uses, Side Effects, Interactions and Warnings.* Available at: http://www.webmd.com/vitamins-supplements/ingredientmono-300-garlic.aspx?activeingredientid=300&activeingredientname=garlic (accessed 3 December 2014).

Weissman, J.S., Blumenthal, D., Silk, A.J., Zapert, K., Newman, M. and Leitman, R. (2003) 'Consumers' reports on the health effects of direct-to-consumer drug advertising', *Health Affairs (Project Hope), Suppl Web Exclusives.*

WHO (2010) *More Developing Countries Show Universal Access to HIV/AIDS Services is Possible.* Available at: http://www.who.int/mediacentre/news/releases/2010/hiv_universal_access_20100928/en/ (accessed 3 December 2014).

Wilyman, J. (2013) 'HPV vaccination programs have not been shown to be cost-effective in countries with comprehensive Pap screening and surgery', *Infectious Agents and Cancer,* 8(1): 21.

Wong, W.W. and Gupta, S.C. (2011) 'Plastic surgery marketing in a generation of "tweeting"', *Aesthetic Surgery Journal,* 31(8): 972–6.

Wosinska, M. (2005) 'Direct-to-consumer advertising and drug therapy compliance', *Journal of Marketing Research,* 42(3): 323–32.

10 Tourism, Heritage, Cultural, Arts and Cause-related Marketing

Lynne Eagle, Tracey Mahony and Stephan Dahl

CHAPTER OVERVIEW

In this chapter, we will discuss:

- Ethical criticism of the tourism industry, including contributions to greenhouse gas emissions and other environmental issues
- Specific criticisms of specialised tourism activity
- The challenge of gaps between attitudes and behaviours in the tourism sector
- Ethical challenges within the arts and heritage sectors
- Ethical challenges within the cause-related sector

SECTOR OVERVIEW

Tourism, heritage and arts marketing are also facing increasingly ethical issues, such as potential contradictions between environmental protection and the profitability of tourism. Similarly, funding and the promotion of arts and heritage attractions can cause potential ethical issues, while non-profit organisations face ethical dilemmas such as what images to use to communicate the impact of extreme poverty or the use of stereotypical representations of cultural groups (e.g. when depicting African children in fund-raising campaigns).

We now examine each of these sectors in turn, looking at the ethical issues involved in each, and the major ethical criticisms that have been raised in relation to them.

OVERVIEW OF THE TOURISM INDUSTRY

The tourism industry is one of the largest in the world, being the leading source of foreign exchange in at least 38% of countries and the top five industries for exports in 83% of countries (Donyadide, 2010). Consider the following statistics from the World Travel & Tourism Council (2013):

- *GDP direct contribution:* The direct contribution of travel and tourism to GDP was US$2056.6bn (2.9% of total GDP) in 2012, was forecast to rise by 3.1% in 2013, and to rise by 4.4% pa, from 2013–2023, to US$3249.2bn in 2023 (in constant 2012 prices).
- *Employment direct contribution:* In 2012 travel and tourism directly supported 101,118,000 jobs (3.4% of total employment). This was expected to rise by 1.2% in 2013 and by 2.0% pa to 125,288,000 jobs (3.7% of total employment) in 2023.
- *Investment:* Travel and tourism investment in 2012 was US$764.7bn, or 4.7% of total investment. It was expected to rise by 4.2% in 2013, and by 5.3% pa over the next ten years to US$1341.4bn in 2023 (4.9% of total).

We will review the major criticisms of this industry in the next sections. These need to be considered both in terms of a balance between what might be held to be desirable against what is practical and achievable (Buckley, 2012), and a sustainability–profitability trade-off (Moeller et al., 2011).

Contribution to greenhouse gas emissions

Parts of the industry are subject to criticism, such as air travel due to use of fossil fuels and the emission of greenhouse gases by aircraft. It is claimed that tourism contributes approximately 5% of **anthropogenic** (i.e. caused by humans rather than natural events) climate change (Buckley, 2012) and 5% of CO_2 emissions' (Gössling, 2009). CO_2 accounts for 77% of global anthropogenic global warming (Hall, 2009). Thus it has been suggested that the industry's activity is incompatible with CO_2 emissions reduction targets (Cohen and Higham, 2011). If air travel is allowed to continue unrestricted, estimates of the contribution of aviation to global CO_2 emissions are a minimum of 15% by 2050 and possibly as high as 40% if other industries reduce their emissions (Cohen and Higham, 2011). Even if aircraft become more fuel efficient and biofuels become more widely available, growth in overall passenger numbers is projected to outweigh these gains (Higham et al., 2014).

The industry's response to these criticisms has itself drawn criticism, with accusations that it makes unrealistic claims over emissions reductions (Buckley, 2012) and also that it mismanages data in order to be seen in a positive light environmentally. 'Facts' presented only partially match scientific insights, for example:

(1) Air travel is energy-efficient. Globally, it accounts only for marginal emissions of CO_2.

(2) Air travel is economically and socially too important to be restricted.

(3) Environmental impacts exist, but technology will solve the problem.

(4) Air travel is treated 'unfairly' in comparison to other means of transport. (Gössling and Peeters, 2007: 405)

Further, it is also claimed that the industry has made only small changes to sustainability practices that lead to cost reductions – and then to accusations of greenwashing (Higgins-Desbiolles, 2008), a practice discussed initially in Chapter 2. Thus practices such as asking hotel guests to reuse towels may be motivated more by reductions in laundry bills than environmental concerns. While industry cannot ignore strategies to mitigate the contribution of tourism to climate change, government will need to act with the industry to agree appropriate and affordable strategies to reduce greenhouse gas emissions – not an easy or quick task!

The link between tourism studies and the interest of economies seems to have strengthened in the last decade due to the recognition of the industry's contribution to employment and overall GDP, yet there is no evidence of joint industry/government action as yet. Environmental policies have had little or no impact on the tourism industry at least partially because of a lack of consensus on what sustainable tourism involves and how the concept might be operationalised. This has led to sustainability activity being dependent on individual tourism operators and firms (Gibson, 2010).

Tourist responsibilities

Does the consumer have an ethical responsibility here? Research has indicated that airline passengers were, in principle, willing to pay to offset CO_2 emissions, but when voluntary schemes were introduced by airlines, they were not popular due to feelings that everyone should pay (Brouwer et al., 2008). The majority of air travellers see aircraft manufacturers and airlines themselves as being responsible for the effects of CO_2 emissions (Gössling, 2009). Less than 1% of outgoing holidays booked within the UK gave priority to the environment; most tourists do not consider climate change impacts within their travel plans (McKercher and Prideaux, 2011). In one UK survey, only 22% of respondents were willing to fly less (i.e. one holiday destination per year rather than the average of two) in order to help protect the environment.

Proposed eco-taxes have also proved to be extremely unpopular and there is now recognition that their implementation in a destination market may reduce that market's competitiveness and attraction as a destination relative to non-taxed destinations

(Holden, 2009). Part of the reason for the reluctance to change air-travel behaviours appears to be that the behaviour of highly mobile travellers is rewarded by aviation marketing activity which stresses and reinforces the status, self-image and both self and social identity of those who fly frequently and/or substantial air miles (Hibbert et al., 2013).

Some destinations have promoted themselves as carbon neutral. This does not imply that the destinations do not emit carbon – just that emissions are compensated for (offset) (Gössling, 2009). How well potential travellers understand this concept has yet to be determined.

Think points

What do you believe should occur to reduce the impact of tourism-related travel on greenhouse gas emissions? Whose responsibility should this be and how should success be measured?

Two of the bestselling guide books for independent tourists, the *Rough Guide* and *Lonely Planet* series (together selling some 6 million copies per year), now contain warnings about the impact of flying on global warming (Holden, 2009). What impact do you believe this will have on air travel decisions?

IMPACT OF TOURISM ACTIVITY ON ENVIRONMENT AND 'HOST' COMMUNITIES

Positive and negative impacts

Many authors note the combination of both positive and negative impacts of tourism activity, such as the support of conservation efforts through income for parks and reserves and the protection and management of wildlife habitats, against pollution of the atmosphere and waterways, and vegetation damage and injury, disease, distress and disruption of wildlife natural behaviours (Ballantyne et al., 2011b; Buckley, 2012), erosion through high visitor numbers to some sites and coastline damage from the construction of hotels and other facilities and the loss of cultural heritage in sites due to the adoption of 'external' cultures (Lansing and De Vries, 2007). Other issues include the unintended spreading of weeds through seeds dropped from tourist clothing (Pickering and Mount, 2010).

Carelessness rather than deliberate unethical behaviour by tourists can also damage the environments they visit, such as damaging corals while snorkelling or diving by careless placement of flippers (Krieger, 2012) or damaging fragile ecosystems while engaging in activities such as fossil collecting (Kim and Weiler, 2013). More serious damage may be deliberate – but not necessarily malicious – behaviour such as carving initials (and more) on ancient stonework, or leaving rubbish on sites – even on the slopes of Mount Kilimanjaro in Tanzania (Holden, 2009). Managing tourist behaviour and helping visitors to sites make the connection between their individual behaviours and the long-term impact on the sites is necessary.

More serious negative impacts occur as the result of brazen illegal activity, such as stealing parts of structures, for example, the deliberate theft of part of a wall mural at Pompeii in early 2014 (ABC News, 2014). Unfortunately this is not an isolated incident; the authors of this chapter have personally witnessed visitors to the site removing small pieces of stone from walls and similar behaviour at other ancient sites. This behaviour is of course far more than unethical – it is illegal! If all visitors were to behave in this way, the attraction of the sites would vanish very quickly. To protect sites from such damage, access is now often limited or visitors kept at a distance, such as at Stonehenge.

Mini case study 10.1   Wreck diving and illegal souvenirs

While snorkelling or diving on shipwrecks may have an obvious appeal, there are a number of potential ethical issues that may not be considered by wreck visitors until damage has been done to sites – and even then, visitors may not be aware of the damage they have caused. Among the issues that have been identified are:

- Removal of artefacts as souvenirs, not only cumulatively reducing the appeal of site visits, but also potentially disturbing other objects and destabilising the site, and accelerating deterioration of the wreck itself.
- Disturbing fragile marine ecosystems, and damaging corals and other marine growths.
- Exhaled air bubbles within a wreck which can accelerate corrosion.
- Damage to wreck structures through careless placement of anchors (Edney, 2006).

The first point is not only unethical – it is also usually illegal in most countries, although legal action is more likely to be taken for brazen looting for the resale of artefacts than 'causal' souvenir collection for personal pleasure. The next three are more likely to be due to carelessness, inexperience and a lack of knowledge – hopefully not from a wider lack of concern. What has not yet been determined is the best strategy to minimise these effects. With whom should the ethical responsibility lie – tourists, tourism operators or regulatory bodies – and who should pay, given the reluctance noted earlier of tourists to acknowledge, let alone respond to, other environmental impacts?

Specific sectors of the industry have been subject to criticisms, such as eco-tourism, defined as a 'form of tourism that focuses on experiencing natural sites, emphasises the appeal of environmental conservation and provides satisfaction with experiences for tourists attracted to natural sites' (Chiu et al., 2013: 2). Uncontrolled visitor numbers due to the increased popularity of sites may lead to the degradation of those sites – negating the reason for visiting them. Conflicts are evident when attempting to balance authentic visitor experiences and wildlife survival, especially when there are instances of humans being injured or killed by the wildlife they want to see (Burns et al., 2011).

As with **carbon offsetting**, evidence of tourists' willingness to pay additional fees to protect the environments they visit are somewhat mixed. Firstly, such fees are only acceptable if tourists agree with the purpose of fee collection and ultimate expenditure and the fees are seen as fair (Chung et al., 2011). General objectives are not favoured – many tourists appear to support fees only if there is a guarantee that the revenue generated will go towards the protection of a specific habitat (Casey et al., 2010).

In addition to the negative impacts noted above, tourism is also accused of failing to deliver on promises such as economic growth and a reduction of dependence on subsistence labour in poor communities (Higgins-Desbiolles, 2008). This is due in part to 'leakage effects' where many of the goods purchased by tourists are not produced locally, and may even be imported. Further, profits from hotels and other tourism-oriented services may not be retained locally but 'repatriated' to overseas owners (Lansing and De Vries, 2007). Lansing and De Vries suggest that more than '50% of tourism money paid either never reaches or leaks out of Third World destination countries' (2007: 82).

There is some debate regarding whether indigenous communities are more ecologically focused than non-indigenous communities, raising questions regarding stewardship and control (Fennell, 2008). As with many other facets in this debate, problems occur when sweeping generalisations are made; there are undoubtedly examples of extremely good indigenous environmental and tourism management initiatives – and of less successful ventures – but the same can be said for non-indigenous ventures!

Questions to consider

Is it ethical to sell souvenirs for a particular country, region or community if they are not manufactured locally and instead mass produced off-shore with revenue from the sales not being retained locally?

The tourist perspective and the attitude–behaviour gap impact in tourism

Research has revealed that people who may be active in environmentally protective behaviours at home may not continue their behaviour patterns while on holiday, and may even engage in behaviours that harm the environment in which they take their holidays (Juvan and Dolnicar, 2014).

One of the strategies proposed (and widely supported) for improving pro-environmental tourist behaviour is awareness raising, but there is extensive evidence that this type of strategy is unlikely to be effective (Miller et al., 2010). Lack of knowledge (i.e. 'information deficit') is cited as causing misconceptions and apathy (Bulkeley, 2000; Owens and Driffill, 2008) and is therefore suggested as an impediment to both attitude and meaningful behavioural change, not just within the tourism sector (Costello et al., 2009; Semenza et al., 2008). However a gap between reported **attitudes** towards environmental issues and actual behaviours is well documented in the literature (Lorenzoni et al., 2007; Ockwell et al., 2009;

Sheppard, 2005). Information is necessary, but does not of itself provide a sufficient condition for change behaviour.

Attitude change towards performing specific behaviours is necessary (Moser, 2010), but also complex. Attitudes are multi-factored and interact with a number of other key factors in influencing behaviour, especially **norms** (Fishbein and Capella, 2006) and **self-efficacy** (Fishbein, 2008). Attitude change alone is unlikely to be effective in achieving sustained behaviour change as a focus on individual voluntary change ignores social, environmental, structural and institutional barriers to behaviour change (Ockwell et al., 2009). Behaviour change, or the lack of it, may be driven by factors other than attitudes, such as financial constraints (Lorenzoni et al., 2007). A further barrier to change may also be a perception that changing one's own behaviour will not make any difference in the face of the magnitude of potential climate change impacts (Semenza et al., 2008).

The weakness of the '**information deficit**' concept in terms of a failure to recognise the complex interaction of values, experience and other factors in achieving (or not achieving) successful and sustained behaviour change is acknowledged in the extant literature, as are the inadequacies of many current theories in capturing and charting the interaction of these factors across different population groups (Lorenzoni et al., 2007).

The role of wildlife tourism

Wildlife tourism is claimed to have the potential for positive long-term impacts on environmental learning (Ballantyne et al., 2011a). Half of the US population and 36% of Australians visit zoos and aquariums each year (Ballantyne and Packer, 2011) and many more participate in organised wildlife watching. Visits to aquariums, turtle viewing tours and other similar operations such as wildlife-based tourism would therefore appear to offer potential for behaviour change programmes, something that is not currently an integral part of most viewing experiences. While close interactions with wildlife are frequently sought by tourists (Ballantyne et al., 2009), experiences are aimed at increasing knowledge and understanding – there is little evidence of deliberate attempts to influence actual behaviours that have environmental impacts (Jacobs and Harms, 2014; Powell and Ham, 2008). Evidence of positive outcomes from environmental education programmes aimed at children is claimed to be largely circumstantial, with few studies isolating 'the characteristics of programs responsible for measured outcomes' (Stern et al., 2013: 1). If the tourism industry is to take their role in changing people's behaviours towards more environmentally friendly actions, there is an ethical responsibility to recognise that activity such as this can build awareness and knowledge, but different strategies are needed to influence behaviours. The research base on which this might be developed also needs refinement.

Many wildlife tourism studies report, albeit somewhat vaguely, that behavioural change aspirations have predicted positive behaviour change potential but have focused on self-reported intentions: these are not good indicators of actual and sustained behaviours (Hughes, 2013), with the probability of socially desirable responses occurring declining, particularly when researchers collect data in face-to-face situations or questionnaires are completed in front of others (Risko et al., 2006). There is some evidence of heightened awareness of environmental issues in the short term in these studies, but enthusiasm declines over time and actual behaviour change is much lower than earlier declared intentions (Hughes et al., 2011); the impact on long-term behaviour appears small if it occurs at all (Lee and Moscardo, 2005). Post-visit resources have some promise, having been found in a single site study to be effective in encouraging people to reflect on their intentions (Hughes, 2011), although further research is needed to determine how far these findings can be generalised and what impact different forms of post-visit resources may have on short- and long-term behaviours. Furthermore, many tourists are ignorant of the environmental impact of their behaviours while travelling as tourists (Budeanu, 2007), let alone the impact of their everyday behaviours on the environment, or the potential impact of behaviour change (Miller et al., 2010).

Among the reasons for the lack of behavioural change is, firstly, this sector has focused since a seminal paper in 1957 on interpretation efficacy, with the aims of influencing knowledge and awareness of environmental issues, but also enhancing visitor experiences and thus their satisfaction (Tilden, 1957, cited in Skibins et al., 2012). It is only in recent years that the assumption of attitudes leading to behaviour change in this sector have been recognised, in particular that a general attitude about a thing has been proven in numerous studies to *not* lead to specific behaviours (Ham, 2009). Moreover, it is now recognised that interpretive and educational experiences will not change behaviours 'unless a specific behaviour is explicitly targeted and communication is designed to address attitudes relevant to that' (Stern and Powell, 2013: 35). A second barrier to change may also be a perception that changing one's own behaviour will not make any difference in the face of widespread problems (Semenza et al., 2008).

A further reason for the lack of behavioural change impact may be the failure to recognise the importance of social norms as a potential barrier to behaviour change. Perceived norms may override knowledge and even individual desire to change behaviour (Barr et al., 2011), particularly if this would be at odds with observed peer behaviour (Armitage and Conner, 2000; Minato et al., 2012). Norms may be injunctive or descriptive; the former focuses on perceptions of what behaviours would typically be approved or disapproved, the latter on perceptions of what behaviours are typically performed (Nolan et al., 2011). Decisions regarding which type of norms to stress can have unintended consequences for message effectiveness, for example, interventions that have attempted to use injunctive norms may have inadvertently reinforced descriptive norms and the belief that individual actions will not have any impact on the problem as noted by Semenza and colleagues above (Cialdini, 2007). The relationship between expected outcomes and self-efficacy judgements has been debated in the academic literature since Bandura's original (1986) work, with conflicting perspectives and entrenched views evident (see, for example, Williams, 2010; Yeo and Neal, 2013).

Does frequent flying for pleasure constitute a form of addiction?

While long-haul flights are usually carefully planned because of the cost and time involved, short-haul air travel such as within EU countries may be based on impulse – to such an extent that some authors suggest frequent short-haul air travel may be a form of behavioural addiction, also termed 'binge flying' (Cohen and Higham, 2011). The difference between this type of addiction and most other addictions is, of course, that there are no negative consequences for the 'addicted' individual who gets short-term pleasure from the experience. The negative impacts accrue to the wider community via environmental damage. These flyers do not recognise any ethical dimensions of their behaviour, let alone any responsibility to change their behaviours.

SPECIFIC TOURISM SECTORS

More than 50 subsets of tourism have been identified – obviously space prevents us from discussing all of them (Zenko and Sardi, 2014). Some tourism sectors have been specifically criticised. We briefly outline only a few of the main sectors to illustrate the type of ethical issues raised. (Note: aspects of medical tourism have been discussed in Chapter 9 and will not be revisited here.)

Volunteer tourism and justice tourism

The **volunteer tourism** sector involves tourists volunteering to take holidays where they work without pay, usually in developing countries, to help restore environments or work on projects aimed at alleviating poverty in groups or communities in which tourists base themselves (Higgins-Desbiolles, 2008; McGehee, 2012). There is evidence that host communities do not always find the experience to be positive, citing examples of arrogance, egoism and displays of perceived personal superiority by volunteers and a lack of understanding of infrastructure constraints (Sin, 2010). Closely related to volunteer tourism is **justice tourism** which aims at promoting mutual understanding between tourists and host communities that have encountered oppression in the past, such as Palestine (Isaac and Hodge, 2011).

Criticisms of activity in this sector centre firstly on ethical concerns that it may lead to exploitation of host communities, and replace (low paid) local labour with volunteers, increasing local unemployment levels. Additional criticisms focus on volunteers lacking an understanding of, or respect for, host communities – at times extending to attempts to spread personal beliefs among cultures whose beliefs may be very different (Smith and Font, 2014; Tomazos and Butler, 2012).

Other authors question whether 'selling' international volunteering activity as a commodity is ethical. This latter concern is due, at least in part, to a significant increase in university students or recent graduates undertaking volunteer tourism activities in order to experience other cultures and to help make a difference to the communities in which they may be based, often over short periods of time such as four weeks or less (referred to as volunteer vacations). Activity in this sector is estimated to be worth US$173 billion per year, with more than 1.6 million annual volunteer tourists spending upwards of US$2bn dollars globally during their volunteering activity, and the sector is expanding rapidly (Hartman et al., 2014; Tomazos and Cooper, 2012).

Drawing on the concerns about the impact of this activity and concepts similar to those within the much wider Fair Trade movement discussed in Chapter 4, Hartman notes that a set of Fair Trade Learning Standards has been proposed for those undertaking volunteer tourism. However, the impact of this on the behaviour of all participants in this activity has yet to be determined.

Think points

Are commercial organisations unethical when they try to make money from arranging for volunteers to travel to work on projects that are in themselves worthwhile? What are the ethical responsibilities of the organisations, the volunteers and the host communities?

Sex tourism

Sex tourism is often narrowly defined in the literature as travel where the main motivation is to seek commercial sexual relationships, although some of the literature has acknowledged that sex tourism isn't always commercially motivated, but can also involve romantic encounters and emotional involvement. Herold and colleagues (2001) have argued that sex tourism takes place on a continuum ranging from a (commercial) sex-only focus with minimum emotional involvement to a romance-framed motivation.

Research into sex tourism has been criticised as being largely focused on the tourist perspective, as well as focusing nearly exclusively on heterosexual tourists (Mendoza, 2013).

Similarly, popular media coverage (and some sex tourism research) has been criticised as depicting sex tourists as older, heterosexual, white European or North American men, who travel to less developed countries in order to take advantage of poorer women of colour and engage in sexual activities with underage partners (Williams, 2012). Fewer scholars have focused on female sex tourism, or indeed sex tourism in developed countries (e.g. The Netherlands, especially Amsterdam).

There are obvious serious ethical concerns where travellers take advantage of more lenient legislation or non-enforcement of legislation, particularly in Asian countries where enforcement and legislation are often seen as lax. Efforts to combat child sex tourism in these countries particularly require greater multinational coordination (Johnson, 2011).

Criticisms of sex tourism often focus on the exploitative nature of commercial sex seeking while on holiday. Because of the particular focus of sex tourism on developing countries in Asia and the Caribbean, some tourism researchers highlight ethical concerns related to sex tourism by framing it as a form of neo-colonial activity, which exploits the lower economic status of sex workers. A more differentiated view is taken by Mendoza (2011) examining gay sex workers in Mexico. He points out that sex work enables access to a previously unobtainable lifestyle, which some enjoy and find hard to give up.

A criticism of a significant proportion of work in the traditional tourism literature is the focus on commercial sex tourism, overlooking tourism where the focus is on consensual sexual encounters. For example, Andrewes and colleagues (2007) describe the highly charged sexual atmosphere in Spanish resorts, which gets no mention as part of the discussion about sex tourism. In what is referred to as 'outrageous tourism', ethical concerns arise from the common mixing of outrageous tourist experiences with other potentially hazardous substances such as intoxication with excessive amounts of alcohol (Munar, 2013) and reports of high sexual risk taking by travellers (Bellis, 2004).

Think points

Where does commercial sex tourism start? What are the ethical responsibilities of the tourism operators to encourage safe sexual environments?

Thanatourism/dark tourism

This is a sector that has received increased focus over the last two decades. **Thanatourism** (the term derives from the ancient Greek term for death) focuses on tourists' fascination with sites associated with death and dying, such as battlefield sites, war cemeteries and sites at which atrocities have occurred. The motivation is claimed to be 'the desire for actual or symbolic encounters with death, particularly, but not exclusively, violent death' (Stone and Sharpley, 2008: 578).

Closely related is **dark tourism** which is, according to Philip Stone, founder of the Dark Tourism Forum, 'the act of travel and visitation to sites, attractions and exhibitions which have real or recreated death, suffering or the seemingly macabre as a main theme' (Stone, 2006: 146).

Some critics feel that there is something unethical about this sector, but Stone points out that 'death has been an element of tourism supply, often through religious or pilgrimage purposes' (Stone, 2006: 147). We question whether the purpose of pilgrimage through the ages – including the current era – had the focus on death that Stone suggests.

We contend that this sector is not inherently unethical but that there are some ethical issues within it. Unfortunately, the academic literature contains many sweeping statements, such as 'Marketing efforts are often kept to a minimum because of ethical issues associated with such activities' (Nawijn and Fricke, 2013: 3). Again, we contend that whether marketing in this sector is unethical depends on the strategy used – many sites with wide historical significance are actively marketed such as the Catacombs in Paris and several other cities. (See, for example, http://www.catacombes.paris.fr/en/homepage-catacombs-official-website.)

Do these sites contribute to a deeper understanding of how and why these events and atrocities occurred? Are they a form of pilgrimage and a way of ensuring that those who died are not forgotten – or merely a form of tourism based on a macabre form of curiosity? Is it ethical to 'sanitise' historical battles via (bloodless) battle re-enactments which seek primarily to entertain viewers? It is probable that different visitor segments have different perspectives and reasons for visits.

The following is an indicative but not an exhaustive list of dark tourism tours and sites:

- Jack the Ripper tours (through the area in London where an unidentified serial killer committed several murders in 1888)
- Battlefield sites such as Waterloo in Belgium (site of the defeat of Napoleon Bonaparte in 1815) and Gallipoli, Turkey (site of an unsuccessful landing by Allied forces in 1915)
- Glencoe (a site in Scotland where members of the MacDonald clan were murdered in 1692, the excuse being that they had been slow to pledge allegiance to the new monarchs) (Knox, 2006)
- Concentration camp sites (WWII) such as Auschwitz (Poland), Dachau (Germany) and Buchenwald (Germany)
- Anne Frank's house in Amsterdam where a Jewish family hid from the Nazi forces for several years during WWII
- Ground Zero New York (site of the 11 September 2011 terrorist attacks)
- The Killing Fields of Cambodia where large numbers of people were killed from 1975 to 1979 during the regime of the Khmer Rouge
- Robben Island, South Africa, a former prison where political prisoners were held during the Apartheid era (a period, 1948–1994, in which racial segregation was rigidly enforced). Prisoners included Nelson Mandela who later became President of South Africa
- Catacombs (underground burial places) in several cities including Paris, Rome and Palermo

For more information on these, see the web-links in the supplementary resources that accompany this book at https://study.sagepub.com/eagleanddhal.

Think points

What are the ethical issues involved in thanatourism/dark tourism from the tourism marketer's perspective and from a visitor perspective?

Trophy hunting

Trophy hunting consists of shooting animals to collect trophies such as horns, antlers, skulls, tusks or teeth (or in many cases the whole head), usually for the purpose of display. (Palazy et al., 2013: 711)

Here we are not discussing wildlife poaching which is illegal. Our focus is on legal forms of wildlife hunting – not for meat but for obtaining trophies of the hunt. Trophy hunting has existed for hundreds of years: the tourism aspect of this activity came to the fore in the nineteenth century with safaris to African countries and to India for the purpose of shooting 'big game' such as elephants, lions and tigers. Today, wildlife safaris are more likely to be undertaken to observe and photograph game rather than to shoot them. However trophy hunting still exists and is subject to vigorous debate regarding whether it is beneficial or harmful to the conservation of species (Palazy et al., 2013). Is trophy hunting inherently unethical? Animal welfare groups argue that it is. A related debate is how to balance the significant revenue that trophy hunting brings to countries and regions, particularly in developing economies, against animal conservation efforts.

A particular concern is evident with the ethics of 'canned hunting', which involves the breeding of wildlife in captivity for the express purpose of enabling hunters to undertake mock safari-style hunts in comparative safety and the (almost) certainty of being able to shoot a beast. This activity extends beyond the native habitat of animals. Sports hunting ranches in the USA (and other places) are based on the importation and/or captive breeding of exotic animals such as African antelopes and gazelles for trophy hunting (Smith, 2013). Animal welfare groups have lobbied against trophy hunting in general and canned hunts specifically, and there are substantial lobbies to prohibit 'hunters' from taking their trophies back to their home countries (Nelson et al., 2013).

Think points

Would the proposed prohibition on taking trophies back to hunters' countries of origin lessen the demand for trophy hunting?

Is trophy hunting inherently unethical? Is canned hunting more unethical than free range hunting?

HERITAGE, CULTURE AND ARTS MARKETING

This is a diverse sector, encompassing visits to historical buildings such as castles or cathedrals, art galleries, museums, a wide range of performing arts centres, folklore sites, cultural centres that portray local songs, dances etc., food and beverage experiences.

Many of the issues in this sector are those we have already discussed in the wider tourism context. There are some issues that are particularly evident in this sector, mainly focusing on authenticity and a genuine reflection of historical events.

Uncritical visitors may accept the entertainment provided as historically accurate. Some may seek credible authentic experiences and resent experiences that do not deliver these – the search for authenticity may be the driving force behind travel decisions (Yeoman et al., 2007). Others, particularly those travelling with children, are claimed to be less concerned about authenticity than having an enjoyable time. This extends from sites visited to food consumed. Many ethnic dishes offered to tourists are simplified versions of their originals, such as versions of goulash served in tourist markets and which 'hardly resemble the traditional Hungarian dish' (Timothy and Ron, 2013: 102).

We have already noted concerns regarding 'sanitising' historical battle re-enactments. Consider now the authenticity of theme parks in historic settings such as castles throughout Europe, or 'pioneer villages' (for example, in the USA, Australia, New Zealand) or Neolithic settlements in many countries throughout the world. Focusing on just one medieval experience, the website for Warwick Castle, built in 1068, offers the opportunity to:

Experience one thousand years of jaw-dropping history at Warwick Castle; great battles, ancient myths, spellbinding tales, pampered princesses, heroic knights ... (https://www.warwick-castle.com/)

How authentic is the actual experience offered (friendly dragons are part of the entertainment)? Is total authenticity possible or desirable? At venues such as Warwick Castle no one is killed during jousting displays or displays of the use of medieval weaponry. Places such as this seek to combine entertainment with education and to give a broad, albeit sanitised interpretation of key aspects of the way sites such as this would have operated in medieval times (up to the fifteenth century).

How authentic is the experience of staying in accommodation in historical buildings that may be many centuries old? What décor style might be considered as authentic given that styles changed substantially over time? Most guests, if self-catering, will be glad of a modern kitchen, bathroom and central heating facilities rather than what might have been available at the time the building was constructed. Dances and songs also change over the years, as often they were passed from one generation to another orally. Does a modern interpretation make them less authentic? It has been noted that 'commercial' performances often keep traditional cultural performance abilities alive when otherwise the skills and knowledge would be lost (Kolar and Zabkar, 2010).

Ethical issues in this very broad sector relate to whether the experience is marketed as strictly authentic if it is not (referred to by some authors as a 'McDisney' experience, see Nelson, 2014).

Think points

Is there an ethical responsibility for tourism providers in this sector to provide in detail information regarding what may or may not be totally authentic?

OTHER ISSUES IN TOURISM

Accessibility/tourists with disabilities

Tourists with special needs generate approximately €166 trillion (£131.2 trillion) (Zenko and Sardi, 2014) and the number of people with disabilities wanting to travel is growing, raising the issue of what facilities and support could and should be provided for them (Navarro et al., 2014). Obviously, some sites will be inaccessible because of access limitations and some forms of transport may not be feasible. There are some substantial elements of the travel experience such as hotels where facilities – and any limitations such as an absence of lifts – need to be clearly communicated and staff need to be trained in how best to ensure that people with disabilities have satisfactory experiences with the hotel facilities.

Ethical issues occur when facilities are marketed as suitable for disabled people when they are not – Navarro and colleagues (2014: 818) note that 'the international symbol for disability is not trustworthy and quality certifications tend to be irrelevant', suggesting that the industry needs to address these issues.

CAUSE-RELATED MARKETING

Cause-related marketing defined

Cause-related marketing (C-RM) involves a marketer becoming involved in the promotion of a specific cause, such as the reduction of poverty, improvement of health and well-being within developing countries or the eradication of a specific disease. It appears to have been first adopted by American Express in the early 1980s when the organisation developed a campaign to help fund the restoration of the Statue of Liberty in New York; a percentage of AMEX credit card use value went to the restoration fund (Ponte and Richey, 2014). It is often subsumed under corporate social responsibility (Sheikh and Beise-Zee, 2011). By demonstrating social responsibility, consumer brand perceptions are expected to become increasingly positive (Moosmayer and Fuljahn, 2013). Positive effects from involvement in specific causes are claimed to include differentiation from competitors and improved brand positioning (Bigné-Alcañiz et al., 2012). There is evidence, however, that these effects are only positive when there is a perceived high fit between the cause being supported and the organisation or brand. Thus poor fits are likely to impact negatively, wasting resources and leading to customer cynicism (Eikenberry, 2009).

Activity to support C-RM initiatives is usually based on the allocation of a specific portion of a purchase price for a product or service being donated to the cause rather than a direct donation being sought, giving the activity alternative names including 'marketised philanthropy' and 'consumption philanthropy' (Nickel and Eikenberry, 2009). Less common are joint promotions with a commercial or not-for-profit organisation working with the selected cause. This can present challenges if the partner organisations do not fulfil their obligations, potentially damaging the reputation of the cause and other organisations associated with it (Liston-Heyes and Liu, 2013).

C-RM offers are usually restricted to a specific time period and a specific brand rather than featuring the parent marketing organisation (Vanhamme et al., 2012). While these types of activity appear to offer a win–win situation for sponsoring marketer and sponsored cause, there is some evidence that funds generated may be at the expense of established income sources for the cause (Smith and Higgins, 2000) and, unsurprisingly, while C-RM may offer both strategic and tactical benefits, it cannot overcome weaknesses in the marketing mix relative to competitors (Vanhamme et al., 2012).

Closely related is **celebrity philanthropy** whereby individual celebrities endorse specific causes and support various fundraising initiatives for the cause, with the attendant media hype focused as much on the celebrity as the cause itself (Nickel and Eikenberry, 2009).

Ethical issues here involve who decides on the cause to be supported, and on what basis that decision is made – the danger is that causes that are likely to attract high levels of media coverage are more likely to be supported than those which may not have the same media appeal, but which could potentially provide much greater benefits to individuals and communities. An example of a cause-related initiative, which received both marketer and celebrity endorsement but which did not achieve the intended positive outcomes, is outlined at the end of the chapter.

C-RM has been criticised in similar ways to greenwashing, particularly in relation to campaigns that appear to be based more on cynical attempts at image building rather than genuinely trying to help specific communities of causes (Brei and Böhm, 2011).

Think points

If a company uses C-RM to communicate that it is fulfilling its social obligations, what ethical issues might arise? What ethical challenges might exist in aligning with a high-profile cause versus one that is less well known?

Mini case study 10.2   Bundaberg Rum – flood relief in parallel with commercial gain

Consider the ethics of the following which has been adapted from the WARC case study *Bundaberg Rum: Watermark* – which won the award for creative effectiveness in the Cannes Creative Lions Awards, 2012.

In 2011, severe and unexpected floods hit parts of Queensland (Australia), flooding many areas including the town of Bundaberg. A significant employer in the town is Bundaberg Rum – their site was flooded. The company devised a programme with the stated aims of:

- Accelerating Queensland's recovery
- Raising money to help Queensland recover

The creative idea was to turn the highest point of the floodwaters into a symbol of resilience and a platform for rebuilding Queensland's community spirit. Taking the point at which the floodwaters peaked, the Watermark was a permanent reminder of where adversity was overcome.

The standard Bundaberg rum bottle was given a redesigned label, 'Watermark', for a limited edition run of production, declaring Watermark as 'The Mark of Resilience'. The initial production run sold out in seven days. Proceeds from every bottle went to help rebuild people's homes. Each bottle carried a message:

(Continued)

(Continued)

We crafted this limited edition bottle to mark the point where the floodwaters peaked. To mark the iron will of ordinary people. To mark those who gave to others when their own lives were gutted. To mark the spirit in every town on the hard road to recovery. We crafted this bottle to mark the day when people came together, shared a story and a laugh and kept going. Bundaberg Rum is contributing all its profits from this rum to flood relief. A limited edition we hope to never repeat.

Benefit concerts were organised to raise money for the flood relief appeal. Proceeds from the sale of Watermark at these concerts were also donated to flood relief. Following the concerts, Watermark was made available for purchase at bottle shops across Australia as well as online. When it went on sale, people queued up for over 96 hours to buy it (this is longer than people queued for the Apple iPad launch).

It is impossible to completely isolate Watermark's impact, but it should be noted that the Bundaberg brand improved across key measures for trial, conversion and consumption in Queensland for 2011, while the same measures declined or stayed flat for key competitors (Jack Daniels, Jim Beam) during the same period. AU$937,359 dollars was raised from Watermark profits for flood relief. Part of their donations went to better equip the Bundaberg disaster relief agencies – SES, police and fire brigade – for future emergencies. Proceeds for SES went to purchase them a new boat to handle area flooding. Bundaberg sales received a positive lift, increasing market share by 3.3% while Watermark was in the market, and Watermark was the dominant limited edition rum sold.

Question to consider

Is it ethical to make commercial gains out of activity such as this?

Mini case study 10.3   Betty Crocker Brand Aid (adapted from Ponte and Richey, 2014)

Betty Crocker ran a campaign in the USA called 'Win One Give One', combining a cause, a branded product and a celebrity, American children (and their mothers) and Rwandan school children. From 15 November 2011 until 31 July 2012, consumers who entered a UPC code from boxes of General Mills' 'Betty Crocker® Fruit Flavored Snacks' ('the branded product') would be registered to win an XO laptop provided through the 'One Laptop per Child' initiative by an organisation founded by Nicolas Negroponte ('the celebrity') with the aim of providing low cost computers for children in developing countries.

For every 100 UPC codes entered on the website, Betty Crocker pledged to donate one XO laptop to a child in Africa, with a maximum of 1725 laptops; a maximum of 259 laptops within the USA was stipulated. Sugar constitutes roughly half the total product weight, so the snacks cannot be considered a healthy option. A website gave details of the project, including photos of a Rwandan child and also advertising content. Criticisms have been levelled at the technology (including software bugs and cumbersome operating systems). Not all countries wanted imported laptops, preferring locally produced computers. The lack of consultation with local communities was also criticised. Evaluations in Peru found that children did not show any improvement in maths or reading.

Questions to consider

Was it ethical to promote the support of a cause in the way that occurred?

What ethical issues arise in relation to the pairing of a product that could be deemed by many to not be a healthy snack food choice because of its high sugar content?

SUMMARY

The discussion in this chapter has highlighted some major issues relating to the marketing and management of a range of tourism sectors. Whilst the chapter has suggested that the implied criticism of several tourism sectors as being inherently unethical is unfair, we have acknowledged that ethical issues do occur in them, as they do in many other marketing sectors. The tourism industry has not been responsive to criticisms of the negative impact of tourist activity such as the impact of air travel on greenhouse gas emissions. Continued failure to address this and other ethical challenges may result in the industry having change forced on them rather than being able to co-create solutions with other stakeholders.

Similarly, cause-related marketing, while not of itself unethical, does present some ethical challenges that need to be addressed.

As in other areas of marketing discussed in earlier chapters, some of the issues we have discussed in this chapter have no simple solution as they have significant economic, contextual and cultural dimensions that make their resolution difficult.

Case study   PlayPumps

This case examines an unsuccessful cause-related marketing initiative, 'PlayPumps'. The case is based on Saunders and Borland (2013).

(Continued)

(Continued)

Access to clean and safe water supplies for drinking and sanitation has long been recognised as a basic human right, yet large numbers of people within developing countries do not have this access. Past initiatives have involved the installation of simple hand-powered pumps at village or small community levels, funded largely through cause-related marketing and supported by celebrities.

In the late 1980s, an alternative technology was identified, whereby the collective power of children playing on a merry-go-round ('PlayPumps') would raise water to an elevated storage tank that would then supply water for the village or community.

The concept was visually appealing and celebrity philanthropists and cause-related marketing activity supported fundraising initiatives to install pumps, particularly within developing African countries. Ongoing funding for pump maintenance was intended to be provided from the sale of advertisements on the storage tanks. Claims such as being able to bring clean water to 10 million people by 2010 were made, but by 2010 it was evident that not only was the target far from being met, but there were also problems with the PlayPump technology itself.

The main faults identified were that:

- The pumps did not pump water at the rate claimed by their manufacturers – in fact, children would have to play for 27 hours a day to pump sufficient water to cover the minimum water required per person per day within a village or community. There is some debate as to whether the outcomes of the performance of the pumps were deliberately exaggerated in order to build hype and publicity for the project. It is surprising that the effectiveness of PlayPumps in delivering the claimed amount of water was not questioned prior to the installation project commencing.

- The design of the PlayPumps also made it difficult for adults to use, with health and safety issues evident in prolonged use, yet the need for adults to supplement or replace child activity does not appear to have been a consideration. Children themselves complained of tiredness and dizziness through prolonged 'play' on the pumps.

- No research was conducted on the effectiveness of the first sites to be established before attempts were made to expand the network of PlayPumps. Had this occurred, some of the subsequent problems may have been prevented. The drive to expand the network of sites also led to the selection of some locations that were not suitable for the technology.

- Existing working hand pumps were removed and replaced by PlayPumps without community consultation or consent, leaving communities with less efficient water supply facilities than were available previously with hand pumps alone. Hand pumps were cheaper to install and operate than PlayPumps, leaving one critic to suggest that in fact 'PlayPumps were a solution to a non-existent problem' (Saunders and Borland, 2013: 328).

- Little advertising support was gained due to the remote location of many of the pumps – and there were concerns about tobacco and alcohol advertisers buying space in some locations.

- The pumps were subject to maintenance problems that were far more time consuming and expensive to repair than the old hand pumps, often meaning that villagers had to travel considerable distances to other communities for water – often creating inter-community tensions and negatively impacting on some small scale food growing.

In 2010, growing criticism of the initiative led to withdrawal of support for the project and the transfer of remaining assets to an organisation, Water for People, which had a long track record of water provision within the countries impacted. Celebrity support ceased, as did fundraising events and initiatives. Some media reports labelled the initiative 'a marketing-driven sham' (Saunders and Borland, 2013: 329).

Water for People have publicly stated that PlayPumps cannot provide water for an entire community and would only be installed as a supplementary water source alongside more effective general sources – such as hand pumps – and only if communities specifically requested the installation of a PlayPump. They have voiced concern regarding the costs of installing and maintaining PlayPumps, and while they have been able to make some design modifications and train local people in repair and maintenance skills, the long-term viability of the pumps remains in doubt (Water for People, 2013).

Saunders and Borland suggest that 'the needs of the poor were conveniently defined in terms of the emotional needs of celebrities and consumers and not in terms of the people's right to access a clean, sustainable source of water' (2013: 331).

Questions to consider

Do you agree with Saunders and Borland's statement?

What lessons can be learned from the PlayPumps experience?

Further Reading

Sage journal articles available for free at https://study.sagepub.com/eagleand dahl include:

Higham, J.E., Cohen, S.A. and Cavaliere, C.T. (2014) 'Climate change, discretionary air travel, and the "flyers' dilemma"', *Journal of Travel Research*, 53: 462–75.

Smith, W. and Higgins, M. (2000) 'Cause-related marketing: Ethics and the ecstatic', *Business & Society*, 39: 304–22.

Weaver, D.B. (2013) 'Asymmetrical dialectics of sustainable tourism: Toward enlightened mass tourism', *Journal of Travel Research*.

(Continued)

(Continued)

Other

Boston, J. and Lempp, F. (2011) 'Climate change: Explaining and solving the mismatch between scientific urgency and political inertia', *Accounting, Auditing & Accountability Journal*, 24: 1000–21.

Gössling, S., Hall, C.M., Peeters, P. and Scott, D. (2010) 'The future of tourism: Can tourism growth and climate policy be reconciled? A mitigation perspective', *Tourism Recreation Research*, 35: 119–30.

Gössling, S. and Peeters, P. (2007) '"It does not harm the environment!" An analysis of industry discourses on tourism, air travel and the environment', *Journal of Sustainable Tourism*, 15: 402–17.

Macbeth, J. (2005) 'Towards an ethics platform for tourism', *Annals of Tourism Research*, 32: 962–84.

Young, W. and Middlemiss, L. (2012) 'A rethink of how policy and social science approach changing individuals' actions on greenhouse gas emissions', *Energy Policy*, 41: 742–7.

Also visit the websites of:

- Greenpeace
- Friends of the Earth
- Tourism Concern
- Volunteer Service organisations
- Dark tourism websites

See also the list of possible sites and organisations in the supplementary resources that accompany this book at https://study.sagepub.com/eagleanddahl.

References

ABC News (2014) *Part of Ancient Pompeii Fresco in Italy Chiselled off by Thieves*. Available at: http://www.abc.net.au/news/2014-03-19/thieves-steal-part-of-pompeii-fresco/5330072.

Andrewes, H., Roberts, L. and Selwyn, T. (2007) 'Hospitality and eroticism', *International Journal of Culture, Tourism and Hospitality Research*, 1(3): 247–62.

Armitage, C.J. and Conner, M. (2000) 'Social cognition models and health behaviours: A structured review', *Psychology & Health*, 15: 173–89.

Ballantyne, R. and Packer, J. (2011) 'Using tourism free-choice learning experiences to promote environmentally sustainable behaviour: The role of post-visit "action resources"', *Environmental Education Research*, 17: 201–15.

Ballantyne, R., Packer, J. and Falk, J. (2011a) 'Visitors' learning for environmental sustainability: Testing short-and long-term impacts of wildlife tourism experiences using structural equation modelling', *Tourism Management*, 32: 1243–52.

Ballantyne, R., Packer, J. and Hughes, K. (2009) 'Tourists' support for conservation messages and sustainable management practices in wildlife tourism experiences', *Tourism Management*, 30: 658–64.

Ballantyne, R., Packer, J. and Sutherland, L.A. (2011b) 'Visitors' memories of wildlife tourism: Implications for the design of powerful interpretive experiences', *Tourism Management*, 32: 770–9.

Bandura, A. (1986) *Social Foundations of Thought and Action*. Englewood Cliffs, NJ: Prentice Hall.

Barr, S., Shaw, G. and Coles, T. (2011) 'Times for (Un)sustainability? Challenges and opportunities for developing behaviour change policy. A case-study of consumers at home and away', *Global Environmental Change*, 21: 1234–44.

Bellis, M., Hughes, K., Thomson, R. and Bennett, A. (2004) 'Sexual behaviour of young people in international tourist resorts', *Sexually Transmitted Infections*, 80(1): 43–47.

Bigné-Alcañiz, E., Currás-Pérez, R., Ruiz-Mafé, C. and Sanz-Blas, S. (2012) 'Cause-related marketing influence on consumer responses: The moderating effect of cause–brand fit', *Journal of Marketing Communications*, 18: 265–83.

Brei, V. and Böhm, S. (2011) 'Corporate social responsibility as cultural meaning management: A critique of the marketing of "ethical" bottled water', *Business Ethics: A European Review*, 20: 233–52.

Brouwer, R., Brander, L. and Van Beukering, P. (2008) '"A convenient truth": Air travel passengers' willingness to pay to offset their CO2 emissions', *Climatic Change*, 90: 299–313.

Buckley, R. (2012) 'Sustainable tourism: Research and reality', *Annals of Tourism Research*, 39(2): 528–46.

Budeanu, A. (2007) 'Sustainable tourist behaviour – a discussion of opportunities for change', *International Journal of Consumer Studies*, 31: 499–508.

Bulkeley, H. (2000) 'Common knowledge? Public understanding of climate change in Newcastle, Australia', *Public Understanding of Science*, 9: 313–33.

Burns, G.L., Macbeth, J. and Moore, S. (2011) 'Should dingoes die? Principles for engaging ecocentric ethics in wildlife tourism management', *Journal of Ecotourism*, 10: 179–196.

Casey, J.F., Brown, C. and Schuhmann, P. (2010) 'Are tourists willing to pay additional fees to protect corals in Mexico?', *Journal of Sustainable Tourism*, 18: 557–73.

Chiu, Y-TH., Lee, W-I. and Chen, T-H. (2013) 'Environmentally responsible behavior in ecotourism: Exploring the role of destination image and value perception', *Asia Pacific Journal of Tourism Research*, 19: 876–89.

Chung, J.Y., Kyle, G.T., Petrick, J.F. and Absher, J.D. (2011) 'Fairness of prices, user fee policy and willingness to pay among visitors to a national forest', *Tourism Management*, 32: 1038–46.

Cialdini, R. (2007) 'Descriptive social norms as underappreciated sources of social control', *Psychometrika*, 72: 263–8.

Cohen, S.A. and Higham, J.E. (2011)' Eyes wide shut? UK consumer perceptions on aviation climate impacts and travel decisions to New Zealand', *Current Issues in Tourism*, 14: 323–35.

Costello, A., Abbas, M., Allen, A., Ball, S., Bell. S., Bellamy, R. et al. (2009) 'Managing the health effects of climate change: Lancet and University College London Institute for Global Health Commission', *The Lancet*, 373: 1693–733.

Donyadide, A. (2010) 'Ethics in tourism', *European Journal of Social Sciences*, 17: 426–33.

Edney, J. (2006) 'Impacts of recreational scuba diving on shipwrecks in Australia and the Pacific', *Micronesian: Journal of the Humanities and Social Sciences*, 5: 201–33.

Eikenberry, A.M. (2009) 'The hidden costs of cause marketing', *Stanford Social Innovation Review*, 7: 51–5.

Fennell, D.A. (2008) 'Ecotourism and the myth of indigenous stewardship', *Journal of Sustainable Tourism*, 16: 129–49.

Fishbein, M. (2008) 'A reasoned action approach to health promotion', *Medical Decision Making*, 28: 834–44.

Fishbein, M. and Cappella, J. (2006) 'The role of theory in developing effective health communications', *Journal of Communication*, 56 (August supplement): S1–17.

Gibson, C. (2010) 'Geographies of tourism: (Un)ethical encounters', *Progress in Human Geography*, 34: 521–7.

Gössling, S. (2009) 'Carbon neutral destinations: A conceptual analysis', *Journal of Sustainable Tourism*, 17: 17–37.

Gössling, S. and Peeters, P. (2007) '"It does not harm the environment!" An analysis of industry discourses on tourism, air travel and the environment', *Journal of Sustainable Tourism*, 15: 402–17.

Hall, C.M. (2009) 'Degrowing tourism: Décroissance, sustainable consumption and steady-state tourism', *Anatolia*, 20: 46–61.

Ham, S.H. (2009) 'From interpretation to protection: Is there a theoretical basis?', *Journal of Interpretation Research*, 14: 49–57.

Hartman, E., Paris, C.M. and Blache-Cohen, B. (2014) 'Fair Trade learning: Ethical standards for community-engaged international volunteer tourism', *Tourism and Hospitality Research*, 14: 108–16.

Herold, E., Garcia, R. and DeMoya, T. (2001) 'Female tourists and beach boys: Romance or sex tourism?', *Annals of Tourism Research*, 28: 978–97.

Hibbert, J.F., Dickinson, J.E., Gössling, S.and Curtin, S.C. (2013) 'Identity and tourism mobility: An exploration of the attitude–behaviour gap', *Journal of Sustainable Tourism*, 21: 999–1016.

Higgins-Desbiolles, F. (2008) 'Justice tourism and alternative globalisation', *Journal of Sustainable Tourism*, 16: 345–64.

Higham, J.E., Cohen, S.A. and Cavaliere, C.T. (2014) 'Climate change, discretionary air travel, and the "flyers' dilemma"', *Journal of Travel Research*, 53: 462–75.

Holden, A. (2009) 'The environment-tourism nexus: Influence of market ethics', *Annals of Tourism Research*, 36: 373–89.

Hughes, K. (2011) 'Designing post-visit action resources for families visiting wildlife tourism sites', *Visitor Studies*, 14: 66–83.

Hughes, K. (2013) 'Measuring the impact of viewing wildlife: Do positive intentions equate to long-term changes in conservation behaviour?', *Journal of Sustainable Tourism*, 21: 42–59.

Hughes, K., Packer, J. and Ballantyne, R. (2011) 'Using post-visit action resources to support family conservation learning following a wildlife tourism experience', *Environmental Education Research*, 17: 307–28.

Isaac, R.K. and Hodge, D. (2011) 'An exploratory study: Justice tourism in controversial areas: The case of Palestine', *Tourism Planning & Development*, 8: 101–8.

Jacobs, M.H. and Harms, M. (2014) 'Influence of interpretation on conservation intentions of whale tourists', *Tourism Management*, 42: 123–31.

Johnson, A.K. (2011) 'International child sex tourism: Enhancing the legal response in South East Asia', *Int'l J. Child. Rts.*, 19: 55.

Juvan, E. and Dolnicar, S. (2014) 'The attitude–behaviour gap in sustainable tourism', *Annals of Tourism Research*, 48: 76–95.

Kim, A.K. and Weiler, B. (2013) 'Visitors' attitudes towards responsible fossil collecting behaviour: An environmental attitude-based segmentation approach', *Tourism Management*, 36: 602–12.

Knox, D. (2006) 'The sacralised landscapes of Glencoe: From massacre to mass tourism, and back again', *International Journal of Tourism Research*, 8: 185–97.

Kolar, T. and Zabkar, V. (2010) 'A consumer-based model of authenticity: An oxymoron or the foundation of cultural heritage marketing?', *Tourism Management*, 31: 652–64.

Krieger, J.R. (2012) *Diving Tourism on Coral Reefs in Florida: Variation in Recreational Diver Behavior and Impacts on Reef Corals*. Alabama: Auburn University.

Lansing, P. and De Vries, P. (2007) 'Sustainable tourism: Ethical alternative or marketing ploy?', *Journal of Business Ethics*, 72: 77–85.

Lee, W.H. and Moscardo, G. (2005) 'Understanding the impact of ecotourism resort experiences on tourists' environmental attitudes and behavioural intentions', *Journal of Sustainable Tourism*, 13: 546–65.

Liston-Heyes, C. and Liu, G. (2013) 'A study of nonprofit organisations in cause-related marketing: Stakeholder concerns and safeguarding strategies', *European Journal of Marketing*, 47: 1954–74.

Lorenzoni, I., Nicholson-Cole, S. and Whitmarsh, L. (2007) 'Barriers perceived to engaging with climate change among the UK public and their policy implications', *Global Environmental Change*, 17: 445–59.

McGehee, N.G. (2012) 'Oppression, emancipation, and volunteer tourism: Research propositions', *Annals of Tourism Research*, 39: 84–107.

McKercher, B. and Prideaux, B. (2011) 'Are tourism impacts low on personal environmental agendas?', *Journal of Sustainable Tourism*, 19: 325–45.

Mendoza, C. (2013) 'Beyond sex tourism: Gay tourists and male sex workers in Puerto Vallarta (Western Mexico)', *International Journal of Tourism Research*, 15(2): 122–137.

Miller, G., Rathouse, K., Scarles, C., Holmes, K. and Tribe, J. (2010) 'Public understanding of sustainable tourism', *Annals of Tourism Research*, 37: 627–45.

Minato, W.L., Curtis, A.L. and Allan, C. (2012) 'Understanding the role and influence of social norms: Lessons for NRM', *Local Environment*, 17: 863–77.

Moeller, T., Dolnicar, S. and Leisch, F. (2011) 'The sustainability–profitability trade-off in tourism: Can it be overcome?', *Journal of Sustainable Tourism*, 19: 155–69.

Moosmayer, D.C. and Fuljahn, A. (2013) 'Corporate motive and fit in cause related marketing', *Journal of Product & Brand Management*, 22: 5.

Moser, S.C. (2010) 'Now more than ever: The need for more societally relevant research on vulnerability and adaptation to climate change', *Applied Geography*, 30: 464–74.

Munar, A.M. (2013) 'Sun, alcohol and sex: Enacting beer tourism', in J. Gammelgaard and C. Dörrenbächer (eds), *The Global Brewery Industry: Markets, Strategies, and Rivalries*. Cheltenham: Edward Elgar. pp. 310–33.

Navarro, S., Andreu, L. and Cervera, A. (2014) 'Value co-creation among hotels and disabled customers: An exploratory study', *Journal of Business Research*, 67: 813–18.

Nawijn, J. and Fricke, M.C. (2013) 'Visitor emotions and behavioral intentions: The case of concentration camp memorial Neuengamme', *International Journal of Tourism Research*, Online: 1–8.

Nelson, F., Lindsey, P. and Balme, G. (2013) 'Trophy hunting and lion conservation: A question of governance?', *Oryx*, 47: 501–9.

Nelson, J.A. (2014) *Issues of Authenticity in Small Scale Tourism: A Study of the McDisney Experience*. Portland University.

Nickel, P.M. and Eikenberry, A.M. (2009) 'A critique of the discourse of marketized philanthropy', *American Behavioral Scientist*, 52: 974–89.

Nolan, J.M., Kenefick, J. and Schultz, P.W. (2011) 'Normative messages promoting energy conservation will be underestimated by experts.....unless you show them the data', *Social Influence*, 6: 169–80.

Ockwell, D., Whitmarsh, L. and O'Neill, S. (2009) 'Reorienting climate change communication for effective mitigation', *Science Communication*, 30: 305–27.

Owens, S. and Driffill, L. (2008) 'How to change attitudes and behaviours in the context of energy', *Energy Policy*, 36: 4412–18.

Palazy, L., Bonenfant, C., Gaillard, J-M. and Courchamp, F. (2013) 'On the use of the IUCN status for the management of trophy hunting', *Wildlife Research*, 39: 711–20.

Pickering, C. and Mount, A. (2010) 'Do tourists disperse weed seed? A global review of unintentional human-mediated terrestrial seed dispersal on clothing, vehicles and horses', *Journal of Sustainable Tourism*, 18: 239–56.

Ponte, S. and Richey, L.A. (2014) 'Buying into development? Brand Aid forms of cause-related marketing', *Third World Quarterly*, 35: 65–87.

Powell, R.B. and Ham, S.H. (2008) 'Can ecotourism interpretation really lead to pro-conservation knowledge, attitudes and behaviour? Evidence from the Galapagos Islands', *Journal of Sustainable Tourism*, 16: 467–89.

Risko, E.F., Quilty, L.C. and Oakman, J.M. (2006) 'Socially desirable responding on the web: Investigating the candor hypothesis', *Journal of Personality Assessment*, 87: 269–76.

Saunders, S.G. and Borland, R. (2013) 'Marketing-driven philanthropy: The case of PlayPumps', *European Business Review*, 25: 321–35.

Semenza, J.C., Hall, D.E., Wilson, D.J., Bontempo, B.D., Sailor, D.J. and George, L.A. (2008) 'Public perception of climate change: Voluntary mitigation and barriers to behavior change', *American Journal of Preventive Medicine*, 35: 479–87.

Sheikh, S-u-R. and Beise-Zee, R. (2011) 'Corporate social responsibility or cause-related marketing? The role of cause specificity of CSR', *Journal of Consumer Marketing*, 28: 27–39.

Sheppard, S.R.J.(2005) 'Landscape visualisation and climate change: The potential for influencing perceptions and behaviour', *Environmental Science & Policy*, 8: 637–54.

Sin, H.L. (2010) 'Who are we responsible to? Locals' tales of volunteer tourism', *Geoforum*, 41: 983–92.

Skibins, J.C., Powell, R.B. and Stern, M.J. (2012) 'Exploring empirical support for interpretations' best practices', *Journal of Interpretation Research*, 17: 25–44.

Smith, P.T. (2013) *Strength From Weakness: How Legalizing Sport Hunting of Endangered Species Could Provide the Conservation Effort Its Greatest Weapon*. Available at: http://scholarship.shu.edu/cgi/viewcontent.cgi?article=1306&context=student_scholarship.

Smith, V.L. and Font, X. (2014) 'Volunteer tourism, greenwashing and understanding responsible marketing using market signalling theory'. *Journal of Sustainable Tourism*, 22: 942–63.

Smith, W. and Higgins, M. (2000) 'Cause-related marketing: Ethics and the ecstatic', *Business & Society*, 39: 304–22.

Stern, M.J. and Powell, R.B. (2013) 'What leads to better visitor outcomes in live interpretation?', *Journal of Interpretation Research*: 9–44.

Stern, M.J., Powell, R.B. and Hill, D. (2013) 'Environmental education program evaluation in the new millennium: What do we measure and what have we learned?', *Environmental Education Research*: 1–31.

Stone, P. (2006) 'A dark tourism spectrum: Towards a typology of death and macabre related tourist sites, attractions and exhibitions', *Tourism: An Interdisciplinary International Journal*, 54: 145–60.

Stone, P. and Sharpley, R. (2008) 'Consuming dark tourism: A thanatological perspective', *Annals of Tourism Research*, 35: 574–95.

Timothy, D.J. and Ron, A.S. (2013) 'Understanding heritage cuisines and tourism: Identity, image, authenticity, and change', *Journal of Heritage Tourism*, 8: 99–104.

Tomazos, K. and Butler, R. (2012) 'Volunteer tourists in the field: A question of balance?', *Tourism Management*, 33: 177–87.

Tomazos, K. and Cooper, W. (2012) 'Volunteer tourism: At the crossroads of commercialisation and service?', *Current Issues in Tourism*, 15: 405–23.

Vanhamme, J., Lindgreen, A., Reast, J. and Popering, N. van (2012) 'To do well by doing good: Improving corporate image through cause-related marketing', *Journal of Business Ethics*, 109: 259–74.

Water for People (2013) *Update on PlayPump Technology*. Available at: www.waterforpeople.or/extras/playpumps/update-on-playpumps.html.

Williams, D.M. (2010) 'Outcome expectancy and self-efficacy: Theoretical implications of an unresolved contradiction', *Personality and Social Psychology Review*, 14: 417–25.

Williams, E.L. (2012) *Sex Tourism*, The Wiley-Blackwell Encyclopedia of Globalization. Available at: http://onlinelibrary.wiley.com/doi/10.1002/9780470670590.wbeog516/abstract.

World Travel & Tourism Council (2013) *Travel & Tourism Economic Impact 2013*. London: World Travel & Tourism Council.

Yeo, G.B. and Neal, A. (2013) 'Revisiting the functional properties of self-efficacy: A dynamic perspective', *Journal of Management*, 39(6): 1385–96.

Yeoman, I., Brass, D. and McMahon-Beattie, U. (2007) 'Current issue in tourism: The authentic tourist', *Tourism Management*, 28: 1128–38.

Zenko, Z. and Sardi, V. (2014) 'Systemic thinking for socially responsible innovations in social tourism for people with disabilities', *Kybernetes*, 43: 21.

11 Ethics in Social Marketing

Lynne Eagle, Stephan Dahl and David R. Low

CHAPTER OVERVIEW

In this chapter we will discuss:

- The unique characteristics of social marketing
- The specific ethical challenges within the sector, including the use of financial incentives and nudging strategies
- The implications of the application of common ethical frameworks to social marketing activity
- The potential role of a Code of Ethics or other ethics resources
- The challenges of enforcement mechanisms for professions such as social marketers

THE NATURE AND SCOPE OF SOCIAL MARKETING

In order to discuss the unique challenges facing **social marketing,** we first need to clarify what social marketing is. To provide a focal point for the following discussions, we have included a brief overview of the major definitions debated in the literature. Like many other marketing-related concepts, there is no single definition of social marketing, the concept having evolved over time from narrow and somewhat simplistic foundations.

The following definitions are drawn from a 2006 National Social Marketing Review but fail to provide guidance for operationalising the concept. It defines social marketing as:

> the systematic application of marketing concepts and techniques to achieve specific behavioural goals, for a social or public good.

and health-related social marketing as:

> the systematic application of marketing concepts and techniques to achieve specific behavioural goals, to improve health and reduce health inequalities. (National Social Marketing Centre, 2006: 1)

A more extensive and more managerial focused definition is provided by Andreasen (2002b: 7), drawing on a definition originally developed in the late 1980s (Kotler and Roberto, 1989).

> A social change management technology involving the design, implementation and control of programs aimed at increasing the acceptability of a social idea or practice in one or more groups of target adopters. It utilizes concepts of market segmentation, consumer research, product concept development and testing, directed communication, facilitation, incentives and exchange theory to maximise the target adopter's response.

Social marketing should not be seen as a specific theory, but rather as a *process* that draws on an **interdisciplinary** range of concepts and theories, such as from psychology, sociology, anthropology and communication as well as marketing itself. This is illustrated by the 2013 consensus definition of social marketing shown below which was drawn up by the (then) three Social Marketing organisations – the International Social Marketing Association (iSMA), the European Social Marketing Association (ESMA) and the Australian Association of Social Marketing. Additional associations have been established in Asia and the USA since that time.

The iSMA, ESMA and AASM consensus definition of social marketing

The following definition has been endorsed by the Boards of iSMA, ESMA and AASM:

> Social Marketing seeks to develop and integrate marketing concepts with other approaches to influence behaviours that benefit individuals and communities for the greater social good. Social Marketing practice is guided by ethical principles. It seeks

to integrate research, best practice, theory, audience and partnership insight, to inform the delivery of competition sensitive and segmented social change programmes that are effective, efficient, equitable and sustainable.

In keeping with other aspects of marketing which are receiving increased focus such as integrated marketing communication (Cornelissen and Lock, 2000), there has been considerable debate as to what social marketing is, where its borders could or should be, and what other behaviour-change interventions might compete against it (Andreasen, 2002a), although the debate has died down since the release of the Consensus Definition. It might be said that conceptual debates and arguments over relatively minor definitional issues detract from areas deserving more focus, such as investigation of the factors leading to interventions with high impact.

Social marketing activity has encompassed a wide range of issues and behaviours; some are relatively uncontroversial and others, such as genetic screening, are more controversial and raise significant ethical issues. While the focus is on encouraging sustained, positive behaviour change among individuals and groups, social marketing also encompasses environmental and policy factors '**upstream**' of actual behaviour change that may be barriers to, or enablers of, that change.

Table 11.1 provides an indicative list of papers, some of which are conceptual discussions, such as genetic testing (Brenkert, 2002), and some of which review research studies which have reported on the impact of social marketing interventions across a number of health and behavioural areas. What these issues have in common is that they focus on forms of actions by individuals that potentially affect, positively or negatively, both their own well-being and that of others. It should be noted that there is far more research within the health sector than within the environmental sector; however the latter sector is now receiving considerable attention within the areas of recycling, energy conservation, and, more recently, the impact of climate change.

It is difficult to compare the success (or otherwise) of factors across the interventions examined due to variations in methodology and reporting procedures. Some critics may challenge whether all of the campaigns are in fact social marketing, rather than **health education**. The latter generally involves the use of a single programme, led by expert knowledge, and provider-driven rather than receiver-driven programmes specifically customised to meet the needs and likely responses of population segments (see, for example, Peattie and Peattie, 2003).

Another misconception is that social marketing equates to **social advertising**, i.e. successful interventions centre around mass media advertising in order to communicate the desired messages. Firstly, in the rapidly changing communication environment in which mass media are no longer as dominant as they once were, advertising is a subset of the wider field of marketing communication as the latter includes the use of new, emerging and **hybrid communication** forms discussed in earlier chapters. Secondly, interventions may indeed use advertising or other forms of marketing communication where this is an appropriate and effective means of communicating with the specific target groups and where resources permit. However, there are many examples of interventions that do not rely on marketing communication, relying instead on other ways of reaching the target groups.

Table 11.1 Indicative list of social marketing interventions and studies examining impact (Eagle et al., 2013)

Issues/behaviour targeted
Safe sex/condom use/contraception
Smoking cessation
Responsible drinking
Seatbelt use
Responsible driving/Anti-speeding
Sun protection/skin cancer awareness
Domestic violence
Immunisation
Medical screening (cancer, cholesterol, etc.)
Genetic testing to reduce the occurrence of inherited diseases
Nutrition
Drug education
Exercise/physical activity
Malaria control
Mental health
Environmental issues, e.g. recycling, energy conservation, pollution
Workplace health
Volunteering
Disaster management and preparedness, e.g. hurricanes, earthquakes, volcanic eruptions

CURRENT SOCIAL MARKETING FOCUS

A number of recent initiatives, all of which place effective communication as the central focus of public health interventions (Bernhardt, 2004), have developed in countries such as the USA and UK and it is recognised that problems – and potential solutions – are not restricted to one specific country. For example, not just pan-European but also global solutions are being sought to issues affecting the health and welfare of individuals (Commission of the European Communities, 2002). In the UK, a government white paper *Choosing Health* (Department of Health, 2004) specifically advocated the adoption of the principles underpinning social marketing in order to more effectively promote public health issues, acknowledging that existing communication strategies were not effective. Issues about the legitimacy of government intervention in individual behaviours and choices are discussed in later sections of this chapter.

The UK Department of Health commissioned an independent study (National Social Marketing Centre, 2006) on the scope and potential of social marketing as a tool by which to help improve health and overall quality of life among the wider population. This study notes that the majority of the population distrust or ignore government advice.

However the study also notes that 'the total annual cost to the country of preventable illness amounts to a minimum of £187 billion. In comparative terms this equates to 19% of total GDP (gross domestic product) for England' (2006: 3). As these data are at least a decade old, the current figures are undoubtedly much higher. While it is difficult to compare data across nations due to differences in the data collected, the problems of **preventable illness** are international. In the USA, approximately 1 million deaths per annum are attributable to **lifestyle** and **environmental factors** (Rothschild, 1999). Some indications of the magnitude of various health and lifestyle issues in the USA are shown in Table 11.2. We have no reason to believe that, in the absence of more specific data, the figures cannot be used as a crude indicator of the potential magnitude of similar issues in other developed countries.

Table 11.2 Magnitude (in USA) of issues social marketing may contribute towards alleviating (Kotler et al., 2002)

Issue	Magnitude
Alcohol use during pregnancy	Estimated 5000 infants born with foetal alcohol syndrome each year
Sexually transmitted diseases	40% of sexually active high school students report not using a condom
Diabetes	About one third of the nearly 16 million people with diabetes are not aware they have the disease
Skin cancer	Approximately 70% of American adults do not protect themselves from the sun's dangerous rays
Breast cancer	More than 20% of females aged 50 and over have not had mammograms in the last two years
Prostate cancer	Only about half of all prostate cancers are found early
Colon cancer	Only about 1/3 of all colon cancers are found early
Seat belts	An estimated 30% of drivers and adult passengers do not always wear their seat belts
Fires	Almost 50% of fires and 60% of fire deaths occur in the estimated 8% of homes with no smoke alarms

You will note from the two tables and from a review of media coverage and academic literature that health-related issues have historically received far more attention than environmental issues; however this is now changing. In the context of environmental issues, there is increasing recognition firstly that continued pursuit of economic growth based on the exploitation of finite resources is unsustainable (see, for example, Burroughs, 2010). Secondly, there is increasing recognition that human activity has disrupted many of the ecological systems on which people depend. For example, it is estimated that '60 per cent of ecosystem services, involving climate regulation, fresh water provision, fisheries and many other services were either being degraded or used unsustainably' (Assadourian, 2010: 187).

Rubbish disposal also creates major environmental challenges. For example, plastic rubbish is responsible for killing 1 million seabirds and over 100,000 sea mammals each year (Leahy, 2004). Some 267 species, including 86% of all sea turtles, up to 36% of seabirds, and up to 28% of all marine mammals have been found with ingested plastic (Derraik, 2002; Müller et al., 2012). This area is only now beginning to receive attention from social marketers.

We discussed wildlife tourism in the last chapter, particularly in terms of claims that it has the potential for positive long-term impacts on environmental learning (Ballantyne et al., 2011). Considerably more work is needed in this area in order to develop potentially effective social marketing interventions such as the use of wildlife tourism as a conduit to help reduce the amount of plastic waste or other litter entering waterways, rivers and oceans.

Another challenge to determining social marketing intervention effectiveness is that it is difficult to assess the relative impact of individual components of many social marketing campaigns, let alone what impact the components may have had, individually or in combination, on factors underpinning behaviour. As has been wryly observed, 'it is more difficult to ascertain usage rates for condoms than for coffee' (Goldberg, 1995: 348).

Think points

What do you see the major challenges faced by social marketers as being? Contrast the ethical issues involved in social marketing with commercial marketing. Contrast the ethical issues within social marketing interventions within the health and environmental sectors. What can each sector learn from the other?

WHAT SOCIAL MARKETING IS NOT

Social marketing focuses on voluntary behaviour change – it is not 'selling', nor is it coercion (Stead et al., 2007); however, there is a level of confusion between social marketing and activities such as **health education** and **health promotion**. We have therefore briefly described these other, related activities to illustrate the differences between them.

Health education

Health education is:

> an activity that seeks to inform the individual on the nature and causes of health/illness and that individual's personal level of risk associated with their lifestyle-related behaviour. Health education seeks to motivate the individual to accept a process of behavioural-change through directly influencing their value, belief and attitude systems, where it is deemed that the individual is particularly at risk or has already been affected by illness/disease or disability. (Whitehead, 2004: 313)

Health promotion

Health promotion is:

> the process by which the ecologically-driven socio-political-economic determinants of health are addressed as they impact on individuals and the communities within which they interact. This serves to counter social inaction and social division/inequality. It is an inherently political process that draws on health policy as a basis for social action that leads to community coalitions through shared radical consciousness. Health promotion seeks to radically transform and empower communities through involving them in activities that influence their public health – particularly via agenda setting, political lobbying and advocacy, critical consciousness-raising and social education programmes. Health promotion tools look to develop and reform social structures through developing participation between representative stakeholders in different sectors and agencies. (Whitehead, 2004: 314)

Environmental management

Environmental management is closely linked to sustainability and focuses on managing, protecting and restoring **ecosystems** that are impacted by human activity, including waterway and air pollution, erosion, damage to plant and animal habitats – and many more related issues such as those discussed in the previous chapter. It also involves maintaining clean water supplies, both for urban and rural populations.

While there are a number of government-administered or sanctioned environmental management groups, there are also private groups whose focus may be on advocacy, education or a combination of the two, such as Greenpeace.

Think points

Given that social marketing, health education and health promotion have similar aims, if not similar strategies and tactics, how do you think they can most effectively work together to achieve synergy? Under what circumstances might health education or health promotion activity hinder social marketing activity and how should these issues be resolved?

USE OF FINANCIAL INCENTIVES

Use of financial incentives (also termed **personal financial incentives** or **PFI**) is the provision of incentives to encourage behaviour change. This type of tactic has been used in a number of areas, including smoking cessation, HIV prevention, exercise and screening programmes and rubbish recycling (Heise et al., 2013; Lynagh et al., 2013), with mixed results, partially due to differences in evaluation methodologies and measurement tools.

Proponents of the use of PFI suggest that it is financially sensible to pay to encourage behaviour change now rather than to incur the costs of treating serious medical conditions later, or the challenges of inadequate water and electricity supplies and rapidly increasing volumes of refuse needing safe disposal – which cannot be solved in short time frames. Criticisms cover two areas: efficacy and ethics. In terms of efficacy, there appears to be a lack of evidence of long-term behaviour change once incentives are discontinued. For example, a recycling programme achieved immediate, significant effects on recycling behaviours but these did not continue once the incentives were stopped (Iyer and Kashyap, 2007).

There is also mixed evidence regarding whether positive rewards or penalties such as taxes on continued behaviour, for example taxes on single use plastic shopping bags (Homonoff, 2012), are more effective. Such taxes are always **regressive**, impacting on those with the least financial resources the most. Negative incentives such as taxes appear less effective than positive rewards, but the behaviours must be seen within the context of the health systems in different countries; most research in this area originates from the USA or the UK and the findings may not be generalisable to other countries with very different health systems. For behaviours such as energy conservation, low socio-economic groups were more motivated by financial savings from lower energy bills than by a conviction that energy conservation itself was a desirable objective.

Ethical dimensions are apparent in relation to the displacement of intrinsic motivations such as feelings of social responsibility, by extrinsic (financial reward) factors. Concerns are also evident in relation to the fairness of PFI. Should the public pay, through their taxes, for some people to be encouraged to change their behaviours when others manage to do so without any financial reward (Lynagh et al., 2013)? Do these types of incentives penalise people with poor health or disabilities as some (see, for example, Schmidt et al., 2012) suggest? In relation to blood donation, PFI have been accompanied by concerns regarding the quality of blood donated, with some potential donors having chronic medical conditions that render their blood unusable for transfusions, and also the negative impact of PFI in this area on people's willingness to donate in the future without PFI (Mortimer et al., 2013).

There are also wider issues relating to equity due to limitations on possible behaviour change because of socio-economic or environmental factors (Stephens, 2013), such as the lack of exercise facilities in some areas, or, more extreme, the futility of trying to encourage hand-washing hygiene in slums that do not have adequate water supplies (Langford and Panter-Brick, 2013).

Think points

Under what circumstances do you believe PFIs may be effective in the short and longer term? What are the major ethical issues that are likely to arise in the use of effective and ineffective PFIs? What role do you believe social norms and group influences may have on the effectiveness of PFIs? What ethical issues may arise as a result of these factors?

Mini case study 11.1   Thai smoking kid

This intervention won a gold medal from WARC for ASIAN Strategy in 2013. The full case study is available on the WARC database.

Encouraging people to quit smoking is a worldwide challenge. This mini case study from Thailand illustrates an innovative approach to the challenge. The Thai Health Promotion Foundation designed a low budget (US$5000) video-based intervention to be run online only. The intention was to increase the number of smokers calling a Quitline for help. Research had indicated that smokers knew about the hazards of smoking, but disregarded their own health risks, believing that their health was under their control. The main barriers that prevented smokers from listening to warnings or taking action were the smokers themselves.

In the video, child actors with cigarettes in hand approached adult smokers in designated smoking areas and asked if the smokers could light their cigarettes. All adults refused the request and lectured the children on the dangers of smoking. The children then asked why the adults were still smoking and handed them a brochure with the message:

> You worry about me, but why not about yourself? Reminding yourself is the most effective warning to help you quit. Call the 1600 hotline to quit smoking.

The video was viewed more than a million times within the first three days after it was posted online, and more than five million times during the first ten days after posting. Media coverage, estimated at more than US$3 million in value, and social media commentaries, all overwhelmingly positive, extended well beyond Thailand. The number of completed calls to the Quitline went up by 62% in the first month after the video was released online, and averaged a 32% increase over pre-intervention levels for the following five months.

Questions to consider

Critique the approach used:

What mechanisms would have been needed to have been put in place to protect the child actors during filming?

What ethical issues do you believe arise in relation to the smokers being filmed without their knowledge? How should these issues be dealt with?

How would you adapt the strategy for the longer term or for possible use in other markets?

CODE OF ETHICS OR OTHER RESOURCES TO AID SOCIAL MARKETING PRACTICE

Given the importance placed on ethical principles in the Consensus Definition of social marketing, there is an obvious need to debate how ethical practice can be supported. We therefore now discuss what can be realistically achieved with **codes of ethics** (CoE), i.e. formal lists of acceptable ethical behaviours for individuals or organisations, and/or other ethical resources, and question whether a global social marketing CoE is achievable, and if so how it could be developed, communicated and enforced. The paper by Sindall (2002) is a response to concerns regarding the lack of CoE for social marketing and related fields such as health promotion which have been evident for over a decade. While several individual health promotion organisations have developed CoEs and ethical standards, they have 'yet to be endorsed by a global health promotion community' (Bull et al., 2012: 9). The establishment of professional associations for Social Marketing (e.g. the Australian Association of Social Marketers (AASM), the International Social Marketing Association (iSMA), the European Association of Social Marketers (ESMA) and newer associations in Asia and the USA) has seen increased focus on the issue. A challenge is whether a single set of ethical resources and/or CoE is possible or, if different approaches evolve for each association, what impact any differences might have on trans-national or trans-cultural activity. How do we guide the development of Aristotle's practical wisdom (**phronēsis**) in knowing 'how, when, where and in what way' (Messikomer and Cirka, 2010: 58) to apply theories, frameworks and other factors in ethical decision making? This discussion is also relevant to wider areas of marketing activity.

Social marketing as a recognised profession is relatively new and professional associations such as those noted above are recognised as having a key strategic role in the process of professionalisation (Thomas and Thomas, 2013). The characteristics of a profession include both professional associations and codes of ethics, as well as education grounded in a theory-based body of knowledge, accountability, public recognition and accreditation or certification systems (Sha, 2011). The discussion of these other aspects of professionalisation is beyond the scope of this chapter but warrants consideration as the profession evolves and matures.

In search of universal moral values

The impact of cultural differences in ethical perceptions has not been studied in the social marketing context; however it has been noted (Lefebvre, 2011: 54) that social marketing thought and practice have 'evolved differently in the developing and developed world', making calls for the development of a common social marketing language challenging (Quinn et al., 2010). Social marketers therefore need to debate and agree on whether a global CoE for Social Marketing can be achieved based on the identification of 'universal moral values' which continue to be sought in the corporate sector (Schwartz, 2005). We note the recent call for a 'transcendental code of ethics' for all marketing professionals (Payne and Pressley, 2013) but suggest these authors grossly oversimplify the magnitude of the task as they merely list broad principles and present an authoritarian approach, such as 'the inability of the marketing decision maker to understand that there may be ethical components to a decision being made' (2013: 69) without considering what ethical resources might be needed and how support for the development and implementation of appropriate resources might be successfully achieved and what outcomes might be achieved as a result.

Think points

How effective do you believe a code of ethics for social marketers might be in guiding practitioners through decisions relating to the ethical dimensions of social marketing interventions they may be planning or implementing? How do you believe the issue of universal moral values should be investigated within the social marketing context?

Examples of social marketing's ethical dimensions

Given that social marketing activity aims to change behaviours in ways that benefit individuals, communities and/or society at large, it surprises novices that ethical issues can arise. A value-neutral perspective of social marketing is noted among some in the sector (Dann, 2007), a view countered by others who stress the **value-ladenness** aspect of activity (Rossi and Yudell, 2012). This relates to the issue of who defines desired behaviour and whether consideration of potential harm to others that may arise as a consequence of a social marketing intervention should be a requirement in the development of any intervention. Indeed, in developing interventions, 'who has the mandate to represent large and diverse populations for the purpose of **informed consent**, and how can this be implemented?' (Guttman and Salmon, 2004: 537). How are individual freedoms of choice and individual rights balanced against the benefits for society as a whole? Who defines or prioritises these benefits (see, for example, Lefebvre, 2011)?

In communicating risk, who decides whether levels of risk that may be acceptable to different segments of society are acceptable to society as a whole (Callahan and Jennings, 2002)? There is a growing body of literature that documents wider ethical issues and unexpected impacts of interventions, including issues regarding targeting, **segmentation**, use of incentive schemes and the consequences of focusing on easy-to-reach or influence groups rather than those with the greatest need, and the needs of low literate groups, and minority groups and cultures (Eagle, 2008; Newton et al., 2013).

The extant literature indicates ongoing debates regarding whether all forms of persuasion are inherently unethical or whether there are boundaries within which these tactics are acceptable, such as when benefits outweigh risks (Rossi and Yudell, 2012). There is considerable debate regarding **behavioural economics** and 'nudge' strategies, i.e. a range of non-legislatory interventions based on altering the contexts ('**choice architecture**') in which behaviour decisions occur. Choice architecture is claimed to alter behaviours in predictable ways through the options intentionally made available or not. It has been asked: 'Is it possible to interfere with individual decision-making while preserving freedom of choice?' (Ménard, 2010: 229). It has been suggested that acceptability is dependent on 'the right kind of nudge for specific circumstances' (Cohen, 2013: 10); the acceptability of nudge strategies may be context-dependent, incorporating the nature of the nudge and both the nudger and nudged (Lucke, 2013).

Missing from this debate is consideration of unintended effects. For example, strategies such as nudge may also lead to reactance effects. **Reactance** occurs when direct or potential perceived threats to personal freedom, such as consumption of specific products or engaging in particular behaviours, are detected and resisted. Furthermore, people may then become motivated by the perceived threat itself, rather than the actual consequences of the threat, to assert their freedom and regain control of their own decision-making and thereby of their threatened freedom (Rains, 2013).

Engaging in the threatened behaviour is one means of re-establishing this freedom (Rummel et al., 2000). Reactance effects appear to be strongest when the threatened freedom is perceived as important and the affected individual perceives that their 'counterforce' efforts will achieve personal control. Conversely, if an individual does not perceive that their actions will be effective in countering the threat, reactance will be minimal (Quick and Stephenson, 2007).

In terms of persuasive communication such as mass media public health intervention programmes, reactance may generate actions that resist or are the opposite of those desired by the individuals or organisations seeking to influence both attitudes and behaviours. Reactance effects explain not only why some public health interventions may not be effective, but also why they may produce effects contrary to those intended (Buller et al., 1998). A further danger is that awareness of attempts to manipulate behaviours may result in the behaviour itself becoming more attractive – the '**forbidden fruit**' problem that has been seen in interventions such as tobacco cessation programmes targeting adolescents (Sussman et al., 2010).

Mini case study 11.2   Act on CO_2

The UK Department of Energy and Climate Change ran an advertising campaign in late 2009–early 2010 to highlight the need to reduce CO_2 emissions. It proved controversial, with 939 complaints made to the Advertising Standards Authority. The ASA's description of the campaign, in their adjudication (ruling), is as follows (ASA, 2010):

a. "A TV ad for the Government's "Act On CO2" campaign showed a young girl being read a bedtime story by her father. Gentle, sorrowful music played throughout. The voice-over stated "There was once a land where the weather was very very strange. There were awful heat waves in some parts and in others terrible storms and floods." Images in the storybook showed a cartoon horse, pig, sheep and other animals staring in dismay at a dried up river bed and a cartoon rabbit crying at the sight of it. The voice-over continued "Scientists said it was being caused by too much CO2, which went up into the sky when the grown-ups used energy." The storybook showed black smoke rising up from an urban scene, from cars on the road and people's houses, and forming a cloud of CO2 in the shape of a monster in the sky. The camera panned to the father and daughter reading the story together. The voice-over continued "They said the CO2 was getting dangerous, its effects were happening faster than they had thought. Some places could even disappear under the sea and it was the children of the land who would have to live with the horrible consequences." The storybook showed a flooded town with people clinging to the roofs of buildings and cars in the rain and a cartoon cat floating on an upturned table and a dog sinking under the water. The voice-over continued "The grown-ups realised they had to do something. They discovered that over 40% of the CO2 was coming from ordinary everyday things like keeping houses warm and driving cars, which meant if they made less CO2 maybe they could save the land for the children." A child in the picture book switched off a light in her house. The little girl turned to her father and asked "Is there a happy ending?" A voice-over stated "It's up to us how the story ends. See what you can do. Search online for Act on CO2".

b. A press ad depicted a drawing of three men floating in a bath tub amidst scenes of flooding which included a floating half-submerged car and houses and a church part underwater. Headline text stated "Rub a dub dub three men in a tub, a necessary course of action due to flash flooding caused by climate change". Two of the men were dressed in the traditional outfits of a butcher and a baker, which recalled the children's nursery rhyme. Text continued "Climate change is happening. Temperatures and sea levels are rising. Extreme weather events such as storms, floods and heatwaves will become more frequent and intense. If we carry on at this rate, life in 25 years could be very different. IT'S OUR CHILDREN WHO'LL REALLY PAY THE PRICE. See what you can do: search online for ACT ON CO2".

c. Another press ad depicted a drawing of a young girl and boy looking for water at a well on a hill. Headline text stated "Jack and Jill went up the hill to fetch a pail of water. There was none, as extreme weather due to climate change had caused a drought". Text continued "Climate change has serious implications for our way of life. For example, extreme weather conditions such as flooding, heat waves and storms will become more frequent and intense. If we carry on at this rate, life in 25 years could be very different. IT'S OUR CHILDREN WHO'LL REALLY PAY THE PRICE. See what you can do: search online for ACT ON CO2".

(Continued)

(Continued)

d. A third press ad showed a drawing of a young girl sitting by her window looking up at the sky and in the top left a star with a sad face. Headline text stated "Twinkle twinkle little star; how I wonder what you are, looking down at dangerously high levels of CO_2 in the atmosphere." Text continued "The science shows that climate change is caused by heat-trapping gases such as CO_2, which is created whenever we use energy like electricity made from gas, oil or coal. As CO_2 levels rise, more and more heat is trapped in the atmosphere, causing changes in our climate. IT'S OUR CHILDREN WHO'LL REALLY PAY THE PRICE. See what you can do: search online for ACT ON CO_2".

e. A fourth press ad depicted a drawing of a cow leaping over a crescent moon whilst reading a booklet labelled "ACT ON CO_2". Text stated "Hey diddle diddle, the cat and the fiddle, the cow jumped over the moon on discovering just how easy it was to reduce our CO_2 emissions". Text underneath stated "CO_2 is produced by many things, but over 40% is caused simply by the way we heat and light our homes and drive our cars. Because we all cause it we can all do something about it. If we start to think about the ways we use energy, and act together, we can help tackle climate change. IT'S OUR CHILDREN WHO'LL REALLY PAY THE PRICE. See what you can do: search online for ACT ON CO_2".

The issues cited in the complaints were wide ranging and included:

1 The ad was political in nature and should not be broadcast.
2 The theme and content of the ad, for example the dog drowning in the storybook and the depiction of the young girl to whom the story was being read, could be distressing for children who saw it.
3 The ad should not have been shown when children were likely to be watching television.
4 The ad was misleading because it presented human induced climate change as a fact when that was not the case.
5 The claim "over 40% of the CO_2 was coming from ordinary everyday things" was misleading.
6 The representation of CO_2 as a rising cloud of black smog was misleading.
7 The claims about the possible advent of strange weather and flooding in the UK, and associated imagery, were exaggerated, distressing and misleading.

In addition there were objections to the press ads:

8 Many complainants objected to the press ads (b), (c) and (d) in respect of (4) above because they believed there was a significant division of informed scientific opinion on the matter.

9 Many complainants objected to the press ads (b), (c) and (d) in respect of (7) above.

10 One complainant objected to the press ad (e) in respect of (5) above.

The complaints on point 1 were referred to Ofcom under CAP (Broadcast) TV Advertising Standards Code rule 4 (Political and controversial issues). There is no specific prohibition in relation to ads which might be classed as political advertising in non-broadcast media (ASA, 2010).

The only part of the complaints to be upheld related to the press ads (b) and (c) which were held to have breached CAP Code clauses 3.1 (Substantiation), 7.1 (Truthfulness) and 49.1 (Environmental claims). Two of the Press ads (b) and (c) were ordered to not appear again in their current form.

Questions to consider

Consider the ASA's description and their decision. What were the ethical issues involved with this campaign?

How might the ASA decision have been altered under different ethical frameworks?

The potential role of a code of ethics or other ethics resources

Adoption of a specific ethical framework can help to identify these issues and guide the evaluation of alternative strategies. Thus, framework selection will impact on the design of interventions, as will be illustrated in a later section of this chapter. Communications strategies also present ethical challenges, such as the impact of fear appeals or other 'execution techniques that may impact negatively on vulnerable audiences' (Donovan et al., 2009), issues that will be discussed in more detail in the end of chapter case study. Codes of ethics (CoE), together with support from professional associations, possibly including specific ethics training, may thus help educate inexperienced practitioners and sensitise them to issues they may face in the future (Eagle et al., 2013), as well as aiding in the development of evaluation tools and in the commissioning of future interventions.

Codes are not panaceas; there is substantial evidence that the existence of a CoE will not of itself prevent unethical behaviour (Messikomer and Cirka, 2010), nor change behaviours in the wider business sector (Painter-Morland, 2010) or in the health care sector (Eriksson et al., 2007). The positive benefits of CoEs and related resources include assisting and empowering individuals to make ethical decisions through being able to apply principles, processes and decision-making models to ethical issues (Sonenshein, 2007), clarifying expectations around decision making and encouraging dialogue regarding ethical issues (Helin et al., 2011). While the issue has not been specifically examined in the social marketing context, examination of the wider business ethics literature indicates clear differences between the characteristics of ineffective and potentially effective codes. These are summarised in Table 11.3.

Table 11.3   Business codes characteristics

Ineffective codes	Characteristics of potentially effective codes
• Based on strategic legitimacy where there is an appearance, but not an embedded alignment of organisational and societal/stakeholder interests and there is only token support from senior management • Collectivist cultures may result in weak support for ethical guidance if this is at variation with observed practices • Codes are used as a means of coercion and control, decreasing the ability to manage ethical ambiguities • Codes do not reflect actual organisational culture (see, for example, Helin et al., 2011; Long and Driscoll, 2008)	• Contain high educational value, are non-authoritarian, provide a clear rationale for ethical behaviour and are empowering for actual decision-making • Clearly state principles and shared values, including what behaviours are desirable versus prohibited • Commitment to codes is embedded within all aspects of associations' and organisations' activity and explicitly endorsed by leaders • Communicated through effective communication channels in readable terms, using positive tones and demonstrating relevance to real-world practice • Discussions of values are open and difficult dilemmas are debated • Violations are seen to be addressed and repercussions are communicated. Failure to do this results in frustration, anger and cynicism (see, for example, Schwartz, 2005; Stevens, 2008)

Codes supported by ethics training and support facilities are perceived positively (Kaptein and Schwartz, 2008); however the literature is silent on which form of training resource and support is effective and there are obvious resource implications for their development and maintenance.

Members of an established, recognised, profession potentially could lose the right to practise in their profession if found guilty by their peers of a significant transgression of professional ethics (Eagle, 2008). Social marketers, and indeed commercial marketers, are not subject to the same level of peer control; there is no requirement that they be licensed and membership of sector organisations is voluntary. The lack of overarching **codified legislation**, and thus the inability to enforce standards or codes in the way that established professional groups are able to do, is therefore missing (Hunt and Vitell, 2006).

Indirect sanctions are possible. These appear to already exist in some consultancy areas, for example, those undertaking social science research on behalf of the UK Government are faced with specific expectations including, for example, obtaining 'valid, informed consent' from research participants, but also the requirement to take 'reasonable steps to identify and remove barriers to participation' and to avoid 'personal and social harm' (Government Social Research Unit, 2005). While provisions for sanctions and redress are noted but not spelt out specifically, an implicit conclusion is that consultants found to be in breach of the provisions would not obtain future commissions. This could readily be extended to include funding from government sources for social marketing intervention development and implementation as well as related research.

Another indirect measure would involve the formal accreditation of members of the social marketing organisations. Positive impacts between accreditation, quality of work and ethical conduct have been found within clinical health (Braithwaite et al., 2010) and counselling (Even and Robinson, 2013); therefore there would appear to be merit in investigating this option within the social marketing context.

Relationship to corporate and other professional codes

A social marketing CoE would not operate in isolation; social marketers work for a range of organisations, many of which have their own CoEs. Professional codes such as in the health or environmental management sectors where boundaries may be unclear (Carter et al., 2011) could also apply and any new social marketing CoE should not conflict with these codes. Research within the accounting profession suggests that professional CoEs have less influence than organisational environments (Somers, 2001). Whether this finding is in any way generalisable will require further research. What is clear is that there will always be an organisational component to code adherence (Malloy et al., 2009). Whether and how professional associations connect professionalism and organisations have been studied in the medical context (Noordegraaf, 2011), but not within social marketing.

Competing theoretical foundations and frameworks

The selection of a framework will impact on the development of an intervention strategy. For example, a social marketing intervention that was driven by good intentions without potential negative consequences being considered would be acceptable under deontological reasoning but not under teleological reasoning. A further problem is the lack of a clear and unambiguous interpretation of the frameworks. For example, fear-based interventions would be acceptable under deontological reasoning, given their positive intentions. If they caused distress, teleological principles would render the approach unacceptable. Indeed, as several social advertisers have found to their cost, marketing communication regulators in many countries appear to operate under teleological principles, resulting in the advertising component of an intervention being withdrawn from the media entirely, or requiring modification before being able to be rescheduled (see, for example, Advertising Standards Authority, 2007).

While space prevents a detailed analysis of all possible frameworks, Table 11.4 reproduces the overview of the main provisions of commonly used frameworks from Chapter 1, together with a brief commentary on the implications for social marketing interventions of the adoption of the different frameworks. How do we guide development of Aristotle's practical wisdom ('phronēsis') in knowing how, when, where and in what way (Messikomer and Cirka, 2010: 58) to apply theories, frameworks and other factors in ethical decision making?

Table 11.4 Application of ethical frameworks to social marketing

Framework and key provisions	Implications for social marketing
Deontology Accepts that actions intended to do good may have unintended negative consequences, such as creating fear or distress. This is contrary to teleological beliefs that interventions should do no harm, particularly to vulnerable groups who may not be the target of the activity.	The actions of marketing communications regulators in ordering the withdrawal or modification of material deemed to cause significant distress indicate that it is not an acceptable framework for mass media activity. Good intentions are held to not be an excuse for inadvertent harm caused, even if the target of the intervention benefits and those who are negatively impacted are not part of the target group.
Teleology/Consequentialism Focuses on the outcomes or effects of actions – we are ignoring egoism and focusing here on *Utilitarianism* in which behaviour is ethical if it results in the greatest good for the greatest number.	Given the focus is on outcomes, the strategies by which successful interventions are implemented would appear to be able to include coercion if it achieves the desired results. Utilitarianism presents challenges when comparing alternative courses of action with different levels of potential impact, for example, a programme that provides minor benefits to all, versus one that provides major benefits to many but no impact, or a negative impact on others. It also raises questions in relation to who has a mandate to decide whether any harm, or what level of harm, might be acceptable. While stigmatising some groups would be unacceptable for many, it is suggested that it can legitimately be used for activities such as reducing smoking rates (Bayer, 2008). The discussion of the regulatory stance regarding distress would appear to render this a dubious strategy.
Relativism (McDonald, 2010) Under this framework, there is no universal set of ethical principles.	Not applicable to social marketing activity.
Social Contract Theory (Kimmel et al., 2011) Under this framework, there is the belief that an implicit contract exists between the state and/or organisations and individuals or groups regarding rights and responsibilities as a member of society.	Given that contracts are implied rather than stated explicitly, there is no shared understanding of which rights, responsibilities and fairness measures apply to the various parties.

As we noted in Chapter 1, some authors suggest that there is no universal set of ethics that can apply across all sectors of society due to the increasing diversity of society and different perspectives that may be held within cultures or groups and therefore each group's ethical perspective should be held to be equally valid. This perspective would make a universal set of social marketing principles unworkable – and present significant challenges for those working on interventions across cultures.

Another key issue that can be influenced by the selection of specific ethical frameworks is the use of intervention strategies that restrict choice or limit personal freedom. While there are claims that coercion and **paternalism** may be justified to stop people harming others or to stop ill-informed actions (Carter et al., 2011), debate is needed over the circumstances under which coercion may be an appropriate strategy.

Think points

Contrast the application of deontological versus teleological principles for social marketing interventions. How would the use of the two frameworks influence decisions regarding the design and implementation of interventions?

Given the rulings of marketing communications regulators against interventions that are based on deontological principles, can this framework in isolation have a role in social marketing interventions that rely on social advertising as a key component?

In our own research, we have found that social marketing practitioners faced with real-world ethical dilemmas rarely referred to a specific professional code of ethics (e.g. ESOMAR and Market Research Society); a small number noted more general implicit codes – 'health promotion and code developed by myself' and 'general ethical code of act professionally and ethically', or the use of university-specific ethics codes, and there was generally not a high level of satisfaction with the way that dilemmas were resolved. There is very little academic material relating to the resolution of ethical dilemmas and none in social marketing. Parallels can be drawn with the findings from a 2011 study of 40 US social workers which concluded:

> Each of these examples reflects an almost idiosyncratic approach to ethical problem solving. While a case-by-case approach has some advantages in that decisions can be tailored to the specifics of the situation, these respondents did not suggest that a body of wisdom was being developed. Instead, there was an ahistorical approach to the use of consultations. (Hyde, 2012: 361)

The lack of use of specific codes may indicate one or more of the following. There may not have been an appropriate code or other supporting resource material available, or respondents did not know where to locate it. Alternatively, existing codes may not have been of any use in providing guidance for pragmatic decisions regarding solutions. Four respondents noted that specific social marketing codes or guidelines would have been appreciated; one extended this to a regulatory system.

Given concerns noted earlier regarding entrenched views, the existence of social marketing-specific resources may not have been sufficient if external (e.g. funding) sources could have prevented their use. This raises a wider issue, noted by one respondent, of clarifying the relationship between 'social marketing-inspired policy and ethical guidelines'.

Code development and communications

The quality of code content and the way in which codes are implemented are factors in ethical performance (Erwin, 2011). For a code to be 'living', it needs to 'get its hands dirty' and address the real-world ethical issues specific to a profession and outline potential courses of action to resolve dilemmas (Smythe, 2012: 48), i.e. Aristotle's practical wisdom ('phronēsis') noted earlier.

It is argued that the development of a CoE will influence its subsequent effectiveness (Messikomer and Cirka, 2010). This area is largely un-researched, even in the corporate sector, although it is asserted that the development process is important for building awareness, support and ownership, with ethics training and personnel support enhancing code implementation (Kaptein and Schwartz, 2008). Communications of CoE appear problematic in other areas; despite widespread effects to communicate the Academy of Management's CoE, they note 'a sizable proportion' of members remain unaware of it and 'only a very small proportion have read it carefully' (Mowday, 2011).

We need to develop strategies to market ethics to social marketers, to gain acceptance of the need and desirability of ethical guidelines, develop a belief that peers will be supportive and that guidelines can empower people to make difficult ethical decisions more effectively (Kirby and Andreasen, 2001). As part of this, research is needed to determine the nature of ethical dilemmas faced by practitioners, satisfaction with existing codes, guidelines or advice for resolving dilemmas and preferences for additional resources and formal or informal support systems (Verbos et al., 2007). While surveys of the association members are a logical starting point, case studies and in-depth interviews with experts have proven useful at the development and implementation stage (Helin and Sandström, 2007) and could add value to the process.

Conclusions regarding ethical guidance

If a CoE or other form of ethical guidance merely lists broad principles, it will, in common with codes in other areas, 'occupy the role of platitude' and be of little operational value (Malloy et al., 2009: 381). If a CoE is to be a living document with value as both an educational and a decision-making support tool, the process of development will require 'thoughtful debate' (Skubik and Stening, 2009: 515) and be lengthy, but potentially rewarding.. The Social Marketing professional organisations will also need, in common with other professions, to consider mechanisms to support those facing significant ethical dilemmas and code enforcement mechanisms – issues with which other professions continue to grapple (see, for example, Sha, 2011).

Think points

What role should practitioners and academics, individually and in tandem, have in the development and dissemination of codes of ethics or other forms of ethical guidelines?

SUMMARY

The discussion in this chapter has highlighted the scope and complexity of social marketing activity, including activity in other sectors that link to it. We have noted the challenges presented by the use of financial incentives and the need to consider the nature of ethical dilemmas faced by social marketing practitioners together with what resources might be appropriate and of practical use in decision making to resolve dilemmas.

As with earlier chapters, it should be noted that some of the issues we have discussed have no simple solution as they have context, values and cultural dimensions that make their resolution difficult.

The challenge presented by competing ethical frameworks is noted, together with the challenges in attempting to develop codes that transcend cultures and national borders.

Case study   White Ribbon Day (WRD)

This case study is based on Donovan et al. (2009).

White Ribbon Day (WRD) is an annual event in Australia, part of international efforts aimed at raising awareness of the costs to victims of domestic violence. The victims are primarily women and children and the costs include medical, emotional, psychological and quality of life factors. WRD also stresses the criminal nature of domestic violence and the severe penalties for perpetrators who are successfully prosecuted.

In 2006, WRD was overseen by a National Leadership Group (NLG) that coordinated a number of individuals, government agencies and non-governmental organisations active in domestic violence prevention. The multi-national advertising agency Saatchi & Saatchi developed a **pro-bono** (i.e. the agency donated their services) media campaign based on what fathers say colloquially they would do for their daughters, such as:

Give my right arm

Swim through shark infested waters

Go to hell and back

(Continued)

(Continued)

The visual components of the campaign displayed graphic scenes or references to self-harm or suicide.

A 60-second television advertisement showed a young girl watching her father in scenes such as:

- Walking in front of, and being hit by a bus;
- Being taken by sharks while swimming;
- Crawling over broken glass;
- Being prepared for surgery to have his right arm amputated.

The advertisement ended with a blank screen and the words:

> If there is nothing you wouldn't do for your daughter .... Start by wearing a white ribbon on November 25, UN Day for the Elimination of Violence Against Women.

Viral electronic postcards and web banner ads such as those shown below reinforced the television messages.

There is substantial evidence that 'media depictions of suicide can encourage vulnerable viewers to make suicide and self-harm attempts, particularly when the suicide method is clearly shown' (Donovan et al., 2009: 7). There are ethical guidelines and codes of conduct for reporting suicide in news reports and for the depiction of suicide in the media, therefore Donovan et al. argue that there 'appears to be an arguably even greater onus on advertisers to not use suicide images because advertising involves repeated exposures to audiences' (2009: 7). Mental health professionals stated that they believed the suicide depictions in the proposed material contravened media guidelines.

Concerns from mental health and suicide prevention professionals about the intended approach were ignored by Saatchi & Saatchi and the NLG who claimed that the imagery 'was necessary to attract men's attention and to motivate men to take

action against violence against women' (2009: 10). They claimed to have pre-tested the material but did not release the actual data for comment.

Donovan et al. conducted their own pre-testing research but ceased the project half way through when it had become apparent that two of the male respondents had demonstrated visible distress when viewing the images. Even with a small sample (24), their research indicated that the creative idea dominated and hampered communication of the key intended messages as regards wearing a white ribbon and reducing domestic violence.

The campaign developers rejected the research and related concerns. Considerable negative publicity ensued and the television advertisement received little support by way of free air time ('community service announcements') usually provided by television channels for charities and non-profit organisations. The WRD public relations team spent time dealing with the controversy rather than disseminating the core campaign message.

Questions to consider

Read the full academic paper and search the Internet for imagery from the campaign and then critique the 2006 campaign. In hindsight, do you believe that the Saatchi & Saatchi creative strategy was appropriate? Justify your response.

(Continued)

(Continued)

If you were to take over the development and coordination of future WRD events – not just in Australia – what would you do differently and why?

Visit the Australian WRD website and contrast the current activity with the 2006 activity. As the WRD initiative is a global one with UN sponsorship, visit other countries' websites and critique their approaches.

What strategies and tactics can you recommend for future activity? How might these vary across cultural groups?

What research would you recommend to aid the development of the strategies and tactics?

How would you evaluate the effects and effectiveness of the activity?

Further Reading

Sage journal articles and chapters available for free at https://study.sagepub.com/eagleanddahl include:

Cismaru, M., Cismaru, R., Ono, T. and Nelson, K. (2011) '"Act on climate change": An application of protection motivation theory', *Social Marketing Quarterly,* 17(3): 62–84.

French, J. (2011) 'Business as unusual: The contribution of social marketing to government policymaking and strategy development', *The SAGE Handbook of Social Marketing*: 359.

Other

Adshead, F. and Thorpe, A. (2009) 'Health inequalities in England: Advocacy, articulation and action', *Perspectives in Public Health*, 129: 37–41.

Barr, S., Gilg, A. and Shaw, G. (2011) '"Helping people make better choices": Exploring the behaviour change agenda for environmental sustainability', *Applied Geography*, 31: 712–20.

Carrigan, M., Moraes, C. and Leek, S. (2011) 'Fostering responsible communities: A community social marketing approach to sustainable living', *Journal of Business Ethics*, 100: 515–34.

Leonidou, C.N. and Leonidou, L.C. (2011) 'Research into environmental marketing/management: A bibliographic analysis', *European Journal of Marketing*, 45(1/2): 68–103.

Marteau, T.M., Ogilvie, D., Roland, M., Suhrcke, M. and Kelly, M.P. (2011) 'Judging nudging: Can nudging improve population health?', *BMJ*, 342: 263–5.

Signild, V. (2012) 'Nudge—A new and better way to improve health?', *Health Policy*, 104: 200–3.

References

Advertising Standards Authority (ASA) (2007) *Adjudication on Department of Health*. Available at: www.asa.prg.uk/asa/adjudications/Public/TF_ADJ_42557.htm.

Advertising Standards Authority (ASA) (2010) *ASA Adjudication on Department of Energy and Climate Change*. Available at: www.asa.org.uk/Rulings/Adjudications/2010/3/Department-of-Energy-and-Climate-Change/TF_ADJ_48225.aspx#.U9XVFLF--9I.

Andreasen, A.R. (2002a) 'Commercial marketing and social change', *Social Marketing Quarterly*, 8: 41–5.

Andreasen, A.R. (2002b) 'Marketing social marketing in the social change marketplace', *Journal of Public Policy and Marketing*, 21: 3–13.

Assadourian, E. (2010) 'Transforming cultures: From consumerism to sustainability', *Journal of Macromarketing*, 30: 186–91.

Ballantyne, R., Packer, J. and Falk, J. (2011) 'Visitors' learning for environmental sustainability: Testing short- and long-term impacts of wildlife tourism experiences using structural equation modelling', *Tourism Management*, 32: 1243–52.

Bayer, R. (2008) 'Stigma and the ethics of public health: Not can we but should we', *Social Science & Medicine*, 67: 463–72.

Bernhardt, J.M. (2004) 'Communication at the core of effective public health', *American Journal of Public Health*, 94: 2051–3.

Braithwaite, J., Greenfield, D., Westbrook, J., Pawsey, M., Westbrok, M., Gibberd, R., Naylor, J., Nathan, S., Robinson, M., Runciman, B., Jackson, M., Travaglia, J., Johnston, B., Yen, D., McDonald, H., Low, L., Redman, S., Johnson, B., Corbett, A., Hennessy, D., Clark, J. and Lancaster, J. (2010) 'Health service accreditation as a predictor of clinical and organisational performance: A blinded, random, stratified study', *Quality and Safety in Health Care*, 19: 14–21.

Brenkert, G.G. (2002) 'Ethical challenges of social marketing', *Journal of Public Policy & Marketing*, 21: 14–36.

Bull, T., Riggs, E. and Nchogu, S.N. (2012) 'Does health promotion need a Code of Ethics? Results from an IUHPE mixed method survey', *Global Health Promotion*, 19: 8–20.

Buller, D.B., Borland, R. and Burgon, M. (1998) 'Impact of behavioral intention on effectiveness of message features: Evidence from the Family Sun Safety Project', *Human Communication Research*, 24: 433–53.

Burroughs, J.E. (2010) 'Can consumer culture be contained? Comment on "Marketing Means and Ends for a Sustainable Society"', *Journal of Macromarketing*, 30: 127–32.

Callahan, D. and Jennings, B. (2002) 'Ethics and public health: Forging a strong relationship', *American Journal of Public Health*, 92: 169–76.

Carter, S.M., Rychetnik, L., Lloyd, B., Kerridge, I.H., Baur, L., Bauman, A., Hooker, C. and Zask, A. (2011) 'Evidence, ethics, and values: A framework for health promotion', *American Journal of Public Health*, 101: 465–72.

Cohen, S. (2013) 'Nudging and informed consent', *The American Journal of Bioethics*, 13: 3–11.

Commission of the European Communities (2002) *Life Sciences and Biotechnology – A Strategy for Europe*. Available at: http://ec.europa.eu/biotechnology/pdf/com2002-27_en.pdf.

Cornelissen, J.P. and Lock, A.R. (2000) 'Theoretical concept or management fashion? Examining the significance of IMC', *Journal of Advertising Research*, 40: 7–15.

Dann, S. (2007) 'Reaffirming the neutrality of the social marketing tool kit: Social marketing as a hammer, and social marketers as hired guns', *Social Marketing Quarterly*, 13: 54–62.

Department of Health (2004) *Choosing Health: Making Healthy Choices Easier*. London: Department of Health.

Derraik, J.G.B. (2002) 'The pollution of the marine environment by plastic debris: A review', *Marine Pollution Bulletin*, 44: 842–52.

Donovan, R.J., Jalleh, G., Fielder, L. and Ouschan, R. (2009) 'Ethical issues in pro-social advertising: The Australian 2006 White Ribbon Day campaign', *Journal of Public Affairs*, 9: 5–19.

Eagle, L. (2008) *Social Marketing Ethics: Report for National Social Marketing Centre*. London: National Social Marketing Centre.

Eagle, L.C., Dahl, S., Hill, S., et al. (2013) *Social Marketing*. Harlow: Pearson.

Eriksson, S., Helgesson, G. and Höglund, A.T. (2007) 'Being, doing, and knowing: Developing ethical competence in health care', *Journal of Academic Ethics*, 5: 207–16.

Erwin, P.M. (2011) 'Corporate codes of conduct: The effects of code content and quality on ethical performance', *Journal of Business Ethics*, 99: 535–48.

Even, T.A. and Robinson, C.R. (2013) 'The impact of CACREP accreditation: A multiway frequency analysis of ethics violations and sanctions', *Journal of Counseling & Development*, 91: 26–34.

Goldberg, M.E. (1995) 'Social marketing: Are we fiddling while Rome burns?', *Journal of Consumer Psychology*, 4: 347–70.

Government Social Research Unit (2005) *GSR Professional Guidance: Ethical Assurance for Social Research in Government*. London: HM Treasury.

Guttman, N. and Salmon, C.T. (2004) 'Guilt, fear, stigma and knowledge gaps: Ethical issues in public health communication interventions', *Bioethics*, 18: 531–52.

Heise, L., Lutz, B., Ranganathan, M. and Watts, C. (2013) 'Cash transfers for HIV prevention: Considering their potential', *Journal of the International AIDS Society*, 16: 1–5.

Helin, S. and Sandström, J. (2007) 'An inquiry into the study of corporate codes of ethics', *Journal of Business Ethics*, 75: 253–71.

Helin, S., Jensen, T., Sandström, J. and Clegg, S. (2011) 'On the dark side of codes: Domination not enlightenment', *Scandinavian Journal of Management*, 27: 24–33.

Homonoff, T.A. (2012) *Can Small Incentives Have Large Effects? The Impact of Taxes versus Bonuses on Disposable Bag Use,* Working Paper. The Wharton School: University of Pennsylvania.

Hunt, S.D. and Vitell, S.J. (2006) 'The general theory of marketing ethics: A revision and three questions', *Journal of Macromarketing*, 26: 143–53.

Hyde, C.A. (2012) 'Ethical dilemmas in human service management: Identifying and resolving the challenges', *Ethics and Social Welfare*, 6: 351–67.

Iyer, E.S. and Kashyap, R.K. (2007) 'Consumer recycling: Role of incentives, information, and social class', *Journal of Consumer Behaviour*, 6: 32–47.

Kaptein, M. and Schwartz, M.S. (2008) 'The effectiveness of business codes: A critical examination of existing studies and the development of an integrated research model', *Journal of Business Ethics*, 77: 111–27.

Kimmel, A.J, Smith, N.C. and Klein, J.G. (2011) 'Ethical decision making and research deception in the behavioral sciences: An application of social contract theory', *Ethics & Behavior*, 21: 222–51.

Kirby, S.D. and Andreasen, A.R. (2001) 'Marketing ethics to social marketers: A segmented approach', in A.R. Andreasen (ed.), *Ethics in Social Marketing*. Washington DC: Georgetown University Press. pp. 160–83.

Kotler, P. and Roberto, E. (1989) *Social Marketing*. New York: The Free Press.

Kotler, P., Roberto, N. and Lee, N. (2002) *Social Marketing: Improving the Quality of Life*. Thousand Oaks, CA: Sage.

Langford, R. and Panter-Brick, C. (2013) 'A health equity critique of social marketing: Where interventions have impact but insufficient reach', *Social Science & Medicine*, 83: 133–41.

Leahy, S. (2004) 'Drowning in an ocean of Plastic', *Wired* [online], 5 June. Available at: http://www.culturechange.org/Petroleum&Plastics.html.

Lefebvre, R.C. (2011) 'An integrative model for social marketing', *Journal of Social Marketing*, 1: 54–72.

Long, B.S. and Driscoll, C. (2008) 'Codes of ethics and the pursuit of organizational legitimacy: Theoretical and empirical contributions', *Journal of Business Ethics*, 77: 173–89.

Lucke, J. (2013) 'Context is all important in investigating attitudes: Acceptability depends on the nature of the nudge, who nudges, and who is nudged', *The American Journal of Bioethics*, 13: 24–5.

Lynagh, M.C., Sanson-Fisher, R.W. and Bonevski, B. (2013) 'What's good for the goose is good for the gander. Guiding principles for the use of financial incentives in health behaviour change', *International Journal of Behavioral Medicine*, 20: 114–20.

Malloy, D., Sevigny, P., Hadjistavropoulos, T., Jeyaraj, M., Fahey McCarthy, E., Murakami, M., Paholpak, S., Lee, Y. and Park, I. (2009)' Perceptions of the effectiveness of ethical guidelines: An international study of physicians', *Medicine, Health Care and Philosophy*, 12: 373–83.

McDonald, G. (2010) 'Ethical relativism vs absolutism: Research implications', *European Business Review*, 22: 446–64.

Ménard, J-F. (2010) 'A 'nudge' for public health ethics: Libertarian paternalism as a framework for ethical analysis of public health interventions?', *Public Health Ethics*, 3: 229–38.

Messikomer, C.M. and Cirka, C.C. (2010) 'Constructing a code of ethics: An experiential case of a national professional organization', *Journal of Business Ethics*, 95: 55–71.

Mortimer, D., Ghijben, P., Harris, A. and Hollingsworth, B. (2013) *Incentive-based and Non-incentive-based Interventions for Increasing Blood Donation*. The Cochrane Library.

Mowday, R.T. (2011) 'Elevating the dialogue on professional ethics to the next level: Reflections on the experience of the Academy of Management', *Management and Organization Review*, 7: 505–9.

Müller, C., Townsend, K. and Matschullat, J. (2012) 'Experimental degradation of polymer shopping bags (standard and degradable plastic, and biodegradable) in the gastrointestinal fluids of sea turtles', *Science of The Total Environment*, 416: 464–7.

National Social Marketing Centre (2006) *It's Our Health! Realising the Potential of Effective Social Marketing*. London: National Social Marketing Centre.

Newton, J.D., Newton, F.J., Turk, T. and Ewing, M.T. (2013)' Ethical evaluation of audience segmentation in social marketing', *European Journal of Marketing*, 47: 1421–38.

Noordegraaf, M. (2011) 'Remaking professionals? How associations and professional education connect professionalism and organizations', *Current Sociology*, 59: 465–88.

Painter-Morland, M. (2010) 'Questioning corporate codes of ethics', *Business Ethics: A European Review*, 19: 265–79.

Payne, D. and Pressley, M. (2013) 'A transcendent code of ethics for marketing professionals', *International Journal of Law and Management*, 55: 55–73.

Peattie, K. and Peattie, S. (2003) 'Ready to fly solo? Reducing social marketing's dependence on commercial marketing theory', *Marketing Theory*, 3: 365–85.

Quick, B.L. and Stephenson, M.T. (2007) 'The Reactance Restoration Scale (RRS): A measure of direct and indirect restoration', *Communication Research Reports*, 24: 131–8.

Quinn, G.P., Ellery, J., Thomas, K.B. and Marshall, R. (2010) 'Developing a common language for using social marketing: An analysis of public health literature', *Health Marketing Quarterly*, 27: 334–53.

Rains, S.A. (2013) 'The nature of psychological reactance revisited: A meta-analytic review', *Human Communication Research*, 39: 47–73.

Rossi, J. and Yudell, M. (2012) 'Value-ladenness and rationality in health communication', *The American Journal of Bioethics*, 12: 20–2.

Rothschild, M.L. (1999) 'Carrots, sticks, and promises: A conceptual framework for the management of public health and social issue behaviors', *Journal of Marketing*, 63: 24–37.

Rummel, A., Howard, J., Swinton, J.M. and Seymour, D.B. (2000) 'You can't have that! A study of reactance effects and children's consumer behavior', *Journal of Marketing Theory and Practice*, 8: 38–44.

Schmidt, H., Asch, D.A. and Halpern, S.D. (2012) 'Fairness and wellness incentives: What is the relevance of the process-outcome distinction?', *Preventive Medicine*, 55: S118–23.

Schwartz, M.S. (2005) 'Universal moral values for corporate codes of ethics', *Journal of Business Ethics*, 59: 27–44.

Sha, B-L. (2011) 'Accredited vs. non-accredited: The polarization of practitioners in the public relations profession', *Public Relations Review*, 37: 121–8.

Sindall, C. (2002) 'Does health promotion need a code of ethics?', *Health Promotion International*, 17: 201–3.

Skubik, D.W. and Stening, B.W. (2009) 'What's in a credo? A critique of the academy of management's code of ethical conduct and code of ethics', *Journal of Business Ethics*, 85: 515–25.

Smythe, V. (2012)' Codes of ethics', in P. Bowden (ed.), *Applied Ethics: Strengthening Ethical Practices*. Prahran, VIC: Tilde University Press.

Somers, M.J. (2001) 'Ethical codes of conduct and organizational context: A study of the relationship between codes of conduct, employee behavior and organizational values', *Journal of Business Ethics*, 30: 185–95.

Sonenshein, S. (2007) 'The role of construction, intuition, and justification in responding to ethical issues at work: The sensemaking-intuition model', *Academy of Management Review*, 32: 1022–40.

Stead, M., Gordon, R., Angus, K. and McDermott, L. (2007) 'A Systematic review of social marketing effectiveness', *Health Education*, 107: 126–91.

Stephens, C. (2013) 'Paying the piper: Additional considerations of the theoretical, ethical and moral basis of financial incentives for health behaviour change', *International Journal of Behavioral Medicine*, 21: 202–5.

Stevens, B. (2008) 'Corporate ethical codes: Effective instruments for influencing behavior', *Journal of Business Ethics*, 78: 601–9.

Sussman, S., Grana, R., Pokhrel, P., Rohrbach, L.A. and Sun, P. (2010) 'Forbidden fruit and the prediction of cigarette smoking', *Substance Use & Misuse*, 45: 1683–93.

Thomas, R. and Thomas, H. (2013) '"Hollow from the start"? Professional associations and the professionalisation of tourism', *The Service Industries Journal*, 34: 38–55.

Verbos, A.K., Gerard, J.A., Forshey, P.R., Harding, C.S. and Miller, J.S. (2007) 'The positive ethical organization: Enacting a living code of ethics and ethical organizational identity', *Journal of Business Ethics*, 76: 17–33.

Whitehead, D. (2004) 'Health promotion and health education: Advancing the concepts', *Journal of Advanced Nursing*, 47: 311–20.

12 Legislation, Regulation and Ethics

Stephan Dahl and Kathleen Mortimer

INTRODUCTION

While the previous chapters have raised potential ethical issues in a variety of contexts, this chapter aims to highlight the role of regulation and other policy interventions to shape, nurture, promote and enforce ethical behaviour. It is notable, however, that most regulatory activities are limited to promotional activities, with far fewer regulations targeting other forms of marketing, for example pricing or distribution. A likely explanation of this is that, as noted previously, marketing communication is the major visible element of marketing, and thus commands most attention from regulators and policy makers.

REGULATION

Most countries of the world have some sort of **self-regulation** for advertising and marketing communications. These include Europe, North America, many South American countries and some countries in Africa and Asia. Projects to develop self-regulation in

China and Russia are presently underway, as well as further adoption in additional South American countries.

Self-regulation

Self regulation is a system which is created and run by the advertising industry, made up of advertisers, agencies and media. The industry agrees on specific rules and standards of practice and creates a self-regulatory organisation (**SRO**) to ensure that the industry adheres to these. The overall aim of these institutions is to ensure that all advertising is legal, decent, honest and truthful. Self-regulation works best if it is within a legislative framework so that it can call on the support of legislation when advertisers are uncooperative and determined to undertake unethical practices e.g. rogue traders (EASA, 2010). The relationship between the SRO and the legislation varies from country to country, and is one of the main challenges in reaching some consistency across borders. For example, in some European countries, e.g. France, there is extensive and quite complicated legislation and one of the main roles of the SROs is to explain the legislation to the advertising industry. In other countries, such as Bulgaria and Hungary, where the advertising industry is young, the legislation and advertising codes are bounded together with the consequence that if the rules are broken then an illegal act has been committed. Taylor and Raymond (2000) suggest that advertising regulations are a result of a combination of legal, political, economic, cultural and religious factors in each country and that these differences are a significant barrier to international advertising.

Most regulatory frameworks, therefore, are country specific, although there is cross-country coordination of some activities and in some economic areas, e.g. the European Union. For instance, the Advertising Standards Authority regulates advertising content in the UK, while the Federal Trade Commission in the US carries out the same function, although local or state laws complement some aspects. For example, the minimum age for advertising and other promotions for alcoholic products targeting young adults is dependent on state provisions in the US. However, due to increases in international business, there have been attempts to ensure some coordination across borders. For example, the European Advertising Standards Alliance (EASA) has been created to support the self-regulatory organisations in each of the member states, share best practice and to encourage consistency whilst being mindful of cultural and legal differences. Its other main role is to deal with cross-border complaints. It presently has 48 members, 21 of whom are from EU countries. Another regional organisation, Asia-Pacific Economic Co-operation (APEC), also strives to encourage and support the self-regulatory organisations of its member states, which consist of 21 countries including USA, Australia, China and Russia. Both these organisations, which between them cover much of the developed and developing world, have obtained their original codes of practice from the International Chamber of Commerce (ICC) – which created a Code of Marketing and Advertising Practice as early as 1937. Its most recent revision of the code was published in 2011. Six of the top 10 contributors to the growth of adspend between 2013 and 2016 are APEC economies, i.e. the USA, China, Indonesia, Japan, Korea and Russia, which indicates the growing importance of these economies to global adspend (OPEC, 2014).

Think points

Go onto YouTube and look at videos of advertisements for the same brand from three different countries. How do they vary? Do you think the foreign advertisements would be acceptable in your country, and if not why not?

While certain promotional activity, especially related to harmful products (see also Chapter 8) and to vulnerable groups (Chapter 9), is most heavily regulated, these SROs also ensure a level playing field, carrying out an important reputational function for the advertising industry. In an environment where advertising is often seen as inherently negative, not least because advertisers are perceived to frequently engage in deceptive practices (for example, through inflated and false claims) (Rotfeld and Taylor, 2009), these organisations are charged with protecting the credibility of marketing communication. Moreover, effective intervention in the case of transgressions can be important, as consumers believe less in contradiction or corrections of false claims then the original (false) claims themselves (Brown and Nix, 1996), and attempting to correct previously stated false claims is tedious and time-consuming (Johar and Roggeveen, 2007).

Regulation focus

There are different ways used to regulate advertising in traditional, and to a lesser extent, online and new media. Restrictions over what can be claimed in advertising (**content restrictions**) and restrictions relating to which products can be advertised (**product restrictions**) are used for both broadcasting media (such as television and radio) and non-broadcast media (such as magazines and direct marketing materials). However, individual regulations may vary. For example, in some countries strong alcoholic beverages (spirits) can be advertised in magazines but not on television. In other countries alcoholic beverages of any kind cannot be advertised on television. For broadcasting media, such as radio and television, in addition to the restriction types above, many countries also have restrictions on the total time or overall amount of advertising (quantity restrictions) that can be broadcast.

Content and product restrictions

In terms of general advertising content, advertising is usually expected to be 'legal, decent, honest and truthful' (ASA, 2014). Further to this, some product categories are heavily restricted in what they can claim when advertised, for example, health claims in food advertising in the European Union (Brennan et al., 2008). The rationale for heavy restrictions of certain claims, such as a ban on any health claims, is that in some cases the claims made are either wholly untrue or deceptive, and that as such can lead to significant societal damage, for example by suggesting that an overall unhealthy product has certain health benefits. For example, in the EU it would not be permissible to claim that potato crisps are an 'excellent source of vitamin E', even if true. This is because crisps are considered a high fat/high salt food and their over-consumption is also considered undesirable. A report by OPEC shows that the most regulated product areas for the economies they represent are alcohol, tobacco, food, medicines and gambling (WHO, 2014). But these regulations vary. For example, in Russia, an alcoholic advert cannot be placed on the first or last page of a newspaper while in Thailand all print advertising for alcohol is prohibited.

In addition to regulation about what can be claimed, advertising for some product categories is banned completely in some countries. Often full advertising bans or partial restrictions on what can be claimed relate to 'undesirable' products, for example demerit goods, such as cigarettes, high-sugar and fat foods, gambling services, guns and alcohol. However, the effectiveness of outright bans or heavy restrictions is disputed. In the case of tobacco advertising, some researchers have found little evidence of a reduction in smoking as a result of complete advertising bans (Capella et al., 2008), while others claim that a reduction in exposure to tobacco promotions as a result of advertising bans leads to a decrease in smoking (Harris et al., 2006). Similarly, content and time restrictions on alcohol advertising are controversial, with some studies claiming little or no effects (Ogborne and Smart, 2006), while other researchers see an urgent need for a full ban on alcohol advertising (Hastings et al., 2010).

Quantity restrictions

For broadcasting media, such as television, the total amount of air-time handed over to advertising is restricted in most, but not all, developed nations. Total advertising time per hour is not restricted in the US, although on average networks air around 11 minutes of advertising per hour (Gantz et al., 2007) . In the EU, the advertising time is restricted by the Audiovisual Media Services Directive to a maximum of 12 minutes per hour (Commission, 2007), although some countries have stricter limitations. Some types of programming have further restrictions on advertising, for example programming aimed primarily at children in Norway and Sweden (Caraher et al., 2007).

From an economic perspective, Anderson (2007) argues that time restrictions may reduce programme quality, breadth of programming, and overall programme choice and diversity by reducing the profits broadcasters can achieve.

Think points

Take a sample of advertisements from a print magazine and compare them with regulatory provisions. For example, look at the alcoholic beverages advertised in a magazine and compare what you see with the appropriate regulations (e.g. the ASA Advertising Code or similar). Discuss your findings.

Non-traditional media

The regulatory framework for traditional media, e.g. television, radio, billboards etc., has been relatively well established in most developed countries. This includes relatively high awareness of complaints procedures, and a system of sanctioning marketers who breach regulations. The effectiveness of dealing with transgressions has been called into question, for example, in the case of alcoholic beverages (Hastings et al., 2010). However, a point to note is that the failure to deal effectively with contraventions can more frequently be found in regulatory provisions, particularly where these provisions have failed to accommodate new media forms. Another potential reason for the perceived failure of regulation particularly in new media formats may be due to the nature of the messages and the context in which they are placed. For instance, regulations, such as the ASA regulations, typically assume that marketing communications focus largely on providing arguments for purchasing a product, e.g. product-related information. Further, they assume that this information is clearly and explicitly articulated.

From an advertiser point of view, such an approach seems logical in a traditional media environment, where much of the information needs to be communicated in a specific and small amount of time (e.g. the time for a television advertisement, or the time a reader pays attention to a print advert). However, in the context of social media, overt sales propositions are less likely to be attractive. Firstly, this is because in a social media context the people who follow and engage with the brand are likely to be brand users. Secondly, from a user perspective, overt sales arguments are likely to be less attractive than entertaining or engaging content (e.g. in the form of content marketing).

Challenge of **simultaneous media usage**

Despite quantity regulation in traditional media forms, advertising messages have become ubiquitous. Especially in broadcast media, the viewers' response to advertising is increasing advertising avoidance (Meurs, 1998), mostly as a learned response to advertising, rather than in response to particular adverts (Speck and Elliott, 1997). Marketers have embraced the possible solution of avoiding avoidance by increasing consumer engagement and interaction, for example by using strategies such as interactive loyalty banners during advertising breaks (Dix et al., 2010).

Most consumers watching television are also using other media, for example engaging in social media interactions, at the same time. Increasingly, viewers access simultaneously used media for additional information, for example searching for information related to advertised products (Zigmond and Stipp, 2010). Thus, a small, but noticeable, number of consumers are bypassing the limitations largely designed for broadcast media by combining different media forms with different regulatory reach. Moreover, engaging actively with advertised products, for example by seeking further product information, is likely to lead to a much stronger attitude towards the product advertised. This is the likely result of information being processed centrally, as described in the **elaboration likelihood model** (Petty and Cacioppo, 1986).

The ELM is a dual process theory of processing information, consisting of a central and a peripheral route. A central route operates when individuals are highly interested or motivated to pay attention to the message. Thus, the individual engages with the message and 'elaborates' on the message content. A peripheral route operates when interest and motivation are low. If a message is processed peripherally, the individual stores sensory (emotional) information related to the advertisement, but does not elaborate on the message. Over time, both routes have the ability to change an individual's attitude. As a generalised rule, centrally processed information will result in a faster and more profound attitude change, while peripherally processed information is likely to result in more subtle, emotional changes over an extended period of time.

Consequently, creating a shift from peripheral to central processing has long been regarded as the most effective way to engage consumers. Increased consumer interactivity, and resulting attention and engagement, are also a major factor explaining why online campaigns have proven to be increasingly more common than campaigns relying solely on traditional media (Kim and McMillan, 2008). Not surprisingly, interactive online campaigns have been found to be more effective than traditional advertising, not least because most information online is likely to be centrally processed. This is especially the case for online word-of-mouth (Trusov et al., 2009), where recommendations come from a trusted source, e.g. a friend or other website users. Trusov and colleagues estimate that word of mouth referrals are 20–30 times more effective than traditional marketing activities. As with traditional media, customer engagement has been identified as the key factor in the success of social media campaigns (Solis, 2010).

User-generated media

A further complicating factor is user-generated media content when much of the regulatory framework has been built around traditional mass media. The ever-changing digital landscape, including the explosion of content created by individuals rather than organisations, has created new challenges for regulators. The European Advertising Standards Alliance (EASA) created 'Digital Marketing Communications Best Practice' guidelines for its members in 2008 to address some of these challenges, and this developed into the Extended Digital Remit that was implemented across most of Europe in 2011. This remit means that the SRO has influence not only over paid-for advertising on the Internet but also over any 'advertising and marketing communications' on an advertiser's website or other non-paid-for space online that is under their control, e.g. blogs and Facebook pages. This distinction of control is an important one when considering user-generated content. The remit explains that if the advertiser has requested the creation of user-generated content or assisted in the distribution of it, then it becomes the advertiser's responsibility to ensure adherence to the code. Notably though, if members of the general public create content which contains reference to an organisation's brand independent of that organisation because of their own accord, then such communication is not covered by the remit. The remit also covers advergames, digital outdoor material and text messaging. In the area of text messaging, many of the complaints are in the area of financial services, particularly the perceived information that loans are easily available with few conditions if any.

An interesting area of challenge is that of Twitter which also falls under the Digital Remit. A number of companies have employed celebrities to tweet on their behalf and some complaints have been made to the Advertising Standards Authority in the UK where it was unclear whether an individual created the tweet independently or the company did, e.g. Wayne Rooney and Nike. One of the rulings of the code is that any marketing communications should be clearly identified as such (see also discussion in the chapter on social media ethics).

However, online word-of-mouth (i.e. the publishing, sharing or forwarding of product relevant information) and additional information seeking are only two of the potential marketing tools used for online, interactive marketing. Other tools include **open source marketing**, where customers create their own advertising campaigns for a product or service, and co-created campaigns based on crowd sourcing. Similarly, online groups and Virtual Worlds, all of which aim to engage the consumers, although to different degrees, offer new and evolving forms of potential marketing and promotional activity.

Table 12.1 summarises the main tools used in advertising, in terms of interactivity (or central processing likelihood), shareability (or likelihood of the tool being used in a 'viral manner'), and hypothetical ability for a regulator to regulate messages and for companies to control marketing messages.

Table 12.1 Different forms of online marketing activities

	Open source marketing	Crowd sourcing/ Co-creation	vWOM	Groups	Virtual worlds	Website
Interactivity	Very high	High	High	Variable	High	Low
Shareability	Very high	Low	Medium	Medium	Medium	Low
Regulation ability	None	High	Low	Low	High	High
Message control	None	High	Low	Low	High	High

As the area of new and evolving media and communication forms is rapidly expanding and evolving, designing a regulatory framework which is able to cover the multitude of different marketing forms will be an increasing challenge.

CROSS-BORDER LEGISLATION

One of the other results of new media is that many marketing communications are now available to consumers outside of the country from which the message was sent. In order to ensure that consumers have the same protection from these communications as from those within their own country, EASA set up a cross-border complaints procedure. Because, as stated above, there are inconsistencies in terms of regulations between countries, this system is based on the premise of 'mutual recognition', which states that marketing communications must comply with the rules of the country of origin and not with the rules of the country in which they are being received. The country of origin is based on the domain name and the registered office address.

The EASA produce a quarterly report on complaints that are based on one country to another in this process. The Quarterly Report for January to March 2014 indicates that there were 27 cross-border complaints during that period, with 26 of them referring to misleading information. For example a consumer in the UK complained about an email communication from Adidas who were based in the Netherlands. The message stated that there was free delivery on all orders over £100. However, the UK consumer was charged £8.95. The complaint was upheld by the Dutch SRO and Adidas was told to not advertise in this way again.

ALTERNATIVE APPROACHES

The SRO approach has been well established in many countries. And while one of the declared principles of SROs is to uphold the honest and fair principles of marketing activities, there are nevertheless frequent criticisms of the advertising industry and marketing as a whole, some of which have been highlighted throughout this book.

The SRO approach have been widely criticised as essentially ineffective by some researchers (Roberts et al., 2014), while others have looked at how effectiveness can be enhanced (Bian et al., 2011). In relation to advertising, but with ramifications into other aspects of marketing such as pricing and distribution, Bian et al. (2011) point out the fundamental dilemma facing regulation – the opposing primary concerns of the parties involved. While marketers are largely driven by self-interest and avoidance of regulator action or lawsuits, consumers are largely driven by a need for accurate and truthful information, respect of dignity and transparency.

The only common concern binding together advertisers, agencies, consumers and the media is the law. Yet, lawmakers are often reluctant to intervene in marketing activities, unless there is a potential for significant political gains. Thus, lawmakers have traditionally focused mostly in a responsive manner on matters of heightened public and media concerns (e.g. rising obesity rates prompting interventions into the marketing of food items), while they have seldom taken a proactive stance.

Thus the question arises which, if any, alternative or complementary methods have the potential to lead to a more ethical, truthful and level playing field for marketers? The answer is unlikely to be found in a single approach, and more likely to be in a combination of different approaches. Throughout this book, alternative approaches have been highlighted, and it is therefore useful to draw together the main three alternatives and discuss them briefly together: codes of practice, from the industry side; media literacy targeting and empowering consumers; and demarketing, from a governmental and industry side.

Codes of practice

Codes of practice (CoPs), sometimes called codes of ethics or conduct, are common in management and marketing. From the Advertising Standards Authority's Code of Practice, to industry specific codes such as the Portman Group's Code of Practice governing alcohol advertising, or the ABPI code for prescription medicines or PAGB Code for over the counter medicines in the UK – to name just a few.

Drawn up by the industry, or industry bodies, while the intention of these codes may be laudable, they are often static. However, to be truly useful CoPs need to be a living document with value as both an educational and a decision-making support tool. The process of development requires 'thoughtful debate', which should be lengthy, but potentially rewarding (Skubik and Stening, 2009).

It is important to realise though that the simple existence of a CoP will not prevent unethical behaviour. Rather, CoPs need an extensive development process, have the potential to raise awareness of issues and require a wide-ranging 'buy-in' to be effective (Messikomer and Cirka, 2010).

The 'buy-in' of all industry parties is important in order to achieve a commitment for exemplary behaviour, a burden increasingly falling on various industries as a whole. Faced with the threat of increasing regulation, industry players cannot rely on the absence of evidence of harm resultant from their marketing activities. Rather, they must realise that legal and statutory regulation is largely based on 'a judgement of probable influence' (Livingstone, 2005: 278).

Media literacy

Media literacy is discussed in detail in Chapter 7. As previously noted, simply developing media literacy campaigns is unlikely to avert potential statutory regulation in the long run.

There is undeniably a need to be seen to be taking positive action to avoid further restrictions on promotions and marketing communication activity (Cincotta, 2005). But further than being seen to be taking action, it is imperative that media literacy campaigns are rigorously tested for their effectiveness, and are able to prove positive outcomes beyond recall and recognition.

Demarketing

Demarketing has been touched upon in the context of sustainable consumer behaviour in Chapter 6. The idea of discouraging demand should be a consideration of not only governmental institutions, but also of industries facing increasing scrutiny of their marketing practices. Using demarketing to achieve sustainable markets and activities is important and not only in an environmental context. In other contexts demarketing with input from industry will help to position industry as part of a solution rather than the problem, especially if a rigorous evaluation of demarketing interventions is carried out. Examples of the potential for demarketing campaigns are wide-ranging, from gun controls (Gundlach et al., 2010) to tobacco products (Lee et al., 2005). But they are also less contentious products. For example, giving rising rates of antibiotic resistance, the medical industry has a real chance to engage in demarketing campaigns for some prescription drugs.

SUMMARY

This chapter focused on existing regulatory frameworks, as well as a brief discussion of potentially complementary tactics to ensure long-term sustainability in marketing.

Ultimately though the burden lies with the marketers and the industry themselves. Facing rising criticism from policy makers and scepticism from consumers, exemplary behaviour by marketers appears to be the most promising tactic to develop a sustainable way forward. No single SRO, code of practice, media literacy or demarketing campaign will appear as convincing as consistent, ethical behaviour from the industry.

Case study   Paddy Power

Paddy Power is an Irish bookmaker operating a chain of betting shops in the UK and the Republic of Ireland, as well as online gambling in the form of casinos, betting and poker games.

Marketing in the gambling and betting market, and especially marketing communication activity, is tightly regulated in the UK as well as in other markets. For example, the Advertising Standards Authority has a specific code for the advertising and promotion of gambling and betting.

Paddy Power is no stranger to controversial marketing campaigns, some of which have resulted in official investigations by the Advertising Standards Authority. For instance, an advert in 2010 showed sight-impaired footballers apparently kicking a cat rather than the ball. A year later, the bookmaker ran into trouble for running a suggestive advertising campaign using the slogan 'Blow Me'. A reoccurring feature of these advertising campaigns is the offer of money off – or a refund on unsuccessful bids. For instance, the 2011 advertising campaign offered refunds if Barcelona beat Manchester United for losing bets (*Guardian*, 2011).

In 2014, Paddy Power ran a one-off advert in the *Sun on Sunday*, showing an image of an Academy Award (Oscar) statue, with the head replaced with that of Oscar Pistorius. This coincided with Pistorius's trial in South Africa for the alleged murder of his girlfriend, and offered to refund all money on losing bets if he was found not guilty.

The advertisement caused outrage among many people, making it the most complained about advert in UK history: more than 5500 complaints were lodged with the Advertising Standards Authority, and an online petition at change.org reached 100,000 complaints within two days.

Despite the outcry, Paddy Power reacted gloatingly to the public reaction. In an interview with the *Daily Mail*, the company revelled in the publicity the controversy had created. A company spokesman described the controversy as 'In your face, KFC!', a reference to an earlier, similarly controversial advertisement (Reilly, 2014).

In an unusual step, the Advertising Standards Authority immediately ordered the advertisement to be withdrawn, and ordered that no further version of the advert could appear in the meantime.

The ASA then considered, under its usual complaints procedure, whether the advertisement had been in breach of the advertising rules. Specifically, it investigated possible breaches against bringing marketing communication into disrepute and causing widespread offence or distress.

The ASA eventually ruled that the advert caused widespread offence and distress and that it further brought advertising into disrepute. In its ruling, the ASA stated that Paddy Power should have foreseen the potential widespread offence caused by the advert.

Questions to consider

Given that none of the complaints were specific to gambling or betting, how do you judge the case?

Considering that Paddy Power has a long-standing history of controversial advertising, how can you address potential harm? What do you think are the potential consequences of Paddy Power's behaviour for other betting and gambling companies?

How do you judge the outcome of the campaign, especially considering that one single advert caused widespread public relations coverage and it was prominently discussed on social media?

Further Reading

Sage journal articles available for free at https://study.sagepub.com/eagleand dahl include:

Gordon, R., Carrigan, M. and Hastings, G. (2011) 'A framework for sustainable marketing', *Marketing Theory*, 11(2): 143–63.

Harker, D. and Harker, M. (2000) 'The role of codes of conduct in the advertising self-regulatory framework', *Journal of Macromarketing*, 20(2): 155–66.

Redmond, W.H. (2009) 'A political economy of regulatory failure in US packaged food markets', *Journal of Macromarketing*, 29(2): 135–44.

Other

Bian, X., Kitchen, P. and Teresa Cuomo, M. (2011) 'Advertising self-regulation: Clearance processes, effectiveness and future research agenda', *The Marketing Review*, 11(4): 393–414.

Rotfeld, H.J. and Taylor, C.R. (2009) 'The advertising regulation and self-regulation issues ripped from the headlines with (sometimes missed) opportunities for disciplined multidisciplinary research', *Journal of Advertising*, 38(4): 5–14.

References

Anderson, S. (2007) 'Regulation of television advertising', *The Economic Regulation of Broadcasting Markets*, Cambridge: Cambridge University Press. Pp 189–224.

ASA (2014) Performance and objectives: Half-year statement, January–June. London: Advertising Standards Authority.

Bian, X., Kitchen, P. and Teresa Cuomo, M. (2011) 'Advertising self-regulation: Clearance processes, effectiveness and future research agenda', *The Marketing Review*, 11(4): 393–414.

Brennan, R., Dahl, S., Lynne, E., Mourouti, O. Czarnecka, B. (2008) 'Regulation of Nutrition and Health Claims in Advertising', *Journal of Advertising Research*, 48(2): 57–70.

Brown, A.S. and Nix, L.A. (1996) 'Turning lies into truths: Referential validation of falsehoods', *Journal of Experimental Psychology: Learning, Memory, and Cognition*, 22(5): 1088–100.

Capella, M.L., Taylor, C.R. and Webster, C. (2008) 'The effect of cigarette advertising bans on consumption: A meta-analysis', *Journal of Advertising*, 37(2): 7–18.

Caraher, M. and Carr-Hill, R. (2007) 'Taxation and Population Health: "Sin Taxes" or Structured Approaches', *Macrosocial determinants of population health*. Springer, pp. 211–231.

Cincotta, K. (2005) *Accord Gets Kids to Munch Right*. B & T Magazine – electronic edition, 8 April. Sydney. Available at: www.bandt.com.au (accessed: 27 April 2005).

Commission of the European Union (2007). Audiovisual Media Services Directive. Vol. 2007/65/EC. Brussels.

Dix, S.R., Bellman, S., Haddad, H. and Varan, D. (2010) 'Using interactive program-loyalty banners to reduce TV ad avoidance: Is it possible to give viewers a reason to stay tuned during commercial breaks?', *Journal of Advertising Research*, 50 (2): 154–160.

EASA (2010) Draft EASA Best Practice Recommendation, Brussels: European Advertising Standards Alliance.

Gantz, W., Schwartz, N., Angelini, J., Rideout, V. (2007) Food For thought: Television Food Advertising to Children in the United States, Menlo Park, California: The Henry J. Kaiser Family Foundation.

Guardian (2011) *Paddy Power Runs into Controversy over Imogen Thomas Newspaper Ad*, *The Guardian*, 27 May. Available at: http://www.theguardian.com/media/2011/may/27/paddy-power-imogen-thomas-blow-me (accessed 11 December 2014).

Gundlach, G.T., Bradford, K.D. and Wilkie, W.L. (2010) 'Countermarketing and demarketing against product diversion: Forensic research in the firearms industry', *Journal of Public Policy & Marketing*, 29(1): 103–22.

Harris, F., MacKintosh, A.M., Anderson, S., Hastings, G., Borland, R., Fong, G.T., Hammond, D. and Cummings, K.M. (2006) 'Effects of the 2003 advertising/promotion ban in the United

Kingdom on awareness of tobacco marketing: findings from the International Tobacco Control (ITC) Four Country Survey', *Tobacco Control,* 15 (suppl 3): iii26–iii33.

Hastings, G., Brooks, O., Stead, M., Angus, K., Anker, T. and Farrell, T. (2010) 'Failure of self regulation of UK alcohol advertising', *BMJ,* 340: b5650.

Johar, G.V. and Roggeveen, A.L. (2007) 'Changing false beliefs from repeated advertising: The role of claim-refutation alignment', *Journal of Consumer Psychology*, 17(2): 118.

Kim, J. and McMillan, S.J. (2008) 'Evaluation of internet advertising research: A bibliometric analysis of citations from key sources', *Journal of Advertising,* 37 (1): 99–112.

Lee, D., Cutler, B.D. and Burns, J. (2005) 'The marketing and demarketing of tobacco products to low-income African-Americans', *Health Marketing Quarterly*, 22(2): 51–68.

Livingstone, S. (2005) 'Assessing the research base for the policy debate over the effects of food advertising to children', *International Journal of Advertising*, 24(3): 273–96.

Messikomer, C.M. and Cirka, C.C. (2010) 'Constructing a code of ethics: An experiential case of a national professional organization', *Journal of Business Ethics*, 95(1): 55–71.

Meurs, L.V. (1998) 'Zapp! A study on switching behavior during commercial breaks', *Journal of Advertising Research*, 38(1): 43–4.

Ogborne, A. and Smart, R. (2006) 'Will restrictions on alcohol advertising reduce alcohol consumption?', *Addiction*, 75 (3): 293–296.

Petty, R.E. and Cacioppo, J.T. (1986) 'The elaboration likelihood model of persuasion', *Advances in experimental social psychology,* 19: 123–205.

Reilly, J. (2014) *Paddy Power Gloats that Oscar Pistorius Ad is 'Most Complained About Advert', Daily Mail* Online, 20 March. Available at: http://www.dailymail.co.uk/news/article-2585179/In-face-KFC-Shameless-Paddy-Power-makes-extraordinary-gloats-disgusting-Pistorius-ad-complained-advert-time.html (accessed 11 December 2014).

Roberts, M., Pettigrew, S., Chapman, K., Quester, P. and Miller, C. (2014) 'Children's exposure to food advertising: An analysis of the effectiveness of self-regulatory codes in Australia: Children's exposure to food advertising', *Nutrition & Dietetics*, 71(1): 35–40.

Rotfeld, H.J. and Taylor, C.R. (2009) 'The advertising regulation and self-regulation issues ripped from the headlines with (sometimes missed) opportunities for disciplined multidisciplinary research', *Journal of Advertising*, 38(4): 5–14.

Skubik, D.W. and Stening, B.W. (2009) 'What's in a credo? A critique of the academy of management's code of ethical conduct and code of ethics', *Journal of Business Ethics*, 85(4): 515–25.

Solis, B. (2010) *Engage: The Complete Guide for Brands and Businesses to Build, Cultivate, and Measure Success in the New Web*. New York: Wiley.

Speck, P.S. and Elliott, M.T. (1997) 'The Antecedents and Consequences of Perceived Advertising Clutter', *Journal of Current Issues & Research in Advertising*, 19 (2): 39–54.

Taylor, C.R. and Raymond, A.M. (2000) 'An analysis of product category restrictions in advertising in four major East Asian markets', *International Marketing Review,* 17 (3): 287–304.

Trusov, M., Bucklin, R.E. and Pauwels, K. (2009) 'Effects of Word-of-Mouth Versus Traditional Marketing: Findings from an Internet Social Networking Site', *Journal of Marketing,* 73 (5): 90–102.

World Health Organization (2014) *Global status report on alcohol and health, 2014.* World Health Organization.

Zigmond, D. and Stipp, H. (2010) 'Assessing a New Advertising Effect', *Journal of Advertising Research,* 50 (2): 162–168.

Glossary

Advergames   computer-based games containing embedded advertising.

Alcohol moderation campaigns   promotional activity aimed at encouraging people to drink no more than recommended daily amounts and to not get drunk.

Alter-globalisation   'alternative globalisation' focusing on supporting cooperation and interaction across developed and developing countries.

Anthropogenic   caused by people (rather than naturally occurring).

Anthropomorphic marketing   marketing strategies whereby a product, service or brand appears to take on human characteristics such as 'talking' directly to individual consumers.

Anti-consumption   strictest form of non-consumption, where all forms of consumption are avoided as far as possible.

Anti-globalisation   movement against global capitalist forces (see also **Alter-globalisation**).

Anti-social behaviour   behaviour that may harm or alarm others, including creating a public nuisance (such as vandalism, graffiti, excess noise, etc.).

Astroturfing   the practice of paying people to create false grassroots support for an organisation or brand.

Attitudes   learned and relatively consistent evaluations of products, services or behaviours. Usually attitudes have three components: *cognitive* (based on actual knowledge acquired), *affective* (emotions or feelings) and *conative* (likelihood that an individual or group will behave in a particular way, such as the intention to make a specific purchase or behave in a specific way).

Bait and switch tactics   tactics whereby a specific product is offered at a low price, but when potential buyers try to make a purchase, the advertised product is not available and they are offered more expensive alternatives instead.

Behavioural economics   see **Nudge**.

Behaviourally Targeted Advertising (BTA)   advertising targeting specific potential purchasers on the basis of their behaviour, such as web-browsing activity. Advertisements will be displayed based on the sites visited or searches made.

Big Data large and complex sets of data requiring more than traditional data processing methods for analysis – now used frequently to refer to data sets derived from Internet and social media-based activity.

Binge drinking consumption of large amounts of alcohol in a short period of time.

Bluetooth technology that enables short-range connections between electronic devices such as smartphones, computers, etc.

Boomerang effects unintended effects from attempts to persuade people to change behaviours, where behaviour changes in the opposite direction to that intended.

Boycott avoiding specific products, often to achieve a social or political outcome.

Brand communities a community or group formed on the basis of their use of, and loyalty towards, a specific brand.

Brand equity a measure of the strength of consumers' attachment to a brand.

Brand image perceptions regarding a brand's personality, strengths and weaknesses.

Bribery giving money, gifts or anything perceived by the receiver as being of value in order to influence the receiver's behaviour, such as purchases or preferential treatment. Regarded as a crime, but subject to different definitions of what is acceptable and unacceptable behaviour across cultures.

Business-to-Business Marketing (B2B) marketing activity involving transactions (e.g. sales) between businesses, such as between two manufacturers, a manufacturer and a wholesaler or retailer or between a wholesaler and a retailer, as opposed to business-to-consumer (B2C) transactions.

Buycott intentionally engaging in the consumption of specific products to support a social cause (opposite of boycotts).

Carbon offsetting schemes designed to compensate for or counterbalance the production of carbon emissions – this may be a tax or other financial contribution, or the production of products that use rather than emit carbon.

Cause-related marketing involves a marketer becoming involved in the promotion of a specific cause, such as the reduction of poverty, improvement of health and well-being within developing countries or the eradication of a specific disease.

Celebrity philanthropy involves celebrities endorsing a specific cause and supporting fundraising activity for the cause such as making public appearances at fundraising events, discussing the cause with the media or making well-publicised donations.

Choice architecture see **Nudge**.

Choice editing process of limiting consumers' choices of undesirable products, for example by imposing taxation or making certain choices unavailable (see also **Nudge**).

Citizenship-based consumption consumers using collective power to achieve socio-environmental outcomes.

Cloud computing in the marketing context, the use of third party organisations to store data such as customer information or profiles.

Codes of ethics formal lists of acceptable ethical behaviours for individuals or organisations.

Codified legislation formal legislation governing the behaviour of a specific group of individuals such as a profession, e.g. accountancy, medicine.

Coercion preventing people from acting in certain ways, or forcing them to act in specific ways without consideration of their wishes.

Cognitive abilities the ability of individuals to understand the information available and to be able to process the information and make decisions regarding whether or how to react to it. This may be age-related or linked to functional literacy issues, or to overall intellectual abilities.

Cognitive development the way in which the ability to understand, process and act on information, including the persuasive intent behind marketing activity, develops with age.

Commercial media literacy the achievement of a greater understanding of the persuasive intent behind persuasive communication such as advertising.

Communicative Approaches approach for resolving ethical conflicts by combining normative and relativist approaches by resolving differences through dialogue.

Comprehensive Model of Consumer Action a complex model of understanding consumer actions developed by Bagozzi.

Conflict of interest situations that arise when a core interest, such as obligations to employers to act in a specific way – e.g. with honesty – is influenced and at times over-ridden by a secondary interest such as personal gain.

Consequentialism see **Teleology**.

Consistency theory theory asserting that individuals tend to behave in ways consistent with their personal norms and beliefs.

Conspicuous consumption consumption with the purpose of displaying wealth or status, e.g. through the purchase of luxury goods.

Consumption   the acquisition, use and disposal of goods or services.

Content restrictions   restrictions on the contents of advertising, e.g. regulation about claims that can be made for a specific product or product category.

Corporate Social Responsibility   a management approach designed to show an organisation's commitment to the social environment in which it operates.

Coupons   vouchers or other documents that entitle customers to a discount on future purchases.

Dark tourism   tourism activity where the focus is on visiting sites which are associated with death or human suffering, such as battlefields, mass burial sites, etc. Also termed **Thanotourism**.

Data mining   extraction of information from a set of data for use in business decisions such as the use of customer historical purchase patterns in order to tailor future promotional activity to meet their needs.

Demarketing   marketing strategies and tactics aimed at reducing demand for goods and services.

Deontology   an ethical framework that focuses on intentions and holds that there are ethical 'absolutes' that are universally applicable, with the focus on means or intentions.

Detailing   direct marketing such as face-to-face contact or promotion of pharmaceutical products to doctors or other medical professionals with the intention of providing specific details about the benefits of a product or service, or showing how it can be used; for example, focusing on specific conditions the drug is indicated for.

Direct-to-Consumer Advertising/DTCA   advertising or other forms of promotional activity of prescription medications by pharmaceutical companies direct to potential consumers, even though the only access to the medication is via a prescription from a medical professional such as a doctor.

Disposition theory   suggests that enjoyment of media often results in strong feelings which may be positive or negative regarding specific characters or the situations portrayed.

Distributive justice   assignments of benefits and burdens from all activity according to some (usually implicit rather than clearly stated and agreed by all parties) standard of fairness.

Ecosystem   a complex combination of living organisms including plants and animals, together with the physical environment in which they exist.

Education events specific education events, such as dinners or presentations, where certain drugs, sponsored by a pharmaceutical company, are presented to health care professionals.

Egoism an ethical framework, a subset of **Teleology**, in which the benefits to the individual undertaking action are stressed and the impact on other people is de-emphasised.

Elaboration Likelihood Model (ELM) a dual process theory of processing of information, consisting of a central and a peripheral route. A central route operates when individuals are highly interested or motivated to pay attention to the message. A peripheral route operates when interest and motivation are low.

Environmental factors in social marketing, factors such as economic conditions or social factors that may positively or negatively influence people's behaviours.

Environmental management management of the natural environment, particularly in relation to the impact human activity may have on it, such as the depletion of natural resources or pollution.

Fair Trade a movement begun in the 1960s in order to offer better trading conditions for small producers and workers in developing countries through guaranteed minimum pricing for produce, minimum labour standards and capacity building.

Fairwashing conveying a (sometimes false) image of a company as a responsible purchaser of Fair Trade/sustainable products, but actually overselling the organisation's commitment to Fair Trade principles.

False positive incidence where a medical or other test shows a positive result, despite the medical condition not being present.

Fast moving consumer goods (FMCG) that is, frequently purchased products such as groceries.

Flashmobs public gatherings, often organised via social media, at which people perform a specific act for a short time and then disperse.

Flogs fake blogs.

Forbidden fruit unintended effects of attempts to manipulate behaviours which result in the behaviour itself becoming more attractive.

Franchising/franchisee and franchisor business arrangements where an organisation (the franchisor) contracts with other firms, individuals or groups (franchisees) to offer products and services under its brand names.

Generic drugs   drugs marketed under their chemical name as opposed to branded drugs without advertising; generally cheaper than branded drugs and usually only marketed once a patent for a branded drug has expired.

Ghost blogging/ghost tweeting   writing blog posts or tweets on behalf of the stated author without disclosing the true authorship.

Greenhouse gases   any of the gases, including carbon dioxide, whose absorption of solar radiation is held to be responsible for the 'greenhouse effect', i.e. warming of the earth's average temperature.

Green consumption   practice of consumption reduction and emphasising sustainable and environmentally friendly consumption practices.

Greenwashing   tactics designed to mislead consumers regarding the pro-environmental stance of an organisation or the environmental benefits of a product or service it markets.

Gross Domestic Product (GDP)   the total market value of all final goods and services produced in a country in a given year, equal to the total consumer, investment and government spending, plus the value of exports, minus the value of imports.

Group influences   see **Social norms**.

GPS   Global Positioning System: a satellite-based navigation system.

Guerrilla marketing   promotion through social networks to promote and popularise a product, service or idea. Traditional mass media are not used. See also **Stealth marketing**.

Health education   activity that seeks to inform the individual on the nature and causes of health/illness and that individual's personal level of risk associated with their lifestyle-related behaviour.

Health promotion   activity designed to promote health/healthier lifestyles, usually based on single messages sent to wider population groups rather than being specifically targeted at individual population segments.

Health tourism   tourism with the primary aim of seeking medical treatment abroad.

Hierarchy of Effects models   suggest that people pass through clearly defined stages of response to advertising messages (e.g. AIDA, i.e. *Awareness, Interest, Desire and Action*).

House brands   brands marketed under the name of a retailer rather than the organisation actually manufacturing the products. Also referred to as Own Label brands.

Hybrid communication new, mostly electronic communication forms that blend advertising and entertainment.

Illicit drugs drugs such as heroin or cocaine that are illegal.

Information deficit lack of knowledge about an issue – held (incorrectly) to be a direct barrier to attitude and behaviour change. However, a gap between attitudes and behaviours is well documented. Information is necessary, but does not of itself provide sufficient conditions for change behaviour.

Informed consent provision of information to research participants or to individuals, groups or communities of the objectives of research or social marketing interventions prior to activity commencing.

In-game advertising advertising content integrated into electronic games as part of the game itself.

Inoculation theory holds that it is possible to immunise people against pressures generated via media content or advertising to act in particular ways or to consume products such as tobacco.

Interdisciplinary involvement of more than one discipline area, such as social marketing psychology and public health or environmental management, in the design and development of social marketing interventions.

Justice tourism aims at promoting mutual understanding between tourists and host communities that have encountered oppression in the past, such as Palestine.

Legislation laws that are universally binding on all citizens and organisations.

Lifestyle how individuals live, including interests, activities and decisions such as quality of diet, amount of exercise undertaken, alcohol consumption levels and decisions regarding smoking and other factors that may impact positively or negatively on health and overall well-being.

Lifestyle drugs medications used to treat non-medical conditions, often because the underlying conditions for these drugs have become medicalised.

Location-based media a component of social networking services that delivers content to mobile devices such as smartphones based on where the user is physically located at the time.

Loss leader selling a specific product at or below cost price in order to draw in customers who will purchase other full price products.

Low involvement processing   processing of persuasive communication with the use of very little cognitive processing. This is not a subconscious or unconscious process.

Manipulation   the belief that advertising is a strong force that is capable of making people act in ways they would not normally do.

Manufacturer brands   brands manufactured and marketed under the name of the manufacturing organisation or its brands (see house brands).

Mash-up   content that comprises material from multiple sources, such as different websites.

Materialism   the desire to possess things for more than their purely functional attributes, such as for status.

Media literacy   the ability to access, analyse, evaluate and communicate messages in a wide variety of forms.

Medicalisation   process through which previously non-medical human conditions and problems become defined, diagnosed, studied and treated as medical conditions.

Medical tourism   involves travelling to locations, usually in developing countries, where medical services are cheaper than in developed countries (see also **Health tourism**).

Mere exposure effects   responses to repeated persuasive communication based on passive exposure to messages rather than active consideration of the message content.

Microfinancing   provision of very small financial loans to people, usually in developing countries, to enable them to set up small businesses.

Mindful consumption   tempered consumption practice based on motivations of caring for oneself, the community and nature.

Moral licensing effects   effect where a consumer feels he or she has acquired an imaginary licence for bad behaviour following previous good or ethical behaviour.

Multi-level marketing (MLM)   marketing strategies whereby products or services are distributed or sold through a number of different supply chain levels. Agents at a high level in MLM distribute products to lower level agents in return for commission or other forms of payment. Payment is also made for recruiting other agents.

Near-field communication   technology that enables communication between devices such as transport fare payments or other small amounts via enabled smartphones.

New media   originally a term used to describe Internet-based communication. Now used to describe any digital device allowing content access, feedback and user-generated content.

Non-consumption   avoidance of consumption or consumption temperance.

Norm-activation model   a model linking pro-social and altruistic behaviour to personal norms.

Normative   ethical behaviour based on perceived, usually ridgid, norms.

Norms   perceived standards of behaviour, often divided into 'injunctive' (what is perceived as being approved or disapproved) and 'descriptive' (what appears to be actually occurring) components.

Nudge (see also Behavioural economics)   a range of non-legislatory interventions based on altering the contexts ('choice architecture') in which behaviour decisions occur. Choice architecture is claimed to alter behaviours in predictable ways through the options intentionally made available or not.

OTC/over the counter   non-prescription medication available over the counter without a consultation.

Open source marketing   marketing practice where customers create their own advertising campaigns for a product or service, rather than marketers.

Own-label brands   see **House brands**.

Paternalism   policies that take decision making away from individuals and places governments or their agencies in the position where decisions are made, as a father might do for young children, hence 'pater' or 'father', on a population's behalf without consultation or their consent.

Patriotic consumption   consumption based on patriotic or ethnocentric principles.

Personal financial incentives   financial incentives such as cash payments made to individuals to encourage behaviour change.

Phronēsis   a term originally attributed to Aristotle and referring to practical wisdom – knowing how, when, where and in what way to apply theories, frameworks and other factors in ethical decision making.

Physician-targeted marketing   sales rep visits to doctors or GPs, where the health professional is presented with new drugs or explained the benefits of prescribing certain drugs.

Pious consumption consumption based on principles derived from religious works or doctrines.

Ponzi schemes illegal investment schemes named after Charles Ponzi who used a scheme in the 1920s.

Predatory marketing marketing activity that is aimed at gaining a significant market share advantage over competitors, or forcing them to leave the market entirely.

Preventable illness illnesses that are caused or aggravated by personal actions and lifestyles, such as smoking, excess alcohol consumption or inactive lifestyles.

Price collusion strategy whereby two or more firms who are dominant in a specific market collectively set and maintain prices at a higher level that would have applied if there had been free competition. This is not only unethical, but also, in many countries, illegal.

Price discrimination a strategy whereby the price of goods or services is different for different groups of people or for different distribution systems, such as online versus conventional retail outlets.

Price gouging a strategy whereby a firm sets the price for goods or services at a level that is seen as unreasonably high.

Price skimming a strategy where a higher price is charged at the time a new product or service is introduced to a market, before competitive activity is likely to drive prices down.

Production the creation of goods and services, historically considered separate from consumption.

Pro-bono work done at no or reduced cost such as the preparation of advertising material for a no-profit organisation.

Product placement the insertion of a recognisable branded product into the content or background of a range of media broadcasting formats.

Product restrictions restrictions on the advertising of specific products or product categories, e.g. restrictions on advertising of tobacco products.

Profits, People and Planet reporting see **Triple Bottom Line.**

Public good see **Social good.**

Puffery obvious, and recognised, exaggeration of a product's benefits such as in advertisements.

Push notifications   notification of new content updates, messages or other activity.

Pyramid selling   strategies whereby people make a financial investment in return for a license to recruit others to the scheme, with the promise of high financial returns. Illegal in many countries.

Reactance   occurs when direct or potential perceived threats to personal freedom, such as consumption of specific products or engaging in particular behaviours, are detected and resisted. Furthermore, people may then become motivated by the perceived threat itself, rather than the actual consequences of the threat, to assert their freedom and regain control of their own decision making and thereby of their threatened freedom.

Rebound effects   effect where a positive behaviour results in a negative behaviour.

Recession   a period of temporary economic decline during which trade and industrial activity are reduced, generally identified by a fall in GDP in two successive quarters.

Regressive (taxes)   taxes that impact most severely on those with the least financial resources.

Regulation   is always subservient to legislation, being used to implement legislation, and is usually 'local' in focus, such as applying only to a specific industry sector. Regulation can never be used as an alternative to law, or to supersede legal rulings. It may be enforceable by a governmental authority, or by industry bodies, i.e. self-regulation.

Relationship-based sales   sales activity that moves beyond mere immediate transactions to build long-term positive relationships between buyer and seller.

Relativist Approaches   approaches for resolving ethical issues based on the assumption that there is no universal set of ethical principles, and that individual cultures or groups have their own moral guidelines and perception.

Responsible consumption   a combination of green consumption and socially conscious consumption practices.

Sales tax   tax applied at the point of purchase – called 'Value Added Tax' (VAT) in some countries, 'Goods and Services Tax' (GST) in others.

Sampling   providing samples of products, such as providing samples to prospective clients.

Segmentation   a technique used by marketers to split a population up into homogeneous groups (i.e. groups with similar characteristics) so that the marketer may concentrate on meeting the needs of each segment as well as possible. Different segments may have different attitudes, believes, behaviours and media usage habits, thus focusing on meeting the needs of specific segments can be more effective than trying to communicate to the entire population with one strategy and set of messages.

Self-efficacy   perceived or actual ability of an individual or group to change behaviour or undertake a specific course of action.

Self-identity   perceptions of oneself and one's unique identity relative to others (including groups).

Self-regulation   regulation of business behaviour of members of an industry sector by its own members who set desired standards for the behaviour of their sector members.

Service-Dominant Logic (S-DL)   a framework first developed by Vargo and Lusch in the early 2000s. It holds that service is the fundamental basis for exchange, that service provision is a part of goods distribution, that all economies are service economies and that customers co-create value.

Sex tourism   travel and tourism with the specific intent of engaging in sexual activity.

Sharing economy   economic model based on temporary, rented ownership of goods, rather than full and exclusive ownership (e.g. car clubs).

Simultaneous media usage   the use of two or more media forms simultaneously, such as watching television or listening to the radio while simultaneously using the Internet or mobile devices.

Single action bias   focusing positive behaviour on a single action rather than several, or on several connected behaviours or actions.

Slack packaging   the practice of using large packages to visually overstate the quantity of product the package contains.

Slotting allowances   lump sum payments made by manufacturers to retailers, especially, but not restricted to, the fast moving consumer goods (FMCG) sector in return for shelf space ('slots').

Social advertising   a component of social marketing focused on the use of advertising or wider forms of marketing communication. Seldom used on its own, but often a prominent part of overall social marketing activity.

Social contract theory   the belief that an implicit contract exists between the state and/ or organisations and individuals or groups regarding rights and responsibilities as a member of society.

Social good (also termed Public good)   the target of social marketing – i.e. not to make commercial sales, but rather to improve the health or well-being of individuals, communities or wider population groups through improving positive behaviours and minimising negative behaviours.

Social identity   a person's perception of their identity within a social group of importance to them, such as peer groups, friends, etc.

Social marketing   interventions aimed at influencing behaviours that benefit individuals and communities for the greater social good.

Social media   websites and applications that enable users to access, share or create content for users within social networks, i.e. networks of people connected to each other because of similar interests.

Socially conscious consumption   focus on the consumption of socially desirable products – and avoidance or boycotts of undesirable products or organisations.

Social norms   perceptions regarding desirable behaviours – may be based on what individuals perceive others as doing or on what they believe those whose views are important to the individual believe individuals should do.

SRO   Self Regulatory Organisation (see **Self-regulation**).

Spillover effect   effect of one behaviour on another, usually a following behaviour.

Stakeholder theory   holds that there are groups beyond shareholders to whom an organisation has obligations; however which groups should be included as stakeholders is open to debate.

Stealth marketing (closely related to Guerrilla marketing)   tactics used to promote products or services in ways that will not be immediately obvious to recipients as promotional activity, such as paying people to write positive reviews in blogs or via Twitter, or to use a product in a highly visible manner.

Subliminal advertising   advertising messages presented in a way whereby people are not consciously aware of them. See also **Low involvement processing**.

Supply chain   the organisations involved in all stages of the provision of products and services, from the provision of raw ingredients or components, transportation, warehousing, and final production and delivery, or access to the finished product or service. Closely linked to **Value chain** which focuses on the value added by each member of the supply chain.

Sustainability   consumption of goods and services that can continue over time without the degradation of natural, physical, human and intellectual capital. Increasingly linked to **Triple bottom line** reporting.

Tax revenue income gained by governments through taxes such as income tax or from taxes placed on the sale of products or services and included in the purchase price.

Teleology (also called Consequentialism) focuses on the outcomes or effects of actions and is usually divided into two sections, **Utilitarianism** and **Egoism**.

Thanotourism see **Dark tourism**.

Theory of Planned Behaviour theory for understanding different norms, drivers and motives leading to specific behavioural outcomes.

Third-party an organisation, group or individual that operates in ways that will encourage potential customers to visit websites or physical stores.

Transaction-based sales sales situations where the emphasis is on completing a specific transaction with no consideration of the implications for future sales opportunities such as through building trust and confidence and thus long-term positive relationships between buyer and seller.

Transit media advertising on the outside of vehicles such as buses or trucks.

Triple bottom line corporate reporting of an organisation's performance incorporating economic, social and environmental impacts over a specific period of time. Also referred to as **Profits, People and Planet (PPP) reporting**.

Trust in the context of marketing, an expectation that a supplier, retailer or other member of a supply chain will treat others, including customers, honestly and fairly.

User-generated content a term encompassing the use of a range of media to enable people to place their own content on websites, such as social media activity, product or service review sites, etc.

Unsustainable consumption consumption that uses raw ingredients or other resources that cannot be renewed at a rate that will keep up with consumption – thus eventually leading to lack of availability of the products concerned.

Upstream socio-economic or environmental factors that may act as barriers to, or potential enablers of, sustained behaviour change.

Utilitarianism an ethical framework, a subset of **Teleology**, in which behaviour is ethical if it results in the greatest good for the greatest number.

Value-added promotion promotional activity that increases a product's or service's perceived value to potential customers such as 'buy one, get one half price' offers, or the provision of free extended warranties.

Value-Belief-Norm theory   theory linking participation in causes or the consumption of products to underlying personal values.

Value chain   see **Supply chain**.

Value-laden   decisions based on the perception of what is right or best in the interests of individuals or population groups without consideration of whether the targeted groups share these values or agree with the proposed actions. Often the values are implicit rather than being clearly stated.

VAT   see **Sales tax**.

Viral marketing   marketing strategies whereby information about goods or services is passed from one Internet or mobile device user to others who then pass it on to others in their networks.

Volunteer tourism   involves tourists volunteering to take holidays where they work to help restore environments or work on projects aimed at alleviating poverty in the groups or communities in which tourists base themselves.

Wikis   websites developed collaboratively by users.

Wildlife tourism   tourism activity such as cruises to watch dolphins or whales, or visits to wildlife reserves where the focus is on close encounters with wildlife in as close to their natural environment as possible.

Index

Made in the USA
San Bernardino, CA
01 September 2018